Proceedings of the Fourth European Conference on Computer-Supported Cooperative Work

10-14 September, 1995, Stockholm, Sweden

ECSCW '95

Edited by

HANS MARMOLIN, YNGVE SUNDBLAD
Interaction and Presentation Laboratory,
Department of Numerical Analysis and Computing Science,
KTH, Stockholm, Sweden

and

KJELD SCHMIDT
System Analysis Department,
Risø National Laboratory,
Roskilde, Denmark

SPRINGER SCIENCE+BUSINESS MEDIA, B.V.

A C.I.P. Catalogue record for this book is available from the Library of Congress.

ISBN 978-94-010-4155-3 ISBN 978-94-011-0349-7 (eBook)
DOI 10.1007/978-94-011-0349-7

Printed on acid-free paper

Cover Design by Gary Newman,
Newman IAF Designs, Stockholm, Sweden

Proceedings of
the Fourth European Conference on
Computer-Supported Cooperative Work

From the editors and chairs

Welcome all readers of these Proceedings, participants at ECSCW'95 as well readers after the conference! We hope that you find the papers interesting, informative and stimulating contributions to the multi-disciplinary Computer-Supported Cooperative Work field.

Out of 95 papers submitted to ECSCW'95 the Programme Committee had the difficult task of chosing the 21 papers to be presented at the conference paper sessions and in these Proceedings. The review process has been very thorough. Each paper was reviewed by at least three Programme Committee members. The final decisions were made at an extensive Programme Committee meeting after deep discussions. Many interesting papers could not be accommodated because of the limitations imposed by the choice to maintain an interdisciplinary single-track.

Note that the papers in these Proceedings are but one prominent part of a wide set of activities at ECSCW'95 which also comprises Workshops, Tutorials, Demonstrations, Videos, Posters as well as a social programme. We hope that all participants, academics as well as professionals, will find rich opportunities to discuss, to learn and, consonant with theme of the conference, to *interplay*.

Demonstrations, Posters and Videos that have been accepted for the conference are presented in a supplement to these Proceedings.

ECSCW'95, and these Proceedings, would not have been possible without dedicated work from the following persons, who we gratefully thank:

- All those who submitted a paper: Receiving many good submissions from contributors that accept a rigorous selection procedure is necessary for a good conference.
- All those who proposed and contribute with Workshops, Tutorials, Demonstrations, Videos and Posters: A rich programme containing those components is crucial for a stimulating conference.
- All those who contributed to the organisation of ECSCW'95: Planning and carrying through an international conference is complicated and required careful attention to a lot of details.
- All the student volunteers: The contribution of the volunteers to making the conference run smoothly and in good spirit is of great value.
- All those who sponsored ECSCW'95: This kind of conference needs a lot of resources where sponsors help so that fees can be held at a reasonable level.
- All those who contributed to the definition of the technical programme: The Programme Committee did a great and difficult job. We hope that the written reviews returned to the authors of submitted papers (whether accepted or not) help them in their work.

- The publishers and designer of the Proceedings: A well designed, printed and distributed book is an important and attractive source and transfer medium of knowledge to the international CSCW community.
- The promoters and organisers of the North American ACM conferences on CSCW: The tacit agreement to interleave their bi-annual conferences with our bi-annual European conferences and the opportunity to announce each others' conferences as if they were a single track, of which ECSCW'95 is the 9th, significantly contributes to make the ECSCW conference the international CSCW research conference of that year and to defeat geographic barriers.

Hans Marmolin, Kjeld Schmidt, Yngve Sundblad

Sponsors of ECSCW '95

NUTEK (Swedish Board for Technical Development), Sweden

Ericsson, Sweden

Tele 2, Sweden

Telia, Sweden

KTH (The Royal Institute of Technology), Sweden

The Graphics Institute, Stockholm University, Sweden

ECSCW '95 Conference Committee

Chair: Yngve Sundblad, KTH, Stockholm
ECSCW'93 (in Milano) Past Chair: Carla Simone, University of Torino
Technical Programme Chair: Hans Marmolin, KTH
Proceedings: Kjeld Schmidt, Risø National Laboratory, Denmark
Demonstrations/Videos: Konrad Tollmar, KTH
Panels: Lennart Fahlén, SICS, Stockholm
Tutorials: Kai-Mikael Jää-Aro, KTH
Workshops: Pål Sörgaard, Norwegian Computer Centre, Oslo
Treasurer: Nils-Erik Gustafsson, Ellemtel, Stockholm
Student volunteers: Ann Lantz, KTH
Local arrangements: JoAnn Gerdin, KTH
Conference Support:
Jacqui Forsyth, Lancaster University,
Kristina Groth, KTH
Thierry Reignier, KTH
North American publicity: Karen Ruhleder, Worcester Polytechnic

Proceedings editors

Kjeld Schmidt, Risø National Laboratory, Denmark,
Hans Marmolin, KTH, Sweden
Yngve Sundblad, KTH, Sweden

ECSCW '95 Program Committee

Liam Bannon, University of Limerick, Ireland
Steve Benford, University of Nottingham, U.K.
Jeanette Blomberg, Xerox PARC, Palo Alto, USA
John Bowers, Manchester University, U.K.
Tone Bratteteig, University of Oslo, Norway
Susanne Bødker, Aarhus University, Denmark
Matthew Chalmers, Ubilab, Zürich, Switzerland
Claudio Ciborra, Theseus Institute, Sophia Antipolis, France
Prasun Dewan, University of North Carolina at Chapel Hill, USA
Lennart Fahlén, SICS, Stockholm-Kista, Sweden
Jonathan Grudin, University of California at Irvine, USA
Christian Heath, King's College, London, U.K.
Hiroshi Ishii, NTT, Kanagawa, Japan
Simon Kaplan, University of Illinois at Urbana-Champaign, USA
Viktor Kaptelinin, Umeå University, Sweden
John King, University of California at Irvine, USA
Laszlo Kovacs, MTA-SZTAKI, Budapest, Hungary
Kalle Lyytinen, University of Jyväskylä, Finland
Marilyn Mantei, University of Toronto, Canada
Hans Marmolin, KTH, Stockholm, Sweden **(Chair)**
Giorgio de Michelis, University of Milano, Italy
Christine Neuwirth, Carnegie-Mellon University, Pittsburgh, USA
Agneta Olerup, Lund University, Sweden
Encarna Pastor, University of Madrid, Spain
Atul Prakash, University of Michigan at Ann Arbor, USA
Wolfgang Prinz, GMD-Bonn, Germany
Mike Robinson, GMD-Bonn, Germany
Tom Rodden, Lancaster University, U.K.
Yvonne Rogers, University of Sussex, Brighton, U.K.
Kjeld Schmidt, Risø National Laboratory, Roskilde, Denmark
Carla Simone, University of Torino, Italy
Norbert Streitz, GMD-Darmstadt, Germany
Lucy Suchman, Xerox PARC, Palo Alto, USA
Yngve Sundblad, KTH, Stockholm, Sweden
Yvonne Waern, Linköping University, Sweden

Table of Contents

Distributed Social Worlds

Cooperation and Power

Collaborative Activities

CSCW Mechanisms I

Electronic Meetings I

CSCW Mechanisms II

Proceedings of the Fourth European Conference on Computer-Supported Cooperative Work,
September 10–14, Stockholm, Sweden
H. Marmolin, Y. Sundblad, and K. Schmidt (Editors)

Work, Locales and Distributed Social Worlds

Geraldine Fitzpatrick[1]
Dept. of Computer Science, The University of Queensland, Australia.

William J. Tolone and Simon M. Kaplan
Dept. of Computer Science, University of Illinois at Urbana-Champaign, IL, USA.

Efforts to build systems to support the complex social reality of cooperative work need both a *grounding* in the social i.e., a rich abstract basis for understanding work, and a *bridging link* between the social and the technical to provide new insights into how to approach designing systems based on this understanding. We propose Anselm Strauss' (1993) Theory of Action as a candidate from which to evolve a framework to ground an understanding of work. Insights from Strauss' work on the importance of structural conditions for social world (cooperative ensemble) interactions can help us to view support systems in a new role as setting/locale for cooperative work interaction, thus providing a bridge between the social and the technical. We briefly overview a locales-based environment called WORLDS we are building concurrent with our theoretical exploration.

Introduction

The Computer Supported Cooperative Work (CSCW) community has two predominant strands of research: the *social*, i.e., the study of how people work in cooperative arrangements, and the *technical*, i.e., the study/practice of building systems to support this work. In order to build systems that are grounded in the real world, systems developers look to the *social* for abstractions which capture the nature of work to be supported. To date, the *social* has provided insights such as the notion of 'situated action' (Suchman, 1987) and the complex contingent nature of work,

1. The author participated in this work while visiting the Uni. of Illinois at Urbana-Champaign.

as well as many focussed studies showing the complexities of real-life workaday situations. These insights have not, however, led to CSCW systems that satisfactorily support them. CONVERSATIONBUILDER is an example of a system where the designers have explicitly cited support for the situated, contingent nature of work as an important goal, but have found achieving such support in practice to be elusive (Bogia et al, 1993).

We suggest that efforts to build systems to support the complex social reality of cooperative work need both a *grounding* in the social i.e., a rich abstract basis for understanding work, and a *bridging link* between the social and the technical to provide new insights into how to approach designing systems based on this understanding. The principled development of CSCW support environments is predicated on the existence of such a framework.

In the first section of this paper, we propose Anselm Strauss' (1993) Theory of Action as a candidate from which to evolve a framework to *ground* an understanding of work for the following reasons: (1) it already exists as a coherent, related set of abstractions - a big picture - which makes the social more accessible, and provides a background against which other concepts from CSCW can be mapped or be seen to complement; and (2) it provides analytical leverage for systems developers who do not have a social science background nor the services of a social science team member. In the second section, we propose that insights from Strauss' work on the importance of structural conditions for social world (cooperative ensemble) interactions can help us to view support systems in a new role as setting/locale for cooperative work interaction, thus providing a *bridge* between the social and the technical. We then provide a brief overview of WORLDS, a locales-based environment we are building concurrent with our theoretical exploration.

Action, Social Worlds and CSCW

We focus on Anselm Strauss rather than other action theorists for our understanding of work, not just because he is a prominent sociologist, but because his theory of action is grounded in and abstracted from a lifetime of 'real-world' observations of how people work. Various concepts have evolved in his work, such as 'articulation work', often quoted in CSCW literature, but it is only recently that Strauss has attempted to draw out a rich coherent, related set of abstractions, concepts and assumptions about action and work as action/interaction. It is the 'groundedness' of this framework, and hence by definition its incompleteness, that we believe makes it a good candidate on which to ground systems developers' understanding of the social, and to build links between the social and the technical. We consider it a valuable exercise for our own research program to investigate as fully as possible the ways in which Strauss' theory can positively influence CSCW systems development, both to move the field forward and to identify problems that can act as springboards for further research.

We wish to stress here that Strauss is not the only candidate for this task, nor does the task demand a sociological framework. Indeed, Nardi (1995) proposes Activity Theory as a basis for studies of context in the HCI community. In a similar vein, Shapiro (1994) proposes a set of core propositions drawn from many different social science disciplines which he considers to be relevant to systems design. Other related work is discussed below. Our work based on Strauss' theory should be seen as complementary to these alternatives.

Strauss argues that the operative criterion by which his theory should be judged is not truth but usefulness. We take up Strauss' invitation to explore the usefulness of his theory in relation to the actions/interactions of cooperative work ensembles, and for the purpose of informing CSCW systems development.

Strauss' Theory of Action/Interaction

While acknowledging that it is impossible to do justice to a lifetime of research and theory evolution in a few short lines, we attempt here to summarize Strauss' (1993) main assumptions and concepts. There are two aspects of Strauss' work that we wish to emphasize: first is the foundational notion of *actions/interactions*; and second is the related notion of *social worlds*, which we argue is central to the understanding of actions within many cooperative work ensembles.

Actions and **interactions** (which are actions towards others) are pivotal concepts. Actions are always embedded in interactions and in systems of meaning - past, present and imagined future. Actions and interactions are carried out by one or more *interactants*. An interactant can be an individual, an aggregation of individuals or a collective, bringing a particular identity, biography and perspective to an interaction. Interactants are able to shape and manage the interactional course and systems of meaning by their actions.

Actions take place within the context of both direct and indirect *structural conditions* which are able to change with time and/or in response to contingencies, and which may either facilitate or hinder the interactional course. Thus, structural conditions and actions/interactions mutually shape and evolve one another. Ultimately, actions and interactions are directed at shaping various *orders* - spatial, temporal, work, technological, informational, sentimental and moral.

Actions also have *temporal* dimensions, filled with "contingencies, changes of projections and plans, even ... goals" (p. 32). Courses of interaction can be characterized along a broad spectrum of dimensions, e.g., from being relatively routine to relatively changeable and problematic. Even for routine interactions, it is likely that *contingencies* will arise which "can bring about change in ... [an interactional course's] duration, pace and even intent, which may alter the structure and process of interaction" (p. 36).

Courses of interaction may be decomposed into *sequences* of connected actions. When there are several participants in an interactional course, *articulation* or alignment of their respective actions (and/or perspectives, interpretations of shared goals, definition of interactional courses etc.) is required.

Trajectory is Strauss' central concept for exploring work as interaction, embodying all of the assumptions of a theory of action. A trajectory is both the course of action as it evolves over time and the actions and interactions contributing to its evolution. Important subconcepts associated with trajectory include trajectory phasing, projection, scheme, arc of action and management.

The evolution of interactional courses and trajectories is shaped and carried out by interactants via two forms of processes: *interactional processes* or strategies such as negotiation and manipulation; and *action or work processes* such as division of labor, supervision, and the actual performance of tasks.

Thus, the two main ways in which Strauss explores and understands actions and interactions are via structure and process, i.e., structurally in terms of the conditions which influence and are influenced by actions, and processually in terms of the response to changes in those conditions over time (Corbin, 1991). This dualism exists at a theoretical level only, structure and process being united in the moment of action (Soeffner, 1991).

The second main notion of Strauss' theory we wish to emphasize is **social worlds**, "the fundamental building block(s) of collective action" (Clarke, 1991, p. 131). A social world is an interactive unit that arises when a number of individuals strive to act in some collective way, often requiring the coordination of separate perspectives and the sharing of resources. It has "at least one primary *activity* (along with related activities), ... *sites* where activities occur ... [and] *technology* (inherited or innovative means of carrying out the social world's activities)" (Strauss, 1978; cited in Clarke, 1991, p. 131).

Membership of a social world is constrained by the limits of effective communication rather than by geography or formal structure (Clarke, 1991). Social worlds may be well defined, e.g., an organizational hierarchy, or they may be loosely defined, e.g., the community of World Wide Web users or the participants at a conference workshop. They may be short or long lived, depending on the purpose for which they have come together. Their shared goal may not necessarily be well developed and completely knowable. They may be composed of sub-worlds, which may in turn contain sub-worlds and so on. People may be involved in many social worlds simultaneously, this membership having a significant bearing on their perspectives and thus their interactions.

The work undertaken by the members of a social world can be characterized using the action/interaction concepts and assumptions outlined previously.

Cooperative Work and Social Worlds Interactions

We suggest that Strauss' theory of action gives us a framework to describe cooperative work ensembles as social worlds that have been formed (to whatever degree of formality) to meet some shared objective (however that may be defined or agreed upon) via a commitment to collective action (however that course of action proceeds), and whose members can be co-located or distributed, to the extent that effective communication can be facilitated[2].

Further, we view cooperative work as taking place in the context of particular structural conditions and contingencies (c.f. the notion of situated action in (Suchman, 1987)), by interactants with particular selves and perspectives, in such a way that conditions, interactants and courses of action mutually shape and evolve one another. The evolution of cooperative work involves both action and interactional processes, not only to perform actions, but to manage the interdependencies entailed in collective action, and negotiate common perspectives of the shared commitment and ongoing interactional course in response to contingencies and changes in conditions (c.f. the notion of double-level nature of work (Robinson, 1993a)).

In one sense, many aspects of Strauss' work seem familiar to us because we have seen or heard similar things before and/or we have already come across references to concepts of his, such as articulation work, e.g., in Bannon and Schmidt (1991). However, while many of the individual concepts may not be new, what is new is their positioning within a broad coherent framework of principles and concepts pertaining to action and interaction which can be related to a host of different phenomena from the most macroscopic to the most microscopic.

This highlights one of the basic problems with the theoretical work in the CSCW community to date, especially for systems developers who struggle to produce actual systems - there has been no framework against which to make sense of and work with the various concepts, approaches and experiences reported in CSCW literature. While each of the insights provided might be 'true' for the phenomenon they describe, they tend to be 'true' in the small or in isolation. Ethnographic[3] studies, describe very specific work situations at particular points of time, e.g., Heath and Luff (1992). Studies of systems in use relate to a particular instance of use of a specific system, e.g., Orlikowski (1992). Conceptual papers, while convincingly argued, offer important but isolated concepts, e.g., Robinson (1993a). While each is valuable and indeed necessary if work in CSCW is to make a difference, they are like pieces of a puzzle, without a broader context in which to position them. We believe that Strauss' work is worth exploring as a possible foundation from which a CSCW-specific framework linking action and systems can be evolved, drawing on the synergy between Strauss and the work of the CSCW community.

It could be argued that Strauss' work offers little more than what could be gained from modest inductive generalizations over a growing corpus of ethnographic studies in CSCW. This corpus, as advocated by Hughes et al (1994),

2. This coincides with Bannon and Schmidt's (1991) definition of cooperative work as being "the general and neutral designation of multiple persons working together to produce a product or service. It does not imply specific forms of interaction or organization ..." (p. 7).

3. We use the term 'ethnographic' very loosely here to denote observational studies of work in situ independent of the particular methodology or theoretical framework employed.

should play an important role in informing an understanding of work and 'good practice' in the design of CSCW systems. However, generalizations to date have been slow in coming. Implications for systems development have similarly been reticent (Shapiro, 1994). Since Strauss' theory of action itself has been inducted from many studies, we believe it can help frame and complement this growing corpus of work. It will not take the place of such a corpus. Rather, by definition being incomplete and inadequate, it will be challenged, reinforced and evolved by a growing body of knowledge about work in the particular. We believe that each ethnographic study can be viewed as an in-depth exploration of the interactions of social worlds and the continual permutations of action, from which new and relevant concepts may be uncovered.

The role of artifacts in work, particularly computer artifacts, is one area where Strauss' framework can be complemented and evolved by current CSCW work. Schmidt and Simone (1995) take Strauss' concept of articulation work and explore the role of protocols embodied in (computational) artifacts as mechanisms of interaction to reduce the complexity and overhead that articulation entails. Robinson's (1993b) common artifacts can be interpreted as part of the structural conditions for work, as well as part of the mechanisms to mediate interaction and effective communication among members of social worlds. What Strauss' theory offers in return is a rich understanding of the interactional contexts in which these artifacts will be used. There are other theoretical frameworks that can also offer particular perspectives on artifacts in work. Distributed cognition (Hutchins, 1995) focuses on work at a system level where the system is a collection of interacting individuals and artifacts in the propagation of knowledge. Actor-network theory, e.g., see Law and Callon, 1988, explores the role of actants, human or non-human, in an interactional network without making *a priori* distinctions between what is social and technical.

Strauss' framework can also provide analytical leverage. For example, the problems of rigidity and inflexibility associated with systems such as THE COORDINATOR (reported in Robinson, 1993a), DOMINO (Kreifelts et al, 1991), CONVERSATIONBUILDER (Bogia et al, 1993), and PSS (Wastell and White, 1993) can be analyzed using the trajectory concept. With all of these systems, there is an implicit assumption that work could be predicted and prescribed *a priori* via a *trajectory projection* (vision of the expected course) and *scheme* (plan based on the vision). Change and evolution are interpreted as isolated or unwanted events, or as happening in a controlled manner that can be dealt with *post hoc* by the process engineer. Such rationalizations of work render invisible the work that is performed in *trajectory management* (carrying out the scheme, with a re-casting of the trajectory projection and scheme as required) in light of the actual *arc of action* (the cumulative actions and conditions arising from previous interactions and contingencies (Star, 1991)). Not only does this framework help identify what went wrong, it also points to possible solutions by highlighting 'new' areas that need to be accounted for in future support systems. Trajectory projections and schemes, such as workflow representations, are a necessary, but not sufficient condition for the support of work. Facilities for trajectory management are required to support the evolution of projections and schemes.

Perhaps closest to Strauss' theory of action in the CSCW domain is activity theory e.g., see Kuuti, 1992. This theory has a much longer history of adaptation for use in the CSCW/HCI fields than Strauss' work. One strength is its emphasis on the change, unpredictability and continuous development of activity. The fundamental unit of analysis here is an activity, similar to Strauss' interactional phase, which exists in a material context, similar to Strauss' structural conditions, and transforms that context. Activity components include a distinguished object, an active actor (individual or collective) who understands the activity, and a community who share the same object (similar to Strauss' social worlds concept). The relations between activity components are always mediated by artifacts such as tools, rules, and division of labor. An activity is realized through purposeful actions and subconscious operations by participants, resulting in a transformation of the object.

However, while the vertical decomposition of an activity is well defined, the processes by which a community of actors articulate actions and operations in context, and develop (evolve) them in the face of contingencies are not well defined. This is because, despite more recently added notions of community and division of labor, activity theory primarily gives an individualistic perspective on work[4]. We believe that Strauss' action theory has advantages in its understanding of the interactional and processual aspects of work where more than one person is involved, and in its interpretation of the permutability of activity and the interplay of activity, actor and environment.

There are numerous other theoretical frameworks that we could explore in relation to Strauss' theory, e.g., distributed cognition, language-action perspective, actor-network theory, etc. While some have been touched upon, space does not permit a full exploration. Suffice it to say that each has its own particular strengths, weaknesses, emphases and uses, and can offer particular insights into the link between the social and the technical. A CSCW-specific framework can be evolved from Strauss' work by drawing on the complementary strengths of these many approaches.

The reader must always bear in mind that Strauss' theory is a starting point only, not a fixed point. The theory itself will undergo continual permutation as it becomes part of the structural conditions of the CSCW social world, to both shape and be shaped by the interactions in and with that world. Also, concepts such as actions, interaction, processes, trajectories, structural conditions, social worlds etc., exist as entities only in the analytical world of the researcher. They are tools to aid the uncovering and understanding of the nature of work. In the real world of the interactant, no such distinctions exist. Work is carried out in semantically rich and continually evolving social contexts, with complex interdependencies and conse-

4. We are grateful to Jesper Doepping for highlighting this notion.

quences of actions. Interactants move fluidly and unselfconsciously around the spectrum of different types of work: individual - group; structured - unstructured: routine - problematic and so on; and among different activities and social worlds. When designing computer-based support, we must respect these realities.

Bridging the Social and the Technical

At one level, Strauss' theory reinforces the need for CSCW systems to support the seamlessness of work, the continual evolution of work in response to local contingencies, and the social processes involved. Moreover, it provides us with a rich theoretical framework in which to understand these. However, we are still left with the question of how to actually go about designing systems to do this. In Straussian terms, many past efforts have focussed on the processual elements of work, usually either action (work) processes with *post hoc* attempts to add support for the above factors, or interactional process such as negotiation support. In these approaches, the computer can be seen primarily as a tool to enforce *a priori* conceptions of work, or as a mediating artifact, where interactions take place through, but in some sense external to, the artifact.

We propose that Strauss' emphasis on the structural conditions of work, as well as his notion of social worlds, gives us a way to view the computer in a different primary role - as *setting* for social world interactions. More specifically, we draw on the assumptions that: (1) interactions take place in some structural context, the conditions there shaping the possibilities for interactions; (2) many cooperative work ensembles can be viewed as social worlds whose activities require site and means; (3) site and means are part of the structural conditions for work; and (4) structural conditions, constituting the more stable, persistent elements of situations, are far more amenable to instantiation in a computer-based system than representations of continually permuting actions (noting, of course, that structure still changes, but at a slower rate, as it shapes and is shaped by interactions).[5]

We view the role of the system as providing setting rather than structure because structural context for actions embodies far more than can be meaningfully or usefully captured in a computer, e.g., power relationships, moral codes, social norms, personal biography and so on. Hence, the computer system, as setting for interaction, is a configurable subset of conditions for action, e.g., roles, resources, tools, artifacts, action possibilities, etc. The computer can now play out multiple other roles as well, e.g., as tool or mediating artifact, part of the means available to social world interactions, but does so in relationship to the setting and the other conditions found there.

---

5. We note here that Strauss is not the only route by which one could have arrived at this view of computer as 'setting for interaction'. Many other approaches emphasize the importance of context in work. Indeed, we have previously explored spatial metaphors for the support of work. However, the work of Strauss, for us, brought these notions into the sharpest focus.

Further, we view setting as being more than just a spatial/physical dimension of work or a collection of actions and resources. It also embodies conditions for work in relationship to one another, and it embodies the way in which members of social worlds use, evolve and make sense of the setting in their interactions. Hence, actions in and with settings create context. To capture more of this notion, we call our settings *locales*[6], influenced by Giddens' use of the term to refer to the "use of space to provide *settings* of interaction, the settings of interaction in turn being essential to specifying its *contextuality*" (Giddens, 1984, p. 118). In short, locales are collections of conditions which both enable and constrain action possibilities, that together with 'action in/with setting', become context for further actions.

The nature of locales can vary greatly and can span both space and time. For example, some locales may correlate with physical domains such as meeting rooms, offices, libraries, streets, and cities. Not constraining locales by physical co-location, we may also correlate them with activity domains such as discussion locales, and code development locales, or with other social worlds, such as a locale for the editorial board of a particular journal.

WORLDS: Computer-Based Locales for Social World Interactions

As systems developers, we are in the process of translating this notion of locales to a computer-based support environment by creating virtual locales for social worlds interactions. Our basic approach is to draw on Strauss' framework to understand the abstract nature of the interactional, processual and temporal aspects of the work that may take place, and the social worlds that may be involved, to thus inform what 'site' and 'means' may be needed to support this. The resulting system, called WORLDS (**WOR**k, **L**ocales & **D**istributed **S**ocial WORLDS), is a CSCW environment that provides aggregations of facilities/resources (structural conditions), called locales, to facilitate social world interactions. The primary ways in which WORLDS achieves this is through support for: the definition and evolution of locales and trajectory schemes; navigation around locales; rich communication channels; and an open extensible architecture[7]. From this general system architecture, specific support environments can be developed guided by an understanding/analysis of the particular work situations.

We do wish to make some points explicit before we proceed. Social worlds are not contained within computer-based locales, nor are all social world interactions and conditions limited to our locales. We do believe, however, that computer-based locales can extend the limits of effective communication across time and space for existing social worlds and can facilitate the creation of new forms of social worlds.

6. Strauss (1961) has also employed a locale concept in earlier work to describe urban places drawing people from different urban worlds where more sociable, lasting contact can occur.

7. WORLDS is implemented using an Object Request Broker supplied by HP Distributed Smalltalk. This architecture provides WORLDS with a distributed, shared object model. External messaging capabilities are provided through a message bus, HTTP, NNTP, email and multicast services.

Appropriate computer-based locales can provide rich settings to enable and augment social world interactions[8]. This is not to mean that the computer 'understands' these settings in any way; rather, our view is that by providing access to shared workspaces populated by appropriate artifacts and tools, with facilities for manipulation and means for synchronous and asynchronous communication, members of social worlds can interact with and through the setting to build and evolve their own work contexts.

WORLDS Locales

To facilitate an integrated work environment and seamless transition among different work settings, we provide each person with a home locale, as well as create locales that are more generally used by larger social world ensembles. We propose that a locale can be characterized by four components. In the following discussion of these components, we make reference primarily to the *locale pane* notebook widget in the WORLDS screen (see Figure 1(a)).

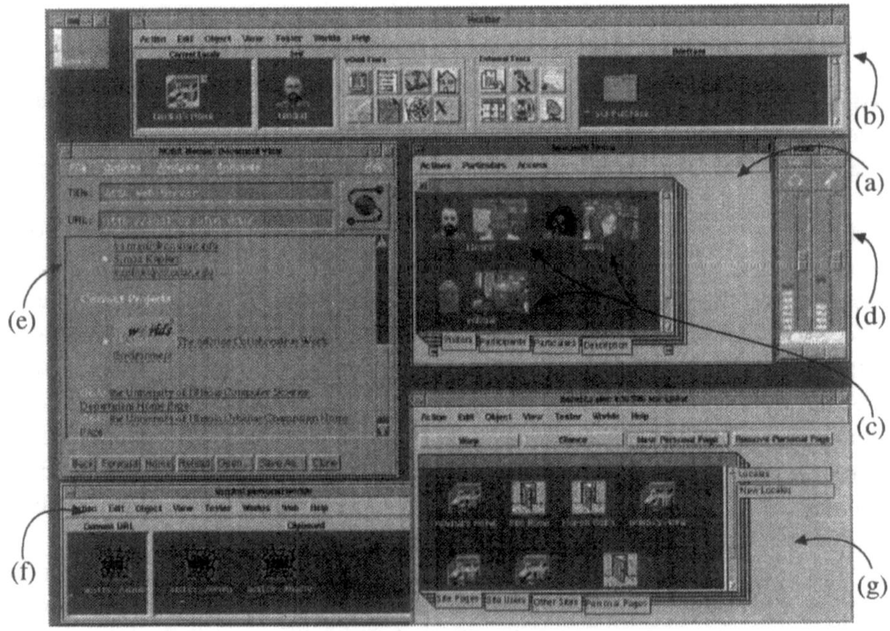

(a) Locale Pane (c) NV (e) Mosaic (g) Site Navigator
(b) Tool Bar (d) VAT (f) Web Tool

Figure 1. Screen-shot of example locale in WORLDS

8. Wagner (1994) uses Gidden's concept of locale within an actor-network framework to analyze how computer networks create new regionalized space-time-geographies in which people interact. She uses locale in the sense of the new ways people can be connected together.

The first component is the *primary work activity/activities* for which the setting is created or for which it is being used, as outlined in the description page of the locale pane. This work activity description is relative to the possible actions facilitated by the collection of conditions/resources in the locale rather than to the shared objective of any particular social world. Hence, it shapes rather than enforces how the setting will be used. For example, a locale set up for office work would be difficult to use for a game of tennis, though people are quite free to use the locale as they please.

The second component is the *particulars* of the setting, drawn from those aspects of the structural conditions of work that are more amenable to computer-based representation. Hence, we refer specifically to the family of artifacts, tools, resources, and possible actions that shape and populate the landscape of a computer-based locale. Meanings associated with the particulars are embedded in a web of interactions, and in interdependencies which evolve with use.

The particulars page of the locale pane holds the family of shared objects relevant to that locale, e.g., applets, which are small application objects (such as an issue-based discussion manager, a shared document annotator or a bug report); integrated external tools (such as word processors, calendars, or spreadsheets); and external objects (such as files, URLs, or database objects).

The third component is the *people* who will participate in, and interact with, the setting. Here we do not mean to specify all the individuals by name, but we do differentiate between potential participants defined by role and actual visitors present in a locale at a particular time. In the following, we clarify this distinction.

A locale has a set of *roles* that are defined in relation to the social world's negotiated division of labor for the primary activity. *Participants* in a locale are people, usually from the same social world, who have been assigned one or more of these roles. Their iconic representations are found on the participants page of the locale pane. When participants are actually present in a locale at a particular time, their video image is displayed in the visitors page of the locale pane. *Visitors* are all the people who are actually present in an locale at the current moment. Visitors are not necessarily participants. For example, a bridge game locale may have five visitors: the four participants who are playing the game, and a novice player who does not have an active role to play but is watching how the others are playing the game so that she can learn from them.

Rich communication channels are provided to support synchronous and asynchronous communication within and across social worlds. Each locale in WORLDS supports an video/audio conference (provided by standard conferencing tools such as NV and VAT, see Figure 1(c) and (d)) to which visitors are automatically added and removed as they enter and leave the locale, respectively. Audio and video channels enable visitors to be aware of each others presence and to support the interpersonal communication processes involved in work. For asynchronous communication, e.g., between participants who are not co-present, support is provided via channels such as email, post-it notes and an 'answering machine' facility.

The fourth component is *process*, the co-evolution of setting and action over time. Here we start to draw on the notion of trajectories (where trajectory schemes may be part of the resources for action available in the setting), and on the notion of the mutual shaping of action and structure. Note that process is not necessarily contained within locales but often spans multiple locales over time.

To support the definition of domain specific locales and the representation of trajectory schemes that exist within and across locales, WORLDS provides a visual/ textual specification language called Introspect (Tolone et al, 1995). Cognizant of contingencies, change and the continual evolution of work, and of the way interactions can shape and evolve settings, Introspect employs a meta-level architecture. This architectural design is based on the principle of reflection to enable run-time modifications to locale definitions and trajectory scheme representations. Environments tailored to support the construction and modification of these specifications are themselves locales within WORLDS. The interactional processes involved in these activities are supported by the availability of rich communication channels.

Thus, locales are uniquely defined, and continually re-defined, not only by their expected primary activity and family of tools and artifacts, but also by people and their interactions in and with the locale over time. Two meeting rooms can be established in separate locations, furnished with the same set of tools and artifacts, but the process and outcomes of meetings in those rooms, can be entirely different because of the different people and social worlds, and different use of the setting.

Additional Aspects of the WORLDS Environment

In addition to the locale pane outlined above, the representation of a locale to users is also minimally characterized by a tool bar. The *tool bar*, see Figure 1(b), has four main components: the *current locale* pane which contains an iconic representation of the user's current locale, copies of which may be created (e.g., via drag-n-drop) and passed around as references to the locale; the *self pane* which contains an iconic representation of the user, copies of which may also be created and passed around; a collection of *tool icons* which provide users with some standard set of tools and actions, e.g., this prototype includes an XEmacs editor, an issue-based discussion applet, a 'warp to home locale' button, a mailer, a network news reader, a Web Tool which opens a web conference using Mosaic 2.5b3 (see Figure 1(e) and (f)), and a navigation tool; and a *drop area* called a briefcase which can accommodate any object you want to carry around from locale to locale.

Unlike a locale pane, the tool bar is unique to a particular user, who can extensively tailor both the bar, and the binding of buttons to tools and applets. Since social worlds are made up of individuals with particular identities, preferences etc., it is important to support flexibility at the individual as well as the social world level.

As stated previously, each user has a home locale. However, a working WORLDS environment may contain any arbitrary number of locales. Movement among locales is facilitated by *warp* and *glance* mechanisms and a *navigator* facility.

People first enter WORLDS by warping into their home locales. Warping is the most primitive way within WORLDS of moving from one locale to another. It is similar to walking straight into a room. Glancing is a more polite way of entering a locale where a person can glance a locale to see who is currently present, at which time a temporary audio/video connection is established between the glancer and those present. Those people present can then warp the glancer into the locale if they so desire. Our glancing model is similar to the work of Tang et al (1994).

As people can be members of multiple social worlds simultaneously, and can be engaged in multiple concurrent activities, WORLDS provides a *Navigator* to promote awareness of and access to other locales and users. We define the WORLDS universe as being partitioned into collections of locales called sites. Sites can be defined logically, e.g., all the locales on a particular server, or semantically, e.g., all the locales related to WORLDS code development. The Navigator, see Figure 1(g), has four components: *site pages*, one page per site, containing icons of all the locales registered at that site, from which users can warp or glance other locales; *site users* containing iconic representations of all the users who are registered at the site being navigated, plus a 'call' feature to allow users to establish audio/video conferences with other users independent of locale; icons representing *other sites* in the WORLDS universe; and *personal pages*, a 'hot-list' of locales of interest for that user.

The Navigator is not the only means of navigation within WORLDS. We support a variety of methods by which people can access one another and other locales. Users and locales can be registered with an HTTP server, accessed from the world-wide web or referenced through MIME-compliant mail messages. We seek to provide a rich family of options without enforcing any particular one because we are aware that our computer-based setting is only part of a broader structural context of work where interaction within the system as setting will be shaped not only by technical possibilities but also by social norms etc.

Support for the collective action of social worlds also requires that users be aware, subject to access constraints, of state changes to other users, artifacts, locales, etc. For example, within a locale users must know what objects are available in the locale, how they are shared with other visitors to the locale, and what actions are being performed on them. Similarly, where trajectory schemas are in use, the actual arc of action to date, the projected schema, and the range of action possibilities need to be made visible to the user. Such awareness information, often subtle and indirect, is critical for users of WORLDS to maintain their sense of what is happening in locales, and is critical in support of the temporal and processual aspects of collective work.

As part of our research and evolution of WORLDS we are investigating several mechanisms, beyond audio and video support for informal communication, to facilitate user awareness in both asynchronous and synchronous modes of work. Examples include: tracking shared object manipulation and making these manipulations visible to any user accessing the shared object; monitoring events outside WORLDS (such as manipulation of files in the filesystem) and making these events, where relevant, available within WORLDS; and icon morphing to provide visual feedback to show, for example, trajectory state.

Evaluation and Future Work

Current development on WORLDS is at a 'proof of concept' level, deploying many general tools and facilities that may potentially be useful in supporting a variety of Strauss' action and interaction processes. A formal evaluation of WORLDS is planned. In parallel with the development of WORLDS we have been conducting an ethnographic study of the work practices of a group of systems support staff responsible for the computing needs of a large computer science department, framing our study in terms of Strauss' action theory. We now plan to deploy WORLDS into this group, both as a usability study of the system and to discover how using an environment such as WORLDS can evolve the practices of the group. Additionally we anticipate that this deployment will affect the design and development trajectory of our project.

In the meantime, our development team has used WORLDS as its work environment and we have made several informal observations based on this use. Firstly, once we reached a critical mass of tool integration within the system, we experienced a usefulness that was absent when these tools were used in isolation. For example, the combination of locales with audio/video conferencing, the ability to navigate easily among locales, and the ability to manipulate shared objects (internal or external to WORLDS), where the system takes care of much of the administrative overhead of maintaining consistency in locales, resulted in an environment which allowed us to work on multiple levels simultaneously.

Other observations include how quickly people adapted to using WORLDS and how adapting to the system changed communication practices among our group after only a short period of time - although we were in the same large room comprising our laboratory often we communicated via the system rather than by others means, e.g. traveling or shouting across the room.

We also experienced the normal difficulties one would expect when deploying a system of this complexity. The main issues of current concern center on the time lags in establishing connections with people and warping between locales, and the addition of more functionality via applets, together with the urgent need for wider deployment and evaluation of the system. While our framework has held up well under initial use there is no doubt that as the WORLDS user community grows stresses will appear and evolutions of many different types will be necessary.

Ongoing plans for the continual permutation of WORLDS include addressing technical issues such as: improved warping, glancing, calling and navigation; persistence; messaging, object trading, and reliable operation over the internet; security; integration of a larger range of external information sources; and more, improved applets. We are also exploring other issues such as: regionalization, overlapping, intersection and composition of locales; presence; and availability.

Conclusions

We realize that we are embarking on an ambitious task, yet we believe that this task is not only worthwhile but essential to the advancement of CSCW systems research if the technical is to be grounded in a good understanding of the social. We do not suggest that we have found *the* answer in using the insights from Strauss' work as our starting point for bridging the gap between the social and technical. However, we believe that there is value in continuing this pursuit as we can learn from the ways in which we both succeed and fail to meet our goals.

Acknowledgments

We wish to thank: others who have contributed to the development of WORLDS - Mark Kendrat, Mark Fitzpatrick, Donald Cook, Ted Phelps, Doug Bogia, Annette Feng, Xinjian Lu, Ken Hu; Leigh Star and Kjeld Schmidt for extensive discussions and insights; and the anonymous reviewers whose feedback was invaluable. This work supported in part by the Advanced Research Projects Agency under grant F30603-94-C-0161, by the National Science Foundation under grants CDA-9401124, CCR-9108931 and CCR-9007195, by the US Army Corps of Engineers, and by Sun Microsystems, Bull, Hewlett-Packard, DEC, Intel and Fujitsu/Open Systems Solutions. The views and conclusions contained in this document are those of the authors and should not be interpreted as representing the official policies, expressed or implied, of the Defense Advanced Projects Research Agency or the U.S. Government. The first author also acknowledges the support of an Australian Commonwealth Postgraduate Research Award and an Australian Telecommunications and Electronic Research Board Scholarship, as well as the support provided by the Computer Science Department at the University of Illinois.

References

Bannon, L. J., & Schmidt, K. (1991): "CSCW: Four Characters in Search of a Context.", in J. M. Bowers and S. D. Benford (eds.): *Studies in Computer Supported Cooperative Work. Theory, Practice and Design*, North-Holland, Amsterdam, 1991, pp. 3-16.

Bogia, D. P., Tolone, W. J., Bignoli, C., & Kaplan, S. M. (1993): "Issues in the Design of Collaborative Systems: Lessons from ConversationBuilder", in *Schaerding International Workshop on Task Analysis and CSCW*, Schaerding, Austria.

Clarke, A. E. (1991) : "Social Worlds/Arenas Theory as Organizational Theory" in D. R. Maines (ed.) : *Social Organization and Social Processes: Essays in Honor of Anselm Strauss*, Aldine De Gruyter, New York, 1991, pp. 119-158.

Corbin, J. (1991): "Anselm Strauss: An Intellectual Biography" in D. R. Maines (ed.): *Social Organization and Social Processes: Essays in Honor of Anselm Strauss*, Aldine De Gruyter, New York, 1991, pp. 17-42.

Giddens, A. (1984): *The Constitution of Society*, University of California Press, Berkeley, CA.

Heath, C., & Luff, P. (1992): "Collaboration and Control: Crisis Management and Multimedia Technology in London Underground Line Control Rooms", *Computer Supported Cooperative Work*, vol. 1, pp. 69-94.

Hughes, J., King, V., Rodden, T., & Andersen, H. (1994): "Moving Out from the Control Room: Ethnography in System Design" in *ACM Conference on Computer-Supported Cooperative Work*, Chapel Hill, North Carolina: ACM Press, 1994, pp. 429-439.

Hutchins, E. (1995): *Cognition in the Wild*, MIT Press, Cambridge, MA.

Kreifelts, T., Hinrichs, E., Klein, K., Seuffert, P., & Woetzel, G. (1991): "Experiences with the DOMINO Office Procedure System" in L. Bannon, M. Robinson, & K. Schmidt (eds.): *Second European Conference on Computer Supported Cooperative Work*, Amsterdam: Kluwer, 1991, pp. 117-130.

Kuuti, K. (1992): "Identifying potential CSCW Applications by Means of Activity Theory Concepts: A Case Example" in J. Turner & R. Kraut (eds.): *ACM Conference on Computer Supported Cooperative Work*, Toronto, Canada: ACM Press, 1992, pp. 233-240.

Nardi, B. (1995): "Studying Context: A Comparison of Activity Theory, Situated Action Models and Distributed Cognition" to appear in B. Nardi (ed.): *Context and Consciousness: Activity Theory and Human Computer Interaction*, MIT Press, Cambridge, MA, 1995.

Orlikowski, W. J. (1992): "Learning from NOTES: Organizational Issues in Groupware Implementation", in J. Turner & R. Kraut (eds.): *ACM Conference on Computer Supported Cooperative Work*, Toronto, Canada: ACM Press, 1992, pp. 362-369.

Robinson, M. (1993a): "Computer Supported Cooperative Work: Cases and Concepts" in R. M. Baecker (ed.): *Readings in Groupware and Computer-Supported Cooperative Work*, Morgan Kaufmann, San Mateo, CA, 1993, pp. 29-49.

Robinson, M. (1993b): "Design for Unanticipated Use ..." in G. de Michelis, C. Simone, & K. Schmidt (eds.), *Third European Conference on Computer Supported Cooperative Work*, Milan, Italy: Kluwer, 1993, pp. 187-202.

Schmidt, K., & Simone, C. (1995): "Mechanisms of Interaction: An Approach to CSCW Systems Design", in *COOP'95. International Workshop on the Design of Cooperative Systems*, Notables-Juan-les-Pins, France, 1995.

Shapiro, D. (1994): "The Limits of Ethnography: Combining Social Sciences for CSCW" in *ACM Conference on Computer-Supported Cooperative Work*, Chapel Hill, North Carolina: ACM Press, 1994, pp. 417-439.

Soeffner, H. (1991): "'Trajectory' as Intended Fragment: The Critique of Empirical Reason according to Strauss" in D. Maines (ed.): *Social Organization and Social Processes: Essays in Honor of Anselm Strauss*, Aldine de Gruyter, New York, 1991, pp. 359-371.

Star, S. (1991): "The Sociology of the Invisible" in D. Maines (ed.): *Social Organization and Social Processes: Essays in Honor of Anselm Strauss*, Aldine de Gruyter, New York, 1991, pp. 265-283.

Strauss, A. (1961): *Images of the American City*, The Free Press of Glencoe, New York.

Strauss, A. (1993) : *Continual Permutations of Action*, Aldine de Gruyter, New York.

Suchman, L. (1987): *Plans and Situated Action*, Cambridge University Press, Cambridge.

Tang, J. C., Isaacs, E. A., & Rua, M. (1994): "Supporting Distributed Groups with a Montage of Lightweight Interactions" in *ACM Conference on Computer Supported Cooperative Work*, Chapel Hill, North Carolina: ACM Press, 1994, pp. 23-34.

Tolone, W. J., Kaplan, S. M., & Fitzpatrick, G. (1995): "Specifying Dynamic Support for Collaborative Work within WORLDS" to appear in *ACM Conference on Organizational Computer Systems*, Milpitas, CA, 1995.

Wagner, I. (1994) : "Networking Actors and Organisations", *Computer Supported Cooperative Work*, vol. 2, pp. 5-20.

Wastell, D. G., & White, P. (1993): "Using Process Technology to Support Cooperative Work: Prospects and Design Issues" in D. Daiper & C. Sanger (eds.): *CSCW in Practice: An Introduction and Case Studies*, Springer-Verlag, London, 1993, pp. 105-126.

Proceedings of the Fourth European Conference on Computer-Supported Cooperative Work, September 10–14, Stockholm, Sweden
H. Marmolin, Y. Sundblad, and K. Schmidt (Editors)

POLITeam Bridging the Gap between Bonn and Berlin for and with the Users

K. Klöckner, P. Mambrey, M. Sohlenkamp, W. Prinz, L. Fuchs, S. Kolvenbach, U. Pankoke-Babatz, A. Syri
GMD, FIT Institute, Schloß Birlinghoven, D-53757 Sankt Augustin
Email: politeam@gmd.de

Abstract: Supporting the cooperation of people in large organizations which are distributed geographically is one of the great challenges for the CSCW research. With POLIKOM, the German Federal Ministry of Education, Science, Research, and Technology launched a framework in which telecooperation applications will be developed to support the distributed government in Bonn and Berlin. POLITeam is one project embedded in that framework. Its aim is to support asynchronous cooperation in administrative or industrial settings by an integrative groupware system that applies the metaphors of electronic circulation folders and shared workspaces. The development process is based on the approach of using an existing groupware system that is evaluated and redesigned in close cooperation with selected pilot partners. This paper describes the initial design, our development approach and the first experiences of the POLITeam project.

Introduction

In 1991 the German parliament decided to move the government from Bonn to Berlin. As a consequence ministries and other public organizations will be distributed between Bonn and Berlin, as not all of them will move to Berlin in the next decade. Because of these changes the German Federal Ministry of Education,

Science, Research, and Technology has launched the research framework POLIKOM (Hoschka et al., 1993). In this framework the required telecommunication and telecooperation technology will be developed to support the distributed government. One of the projects in this framework is the POLITeam project.

The project involves industrial partners (VW-Gedas), research institutes (GMD, University of Bonn) and application partners. Special attention will be paid to the application partners who will be closely involved in the design process from the beginning. The application partners are the Federal Ministry of Family Affairs, Senior Citizens, Women, and Youth as well as the Ministry of Justice of the state Mecklenburg-Western Pommerania. Both partners contribute experiences in ministerial, i.e. administrative and political office work. As industrial application partner the AUDI AG is involved. The focal point of that application partner is to enhance the support of concurrent engineering between project groups located at different cities.

The objective of the POLITeam project is the development and introduction of a system which effectively supports the cooperative work in large organizations distributed geographically. The processes at which POLITeam aims are workflows in business and public organizations. These are supported by a workflow component which follows the metaphor of electronic "circulation folders". This is augmented by the support of coordinated document and task processing. Here the guiding metaphor is that of a "shared desk". Both components will closely interact with an event and notification service which supports awareness of the cooperative environment.

In this paper we first describe the envisaged design of the POLITeam system. Then we describe the methodological and technological approach towards the implementation of this design. Finally, we describe the first experiences and impressions gathered from the use of the initial system and the cooperation with our pilot partners.

The Design of POLITeam

Overview

The POLITeam system implies several functional components which are illustrated in the following architecture diagram (Fig. 1). We will concentrate on the description of those components which are most visible to the user: the workflow support, the coordinated document and task processing, and the notification and information service. Further services are archive and registration, organization information and management (Prinz, 1993), and technical management. None of these components represents a completely new application in its own, however their combination and integration into a comprehensive support system that can be tailored to different application areas is challenging (Navarro et al., 1993).

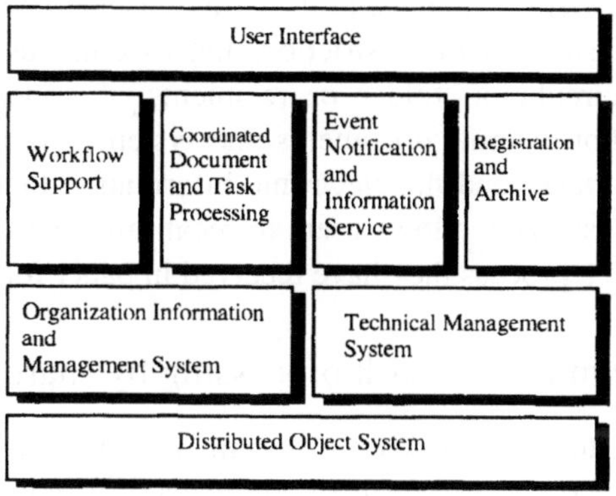

Fig.1: The POLITeam architecture

Workflow support by electronic circulation folders

Workflows are supported by means of *electronic circulation folders* in correspondence to the internal mail folders used in the real office world. Similar approaches can be found in (Shephard et al., 1990, Karbe, 1993). Circulation folders contain documents of arbitrary content; their contents can be changed during the workflow. Addressees can be individual users of the system, or role descriptions, represented in an organization management system, which are then resolved at runtime. Informal annotations can be attached by any user to the circulation folder and can be deleted later. A circulation slip prescribes in an arbitrarily and dynamically configurable way the route of a circulation folder. Since these are easily modifiable at runtime according to the actual cooperative situation, the folder can provide flexible mechanisms for the coordination of workflows. This satisfies the requirements drawn from experiences gained by office procedure systems (Kreifelts et al., 1991).

The envelope and contents of a circulation folder can be protected with access rights. In the case of the envelope, this concerns the adding and removing of documents and the inclusion and deletion of addressees on the circulation slip as well as of annotations. Access rights on documents specify who may read, modify, or delete them.

It will not be possible to supply all relevant employees of an organization with the POLITeam system in the initial phase. Nevertheless, all users must be able to participate in workflows. Furthermore, interviews with our application partners have shown that documents are often processed which are not available or are unwieldy in an electronic form due to their size (e.g. construction plans) or their large number of pages (e.g. catalogues). These documents must still be circulated in paper form. Therefore, the system must provide mechanisms to integrate both external users and paper documents. In the case of users, obvious limitations apply to this integration, such as the restriction that external users can only be end recipients of the circulation folder or recipients of concurrent copies of the circulation folder. For external documents, the system will provide means for the combination of the paper and the electronic information that is exchanged in the context of the process. This allows users to recall all electronic information, e.g. related messages, to a process they have received in paper form.

Coordinated document and task processing by shared workspaces

As a supplement to the workflow system and to support less structured cooperative work, a component for the coordinated document and task processing is developed in the form of a *shared workspace*. A shared workspace (which also can be seen as a shared "desk") offers an environment for the coordinated document and task processing in a group; it integrates, but does not implement the tools for document processing.

In contrast to the circulation folder of the workflow system, the members of a shared workspace (Fuchs et al., 1995) have a non-sequential, time-unlimited, access to its contents. It supports the handling of tasks for which group members require continuous access to common background and work documents. The access to the contents of the workspace can be freely specified which enables a broad spectrum from private up to public workspaces.

An essential difference between a shared workspace and a file or archiving system is the continuous processing possibility of its contents by different, often remote, members of the workspace. That raises special requirements for consistency, as well as for the representation of the events within the workspace, following the last access or visit of a user. An overview of past actions in the workspace, and the most recent state, is therefore offered to the user by special visualization techniques. The members of a workspace can further access the history of individual objects for more detailed information.

As a special service, the combination of task descriptions with shared workspaces is provided. This is achieved using task lists which assign tasks, related resources, and deadlines to individual workspace members. Thus cooperative task management can be supported the same way as proposed by Kreifelts (Kreifelts et al., 1993). This is useful, for example, if the shared workspace was set up for the production of different documents. Members can be assigned to different tasks of the document production and the responsibilities can be recorded visually. During the task execution, the current processing status is recorded within the task list, which enables a rapid overview of the status of the task, or of future tasks to be accomplished.

The history of processing contents is recorded and it can be inspected by the users, controlled through access rights. Archived documents or external message sources (e.g. internal distribution lists, press releases, news) can be integrated via filters into a workspace if these sources are available electronically. In this way, background information, which is useful for task handling, can be automatically supplied to the group.

Awareness by the event notification and information service

One of the main design goals of the POLITeam system is to provide users with information about the activities of others, as far as it affects their cooperation. In this way, the dynamics of the working environment is presented at the user interface - providing awareness. Awareness is a key mechanism to coordinate and fine-tune cooperative work, as well as a base mechanism to establish communication by showing the availability of other users (Dourish, Bellotti, 1992). POLITeam supports both an active approach (notification service), where the system automatically notifies users of relevant events, and a passive approach (information service) where users can query the system for specific facts. Since this component is used by all other parts of the overall system, for example the shared desks and the electronic circulation folders, there are several key issues for its design that must be considered.

Many problems related to the notification and information service are concerned with the design of the user interface. For the active component, the information must be visualized in the working context in an as unobtrusive and non-disruptive manner as possible. Adequate visualization and animation techniques must be used to take maximum advantage of the screen area and to allow peripheral viewing of the displayed events (Sohlenkamp, Chwelos, 1994). Furthermore we must ensure that important events are always noticed by users. Another problem is the compression of event history: users should be able to get a summarized version of past events to learn about previous actions and to catch up to the current state of the working process.

For any system providing information about users to others, adaptability is a crucial issue. A user must be able to control outgoing, as well as incoming information, the former to provide privacy where needed, the latter to prevent disruption and information overload. POLITeam addresses these problems by providing user-definable filters, allowing the specification of interesting events together with definable access rights for specific classes of events. The challenge is to design a system that is flexible enough to support the usual forms of cooperative work and the evolution of social protocols analogous to those used in real-world collaborations.

Finally, POLITeam is designed to be expandible - additional services and hardware should be easy to integrate into the system when necessary. Since these additional components should use the same basic mechanisms to signal events to users, it is especially important that the notification system provides a well-defined, open interface to other parts of the system.

The POLITeam Design Approach

The methodological approach

The objective of the POLITeam project is the introduction, evaluation and further development of a system to effectively support coordination of asynchronous group work and office procedures. The leading metaphors are the "shared desk" and the "electronic circulation folder" in a virtual office as introduced before. Although academic laboratory research will be done, the main focus lies upon the users who will use the system in a real world setting, i.e. their workplaces. The users work for the three pilot-partners of the project: a German federal ministry, a German state ministry, representing the public administration, and a car manufacturer, where concurrent engineering will be supported. The three organizations have outlets located in different cities, which will be connected closely to their headquarters, bridging the gaps which derive from the differences in time and space. In the following we concentrate on the experiences gained from the ministerial application partners.

The basis for the workflow support and the coordinated teamwork is a product available in the project consortium (see next section), which offers a sufficient basic functionality for the workflow control in order to be able to begin the project in a real life setting. Several steps were planned in advance:

- to analyse work and organizations at a first glance;
- to begin with a short adoption phase in the laboratory to shape the existing CSCW-system (named POLITeam I) to the obvious users' and organizations' needs;
- to introduce the system into the organizations by teaching and guiding the users, which will lead to the usage of the system as an instrument of daily work;
- to evaluate the experiences of the users made with the system in work practice and to redesign the existing system directly, or alternatively to take the experiences as future system requirements for the enhanced system (POLITeam II).

The next milestone will be the introduction, usage and evaluation of this new system POLITeam II, which again will lead to a reshaping of the system, to new requirements and to evolutionary steps of design.

This approach enables stepwise modification and development of the system and guarantees that both, users and developers, maintain control over the process. They can decide about system alternatives and consequences, during a long term learning period, and not just at one, irreversible decision point. This enhances participation in the design process. Furthermore, studies show that user participation also has a direct relationship to user satisfaction (McKeen, Guimaraes, Wetherbe, 1994). The approach, planned as an open process, takes into account the dynamics of the organization such as the organizational goals, organization of group work, careers, fluctuation of personnel, cognitive access to the system, qualification process, the state of the art of technology, etc. (Mambrey, Oppermann, Tepper, 1986).

The development of the POLITeam project will be done in close cooperation with users. The definition of the requirements for the system components is done such that an already existing system is installed at the users workplace, and that the requirements are determined by means of the practical experiences gained by using this system. The strategy of the project follows the helical model of cooperative evolutionary system design represented in figure 2.

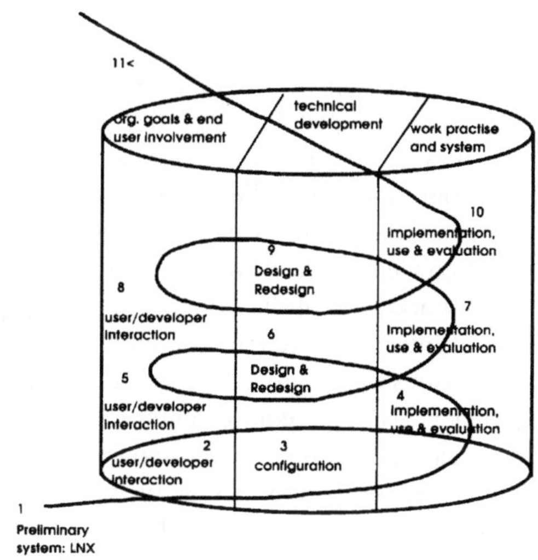

Fig. 2: The helical model of cooperative evolutionary system design

This development strategy of POLITeam is based on previous work done by Eason (Eason, 1982) and Floyd (Floyd, Keil, 1983). To achieve these ambitious goals some basic methodological development ideas structure the development process of the system. We call this a cooperative and constructive design philosophy. This includes a set of activities, methods and tools characterized as follows:

- We start with an existing system which gives us the opportunity to evaluate it under working conditions and not only in the laboratory (Bowers, 1994). We are interested in how work practices match, or mismatch, the system.

- Evaluation criteria of the system are: the usage in existing organizations, how they assist users in their tasks, and how they help to meet the requirements they have towards organizational goals and working life.
- We apply an evolutionary system design cycle, which is more open to changes than a fully, structured top down design approach.
- We reshape existing functionality, and shape new ones, by intensive end-user involvement. The users are the experts of the group work. We apply interactive methods like workshops, meetings, group discussions etc. during the whole development process, instead of a theoretical requirement analysis at the beginning of the process.
- Methods and tools we use take into account that the users are partners and not research objects. I.e. methods and tools must be transparent for the users, approved by them, and must take ethical considerations into concern, e.g. data protection laws, right of informational self-determination, rules and etiquette of the working place, etc.
- We design the cooperative development process as a mutual learning process for users and developers to exchange experiences of design and work practice, and to enhance people's cognitive access to the changes.

Based on this approach, how did we proceed practically in the federal ministry? We started with discussions about CSCW for the government with external experts in this field to get a rich picture of the work practice and further aims in general. Based on this knowledge we developed semistructured guidelines to analyse the structures and workflows of the organization and the work practice of the users. Special points of interests were the individual organization of work and the use of office media, obvious office procedures, non-obvious office procedures, interaction partners, privacy aspects, requirements, expectations, hints, wishes, obstacles. Because in this case the number of participants was limited, we decided to talk with every user (19 persons, approximately two hours per interview, at their workplace) about their work before the introduction of the system. Although we wrote minutes to document the basic requirements, needs, or statements for the team of developers we did not apply a known office analysis methodology (e.g. Sirbu et al., 1984). We were interested in the narrative descriptions of the users about their workplace and work.

The risks of decontextualization of information, overemphasizing of the formal workflows, overestimating the users knowledge about the benefits or problems of a CSCW system theoretically without practical knowledge led us to the following approach: Each designer had to take part in the interaction process with the users and got a personal impression of the workplaces, the employees, and the employees' description of their work practice. Via these personal impressions developers could interpret written information more adequately and design based on the insights of the work practice. After this first interaction phases we did not try to represent all office procedures by formal models but designed some rich scenarios of semistructured workflows like an incoming letter to a unit leader, a speech for the minister, or a registration process. We discussed these scenarios with the users in workshops and asked for the adequacy of the procedures, tested the appropriateness, and discussed the aspects the users required for reshaping work with the assistance of computers. The workshops are another important platform for the cooperative user/developer interaction in this project.

The technological platform

The platform required for our evaluation had to fulfil the basic functionality requirements identified in the design section. Furthermore, it was important that the platform provided a tailorable, programming interface which allowed modifications and extensions to its functionality and its usage as the platform for the realization of future POLITeam versions.

Our industrial project partner, VW-Gedas, contributed LinkWorks[1] which turned out to be a suitable basis for evaluation, as well as for realization of additional functionality, for the following reasons.

LinkWorks provides an open framework for the integration of various office applications. This aspect together with its availability on different hardware platforms, allows the integration into the already existing, and often heterogeneous, office environments that we have found at our application partners (Unix servers; Windows, OS/2 and Macintosh clients). Furthermore, its functionality can be tailored, to a certain extent, to the specific needs of a user group. This is possible without programming due to a graphical administration interface. Further functionality extensions can be realized using the APO (Applications plus Objects) interface which provides programmers access to the internals of the system.

Having described some underlying technical properties let us turn our view to the features which affect the user.

LinkWorks uses the "desk" metaphor. After a user has logged in, the system presents his personal desk, which is the same for every client machine to which a user logs in. The configuration, appearance and the default contents of the desk can be configured, either by the users themselves or by a system administrator, according to the requirements of the users. For the organization of the structure and content of the desktop the user is offered different filing facilities, e.g. cabinets, drawers, registers and folders. These are based on a configurable object model, making it easy to introduce new filing objects which apply metaphors from the pilot partners' office environment.

Communication and cooperation between users is supported by the provision of email, workflow, and shared container components.

---

[1] LinkWorks™ is a groupware product by Digital

The workflow component allows the attachment of circulation slips to arbitrary LinkWorks objects, e.g. files or folders. The circulation slip describes the path for the attached object. Each user who receives the object can easily modify the circulation slip, which provides a flexible mechanism to react on new circumstances. In addition to the path description, users may add annotations, remarks and dates to the slip. If the circulation slip is attached to a container object, e.g. a folder, users can also add new objects, e.g. documents or spreadsheets, to the container. Thus, the transported content of a workflow can easily be modified. We adopted this functionality to create an electronic circulation folder object which models the behaviour of circulation folders, as known to our pilot partners. This allows us to evaluate the applicability of that concept within the pilot system.

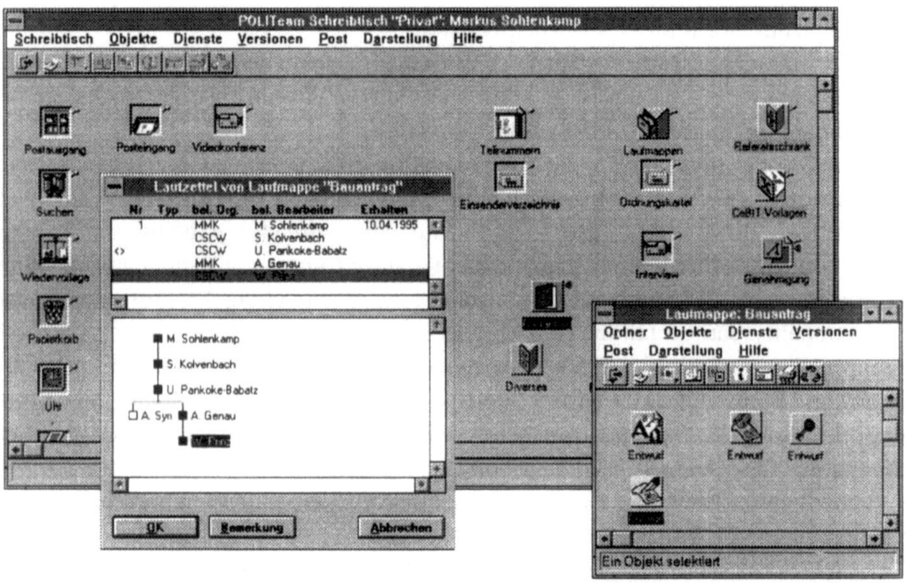

Fig. 3: The initial POLITeam desk, showing the contents of a circulation folder and the attached workflow

The shared container component enables the sharing of filing facilities among users. This provides an easy way of document exchange and group editing: every object put into a shared folder, for example, is visible to every person that has access to the folder. The system prevents concurrent document write access, but allows concurrent read accesses. To receive information about the actual work process, users are offered the opportunity to register interest in particular objects (filing facilities as well as documents) that they are interested in. The registered users get informed about changes that affect these objects. By these means

LinkWorks already provides a rudimentary form of awareness service, which however is inadequate to realize the goals described before.

This short description of LinkWorks gives only a little insight. What should have become clear is that LinkWorks provides the basic functionality for the goals of the future POLITeam system. Actually the complete functionality of LinkWorks had to be reduced for the first pilot phase to provide a comprehensible, easy to learn and easy to use system. This included the adaptation of the system to the terminology known by the users, the removal of unneeded functionality and the configuration of appropriate access rights. The first installation of the POLITeam system will include approximately 55 clients and 6 server components.

First Experiences and Impressions

Based on the results of our empirical work, we gained a deeper insight into the working procedures of our application partners and were able to make rich pictures about several aspects of the organizations, users, tasks, and their work practice.

A general problem we encountered were the elections for the new governments in Germany which took place between the start of the project and the installation of the system and resulted in the change of the relevant ministers and some of our pilot users. This had serious consequences for the organizations of our ministerial partners showing that extensive organizational changes may occur and that our system has to be flexible to be adapted to new situations.

In the following sections we concentrate on further experiences before and after the introduction of the system.

First impressions from the preparation of the system introduction

The interviews confirmed that German federal and state ministries are organized by rules and procedures that precisely describe how (paper)work has to be done, and who is responsible for each activity. On the other hand unwritten rules exist how those tasks have to be done, which do not fit into the general, prescribed scheme. Officially, we are dealing with strict hierarchies, assuming the Weberian, top-down model of bureaucracy. Informally we have to analyse the actual work practice: how things are really done. Consequently, systems have to match both requirements if they are supposed to be used in daily work.

Office procedures in the ministries involve a sophisticated use of paper, folders, colour pens, stamps, annotations, initials, and signatures. Furthermore, persons at higher hierarchical levels have to deal with large quantities of paper in a very short time every day. It will be difficult to develop computer applications which offer a similar functionality combined with the ease of use paper offers.

Accordingly, our current design approach proposes the use of pen-based computers, particularly for the support of managers.

When we discussed features of the system before its introduction, our ministerial pilot users considered shared workspaces to be not as important as circulation folders, since those are closer to the way of working they are used to. Interestingly, their opinion changed after the introduction of the system (see below).

The discussion of the event and notification service was always very lively and interesting. In reality, people walk from office to office in search for a folder, therefore almost everyone considered it very useful to be able to check the current location of a circulation folder. Interestingly, this was not a demand from the department leaders but from normal office clerks who are often asked for the current location and status of a folder. However, after it became clear that with the start version of POLITeam users can observe others without being noticed, their opinion about this functionality changed. In accordance with real life where the owners of requested folders are aware of their colleagues searching for the folders, our design approach for the next version of POLITeam is to notify the users about these searches. Other design approaches are based on the idea of negotiating the status and notification information that is visible and exchanged within a group (Wulf, 1995).

During the workshops one of the main factors for success or failure of our project turned out to be the solution of problems like secure procedures for routing, signing, annotating documents and the authorisation of documents. This was an aspect we had not considered to be of this importance at the beginning of the project.

Adapting the pilot system to the demands of the users required a deeper knowledge about the target organizations and the processes to be supported. It took more than six months to get acquainted to the organizations, to identify the final pilot users and to inform them about our project and to close the first phase of interviews.

Designing office procedure scenarios helped us to understand the application domain. Describing office procedures, and discussing them with the users involved in the procedures, gave furthermore a good opportunity to correct our view of the organization.

Our approach to involve all members of the POLITeam project in the interviews, giving them the chance to come personally into contact with our users, proved to be a valuable experience especially for the designers, allowing them a better understanding for the rationales behind a specific user requirement. The experiences reported in (Heinbokel, 1994) support this approach. In particular the knowledge gained from the interviews and workshops allows us to understand how the system should look in the following application domains:

- the organization of the electronic desk (e.g. organization of folders and tools, access to information services),
- organizational procedures (e.g. signing process, history mechanism informing about past actions),
- mail services,
- shared access to documents and folders (e.g. specific access rights),
- specific hardware/software demands (e.g. scanners, colour printers, extensions of the word processor).

This allowed us to configure a suitable start version for POLITeam I.

First impressions from practical use

The introduction of the system in one ministry began in February 1995 and was accompanied by a very intensive user service. Two members of our project team are permantly assigned to this service. This allows to have some continuity for the users. Their personal presence at the ministry - every day in the first week and once a week later on (the so-called " jour fixe") - turned out to be very useful. It allows us to gain an insight into the usage of the system and it allows our users to ask questions appearing during their daily work. Despite their qualified training, the users were not able to directly use the groupware functionality of the system for their daily work, since they had no experience in electronic group work. While our personal presence was very useful, an additional telephone hot-line was used only sparingly.

At the beginning we were asked to help arranging the users' work settings. They started on their own to establish several shared workspaces, where cooperation partners could deposit papers they work on jointly. Their first problems were "unpredictable" and "irreproducible" effects that happened to the objects in the shared folders. We could clarify that this was caused by the usage of the same object by another user and advised them to be very explicit and disciplined when using shared folders, as well as to negotiate the purpose and the handling of each shared folder among the cooperating partners. There are two important lessons we have learnt: First, a suitable event information service is crucial to efficiently work with shared folders. Second, although our users claimed to have no need for a shared workspace feature in the first interviews, it turned out that this functionality is heavily used for their daily work. This shows the difficulty of users to express their needs without having the possibility to actually experiment with the system.

Currently the groups of our pilot users are limited to small parts of the ministerial hierarchy. We expect further results when the user groups will grow and begin to span hierarchies.

Conclusions and Outlook

The initial design of the POLITeam system has been presented in this paper. This includes the electronic circulation folder and the shared workspace component which interact with an event and information service that aims to provide awareness about the ongoing affairs in the cooperative setting. In particular, the design of the last component requires more knowledge about the needed functionality, and about necessary constraints and limits. Our first experiences show that the integration of the coordination facilities into the personal working environment is more important than sophisticated coordination mechanisms themselves. We expect that this raises new requirements for the openness of interfaces to standard office applications, which go far beyond the usual cut and paste.

Future research will additionally focus on answering some basic questions: Does the new software influence work practices and organizations? To what extent do organizational changes in public organizations result from applying these techniques? And in more detail, reflecting the security and reliability focus of this project: How will coordinated document processing functionality be taken over by the users after learning about their advantages? How will authorizing procedures, based on electronic document processing facilities, be accepted in organizations?

We expect the following years to be very interesting but also involving great responsibility since we have to satisfy the current enthusiasm of our application partners.

Acknowledgements

We wish to thank all those participating in the POLITeam project, in particular our application partners.

References

Bowers, J., "The Work to Make a Network Work: Studying CSCW in Action". In Proceedings of the ACM 1994 Conference on Computer Supported Cooperative Work - CSCW '94, Chapel Hill, USA, ACM, NY, 1994, pp. 287-298.

Dourish, P. and Bellotti, V., "Awareness and Coordination in Shared Workspaces". In Proceedings of the the ACM 1992 Conference on Computer Supported Cooperative Work - CSCW'92, Toronto, Canada, ACM/SIGCHI, NY, 1992, pp. 25-38.

Eason, K. D., "The Process of Introducing Information Technology". In Behaviour and Information Technology. 1(1982)2, pp. 197-213.

Floyd, C. and Keil, R., "Softwaretechnik und Betroffenenbeteiligung". In Beteiligung von Betroffenen bei der Entwicklung von Informationssystemen, P. Mambrey and R. Oppermann, Campus Verlag, Frankfurt, New York 1983, pp.137-164.

Fuchs, L., Pankoke-Babatz, U., Prinz, W., "Supporting Cooperative Awareness with Local Event Mechanisms: The GroupDesk System". In Proceedings of the Fourth European Conference on Computer-Supported Cooperative Work - ECSCW '95 (this volume).

Heinbokel, T., "Benutzerbeteiligung: Schlüssel zum Erfolg oder Hemmschuh der Entwicklung?". In Produktivität und Qualität in Software-Projekten, Brodbeck, Frese, (eds.), Oldenbourg Verlag, 1994, pp. 105-124.

Hoschka, P., Butscher, B., and Streitz, N., "Telecooperation and Telepresence: Technical challenges of a government distributed between Bonn and Berlin". In Informatization and the Public Sector, 1993. 2(4): pp. 269-299.

Karbe, B., "Flexible Vorgangssteuerung mit ProMinanD". In CSCW-Konzepte, Methoden und Anwendungen, S. Kirn, U. Hasenkamp, and M. Syring (eds.), Addison Wesley, 1993.

Kreifelts, T., Hinrichs, E., Klein, K.-H., Seuffert, P., Woetzel, G., "Experiences with the DOMINO Office Procedure System". In Proceedings of the Second European Conference on Computer-Supported Cooperative Work - ECSCW '91, Amsterdam, Netherlands, Kluwer Academic Publishers, 1991, pp. 117-130.

Kreifelts, T., Hinrichs, E., and Woetzel, G., "Sharing ToDo Lists with a distributed Task Manager". In Proceedings of the Third European Conference on Computer Supported Cooperative Work - ECSCW '93, G.d. Michelis, K. Schmidt, and C. Simone, eds., Kluwer, Dordrecht, 1993, pp. 31-46.

Mambrey, P., Oppermann, R., and Tepper, A., "Computer und Partizipation". Westdeutscher Verlag, Opladen 1986.

McKeen, J. D., Guimaraes, T., Wetherbe, J. C., "The Relationship between User Participation and User Satisfaction, an Investigation of four Contingency Factors". In MIS Quarterly, December 1994, pp. 427-451.

Navarro, L., Prinz, W., Rodden, T., "CSCW requires open systems". In Computer Communications, 1993, Vol. 16, No. 5, pp. 288-297.

Prinz, W., "TOSCA: Providing Organizational Information to CSCW applications". In Proceedings of the Third European Conference on Computer Supported Cooperative Work - ECSCW '93, G.d. Michelis, K. Schmidt, and C. Simone, eds., Kluwer, Dordrecht, 1993, pp. 139-154.

Shephard, A., Mayer, N., and Kuchinsky A., "STRUDL - An extensible Electronic Conversation Toolkit". In Proceedings of the ACM 1990 Conference on Computer Supported Cooperative Work - CSCW '90, Los Angeles, ACM, 1990, pp. 93-104.

Sirbu, M., Schoichet, S., Kunin, J. S., Hammer, M., and Sutherland, J., "OAM: an office analysis methodology", In Behaviour and Information Technology, 1984, Vol. 3, No. 1, pp. 25-39.

Sohlenkamp, M., and Chwelos, G., "Integrating Communication, Cooperation, and Awareness: The DIVA Virtual Office Environment". In Proceedings of the ACM 1994 Conference on Computer Supported Cooperative Work CSCW'94, Chapel Hill, USA, ACM, NY, 1994, pp. 331-343.

Wulf, V., "Negotiability: A Metafunction to Tailor Access to Data in Groupware". In Behaviour and Information Technology, 1995, in press.

Authors list

Ludwin Fuchs
GMD - German National Research Center for Information Technology
FIT Institute
Schloß Birlinghoven
D-53757 Sankt Augustin
Phone: (+49) 2241 14 2721
Fax: (+49) 2241 14 2084
Email: ludwin.fuchs@gmd.de

Konrad Klöckner
GMD - German National Research Center for Information Technology
FIT Institute
Schloß Birlinghoven
D-53757 Sankt Augustin
Phone: (+49) 2241 14 2055
Fax: (+49) 2241 14 2084
Email: kloeckner@gmd.de

Sabine Kolvenbach
GMD - German National Research Center for Information Technology
FIT Institute
Schloß Birlinghoven
D-53757 Sankt Augustin
Phone: (+49) 2241 14 2721
Fax: (+49) 2241 14 2084
Email: kolvenbach@gmd.de

Peter Mambrey
GMD - German National Research Center for Information Technology
FIT Institute
Schloß Birlinghoven
D-53757 Sankt Augustin
Phone: (+49) 2241 14 2710
Fax: (+49) 2241 14 2084
Email: mambrey@gmd.de

Proceedings of the Fourth European Conference on Computer-Supported Cooperative Work,
September 10–14, Stockholm, Sweden
H. Marmolin, Y. Sundblad, and K. Schmidt (Editors)

Fragmented Exchange: Disarticulation and the Need for Regionalized Communication Spaces

Andrew Clement
Faculty of Information Studies, University of Toronto, Canada
Ina Wagner
Abteilung für CSCW, Technische Universität Wien, Austria

Abstract:
This paper relates the discussion of articulation work (and of disarticulation) to issues of the creation and control of collective communication spaces. Four different types of settings are examined - occupationally segregated terrains, emergency situations, scarce-resource settings and performance-intensive settings. What is articulated in such settings is seen as depending on the properties of the communication spaces actors build, their zoning and contextuality; while instances of disarticulation within this space can be interpreted as a consequence of both regionalisation and/or a deterioration or even breakdown of envisioning and interrelating. CSCW design needs to take account of the regionalised character of "real world" communications by offering tools for creating a corresponding multiplicity of communication spaces.

1. Background

While CSCW derives from a commitment to establishing shared contexts, it is important to examine carefully and respect the control requirements of different groups of users along with the "politics" of sharing and withholding, inclusion and exclusion. The impulse to develop technical ways of removing barriers to communications derives from various sources ranging from quite personal desires to keep in touch with others to the corporate drive to exercise control over far-flung empires. But whatever the origins of these powerful forces, they all tend to overlook the virtues of communicative forms that are not as fully open as the co-operative ideal would imply. The great variety of practices described in the growing collection of CSCW case studies points to the need to distinguish between interactions that aim at sharing, exposing, making explicit, or prying open, and those that seek to hide, create privileges, or maintain boundaries, but also to preserve privacy, autonomy, confidentiality and solitude.

A principal aim of this paper is to examine a variety of contexts with respect to actors' practices of articulation and "disarticulation". While articulation work is often a necessary but overlooked aspect of productive performance, we seek to show that its obverse, disarticulation, is not necessarily dysfunctional. We will refer to a variety of case studies, among them previous studies in hospitals, research in "media space" environments and a current project on "telework", to exemplify distinctive contexts for communicative work. Based on this analysis, we will draw conclusions for the design of CSCW systems that support work within complex organisations.

2. Between articulating and disarticulating

People's "good reasons" for sharing or withholding information seem not only to be tightly related to the organisational structure and the nature of the tasks to be performed, they also reflect the political culture of the organisation and the environment into which it is embedded. Most of these "good reasons" for protecting or opening up are highly contested and contestable.

Much effort within CSCW (notably within the COMIC project) focuses on the support of articulation work in complex work environments. Complexity is understood as a result of the multiplicity of actors involved in a task, the distributed nature of these activities and the relative autonomy of actors in performing their part of a task. The idea is that technology be used for "reducing the complexity of articulating distributed activities of large co-operative ensembles by stipulating and mediating the articulation of the distributed activities" (Simone, 1993: 110). The authors introduce the notion of "mechanisms of interaction", abstract devices (such as plans, classifications schemes, procedures or schedules) that are embedded in a software application and provide generic facilities for articulation work.Articulation in this perspective is conceptualised as a work process or even a "supra work process" in its functionality for the performance of distributed activities.

The political and cultural context into which these activities are embedded (the coalitions people forge, the boundaries they erect, the relationships they activate or ignore) is implicitly dealt with in the "sharing and access policy" part of a CSCW system and/or in terms of roles which represent different sets of activities (Trevor, 1993). In this paper we seek to develop a conceptual framework which allows us to construct rich representations of "sharing and access" within and in between communities of practice. "Privacy" has some value here, but seems insufficiently to grasp the complexity of the issues at stake. It focuses primarily on protection against violations (of rights, sensitivities etc.) rather than on people's practices of actively structuring the communication spaces they create, occupy, or have access to.

We think that discussion of articulation work within CSCW has to be related to issues of the creation and control of collective communication spaces. The space metaphor we use here connects practices of sharing or withholding information to the location of (collective) actors, the cultural and geographical terrains they occupy, use and shape, and the zoning of these terrains in space and time. Like all representations the space metaphor is partial. It counterbalances the view of the world as a "seamless web" in which actors are in ceaseless, fluid, interactive motion. The spatialisation of social action "refers to those ways in which social life literally 'takes place': to the opening and occupation of different sites of human action and to the differences and integrations that are socially inscribed through the production of place, space, and landscape" (Gregory, 1994: 104).

Based on Hägerstrand's (1975) mapping of interactions in time-space diagrams, Anthony Giddens developed an analytical framework for describing the social organisation of interactions. He introduces two key terms: *locale* which "refers to the use of space to provide the settings of interaction, the settings of interaction in turn being essential to specifying its contextuality"; and *regionalisation* which describes "the zoning of time-space in relation to routinised social practices." "Locales may range form a room in a house, a street corner, the shop floor of a factory, towns and cities, to the territorially demarcated areas occupied by nation states. But locales are typically internally *regionalized*, and the regions within them are of critical importance in constituting contexts of interaction." (Giddens, 1984: 118f) Location captures the here-and-now situatedness of social action, including the specific vision this locatedness provides. Feminist theories insist on the presence and vision of particular subjects in geographically, culturally and historically distinct places, articulated in a "politics of location" (Haraway, 1991; Probyn, 1990).

Hospitals, for example, are highly regionalised interaction spaces with physical boundaries between different regions such as wards, the surgical tract, laboratories, kitchen and laundry. Most of these regions are inhabited by people with different occupational backgrounds and will physically never be entered by others. The interactions of physicians and nurses can be located in specific regions of the hospital, e.g. an outpatient department, in which they convene from different parts of the hospital to pool their knowledge for the treatment of patients. The regionalisation perspective spatially operationalises issues of interdependence and power. Patterns of access and exclusion in an hospital reflect a complex web of occupational hierarchies inscribed in the distribution of competencies and responsibilities.

Spatialisation, or the use of space, place, and landscape as categories for describing and analysing social interaction, helps us focus on the multiple visible and invisible closures of interaction spaces. It assists in identifying the dense, complex and multi-layered connections between people who are not necessarily co-present in space and time. Some studies of co-operative work implicitly build upon a space metaphor. So does Fagerhaugh et al.'s analysis of hazards in hospital care in which they refer to "the fragmentation effects of specialisation (that) arise because multitudes of departments and layers and layers of workers must be co-ordinated within the chain of tasks necessary to complete a treatment or a diagnostic test" (Fagerhaugh, 1987: 14).

Regionalisation in their view is closely connected to the failure to articulate or "disarticulation" - "misassessing, mismonitoring, mistiming, misbalancing of risks, misrectifying, and miscommunication" (139). Disarticulation in complex organisations can occur due to the fact that disruptions of the work process can come from multiple and often interactive sources and affect multiple interrelated lines of work. In addition to complexity, there is a multiplicity of perspectives which are not necessarily shared but may be protected, suppressed or used to dominate others. Finally, not everything can be articulated, as "the errorless imperative", a strong and unreasonable demand for infallibility, shows. The collective communication space in a hospital is neither homogeneous nor complete nor equally accessible to all actors.

In their study of "heedful interrelating" on aircraft carrier flight decks, Weick and Roberts conceptualise a shared communication space which results from actors' ability to construct their own contribution to a shared task "while envisaging a social system of joint actions ..., and to interrelate that constructed action with the system that is envisaged" (Weick, 1993: 363). The envisaged system (e.g. for launching a series of aircraft in quick succession) emerges as the activities are interrelated. When interrelating and the images that feed it break down, actors' attention tends to focus on the local, rather than on the joint situation: "As interrelating deteriorates and becomes more primitive, there is less comprehension of the implications of unfolding events, slower correction of errors, and more opportunities for small errors to combine and amplify" (Weick, 1993: 371). Actors' communication space becomes fragmented, their vision partial and insufficiently connected to the perspectives and interpretations of others.

In contrast to these analyses which focus on the detrimental effects of disarticulation, we look at it in a more "neutral" way. We see disarticulation not just as a failure to communicate openly and effectively but as a phenomenon which highlights the fact that the regionalisation of communication spaces may help actors to get focused and/or to protect their view. In this framework we can think of a large computer network which links and interconnects different communities of practice as consisting of a variety of locales and regions, some of them overlapping. Access to these territories will be highly selective, depending on actors' strategies. What is articulated will depend on the properties of this communication space, its zoning and contextuality, while instances of disarticulation within this space can be interpreted as a consequence of both regionalisation and/or a deterioration or even breakdown of envisioning and interrelating.

3. Contexts of sharing or withholding

Our approach to understanding how the properties of communication spaces influence articulation work is to distinguish between archetypal settings. It is inspired by Weick and Roberts' analysis of high-reliablity and high efficiency organisations (Weick, 1993). They argue that, in addition to structure and technology, organisations differ with respect to the microdynamics of interrelating and style and manner of performance. We wish to expand their distinction on the basis of our case-study material. Each of the four settings we discuss will highlight a specific set of relationships between organisational 'micropolitics', the structure of communication spaces and the technological support of articulation work. We speak of settings rather than of organisations since several types of settings may be found in one and the same organisation. The first setting, characterised by strong *occupational segregation*, is commonly found in large, mature, formal organizations operating in relatively stable environments. The other settings can be regarded as variations – *emergency* settings arise on occasions when action must be taken quickly in the face of high risk of serious failure; *scarce-resource* settings are becoming more common as funding, particularly in public sector organizations, is reduced; and *performance-intensive* settings emerge when there are strong competitive pressures.

3.1. Segregated terrains

A particular type of communication space can be found in Crozier and Thoenig's study of processes of organisational fragmentation. In their analysis they describe the fragmented organisation as building upon and also encouraging the development of a diversity of practices and perspectives. As such it reflects a recognition of the multiplicity of organisational realities. On the other hand it does not support the sharing of these perspectives. Often the information flow in these types of organisations is low and there is little direct co-operation. Although there are multiple dependencies, the games actors play are games of "defence, protection and non communication" (Crozier and Thoenig 1976: 550). Where actors co-operate, they build on complicity, based on shared mutual experiences and complementary interests.

Hospital work typically takes places in a fragmented organisational context. Apart from the traditional subdivision of hospitals into wards, medical departments and a central administration, each of which constitute their own parallel organisation, medical specialisation and new technologies based on impressive machines have generated an increasing number of specialised services and associated work and procedures. Each of these groups, through their professional training and highly specialised work tasks, develop their own thought worlds and form distinct occupational 'milieus'. For instance, when we look at patients' location within this highly regionalised interaction space, we see that patients are frequently moved to and from specialised machines and areas. However, the knowledge of patients that has been interactively accumulated in one region of the hospital does not follow their physical movements, unless special effort at articulating this knowledge is made. This multiplies the possibilities of misinformation and of confusion over the co-ordination of regionally distributed work.

Resistance against building a shared communication space across regions is strong. An example is the difficulties in dealing with technology-associated medical hazards in hospitals. In their analysis of safety critical situations in hospitals, Fagerhaugh et al. understand the present mismanagement of clinical safety as a result of the multiplicity of the domain (which may result in contradictory functional requirements) and of health workers' perspectives (Fagerhaugh, 1987). The complex nature of safety work, they argue, calls for much sharing and overlapping among the various services, departments and occupational groups within a hospital – nurses, medical specialists, a host of ancillary services, and multitudes of regulatory agencies with their distinctive guidelines. Each of these groups creates its own modes of perceiving and interpreting hazards and often holds discrepant views on basic issues pertaining to clinical safety and the work of maximising it. Practices of safety articulation are ill-developed. This is partly due to the fact that actors are not encouraged to build a shared understanding of clinical safety; partly it results from the distribution of safety work over regions that develop distinct contextualities.

In segregated terrains, people's communication spaces are highly regionalised. The records that populate these spaces are a product of selective co-operation, of access as well as exclusion. What is visible and shared throughout the organisation is carefully defined and restricted. This can be seen as an attempt at protecting special locations and the vision they provide from powerful, potentially overriding views and interests. This zoning also supports existing power structures and dependencies.

Shared communication spaces in such settings are typically restricted to local contexts where interaction is dense and levels of articulation are high. Articulation work across regions is confined to restricted communication channels and facilitated by standardized mechanisms of interaction. An example is a central application linking the hospital's wards with the laboratories and the pharmacy. In combination with an automated transportation system, it regulates the transfer of medical orders, specimen, diets, drugs and lab results. Forms, procedural rules, and thesauri provide some of the common ground for such border crossings.

3.2. Emergency (High-Reliability) Situations

While regionalization can help in the smooth conduct of routine operations, it can get in the way on the occasions when decisive action is urgently required. In health work, for instance, co-operative relationships are often centred around such acute situations. A "crisis" elicits patterns of dense co-operation and sharing which cannot be observed in the handling of daily routines. Practices of time-management also change dramatically as soon as an emergency arrives. The staff's ability and willingness to synchronise their activities and to improvise by circumventing routine procedures of generating, retrieving and sharing information greatly differs from what is considered routine practice. These two temporal orders (and the associated practices) are selectively activated and they only partially overlap (Wagner, 1994).

Emergencies can be of varying kinds: they can be an intricate feature of a work situation as is the case in air traffic control; they also can occur spontaneously and unexpectedly, pushing people to extend their communication space in order to be able to cope with a problem. In some of the impressive examples of co-operative work in the CSCW field (such as air traffic control (Hughes, 1992) or the London Underground control room (Heath, 1992)) routine procedures seem to incorporate the experience of emergencies and their handling. Staff's level of peripheral awareness of each other's work is such that they can immediately evaluate and react upon an incident. Emergencies require the kind of interrelating which Weick and Roberts see as typical of high-reliability organisations in which errors can have fatal consequences. Often this is coupled with a preoccupation with perfection - activities need to be perfectly attuned not only to avoid mistakes but also to keep the unfolding flow of events comprehensible.

Although emergency settings create a strong incentive for building a shared communication space, instances of disarticulation are widespread and in some cases (such as aeroplane crashes) attract a lot of attention. In their analysis of such an incident, Weick and Roberts offer a detailed description of how the boundaries of actors' shared communication space (or in their language: "collective mind") were drawn more and more narrowly and their ability "to envision their contributions in the context of requirements for joint action" (Weick, 1993: 373) broke down. The incident happened during a night-time launch and recovery of several aircraft, a typical emergency situation. A cumulation of incomprehensible events made interrelating more and more difficult. Actors and activities became isolated and the system of distributed action rapidly lost its form. This is an example of how a shared communication space is split into ill connected fragments that no longer support a vision of the whole task.

In emergency situations, the communication space need not be restricted to the immediate local context. Examples of this can be found in the uses of corporate bulletin board systems and groupware products such as NOTES. There are reported cases of technical personnel posting requests for help on particular problems, and quickly getting pertinent responses from others scattered throughout the corporation. Similarly, reports on Internet news groups give examples of immediate, focused attention on certain topics. The August 1993 issue of Newsweek describes how participants of a parent support group distributed throughout the US helped someone through a family crisis. During the most dramatic phase of the war in Slovenia, an academic network (Usenet) was spontaneously converted into a means of distributing the unofficial views of independent individuals and of providing personal and moral support to colleagues (Lubich, 1993). These are examples of spontaneously formed communication spaces for people who otherwise would not have had the incentive nor the opportunity to reach out at each other. The Slovenian case is particularly interesting since an already well-defined communication space for scientists was extended to journalists who quickly became aware of the value of this source for their assessment of the situation. There was even the notion of "misuse", questioning the right of people to appropriate an electronic forum which was designed for academic exchange for their political and personal purposes (Wagner, 1995).

Regionalisation is low and boundaries permeable. In a segregated environment, such as an hospital, emergencies are handled by pooling knowledge situationally and locally without touching upon those boundaries and selected cooperations that govern routine interactions. Even in a control room context (connecting a variety of physically separated locales), there are distinct regions which are reserved for specific sets of actors and events. Still, boundaries are 'spongy' and relationships between distant actors can be easily activated through a variety of communication channels and a broad array of mechanisms of interaction (prespecified as well as open and flexible) . In emergency settings we will often find rich common artefacts (Robinson, 1994) which support the envisioning of the whole task and capture as much contextual information as possible.

3.3. Scarce-resource settings

An increasingly common variant of occupational segregation are scarce-resource settings. The scarcity of time, money, people, technologies, or access to information may constrain the performance of an organisation and create a strong pressure to co-operate and share across boundaries.

A good example is reported by Sørensen in her account of an action research project in a Norwegian hospital. At the start of this project, the staff was clearly reluctant to make performance data explicit and to share them with other organisational units. As long as this fear prevailed, surgical departments suffered from recurrent severe bottlenecks. Patients had to be sent away and the hospital lost part of its income. A major step forward was taken when the responsible head nurses came to realise that sharing information would help them to cope better with their dwindling resources. They initiated the development of a small computer system whose main rationale was to provide an overview of the actual and projected need of resources which would otherwise not be available (Sørensen 1993).

This example also shows that a strong incentive for complex organisations to strengthen co-operation are economic sanctions in case of under performance. Distributing resources according to achievement criteria which apply across individuals or groups, provides motivation to share, adjust flexibly and negotiate. For example, in the Norwegian case all patients in the waiting list that have not been treated within six months (and the income that they would generate for the hospital) are transferred to another hospital. This may result in a substantial loss of resources (e.g. a unit may lose some of its already scarce nursing staff).

Scarce resource settings can be found in many types of organizations, apart from the highly segregated environments illustrated by this hospital case. The patterns that characterize them are distinct, as cooperative relationships center around the need for negotiating and aligning resources, often under time constraints. Representations of work are partially integrated. They provide an overview which both exposes units and individuals to scrutiny and assessment from outside and helps to limit the risk of an unexpected shortage or variation of resources. They connect different regions (e.g. surgical departments), allowing actors to envision them as a system of shared resources and to interrelate their planning of operations and personnel. A key feature that supports this cooperation is the common stake that particpants have in the outcome. If there weren't trusted assurances of relatively equitable outcomes, such as those offered by job security or adjustment provisions, there would be much less incentive for individuals to give up exclusive control of their local resources.

3.4. Performance-intensive settings

Surgical teams and air traffic controllers are good examples of settings in which high performance levels are required for the monitoring of risk situations. Other types of performance-intensive situations are more difficult to assess with respect to articulation and disarticulation.

In her account of the design of a prototype "electronic file cabinet" for a law firm, Lucy Suchman discusses the "good reasons" of Mark, a lawyer who has built up an enormous "private" paper file together with highly developed text searching skills, for making this file electronically available and searchable to everyone in his firm (thereby renouncing his information monopoly). As in many other organisations, there was a strong and increasing pressure towards "high performance." This is closely associated with management's interest in making individual expertise more readily accessible and exploitable in the pursuit of profit..

A good example of this pressure is to be found in Quinn and Pacquette's account of a global management consulting fiorm, which they characterise as a "spider's web" organisation. It has been building a database that systematically captures the histories of its contacts with clients and practical solutions for special problems (Quinn and Paquette 1990: 73):

> The firm operates in a highly decentralised, real-time mode. Each local office is as independent as possible. Partners say that AA&Co.'s distinctive competency has become "empowering people to deliver better quality technology-based solutions to clients in shorter time". ... Yet professionals who leave AA&Co. immediately lose access to its system and accumulated experience.

> Within wide ranges, each node (team) may function quite independently in serving a particular client base. However, in certain circumstances, the individual nodes may need to operate in a highly co-ordinated fashion to achieve strategic advantage for a specific purpose.

People working in performance-intensive settings often have to operate in a "profit-centre" mode. Case studies of information-sharing practices in two large computer firms (work in progress) suggests that in such situations people often endorse and practise "open access" strategies. The growth of LANs, personal but shared databases, and Internet connections is part of this strategy. It reflects people's need for immediate access to a wide array of distributed standardised information as well as informal information, in order to be able to act as 'high performers.' However, as Orlikowski (1993) observes in her study of a firm remarkably similar to AA&Co., unless such structural properties as reward systems and workplace norms are consistent with openness and sharing, the desired collaboration is unlikely to emerge.

Redrawing regions

A particularly good example of how performance-intensity influences actors' communication space is the case of a software house which has started to shift part of its employees' activities to their homes[1]. In-depth interviews were carried out with eleven of its staff, most of them marketing specialists for different types of clients as well as some systems engineers. These people's tasks largely consist of well-defined, short term "actions" which require considerable co-ordination effort, but there is little time and social space for managing tasks co-operatively. This in turn strengthens people's dependence on technical support systems such as computer networks and the variety of services provided through them. Over time, people who in another type of organisation would have managed their "action items" in intense, partly face-to-face co-operation within a team and across organisational units, have come to rely almost entirely on their own capacity for self-organisation, backed up by a shared information system.

Practices of self-organisation are reinforced by the company's reward structure. Rewards are extremely output-oriented. Employees are not paid primarily for the time they work, but for their results. Much of the effort spent on creating organisational and technical support for colleagues within the company remains invisible and unrewarded. Relations with clients have clear priority over internal contacts. Patterns of communication and co-operation reflect the fact that employees operate within this "weakly attenuated" social environment. A particularly interesting feature of this environment is the use of network-based services, above all email. Email is heavily used for managing time and tasks. All employees have access to individual electronic calendars and discipline in updating seems to be high. When people have very little shared time in the office, this opening up of individual calendars becomes vital. In order to be included in ad-hoc meetings and at the same time to be able to call in an urgent meeting, people simply have to share information about their individual use of time.

Email is valued as helping to increase the completeness and reliability of information, even among people who are spatially close to each other. Requests in the cafeteria or in the corridors are often not answered unless written up and fixed on email. Email is also associated with a certain communication discipline. People expect others to concretise their requests. For managers, it has a documentary function and helps to ensure consecutive action. Even people who have agreed on something on the phone or face-to-face use email to confirm. Email is also used for

---

[1] This case description refers to ongoing research by Andrea Birnbaumer, Martin Kompast, Hilda Tellioglu and Ina Wagner, Abteilung für CSCW, Technische Universität Wien.

establishing discipline, e.g. through forwarding reminders to a person's manager - as one of them phrases it "a wonderful escalation tool which really works" (KL, 15).

The telephone is the second most used communication tool in this environment. People call each other even if they sit in adjacent rooms. A switchboard operator is responsible for the efficient routing of incoming calls. She and a system of voice boxes are trusted with ensuring availability to important contacts (mostly clients). Portable phones make it possible to use otherwise unused time (e.g. en-route in a traffic jam) for answering urgent calls.

Moreover, much of the most important information is no longer provided by the co-inhabitants of people's office but by spatially distant partners. This culture of communication reflects an organisation which expects its employees to develop a high level of self-reliance and self-organisation and provides little time and space for the social management of tasks. The whole array of technologies available to its employees is designed to support "the parallel management of multiple tasks" at a distance. Co-presence is no longer a specific value. On the contrary, it is often associated with disruption, overload, and unwanted intrusion. Protecting and drawing boundaries in such an environment is connected with the danger of cutting oneself off from a multiplicity of only partially knowable and predictable sources.

Comparing this environment with a performance-intensive, but occupationally segregated setting highlights some of the differences between organisational communication spaces. In our case study on scheduling surgical operations, for example, introducing a shared electronic calendar was a highly contested issue. In particular, the group with the highest level of time autonomy, surgeons, had the power to insist on keeping information about their availability private, while nurses and anaesthesiologists voiced an interest in making their use of time publicly visible (Egger and Wagner 1993). Temporal transparency was constrained by the hospital's hierarchy and compartmentalisation. There is a strong contrast between the communication space for the planning of surgical operations in this clinic which remained strictly regionalised, and the level of simultaneous envisaging and interrelating attained locally, in the operating theatre.

Overriding personal boundaries

Whereas the previous example showed how common electronic spaces could support articulation work across physical and temporal locales that were increasingly regionalised because of growing performance requirements, a field study conducted by Laura Garton (Garton and Moore 1994) suggests that this approach can be taken too far[2]. The study, involving an experimental use of media space technologies to link the central and satellite offices of a small research institute, provides a vivid example of difficulties that can arise when open

---

[2] This account draws heavily upon materials presented by Laura Garton and Gale Moore at the CSCW'94 Workshop on Critical Considerations in the Creation and Control of Personal/Collective Communications Spaces, Chapel Hill, NC, October 22, 1994. We appreciate their willingness to allow us to make extensive use of this insightful report.

communication spaces are overlaid across disparate physical, status and personal boundaries in response to a desire for intensified performance.

The technologies involved in this case were developed with the aim of gaining early insights into the social implications of media space technologies through rapid prototyping, and workplace-based field research. The prototype media space is a form of Multi-Media Communication Service (Clement 1994, Dourish 1993) and interconnects a variety of technologies such as video cameras, microphones, VCRs, and computers, and a variety of spaces such as conference rooms and offices, providing services such as video-conferencing.

The principal field trial of the media space took place within a research administration organisation, whose primary work is to support the growth and development of a regional IT industry. Funded on a contract basis, this organisation was under constant pressure to demonstrate its effectiveness and promote `leading edge technologies.' The Director and most of the other 11 employees work at the headquarters, while the Associate Director and one site co-ordinator work in a satellite office located beyond reasonable commuting distance. The recently hired Director, who had a background in marketing came to see the media space as a way to advertise the mission of the organisation, and hopefully to help create technologies that 'empower human beings'. The Director believed that the office in the periphery would like to be more involved and in touch with the core group at headquarters.

The Co-ordinator at the satellite office considered the work as independent from headquarters and prior to installation, did not feel the media space technology was needed to accomplish work tasks. A personalised desktop video connection between sites was viewed as uncalled-for: it wasn't necessary to get on a TV to talk to the headquarters staff about ordering supplies. It also seemed like `Big Brother' and the Co-ordinator didn't want to spend extra time with what would likely be lengthier interruptions from headquarters. Coupled with the concern that the media space would cost extra time was the concern that the Associate Director might become too available for more work from the Director. Since the Director had come on board it seemed they were swamped and the Co-ordinator felt discouraged about the whole idea that headquarters would have more access to them at the satellite site. From the Co-ordinators perspective, lack of access to headquarters was not a problem. Rather than improve connectivity through the media space, the strong preference was to manage the connectivity they already had. The Associate Director assumed the role of protecting staff from the direct requests of headquarters and supported staff attempts to control the work flow.

With this set of social relations between the periphery and the core, when the media space was installed, the Co-ordinator simply closed the electronic `door', thus indicating unavailability via the software. Masking tape applied to the camera lens ensured no unwanted viewing, and was eventually replaced by a camera lens cover. Interestingly, the closed `door state' behaviour was not considered particularly unusual by the staff at headquarters. They referred to the satellite office Co-ordinator as someone who prefers to work separately form central office. Even though no one else kept their door state closed, this behaviour was not considered deviant or even particularly noteworthy. As long as there was access by phone or email, no one expressed concern.

However, with the Associate Director connected to the Director via the media space, the periphery was no longer as isolated as it had once been. The Associate Director who was an early promoter of the technology because of its ability to reduce travel needs, was also generally pleased with the new accessibility to the Director. In fact, both parties felt the system was invaluable during the first summer of operation when they had to make a number of important budget decisions, such as staff allocation for the upcoming year. However, toward the end of the summer the Associate Director's enthusiasm for the system began to wane. There were times when the Director `popped' into the office unannounced,and once during a phone call remained `on the desk' until the call was finished. The Associate Director found these spontaneous episodes somewhat disconcerting and not quite what had been expected when anticipating a `shared workspace'. At that time, the Associate Director may have felt it was not judicious to adjust the door state and thereby make explicit to the Director a desire to maintain more control over this new shared work environment. Instead, the Associate Director would occasionally disconnect the camera. This resulted in the person who was trying to connect to get a message that there were problems with the video connection. The general interpretation by the caller was that there was some sort of system failure.

Since the system, a research prototype, did on occasion fail, it became an accepted belief that the media space technology was not reliable. This grey area of system reliability allowed users to manipulate their accessibility without using the more explicit protocols of door states. For the technical group it unexpectedly became a support nightmare trying to disentangle what was a true technical problem, from a technical problem due to something not under their control, or what was possibly deliberate `sabotage' by a user.

We see in this case an example of how a CSCW application, introduced on the presumption of the value of seamless communication, interferes with the prior and apparently legitimate patterns of regionalisation, and leads to some technical dysfunction. We can also see how, in Weick and Roberts terms, the lack of shared vision (of a particular form of organizational functioning) can lead to a deterioration of interrelating to the point that measures, such as resorting to lens covering and plug pulling, became desirable.

The technical features that were built into the system to afford some degree of protection against unwelcome intrusion and exposure, proved to be only partly successful. A more careful attention to the social dimensions of the communication spaces and in particular a more critical examination of assumptions concerning the overriding of boundaries would be helpful. In this experimental setting, such unintended consequences are to be expected and may be handled through ongoing adjustments, but it is likely that in more conventional settings there will be similar needs for continuing adaptation. In performance-intensive settings people have strong incentives to build up communication spaces which help them to envisage and interrelate while acting for a common task and/or to have access to a multiplicity of only partially knowable and predictable sources. Still, regionalisation in such settings is variable, depending on the situation and on power relations. The representations of work of superiors are not necessarily as open and immediate to subordinates as they are the other way around.

The four settings discussed above are not distinct in all dimensions, nor are they mutually exclusive. Rather, they highlight specific sets of relationships between tasks, organizational culture, the structure of communication space and technological support for articulation work. Table 1 summarizes some of the main differences and similarities between these archetypal settings.

Table 1: Archetypal settings - sets of relationships

	SEGREGATED	EMERGENCY - HIGH RELIABILITY	SCARCE RESOURCE	PERFORMANCE-INTENSIVE
Incentives for articulation	intense local interaction boundary crossings	grave consequences of error in acute situation need for perfection	scarce resources economic sanctions	high pressure to perform economic rewards
Incentives for disarticulation	highly specialized perspectives protecting a particular vision, practice	deflect blame claim credit	hoard local resources	information overload protecting personal boundaries
Regionalisation	high on the basis of functions & occupational milieus	low, or flexibly adaptable (at least temporarily)	high, restricted openings	variable, depending on situation
Representations of work	specialized & fragmented partial connections	support envisioning of whole task	partially integrated	open, immediate access
(Technological) support of articulation work	local applications restricted communication channels formalized mechanisms of interaction	open networks rich common artefacts broad array of mechanisms of interaction	resource-sharing facilities	open networks shared databases and planning tools telepresence arrangements

4. Implications for the design of communication spaces

Computer technologies can be seen as opening up new communication spaces, as influencing the distribution of encounters in these spaces, and as supporting the definition of regions and of transitions or barriers between them. One important part of design work is to identify regions and the connections and boundaries between them which may be professional (reflecting the needs of different local communities), political (e.g. seeking protection against powerful actors), or personal. As Schmidt and Bannon (1992) argue, "visibility must be bounded" in order that individuals' activities not be overexposed, but some of these preserves will be more legitimate than others.

Part of the challenge facing developers of CSCW applications that are sensitive to the needs for both articulation and disarticulation, is to distinguish between technically and socially focused prescriptions. There is a common and well founded presumption that the technical infrastructure to support communication should ideally present as few barriers as possible, that it should be 'seamless' in its connectivity. However, this does not necessarily mean that the actual human communication would not often benefit from maintaining barriers and divisions. As we have shown, there may well be very good reasons for doing so. This suggests that there should be technical facilities for allowing participants to erect, shift, blur, harden, dissolve, and strengthen the boundaries to communication spaces. This is already done in conventional (non-electronic) communication spaces by drawing upon the rich resources for accomplishing this that are afforded by the physical world (walls, partitions, locks, windows, doors, furniture placement, etc.). Providing electronic communication facilities should then not be seen only as offering ways to surmount obstacles but also to permit people to rearrange communication spaces according to their changing needs, wants and desires.

The spectacular success and obvious shortcomings of email are instructive here. Because the basic email transactions are dyadic, between a voluntary initiator and an explicitly designated recipient, many of the difficulties outlined above are avoided from the start. Email, in effect, facilitates the spontaneous ad-hoc creation of very many two-person communications spaces. Distribution lists of various forms expand the membership, but participation typically remains voluntary and the boundaries defined by explicit subscriber lists. It is when messages cross these borders that controversies arise – senders accidentally send to the wrong person, a recipient forwards to a third party, a supervisor monitors employee email traffic (giving rise to some high profile court cases in the US), archived messages thought to be deleted serve as incriminating evidence (perhaps just as well in the case of White House agent, Oliver North).

As electronic systems are refined to support various forms of group communication more specifically, then greater attention must be paid to questions of boundary management – especially who is within (and outside) the space for particular types of communication, and how spaces may be linked across the borders. Of course, providing the technical means to define communicative regions under individual and collective control alone is not adequate, as the media space example showed. Very much depends on the social processes by which the participants can bring their own informed voices to bear.

At this point we can only offer a "metaphorical approach" to the question of how to integrate "flexible regionalisation" into a CSCW system. We might envision a layered map of actors' communication spaces, the first layer showing the shared terrains, their contours, the actors and objects that populate them. Successive layers may be more detailed, affording an overview of regions and selected connections between them, or representing the views open to different sets of actors. Negotiations would then result in operations such as visibly removing a barrier, displacing objects, introducing one-way roads and dead-ends, and inserting temporal constraints for certain actions.

Our point is not to say that in general there should be more or less co-operation, openness, withholding, and so on. Rather, CSCW design should take account of the regionalised character of "real world" communications and by offering tools for creating a corresponding multiplicity of communication spaces, provide the technical basis for the necessary negotiations between the actors involved.

References

Clement, Andrew (1994): "Considering Privacy in the Development of Multimedia Communications", *Computer Supported Cooperative Work*, vol. 2, pp. 67-88.

Crozier, Michel and Jean-Claude Thoenig (1976): "The Regulation of Complex Organized Systems", *Administrative Sci ence Quarterly*, vol. 21, pp. 547-570.

Dourish, Paul (1993) "Culture and Control in a Media Space", *Proceedings of the Third European Conference on CSCW*, Milan, Kluwer, pp. 125-137.

Egger, Edeltraut and Ina Wagner (1993): "Negotiating Temporal Orders. The Case of Collaborative Time-Management in a Surgery Clinic", *Computer Supported Cooperative Work. An International Journal*, vol. 1, pp. 255-275.

Fagerhaugh, Shizuko, Anselm Strauss, et al. (1987): *Hazards In Hospital Care. Ensuring Patient Safety, Jossey-Bass*, San Francisco.

Garton, Laura and Gale Moore (1994): "The Creation and Control of a Media Space: A Case Study", CSCW'94 Workshop on Critical Considerations in the Creation and Control of Personal/Collective Communications Spaces, Chapel Hill, NC.

Giddens, Anthony (1984): *The Constitution of Society: Outline of the Theory of Structuration*, Polity Press, Cambridge.

Gregory, Derek (1994): *Geographical Imaginations*, Blackwell, Cambridge MA.

Hägerstrand, T. (1975): Space, Time and Human Condition, in A. Karlqvist (ed.), *Dynamic Allocation of Urban Space*, Saxon House, Farnborough.

Haraway, Donna (1991): *Simians, Cyborgs, and Women*, Routledge, New York.

Heath, Christian and Paul Luff (1992): "Collaboration and Control. Crisis Management and Multimedia Technology in London Underground Control Rooms", *Computer Supported Cooperative Work. An International Journal*, vol. 1, no. 2, pp. 69-94.

Hughes, John, David Randall, et al. (1992): "Faltering from Ethnography to Design". *ACM 1992 Conference on Computer Supported Cooperative Work*, Toronto,

Lubich, Hannes P. (1993): "IT in Action: The Impact of Electronic Communication Networks on Information Dissemination During the Slovenia Conflict", *European Conference on Computer Science, Communication and Society: A Technical and Cultural Challenge*, Neuchatel, Switzerland,

Orlikowski, Wanda (1993) "Learning from Notes: Organizational Issues in Groupware Implementation", *The Information Society*, Vol. 9, pp. 237-250.

Probyn, Elspeth (1990): "Travels in the Postmodern: Making Sense of the Local", in L. J. Nicolson (ed.), *Feminism/Postmodernism*, Routledge, New York, pp. 176-189 .

Quinn, J.B. and P.C. Paquette (1990): "Technology in Services. Creating Organizational Revolutions", *Sloan Management Review* (Winter), pp. 67-78.

Robinson, Mike (1994): "Reconstructing Understandings of Organisation", in A. Clement, P. Kolm and I. Wagner (eds.), *NetWORKing. Connecting Workers In and Between Organizations*, North-Holland, Amsterdam, pp. 7-16.

Schmidt, Kjeld and Liam Bannon (1992): "Taking CSCW Seriously. Supporting Articulation Work", *Computer-Supported Cooperative Work*, vol. 1, no. 2, pp. 7-40.

Schneider, Karin and Ina Wagner (1993): "Constructing the "Dossier Réprésentatif". Information-Sharing in French Hospitals", In *Computer-Supported Cooperative Work. An International Journal*, vol. 1, pp. 229-253.

Simone, C. and K. Schmidt, Eds. (1993): Computational Mechanisms of Interaction for CSCW. COMIC. Lancaster University.

Sørensen, B.A. (1993): The Health Reserach Programme 1988-'90, 1991-'93. Work Research Institute, Oslo.

Suchman, Lucy (1993): "Technologies of Accountability: Of Lizards and Aeroplanes", in G. Button (ed.), *Technology in Working Order*, Routledge, London, pp. 113-127.

Trevor, Jonathan, Tom Rodden, et al. (1993): "COLA. A Lightweight Platform for CSCW", *Third European Conference on Computer-Supported Cooperative Work*, Milan, Kluwer.

Wagner, Ina (1993): "Women´s Voice. The Case of Nursing Information Systems", *AI & Society*, vol.7, no. 4, pp. 295-310.

Wagner, Ina (1994a): "Networking Actors and Organisations", *Computer Supported Cooperative Work. An International Journal*, vol. 2, no.1-2, pp. 5-20.

Wagner, Ina (1994b): "Zur sozialen Verhandlung von Zeit. Das Beispiel computergestützten Zeitmanagements", *Soziale Welt Sonderband* 9, pp. 241-255.

Weick, Karl E. and Karlene H. Roberts (1993): "Collective Mind in Organizations: Heedful Interrelating on Flight Decks", *Administrative Science Quarterly*, vol. 38, pp. 357-381.

Proceedings of the Fourth European Conference on Computer-Supported Cooperative Work,
September 10–14, Stockholm, Sweden
H. Marmolin, Y. Sundblad, and K. Schmidt (Editors)

Workflow From Within and Without:

Technology and Cooperative Work on the Print Industry Shopfloor

John Bowers
Department of Psychology, University of Manchester, UK.
Computing Department, Lancaster University, UK. (visiting 1994-5)

Graham Button
Rank Xerox Research Centre Cambridge Laboratory, UK.

Wes Sharrock
Department of Sociology, University of Manchester, UK.

This paper reports fieldwork from an organization in the print industry, examining a workflow system introduced to the shopfloor. We detail the indigenous methods by which members order their work, contrast this with the order provided by the system, and describe how members have attempted to accommodate the two. Although it disrupted shopfloor work, the system's use was a contractural requirement on the organization to make its services accountable. This suggests workflow systems can often be seen as *technologies for organizational ordering and accountability*. We conclude that CSCW requirements should acknowledge such exigencies and the organizational status of workflow technologies.

Introduction: Workflow Systems and Work Practice

This paper reports a field study of workflow technology in a nationally distributed organization in the print industry. By 'workflow technology' we understand any technology designed to (in some way) give order to or record the unfolding of work activity over time by, for example, providing tools and information to users at appropriate moments or enabling them to overview the work process they are part of or to design work processes for themselves or others or whatever. The development of workflow technology has been an important part of the research endeavour within CSCW (Medina-Mora et al., 1992; Agostini et al., 1993) arousing much controversy and debate (e.g. Suchman, 1994; Winograd, 1994). However, not all of the discussion of workflow technology has been directly informed by empirical studies of cooperative work or of the use of emerging systems. For example, several systems have been developed on the basis of general theories of communication such as speech acts (e.g. Winograd & Flores, 1986) or abstract process models (e.g. Medina-Mora et al., 1992) rather than empirical studies of talk at work or the details of actually occurring work practice. This exposes such systems to the objection that they are insensitive to the contextual details of work and interaction in ways which inhibit their usability. Indeed, an increasing number of case studies of workflow and groupware technology in CSCW point to this as a critical problem when such systems are implemented in actual organizational contexts (e.g. Bowers, 1994; Orlikowski, 1992).

Our study adds to and extends the emerging literature of empirical studies of workflow technologies in use by examining a workflow system in the print industry. To date studies of technology in use in CSCW have been dominated by office work in adminisitrative and managerial sectors. Indeed, with a few exceptions (e.g. Hughes et al., 1992), 'the office' constitutes the default development context for much of CSCW research. To us, this is an unfortunate narrowing of the horizons of CSCW and one which has influenced the debate over workflow systems. The presence of computers in office work, from familiar word processing and database systems to local area networks and so forth, is ubiquitous. This makes it easy for designers to consider adding to the functionality of office systems with the introduction of workflow applications. Indeed, in some of the most developed visions, workflow will become less another application more an 'embedded enabler' of work invisible to the user much like many of the features of today's workstation operating systems (cf. Abbott & Sarin, 1994). However, it is notable that this vision depends upon the ubiquity of computers as the tool and medium for the work. While this may be becoming the case for much administrative and managerial work, not all work has this character. Indeed, the existence of special purpose tools and materials, not necessarily computational or informational in nature, is precisely part of what makes production and manufacturing work distinct.

For example, on the print industry shopfloor, while computer controlled digital technologies are becoming more prominent, older methods such as lithography and 'hot metal' presses are still deemed essential for various forms of work. Many contemporary print shops are likely to contain a heterogeneous suite of technology to maintain flexibility in how jobs can be done. Thus, currently, in much of the print industry, the vision of ubiquitous computer-based workflow technologies is someway off. This means that workflow technologies in such industries need to be at least in part *external* to the tools and materials of the work. While an office based workflow system can take the approach of providing information and computer based tools as and when they are appropriate, it is not feasible for a workflow system to set up a litho-machine or move a comb-binder onto the shopfloor as and when they are required for the job! In short, we feel that much of the debate surrounding workflow has been specific to *internal* workflow technologies where the tools and materials are not different in kind from those used in the work itself.

Of course, those who criticise workflow systems are often precisely objecting to the internal positioning of the system within the work. It is this, some would argue, that allows workflow systems to overly constrain the work by imposing some process model or theory of interaction on it. If a workflow system were external to the work and did not directly control the availability of resources for the work, then perhaps more flexible support for cooperative work could be offered through workflow. In some respects, this is the approach taken by De Michelis & Grasso (1992) who present a system which separates out support for the negotiation of the nature of the work from support for communication about it.

By going beyond office work into an industrial production context for our fieldwork, we hope to subject such claims to examination while adding to the corpus of empirical studies of workflow systems and bringing cooperative work on the print industry shopfloor to the attention of the CSCW community.

Fieldwork in the Print Industry

Our fieldwork has been conducted at an organization which we shall call 'Establishment Printers' (EP), a nationally distributed printing company in the UK, employing a total of over 2,000 personnel. EP engages in a variety of forms of print production work from large run printing of books and pamphlets to smaller scale reprographic work. It uses a range of traditional print technology including hot metal presses and off-set lithography but has also introduced a suite of technical changes into its printing work, incorporating high end photocopying and digital reprographics machines which offer digital scanning, storage, reproduction and networking functionality.

Recently, EP has won a number of contracts to take over the printing facilities of UK Government organizations who had put out their print services to competitive tender. This paper concentrates on the nature of cooperative work and the use of workflow technology at three sites (two in the North of England, one in London) which are maintained by EP within an organization which we shall call 'The Department'. The commitment to install and use a Management Information System (MIS) with 'real time shopfloor data-capture' to monitor workflow was a requirement of each tender. Subsequently, the demand to use such a system has formed an element of EP's legally binding contract with The Department, alongside stipulated monthly 'audit' meetings where reports from the system are inspected to ensure that EP is delivering the level of service the contract requires. It is this system (which we shall call PRINTFLOW PF2) and its impacts upon cooperative work on the shopfloor that we shall describe.

Maintaining a Smooth Flow of Work

A reprographic site at EP faces great variability in the kind of printwork they may be required to do. They may receive little or no notice of work which may itself have varying degrees of importance to the customer. Additionally, the work can run to different deadlines. At The Department, for example, EP offer a same day turnaround counter service for smaller jobs alongside a ten day turnaround for work requiring shopfloor processes. Furthermore, very little of the scheduling of when jobs come in is under the direct influence of EP themselves. Indeed, as EP has undertaken to diversify its services and to adopt a 'customer centred' business philosophy in recent years, the problem of managing the work has become especially acute. How are these problems to be dealt with? How is the work of the reprographic sites to be ordered so that EP can provide the level of service its customers expect? How can the massive contingencies of printwork be managed?

Our claim is that, in essence, reprographic work is managed by the contingent organization of *a smooth flow of work* through all parts of a site's capability. A smooth flow of work involves ensuring, for example, that no one operator is conspicuously occupied while others are idle, that no one job needlessly ties up the shopfloor while other jobs are waiting, and that machines are appropriately used to their best capabilities. In short, a smooth flow of work consists in ensuring the even distribution of work across operators, machines and jobs.

Crucially, EP personnel will organise their work so that there is a smooth flow of work *through the shopfloor* as jobs typically spend most of their time there rather than in the 'front office' or awaiting dispatch. Hence, time delays there are likely to be more critical. Indeed, people in the front office (who open the mail, process new orders, deal with customer queries by 'phone and fax and so forth) are attentive to the nature of shopfloor work, often having worked there themselves, and allocate jobs with the smooth running of the shopfloor as a major consideration. In our observations, we have identified four major ways in which smooth flow is accomplished on the shopfloor: (1) prioritising work, (2) anticipating work, (3) supporting each other's work and knowing the machines, (4) identifying and allocating interruptible work, and it is these that we shall now explicate in turn.

Prioritising Work

On receiving an order for printwork, administrative staff in the front office enter the details of the job (materials required, cost code, numbers, desired delivery dates etc.) into their records. A copy of the order is then used as a 'docket' accompanying the job in a see-through jacket as it undergoes the various printing processes appropriate for it. Administrative staff allocate the jobs to shopfloor workers, depending on (i) the kind of work it is (e.g. colour work will go to the operator skilled in colour lithography) and (ii) who is currently most able to do the work. Typically, jobs are then placed in an in-tray located near the machinery which the first process will be executed on. Once the first process (say colour lithography) is complete, the operator will consult the docket and pass the job to the operator who is most appropriate (either in terms of their skills or availability) for the next process (say comb binding), again depositing the work in the relevant in-tray. And so forth.

Typically, jobs will be sorted or inserted into in-trays so that date-order is maintained. That is, the work with the soonest delivery time will appear at the top. However, operators do not always process work in date-order. Operators will juggle the contents of their in-trays to ensure that a smooth flow of work will be promoted. Operators will examine job dockets to make assessments about how complicated a job is and how long it will take, whether there are further time consuming processes that the job will encounter later on and so forth - these considerations being balanced against the customer's delivery date. This re-ordering will also be influenced by whether there are outstanding jobs from the previous day's work, whether a regular large scale job is imminent and so forth.

The use of digital reprographics technology makes it especially important that operators carefully schedule their work and do not blindly follow date-order. For example, a job involving several thousands of copies of white A4 paper may only require the operator to make periodic checks on the functioning of the machine and copy quality while replenishing paper. In the mean time, the next few jobs can be scanned into the machine's memory and, if necessary, cropped to size or blemishes can be masked. On the digital machines at EP, scanning and copying can be executed independently. In this way, a skilled operator can set the machine off with a large routine job while at the same time engaging in the more labour intensive processes of scanning, cropping, masking and so forth. Accordingly, operators search their in-trays for such routine jobs and juggle the rest of its contents to enable the machine to be kept in continual and smooth production. Finding a large routine job also helps keep digital machines in continual use over lunch and other breaktimes. One operator will set a long job in train and take a break with another coming back from their break to complete the work. The identification of such jobs within the in-tray and ways of covering each other accordingly is essential for the effective and smooth use of the machine. Thus, very rarely will strict date-order happen to coincide with the ordering that makes for a smooth flow of work.

Anticipating Work

To a limited extent, the flow of work through the shopfloor can be organised by taking regular, known-in-advance work as a 'grid' around which other work can be fitted. While this certainly does not provide a complete solution to the problem of managing the complexity of printwork, the fact that some of EP's work is anticipatable enables shopfloor workers to ready themselves and their machines for when the job does properly arrive. Indeed, some parts of a regular job like a monthly report done to a standard format may be started even in advance of receiving the month's contents. Not only can the materials be ordered in advance, perhaps the front and back cover and standard introductory material can be printed if they are identical month-by-month. In other words, to ensure a smooth flow of work, EP staff will maximise the benefits of scheduling jobs around known-in-advance work by 'jumping the gun'.

'Print-on-demand' work (where EP stores the customer's originals digitally and prints copies to order) especially lends itself to jumping the gun. As the originals are already 'in hand', no setting up is required, merely the production of a specified number of copies. Indeed, some print-on-demand work may involve a fixed number of copies to be produced weekly or monthly. Under such circumstances, EP may often produce copies in anticipation of the order being confirmed. What is more, customers in The Department may merely 'phone through the order rather than themselves complete an order form. An order form may then be completed retrospectively or the details may be inserted into EP's records from a memo taken by EP's own staff at the time the phonecall was taken. Accordingly, by jumping the gun both administrative and shopfloor staff can invest print-on-demand work with the character of regular, known-in-advance work and use this as a way of promoting the smooth flow of work through their hands.

Supporting Each Other's Work and Knowing the Machines

We have already remarked that administrative staff are attentive to the workloads of shopfloor workers and are able to take this into account when allocating work. This awareness is obtained by periodically walking through the shopfloor and checking all is well, by discussing workloads when new jobs are to be allocated, by chatting at break times and so forth. Equally, shopfloor workers are attentive to each other's workloads and take this into account when negotiating with administrative staff or judging whom to pass work on to for its next production process.

Importantly, various architectural, machine lay-out and other features of the shopfloor support this monitoring of each other's work. The 'ecology' of the shopfloor provides lines of sight between workers which enable their awareness of each other's work and which support ad hoc cooperation. In addition, operators are able to *hear* whether the work is progressing smoothly. Many of the machines have 'designed-in' alerts (beeps and so forth) which draw attention to paper jams or empty paper trays. These sounds are available, of course, not only to the operator of the machine but to anyone else within earshot. Accordingly, operators can help each other out by replenishing paper if the operator who initiated a job is elsewhere at the moment. Furthermore, skilled print workers are attentive to the regular noises a machine makes at different stages during production. For example, a change in pitch can inform an operator that a paper tray is about to become exhausted, or a noise of a certain sort might suggest an obstruction in one part of the paper path. In short, both an awareness of the state of the flow of work through the shopfloor and ad hoc cooperation are sustained through listening to and knowing the machines. Not only do these activities acquaint workers with whether the flow of work through the shopfloor is smooth or not, they provide them with resources for the swift and ad hoc remedying of irregularities by, for example, helping someone out.

Identifying and Allocating Interruptible Work

We have remarked that very little of the workload of EP's sites can be thought of as known-in-advance work and that most of the flow of work has to be 'ad hoc-ed'. Knowing that interruptions by urgent work and rescheduling are endemic to print production, EP's staff have evolved ways of allocating and re-allocating work to ensure that such events have as minimal an effect on the work's flow as possible.

We have already seen that local, ad hoc cooperative arrangements will be made by operators to help each other out in times of trouble. A job which turns out to be more labour intensive than anticipated by administrative personnel may be split between two operators by local agreement on the shopfloor. Furthermore, the workers who are normally dedicated to the counter service may be utilised if a job passing through the shopfloor requires extra hands. Counter service work is subject to daily and weekly fluctuation. There can be moments when the counter staff are overworked, in which case staff from dispatch or even the administrative office will 'turn a hand'. But equally, there can be idle moments. Accordingly, knowing this, administrative staff allocate counter service personnel further print jobs but ones which tend (i) not to be urgent, (ii) not to require special materials or techniques not available on the photocopiers in counter service, and (iii) to be interruptible in the event of new counter service work coming in. In short, simple, non-urgent, interruptible jobs will also be allocated to counter service workers to be 'taken up and put down' as and when there are slack moments on the counter.

Not only can administrative staff more fully utilise counter service staff by allocating them interruptible jobs, shopfloor operators may also pass appropriate work to counter service personnel when the workload on the shopfloor is becoming intense. At one of The Department's sites in the North of England, a large window has been positioned between the counter service area, where Mary works, and the shopfloor. This enables both parties to check on the workload of the other and detect moments when work is unevenly distributed. At times, no more than a raising of eyes to Mary and an agreeing nod will ensure that work is quickly passed on. Indeed, as Mary's non-counter work is designed by administrative staff to be interruptible, she is also able to help the shopfloor workers if required and if her or her machine's capabilities are appropriate. Thus, 'passing work to Mary' (or her equivalents) becomes a further means for ensuring the smooth flow of work.

The Promise of Workflow Technology

The practices we have identified constitute the indigenous means by which staff at EP's sites within The Department organise and give structure to their working day. However, EP winning the contract to provide printing facilities to The Department had the major implication that a new MIS with workflow components should be overlaid on the work to support monitoring by The Department. PRINTFLOW PF2, the system proposed and installed by EP, has two basic components.

An administrative component in which jobs are registered in terms of their type, customer, cost code, delivery deadline and so forth. A job name will be assigned by the member of administrative staff registering the job. Specifying the type of job it is involves the entry of how the job will be executed in terms of the series of processes it will go through (e.g. copying, binding, finishing etc.). This information is stored in a database which can be searched in various ways and from which periodic reports can be extracted.

A shopfloor component consisting of a number of 'shopstations' arranged around the shopfloor and locally networked to the administrative database. The shopstations consist of a series of keypads. Some of these keypads are specifically configured with the names of workers. Others refer to the machines in the vicinity of the shopstation. Others name the processes which can be executed by the machines near the shopstation and are used to notify PF2 whether an operator is starting a process or has just completed it. Others name materials which are commonly used by the machines in the execution of their processes. Yet others are used to control an operator's interaction with the shopstation and are labelled 'enter', 'yes', 'no' etc. A numeric key pad is also available. Running across the top of the shopstation is a single line, 20 character display which echoes input and illuminates with system messages while the shopstation is being used.

It is by interacting with the shopstations that shopfloor data is 'captured' by PF2. For example, when a process starts, an operator makes herself and the job number (read from the docket) known to the system. Similarly, when a process is completed, the operator re-identifies herself and the job, followed by recording the details of materials used and wastage (if any).

PF2 was selected because it promised a number of important benefits for EP. As they have been explained to us: (1) it was specifically designed for use on the shopfloor of the print industry; (2) it was consistent with the requirements of the invitation to tender and specifically would enable EP to provide management reports which could detail the time spent on processes, materials consumed and wastage figures, while supporting the production of invoices as well as, if required in the monthly 'audit', the justification for the charge made in the form of a job report; (3) it can, in principle, support stock control, through keeping an accurate and up-to-the-moment record of materials used which can be inspected at the administrative component; (4) it can record worker activity and hence could, in principle, replace clocking on/off; (5) it can support process management by giving administrative staff and site managers a view of shopfloor activity which can be sampled from the administrative component; (6) as the PF2 databases had been networked across all three of The Department's sites, cross-site monitoring would be supported so that sites can be aware of what each other are doing; (7) as jobs are registered and their execution is recorded on PF2 as a series of print processes, this reinforces the quality standards which EP subscribes to as this is how they depict printwork too.

The promises of PF2, then, were many and varied. However, of all these, the most important to EP is that PF2 can provide reports of various sorts on how the work has been done, so that EP can demonstrate to The Department, when required, that they are indeed conducting The Department's printwork to contract.

Workflow Technology: Disrupting Smooth Flow

In various ways, the introduction of PF2 itself disrupted the smooth flow of work through the shopfloor of EP's sites, raising a series of problems about how the technology should be used and whether its use could be legitimately 'suspended' on occasion. At the time of writing, nearly a year after the commencement of EP's contract with The Department, a number of the dilemmas surrounding the use of PF2 in relation to the print workers' indigenous practices for organising their work remain unresolved. Let us give some details.

The Imposition of Procedure

We noted that printwork at The Department often requires jumping the gun. Urgent jobs often need to be started before order forms have been received or job numbers issued. Similarly, much regular, print-on-demand work needs to be started in advance so that, amongst other reasons, more contingent work can be flexibly structured around them. However, a job for which no job number yet exists has the same status as a non-existent job as far as PF2 is concerned: no details of its execution can be recorded at the shopstations because there is no job number to enter. Accordingly, just how jobs which have jumped the gun have actually been completed cannot be made visible to PF2 using it conventionally. This raises some dilemmas. For example, independent records could be manually kept for how such a job is done and its details entered some time later. However, in this case, PF2 would give inaccurate information for process management and cross-site monitoring, as well as out-of-date stock control information. Alternatively, one might not use PF2 at all for such work. But then EP would be seeking to charge The Department for work which, according to the record, had not been done, while keeping independent records with no corresponding version in PF2 would risk defaulting on the contract. Finally, counter service work is especially problematic as

PF2 would seem to require the registration of administrative details before the copying service can be completed. While a solution would be to have all counter work set up as one 'rolling' job, this would not allow separate billing for each customer according to individual customer codes. In short, PF2 imposes a procedure on the work (first register it, then do it) which negates important means for ensuring the work's smooth flow and timely delivery.

Work as Processes in Series

Shopfloor workers soon discovered a major constraint on how PF2 could be used to record data on the execution of print processes. PF2 embodies a process model which depicts jobs as a series of processes, each the responsibility of just one operator, each to be terminated before the next commences. Indeed, as PF2 was proposed as a means for capturing accurate data about shopfloor workers as well as about jobs, it had implemented the constraint that a single operator cannot engage in more than one process at a time. This means that the organization of the smooth flow of work by juggling in-trays cannot be made visible to the system. For example, we noted that operators of digital reprographic technology need to order their work so that a long job can be scheduled alongside one or more labour intensive jobs. However, once PF2 has been notified of the start of the long job, the same operator cannot notify the system of any of the scanning jobs. Again there is a dilemma. Either workers accept PF2's constraints and cease juggling their in-trays or they continue to juggle their workload and not log-in the scanning process. Both of these upshots are problematic: the first because it disables an important means for ensuring smooth workflow, the second because it makes invisible to The Department something which had actually been done and which EP would like to separately itemise in billing precisely because of its labour intensive nature.

The Overhead of Use

Shopfloor workers experienced a considerable overhead in using PF2 to log their activities. An interaction with PF2 consists of much keypad pressing. Indeed, a job involving different materials with non-standard codes and some wastage may require several minutes to register. This, when an operator may get through tens of jobs a day, is a noticeable overhead. Furthermore, the time spent using PF2 is not itself calibrated with the time spent on the job. Twenty thousand copies takes approximately the same time to record as two copies. Small scale print jobs which happened to use three colours of paper would require about three times as many key presses at the shopstation than a big job using one colour of paper. Using shop stations, then, was proportionally a very big overhead for small jobs. This problem was especially acute for counter work, when the use of PF2 directly disrupts the service customers receive as they have to wait a little longer while job details are inserted (even assuming appropriate customer codes can be found for them!).

The Individualization of Work

PF2 conceives of print processes being the responsibility of single operators. However, this means that the contingent cooperative activities so important to organising a smooth flow of work cannot be represented to the system. If a big job is done on a digital reprographics machine, say, by one operator replenishing the paper, while another unloads the copies from the stacker, while a third scans in the next ten pages, they have to discuss amongst themselves which of the three should appear as having done the work and which two would potentially appear as 'idle'! Equally, if a job is taken over by another operator to maintain continual production over lunch, the second operator would have to 'impersonate' the first to be able to register the job done at all, thereby making the first operator's lunch break invisible! Again, PF2 presents problems as to how it is to be incorporated into printwork without either dismantling the ad hoc practices which promote smooth workflow or falsifying the record in a way which is potentially detectable by The Department.

Re-Working the Order of the Shopfloor

How did the staff at EP cope with these problems? It is first worth reminding ourselves that they do *have to* solve them practically because working with PF2 is necessary due to contractual requirements. EP *cannot* discontinue the technology. Accordingly, they have to *re-establish* the order of their work with it (or in spite of it). This has been accomplished by different sites in different ways. At The Department's London site, some built-in workarounds in PF2 were discovered and put to use. In contrast, after experimenting with PF2's own workarounds, The Department's sites in the North of England took a more drastic step and reorganised their entire working day to accommodate the system. Let us take these in turn.

Some aspects of the 'overhead of use' problem can be addressed through a facility called 'gang job'. This involves using the shopstations to define a 'gang' of jobs. While each maintains its own customer code, materials used can be registered in a single total per material type. Thus, if there are a large number of small jobs all using white standard grade A4, all the copies made can be returned as just one overall total. While a little effort is required to define the gang initially, much time is saved finally as separate figures need not be entered for each job. However, this workaround leads to anomalies. In order to assign operator times, materials and wastage to each job, the total time and the rest are divided through by the number of jobs and equal numbers counted to each job. This will mean that a two copy job and a two hundred copy job, if they are part of the same gang, will be equally recorded when there is a hundred-fold difference in materials between them. Furthermore, if the gang involves a range of materials, a job which consisted of only white paper may (absurdly) be recorded as having 0.09 sheets of blue included! Clearly, there is another dilemma here. Easing the burden on the shopfloor may lead to inaccurate management information to present to The Department and potentially incorrect billing. Avoiding this dilemma means that 'gang job' can only be used marginally: e.g. when a number of highly similar jobs do happen to turn up at the same time.

Some aspects of the problems of individualising processes can also be addressed by recording a process as a 'labour charge'. This can be done by an operator even if they are engaged simultaneously on another process which they have initiated by interacting with PF2. To record a 'labour charge', an operator presses a button on the shopstation marked 'labour charge', identifies themselves, types in a job number, confirms the title when PF2 retrieves it, enters a time in hours and decimal parts of an hour, followed by the details of materials and wastage as before. At The Department's London site, this facility is used to workaround the constraint that an operator cannot start up a new process on PF2 while another is active. However, this workaround does have its own problems. Labour charges can only be recorded *after* the process has been completed, so they do not support any moment-by-moment process management or cross-site monitoring and require operators to keep an independent record of when they started a job. Furthermore, whether something is recorded as a labour charge or as a timed process depends (arbitrarily) upon what happens to interrupt what in the unfolding of an operator's work and not necessarily in terms of any other feature of the job.

At the time of our last visits to The Department, the London site was persisting with using PF2's 'labour charge' facility as best they could to record concurrent work, keeping independent, manual records when necessary (e.g. if the gun is jumped) and encouraging the workforce to be as accurate as possible in recording materials and wastage. In this way, a momentary peace has come about between the indigenous practices for maintaining smooth workflow and the demands of using PF2. This 'peace' though has come at the cost of working overtime every week since EP's contract began and of only 'clearing the in-trays' during the working day once in six months. And that was after PF2 had been 'down' for three days!

In contrast, the northern sites have developed a more radical solution. Here jobs are entered at the start of the day into the administrative component of PF2 as intended. However, the system is not used to record how jobs are done while working on them. Rather, manual records are kept on the dockets which accompany jobs and, where necessary, further paper notes are added to the see-through jacket. The shopstations are untouched and work is organized by the methods we have noted. However, at the end of the day or the beginning of the next, one administrative worker takes all the dockets and orders (including those for counter service work) and records the operators, materials et cetera into PF2. Thus, PF2 is not used for real-time data capture, rather it is employed to *retrospectively reconstruct* the work in a form which can nevertheless provide The Department with an account of what occurred and why they have been charged in the way they have, even though this forfeits many of PF2's other promised benefits.

Conclusions: CSCW, Workflow and Design

Our fieldwork suggests to us that extreme difficulties can be encountered when introducing workflow systems into a workplace, even when the system is external to the tools and materials of the work itself. PF2 does not (directly) constrain workers' access to the resources for their work, nor (directly) impose an ordering on the work by insisting that some task be completed before another one. However, it does embody a process model of how printwork is done which makes recording the work problematic in the light of what is actually done. This case suggests, then, that the impacts a workflow system may have on work can be extensive even if there are no 'hard wired' links between the system and the conduct of the work.

Workflow From Within and From Without

We feel that the image of 'workflow' captures well the question of the temporal ordering of work. Indeed, this is how several of EP's staff themselves characterised things when all was well: 'the work flows smoothly' and such like. Work unfolds over time and has to be organised (scheduled, conducted, recorded, managed) attending to this. The question is not whether smooth workflow is to exist or not (at EP it has to) but how this is to be accomplished. In this connection, we offer a distinction between workflow *from within* and workflow *from without*.

Workflow from within accomplishes the smooth flow of work through methods which are internal to the work. To do printwork competently requires that, on receipt of a job, an operator is able to orient to matters such as: Is this job properly for me? Should it be done next? How urgent is it? To whom should I pass it when I am done? And so forth. By resolving these questions in working on the job, not only is the job done, so is the organization of the shopfloor in part accomplished. Workflow from within characterises the methods used on the shopfloor which emphasise the local and internal accomplishment of the ordering of work. Workers juggle their in-trays, jump the gun, glance across the shopfloor, listen to the sounds coming from machines, re-distribute the work in the *here and now* so that what to do next can be resolved. In the here and now, in *real time*, workers encounter multiple jobs of a varied nature, requiring artful scheduling and completion.

In contrast, workflow from without seeks to order the work through methods *other* than those which the work itself provides. In PF2, a formal model of the work is provided which depicts printwork as processes in series such that (i) each process has to be terminated before another can begin, (ii) each process has just one operator associated with it at any one time, (iii) each operator can only engage in one process at any one time, and so forth. It would be inaccurate of us to say that these methods from without are just plain wrong. Rather, they offer *another way of organising printwork*, one which is encountered by the workers at EP's sites as alien to *their* methods of organising printwork. Their methods crucially attend to the problem of the ad hoc, real-time ordering of multiply instantiated jobs. PF2's are concerned with the processual character of individual jobs, engaged with by individual workers, measurable by clock time and so forth.

In the case of EP's sites, workflow from within comes to be in tension with workflow from without as soon as the latter also has to be *reckoned on within the work*. The difficulties with PF2 arise not because some technology merely offers an 'incorrect' workflow model, nor (even) because that model is inserted into the work, but because it is inserted in such a way that makes the accountability of workers and the work that they do problematic in new ways which are themselves hard to deal with. It is because PF2 *has to be* worked with and accommodated that the tensions and dilemmas we have noted arise. These tensions can be negotiated in various ways - distributing them across the shopfloor and throughout the working day (as at the London site, where all shopfloor workers use the system as best they can at the cost of overtime and delays) or allocating them to one worker at a given part of the day (as at the northern sites where the day's work is reconstructed retrospectively). Either way these accommodations arise through the practical necessity of having to use the system. And it is this practical necessity which binds the use of PF2 to printwork at EP just as strongly as any internal 'hard wiring' of a workflow system to the actual conduct of work might do.

Technologies of Accountability and Organizational Ordering

Suchman (1994) argues that many CSCW and workflow systems can be regarded as 'technologies of accountability'.

> By technologies of accountability, I mean systems aimed at the inscription and documentation of actions to which parties are accountable not only in the ethnomethodological sense of that term (Garfinkel and Sacks, 1970), but in the sense represented by the bookkeeper's ledger, the record of accounts paid and those still outstanding. (p.188)

This is a useful way of understanding PF2 with respect to the relations between EP and The Department. PF2 is the required means for producing *accounts* both as records of charges made and as documents which *visibly testify* to EP's efficiency, capability, loyalty to contractual terms and so forth. Management reports from or based on PF2 can be used to provide not just a record but a *justification* for what was charged and what was done, if EP are *called to account* by The Department.

We feel our fieldwork adds some important details to Suchman's concept. In particular, technologies of accountability need to be understood *organizationally* and *inter-organizationally*. Introducing technologies of accountability can be in tension with existing ways of organising work, as well as provoke or fall in line with new ways of constituting the very organization within which the work is done. For The Department, EP are not merely the organization that happens to do their printing. They are the organization who do printing in a visible, inspectable, documentable, accountable way. This is a matter of organizational change not only for The

Department (who have 'lost' their print facility to external contractors through competitive tendering) but for EP (who have not only gained business but business which has to be conducted in a new manner). In all these senses, technologies of accountability can be *technologies for organizational ordering*, as part of how organizations come to be redefined through new trading relationships.

Design Requirements for Cooperative Technology

It is not within the available scope of this paper to offer detailed recommendations for CSCW technology as a result of our fieldwork. In fact, the case of PF2 at EP has caused us to reflect upon the larger issue of the very relationship between fieldwork findings and CSCW systems, and just how the former might influence requirements for the latter.

On the one hand, the methods we have uncovered by means of which print workers organise the flow of work from within can be taken to point to domains for application support. We would not be the first to commend that CSCW systems offer support for awareness and mutual monitoring or at least do not contradict members' own methods (cf. Heath & Luff, 1992). Equally, as a workflow system, PF2 could be criticised for not allowing flexible mappings from processes to operators, for not specifically supporting 'run-time' re-allocations, for not recognising ad hoc collaborative arrangements, and for adding to the work that people have to do (cf. Abbott & Sarin, 1994). These are all familiar emphases within CSCW which our study also underlines.

However, we take it as a more challenging and urgent matter that CSCW research consider the implications for system requirements of understanding workflow technologies as *technologies for (inter-organizational) accountability*. This opens up a whole new set of issues for CSCW requirements. First of all, we feel that CSCW research must be more attentive to the formal (in the sense of 'for administrative and managerial purposes') problems that organizations face and often impact upon not only their technology policies but also the details of usage. Accordingly, we are worried about the equation of CSCW with *informal, non-structural interaction* that some researchers make. It is not that we advocate traditional 'structural' notions of the organization. Far from it. Rather, we wish to draw attention to the multiple considerations which impinge upon the acceptability of technology in actual contexts - considerations which often require very difficult trade-offs. If, for example, there are good organizational reasons for accounting for the work in new and more detailed ways, how are these to be balanced up against the requirements of smooth workflow on the shopfloor or in the office? Indeed, in the current case, one might even argue (after all!) that a workflow system like PF2 *is* a reasonable solution, *provided* an organization anticipates the extra work and reckons on it as a cost in bidding for new business, *provided* those offering work for tender do not incorporate demands which might rebound on them, *provided* tenderers do not make similarly unrealistic promises, *provided* an appreciation of how workflow is organised from within and can be disrupted from without is maintained by all parties and so forth.

If CSCW research is to learn one thing from settings like the one we have studied, it is that a naive view of cooperative work and its support has no place on the shopfloor. Organizationally acceptable technology is achieved not through the pursuit of ideals but by ensuring that the list of *provisos* is tolerably short.

Acknowledgments

We are grateful to all personnel at 'Establishment Printers' for their willingness to have us hang around and ask obvious questions. James Pycock and Tom Rodden have given useful suggestions for improving this paper. John Bowers and Wes Sharrock acknowledge help and support from Rank Xerox Research Centre Cambridge Laboratory and from ESPRIT Project 6225 (COMIC).

References

Abbott, K. & Sarin, S. (1994). Experiences with workflow management: Issues for the next generation. In *Proceedings of CSCW '94, Chapel Hill, USA.* New York: ACM.

Agostini, A., De Michelis, G., Grasso, M. & Patriarca, S. (1993). Reengineering a business process with an innovative workflow management system: A case study. In *COOCS '93, Proceedings of ACM-SIGOIS Conference on Organizational Computing Systems.* New York: ACM.

Bowers, J. (1994). The work to make a network work: Studying CSCW in action. In *Proceedings of CSCW '94, Chapel Hill, USA.* New York: ACM.

De Michelis, G. & Grasso, M. (1992). Situating conversations within the language/action perspective: The Milan Conversation Model. In *Proceedings of CSCW '94, Chapel Hill, USA.* New York: ACM.

Garfinkel, H. & Sacks, H. (1970). On formal structures of practical action. In J. McKinney & E. Tiryakin (eds.) *Theoretical Sociology.* New York: Appleton-Century-Crofts. pp.337-366.

Heath, C. & Luff, P. (1992). Collaboration and control: Crisis management and multimedia technology in London Underground Line Control Rooms. *Computer Supported Cooperative Work,* 1 (1/2), 69-94.

Hughes, J., Randall, D. and Shapiro, D. (1992). Faltering from ethnography to design. In *Proceedings of CSCW '92, Toronto, Canada.* New York: ACM.

Medina-Mora, R., Winograd, T., Flores, R. and Flores, F. (1992). The action workflow approach to workflow management. In *Proceedings of CSCW '92, Toronto, Canada.* New York: ACM.

Orlikowski, W. (1992). Learning from Notes: Organizational issues in groupware implementation. In *Proceedings of CSCW '92, Toronto, Canada.* New York: ACM.

Suchman, L. (1994). Do categories have politics? The language/action perspective reconsidered. *Computer Supported Cooperative Work,* 2 (3), 177-190.

Winograd, T. (1994). Categories, disciplines and social coordination. *Computer Supported Cooperative Work,* 2 (3), 191-197.

Winograd, T. & Flores, F. (1986) *Understanding computers and cognition: A new foundation for design.* Norwood: Ablex.

Proceedings of the Fourth European Conference on Computer-Supported Cooperative Work,
September 10–14, Stockholm, Sweden
H. Marmolin, Y. Sundblad, and K. Schmidt (Editors)

Cooperation and Power

John Sherry
Department of Anthropology, University of Arizona, Tucson, Arizona USA

New technologies are not only transforming workplace practices in familiar settings. They are also finding their way into the types of "exotic" locales which have traditionally been of interest to anthropologists. This paper presents an ethnographic analysis of technologically mediated communication in one such atypical setting, among a grassroots group of activists from the Navajo Indian Reservation in the southwestern United States. As this case illustrates, mere access to technology does not solve all of the problems such groups face in terms of empowerment, access to resources for action, and coordination. The discursive practices embodied in technological design may perpetuate the relations of dominance and subordination which characterize interactions between "marginalized" groups and "mainstream" organizations, and force groups into forms of organization which they find inappropriate.

Introduction

Not long ago, a fax was sent from the deep among the douglas firs in Oregon to a home built in the forests of junipers and ponderosa pines high in the mountains on the Navajo Indian Reservation in Arizona. The fax predicted:

> The grassroots network of the future will be a virtual organization with virtual members. It will exist in cyberspace - everywhere and nowhere. Its currency will be information, and its location a collection of E-mail addresses and fax numbers.

The very presence of this message seemed proof of its own veracity. CSCW, it appears, is coming out of the labs, academic settings and offices where it was developed and winding up in some unusual places. As grassroots organizations, people from non-Western societies, and other users gradually gain access to these technologies, current issues may be viewed in a new light, and unanticipated problems will inevitably arise. As new users bring increased diversity with regards to cultural and linguistic backgrounds, approaches to work, and attitudes towards technology, applying the concepts of participatory design and the democratizing of information may become increasingly difficult but all the more important.

This paper analyzes the use of information and communications technologies by one such non-prototypical group. It represents an attempt to further develop two related lines of investigation which have concerned CSCW researchers in the past, that is, heterogeneity and power in cooperative networks. Much research in CSCW has demonstrated the fact that cooperative work "in real world settings" is marked by considerable heterogeneity with respect to orientation and approaches to work (Kling, 1980: Schmidt & Bannon, 1992). Closely related has been the awareness that cooperative work can be affected by significant differences in the respective statuses of participants. Work in CSCW and in Participatory Design (PD) has emphasized the goal of democratizing the computing process (e.g., Schuler & Namioka, 1993). Participatory design has pointed out that workers' knowledge and multiculturalism in the workplace provide valuable sources for information and innovation (e.g., Greenbaum, 1992). Many discussions in CSCW have likewise emphasized the importance of empowering end users and democratizing information (e.g., Clement, 1990). Analyses of power in CSCW have in this respect primarily focused on issues of organizational relations dealing with information flow, the ability to make or implement technology choices, and local autonomy in the conduct of work (cf. Schmidt & Bannon, 1992).

For this discussion, I would like to examine heterogeneity and power in cooperative networks from a slightly different perspective, one which is currently fairly popular in anthropological discussions of "hegemony", based on such analyses of power as Gramsci (1992) and Foucault (1973; 1977). Ethnographers have demonstrated that relations of power can be constructed through "discursive practice" (cf. Goodwin, 1994), that is, through the practices associated with the construction of knowledge. Since one's "choice of representations limits the sorts of inferences that make sense" (Hutchins, 1995: 82), the construction of knowledge is always - and necessarily - subject to limitations on what can be said, by whom, and in what way (cf. Foucault, 1973). Power and the construction of knowledge are in this respect inseparable.

Discursive practice can include more than simply spoken discourse, encompassing as well the way a group constructs and employs all sorts of representational artifacts and media. As many have pointed out with regards to technology (cf. Norman and Draper, 1986; Suchman, 1987; Adler & Winograd, 1992) the design of technological artifacts can embody particular practices that may or may not be suited to the people who wind up using them. Furthermore, as Brown & Duguid (1994) point out, communities may adopt "border conventions", standards of practice which allow people to derive meaning from more than just "what is said" by an artifact. When artifacts and their accompanying practices are used to connect interactants from divergent communities, the result may be a situation in which one participant is forced to adopt the practices of the other, at the expense of his or her own standards. My concern here is thus "How do the discursive practices embodied in technologies for cooperative work construct relations of dominance?"

This is not to say that the problem of conflicting discursive practices is solely the result of new technologies. "Culture collision" has been a part of the human experience probably for as long as there have been peoples coming in contact who speak different languages and hold different beliefs. The problem has about a five hundred year history for the indigenous peoples in the America. The history of Indian relations with Eruopean colonizers is often thought of as somehow "complete", as if early conquests and the violent contact precipitated by the doctrine of "manifest destiny" were somehow played out. However, for many Indian people, the history of relations - and conflict - with the Euro-American political and economic system is still in progress. Part of this story lies in the different approaches to communication which characterize relations between Indian and non-Indian people. As many researchers have shown, interactional differences in face to face settings - for example, in turn-taking norms, in the structuring of discourse, in the lengths of pauses speakers usually take between utterances or between turns at talk - can serve to disadvantage many Native American speakers in conversational situations with non-Indians, especially middle class Euro-Americans. These patterns have been shown to be fairly consistent among people of different North American tribes (e.g., Philips, 1983; Scollon and Scollon, 1981; Hymes, 1974). Discursive practices have in these situations been clearly shown to affect the construction of power in interactions, as well as the evaluations which participants make of each other. But even while the problem is not new to technology use, it bears renewed interest from a CSCW perspective. It is obviously important to technology users coming from a marginalized community, since foreign ways of representing information can present a barrier to cooperation, or perpetuate their own subordination. This issue may be of interest to CSCW research as well, since it illustrates what Anderson (1994) considers a primary goal of ethnography in CSCW research, that is, to understand the "play of rationalities" that occurs when local and non-local practices collide. As technologies become dispersed, and are used to facilitate interaction among ever more heterogeneous networks, assumptions about what constitute "natural" forms of interaction may be increasingly called into question. The concerns of local communities of resistance and CSCW researchers thus meet when the introduction of foreign technologies and their associated practices results in a "play of rationalities" that is carried out as an explicit (and often morally charged) conflict.

The Research Setting

This paper is based on ethnographic fieldwork among a grassroots organization of environmental activists called "Diné CARE"[1], from the Navajo Indian Reservation in the southwestern United States. I use the term "environmental activists" only provisionally here, because these people themselves do not like the title. They regard their work as the continuation of a centuries-old resistance to foreign colonialism, rather than environmentalism as it has come to be thought of in American - and perhaps Western European - societies. In addition, Navajo "environmentalism" has deep cultural roots, which stem from a fundamentally different way of relating to the environment than that embodied in Western industrial societies (cf. LaDuke, 1983). However, because the group often collaborates with non-Indian environmentalists, and because many Indian ways of thinking have been appropriated by non-Indian environmental movements, distinctions between traditional resistance and these modern movements have been blurred.

The Navajo Nation covers about 23,000 square miles (60,000 km^2 - approximately the size of Ireland) in the American Southwest. There are between 150,000 and 200,000 Navajo people living within reservation boundaries. Many of the people living on the reservation over the age of about seventy are monolingual Navajo speakers. Most adults over age thirty speak both English and Navajo.

The technologies used by the people with whom I worked may not be particularly sophisticated from a CSCW perspective, but they shed light on some important issues about technologically mediated cooperation in novel settings. Cooperation among Navajo communities of resistance can be divided into two types: that between the various, geographically dispersed communities of resistance that form Diné CARE; and that which is carried out between these communities (or the organization Diné CARE as a whole) and

[1] Diné is the word Navajo people use to refer to themselves. CARE stands for "Citizens Against Ruining our Environment".

the numerous sources of technical, legal, financial or other forms of support which lie outside the reservation. Because of the Navajo Nation's size and low population density, members of Diné CARE are geographically dispersed. Contact among communities, or between communities and the "outside world" is limited by the fact that the communicative infrastructure on the Reservation is extremely impoverished by Western standards. Fewer than 30% of all Navajo households have telephones or electricity. For those who do have telephones, the geographical isolation of most Reservation homes is such that most calls carry fairly steep long distance charges. Thus, unsurprisingly, the greatest expenses associated with local resistance efforts are usually for telephone communications and travel. The lack of infrastructure supporting the types of communicative or representational activities required by outsiders thus stands as a significant barrier to cooperation between local communities and outside sources of support.

Because each local community faces unique environmental threats or civil rights problems, their particular needs vary. One community, located on Black Mesa, faced the adverse effects of coal mining and the threat of forced relocation from their ancestral lands, which were the site of a border dispute between the Navajo and Hopi tribal governments. Another community, the one at which Diné CARE started, resisted the installation of a toxic waste incinerator. A third dealt with a proposed asbestos dump on one of the Navajo people's most sacred mountains. While each of these issues was unique, some patterns have emerged in the cooperation such communities require to face these threats.

Such patterns also emerged at the place where I conducted most of my research, a community at the foot of the Chuska Mountains, a small range which runs along the northern Arizona, New Mexico border. The local people there organized in opposition to the Navajo Nation's Tribal sawmill, which had once been a "model" for Indian enterprise but which had outlived its usefulness. Local people considered the mill's annual harvest of the mountain's ponderosa pine forests to be excessive and destructive. In spite of the fact that this was an "intratribal" dispute, and the fact that local people opposed the timber cutting based primarily on traditional Navajo beliefs (the Chuska Mountains represent the Navajo male deity, local people thus considered high volume timber cutting to be a form of desecration), these people were nonetheless required to secure the cooperation of non-Navajo technical, legal and financial support to conduct their resistance. This included, for example, the need to master technical knowledge in their efforts, because "official" Tribal procedures and practices for the setting of forestry policy were mostly patterned after the

U.S. Forest Service, not traditional Navajo principles. It also included the need to know U.S. laws concerning forestry, environmental protection, and Indian sovereignty. As one senior member of Diné CARE put it: "Just as our ancestors, the great Navajo patriots of the past - Manuelito, Barboncito - had to learn how to use the white man's guns to defend our homeland, we have to learn how to use the white man's laws." Thus, even the most local efforts required intensive cooperation with outsiders who provided access to various types of resources.

"Accountability"

Cooperation with non-Navajo organizations often required technologies of representation and discursive practices which local people found foreign, difficult to reproduce, or even inappropriate. In this respect, much of the following discussion deals with issues involved in the production, manipulation and sharing of documents. Documents as representational artifacts have received considerable attention in CSCW research, since they are the basis of so many work practices and since new technologies may affect both the physical substrate of documents and possibly some of the practices associated with them (e.g., Brown & Duguid, 1994; Luff, Heath and Greatbatch, 1992). Analysis of Diné CARE's uses of technologies and their practices surrounding documents suggests some issues which may be characteristic of the use of technologies by groups outside the "mainstream".

First, note that the primary use of computers by Diné CARE members was not for *access* to information (which has been the primary issue in many discussions of paper versus electronic documents), but rather for the providing of information to outsiders according to the latter's demands. One particularly clear example of this occurred in what Diné CARE's treasurer called "the funding game."

The "mechanisms of perception" of many organizations which fund environmental work are primarily limited to formal proposals. Proposals, like application forms and other types of mundane bureaucratic documents constitute what Foucault (1977) has identified as a key instrument of power in modern Western societies - the "examination". This "tiny operational schema" links power and knowledge through a system of limitation: the users of forms "engage in active cognitive work, but the parameters of that work have been established by the system that is organizing their perception" (Goodwin, 1994: 609).

Groups unable or unwilling to accommodate a given system are more likely to remain "invisible" to the funders.

In the funding game, the representational artifacts which allowed funders to distinguish among groups center (not surprisingly) on issues of financial accountability. Budgets and financial statements thus constitute key artifacts in the proposal. One entailment of this concern is the representation of the work of resistance in similarly quantified units - that is work as economic production. This practice has a clearly identifiable history in Western society, especially in the industrial revolution and Taylorist management (Edwards, 1989; Epstein, 1978; Seltzer, 1992)). Yet because the representation of work in monetary terms has come to be so widely accepted in Western society, it seems to most of us to be a perfectly natural way of representing work.

It is not a coincidence that Diné CARE's primary use of computers was for the formatting of documents, the completing of forms, and the manipulation of financial information which funders require. These are all uses to which PC's have now been thoroughly applied in office settings throughout much of the industrialized world; their diffusion into such alternative settings as a sort of "first wave" of computing is perhaps not too surprising. Deeper than this, however, is the relationship between the "examination" as a mechanism of knowledge and power and its ease and usefulness for automation. In fact, the constraining of user input through form-filling has been an important feature in facilitating human-computer interaction historically, and remains a standard interface in many applications to this day. Most important for this discussion, however, is how the examination as a mode of information entails relations of power by allowing some participants to establish what "counts" as information.

How the Funding Game is Problematic

For the Navajo communities of resistance with whom I came in contact, the representation of their work in terms required by the funding system did not come so naturally as it does in mainstream society. Many of the people involved in local resistance do not have extensive exposure to a cash economy (there are only a handful of banking centers on the entire Navajo reservation, and in fact many members of Diné CARE do not even have checking accounts). They are thus unfamiliar with the practices underlying the production of budgets, financial statements, or even expense reports and check registers. As a result, such people either lack the ability to complete formal proposals, or appear "unaccountable". Because virtually none of the local people who were involved with Diné CARE accepted monetary compensation for their work (all funds they raised were for direct operating expenses) they were marginalized as "volunteers" and many institutions had trouble dealing with communities where no "professional organizers" were present.

More importantly, most of the people I encountered viewed their efforts as part of a long history of resistance to colonization by a foreign political and economic system. The members of Diné CARE, like much of North American Indian resistance in general (cf. Churchill, 1983), regard the capitalist system as not only destructive to the environment, but also as embodying practices and "ways of thinking" which undermine the social relationships and types of behavior which place humans in harmony with their social and natural ecologies. Diné CARE's treasurer lamented that "By the time they (local communities) get it right, they're corrupted too." This exemplifies her awareness that, as Lave and Wenger (1990:55) point out, learning involves "embodying, albeit in transformed ways, the structural characteristics of communities of practice." Learning the funding game threatens corruption insofar as it entailed the embodiment of social relations characterized as "coordinated self interest" (Habermas, 1984), rather than traditional Navajo social motivations of duty to family and clan, and a sense of connectedness with - as opposed to mastery over - the natural environment.

Because of their failure to share the discursive practices which funders or other resource providers require, Navajo communities often require the assistance of those who have mastered them. This leaves them vulnerable in cooperative relationships. Regional environmental or social justice groups based in nearby cities often take on the role of advocating "on behalf" of Navajo people, raising funds by publicizing local issues and representing themselves as accountable advocates for the local communities, while providing very little in actual assistance. This happened on numerous occasions to the Chuska mountain community. Outside environmental groups with whom they consulted raised thousands of dollars by publicizing their involvement with the Navajo forestry issue; very little of that money was ever applied to actually helping the local people. A more egregious example of this occurred at the community on Black Mesa. Because that issue was well publicized, urban activists raised over $3 million on behalf of local people between 1986 and 1992. At the end of that period, when no benefits had trickled down to the communities, these outside groups could only account for about ten percent of the funds they had raised. Thus, inequality of status, unequal access to resources, and exploitation in cooperative networks can be a direct result of differences in discursive practice among the respective participants.

Authority in Discursive Practice

Diné CARE attempted to organize on a reservation-wide basis partly because of this pattern of exploitation. The group recognized that mediation was necessary to connect many local communities with outside sources of support, but they sought to replace the mediation of non-Indian groups with that provided by a cooperative alliance of Navajo communities.

Technology and practice presented considerable tensions for Diné CARE in this attempt to organize. Because so few communities had access to the type of infrastructure necessary to support computers or fax machines, because local people did not have access to the types of technical support which have been shown to be necessary for using computers (cf. George et al, 1989; Panko, 1988), and most importantly, because local people did not share the types of discursive practices involved in the production of documents, financial statements and other artifacts (which were by far the most common reasons for needing a computer), technology was of necessity concentrated in the hands of only a few members. Those members who became responsible for applying technology were not only located in places where there was power and phone lines, but were also those who had had extensive experience off the reservation, dealing in the "white man's world". This centralized use of technology created a hierarchy in the organization, concentrating access to information, and power, in the hands of a few individuals who did not want it. Diné CARE's treasurer accepted her role, and the unwanted power of arbitrating funds, only reluctantly, expressing it as a willingness to "corrupt herself" for the sake of other members.

To get out of this predicament, the group was forced to establish more codified procedures for many tasks - including the distribution of funds, thereby shifting authority on certain tasks from particular individuals to artifacts created by the group as a whole. While this alleviated the burden of decision making (for example, on the distribution of funds) it also forced Diné CARE towards a "bureaucratic" approach to operations which members strongly resisted. This development was exacerbated by yet other, foreign documentary practices, brought on by the need to represent Diné CARE as "accountable" to outsiders. Practices in this regard included the production of such foreign artifacts as bylaws, articles of incorporation and mission statements. Producing such documentation proved to be an extremely difficult task for members. I watched as members struggled for over a year to come up with an adequate mission statement, lamenting that their sense of purpose could never be adequately expressed in a written, English paragraph. These practices also ran counter to what members considered traditional Navajo patterns of cooperation, including an emphasis on local autonomy, decentralized authority, and trust built through human interaction. The fact that technology use was right in the middle of this tension suggests that the democratization and decentralization which have been held up as goals in CSCW and PD may rely on degrees of formalization and documentary practices which are not necessarily universally shared.

The Authority of Documents

Various practices combine to establish the authority which documents carry in mediating social relationships in Euro-American settings. Perhaps most important among these are signs of a document's "immutability" as evidence of the institutional power which it represents. Brown & Duguid (1994) provide what might be considered a "native's ethnographic description" of the way in which documents embody authority that extends beyond their propositional content, and which outweighs spoken words in terms of binding relationships in Western societies:

> ...the border, in particular the physical substrate of a communication and its various configurations, helps to embody, preserve, and represent authority. Hence, the king's seal carried more weight than his words alone, a promissory note is more forceful than a verbal promise, a will can be proved but a wish cannot. In all, a border distinguishes between mere words and deeds.

The immutability of documents represents a physical manifestation of institutional power. Their authority derives from signs which suggest that their production and appearance rely on forces which lie "outside" daily human interactions. Immutability allows documents to appear on the scene of social interaction as not just a "given", but rather as transcending the ability of social actors to negotiate their meaning (cf. Mitchell, 1990). Brown & Duguid point out that the switch to an electronic (and more mutable) substrate may undermine the inherent authority of documents. There is, however, a deeper issue which Diné CARE's experience highlights: that is, the question of documentation as the basis of articulation work.

Navajo people often explicitly reject the inherent, transcendent authority of documents. This was starkly illustrated, I recall, on an occasion when a Navajo woman of the Big Mountain community in Northern Arizona received a court summons for herding her sheep on her own ancestral lands - which were politically disputed and thus subject to grazing prohibitions. When asked what she was going to do about it, she replied: "That piece of paper doesn't breathe. It isn't alive. Why should I do what it tells me." Although perfectly literate, this woman did not share the literacy-related practice which attributes institutional authority to documents themselves.

For the people with whom I worked, authority relies instead on the situated practice of oral interaction. Spoken words constitute the means by which relationships are established and maintained. As Diné CARE's President once discussed with me:

> We are an oral people. For us our word is everything. That's why we prefer to speak to each just right here (hands motioning in front of him) without anything written down, without contracts or legal-eze, even without notes or what have you. In that particular manner we know that we are speaking from our hearts.

On several occasions, not only Navajo people with whom I worked but also other American Indians in various settings, maintained a distinction between two ways of communicating, either "from the heart" or "on paper". Linguistic "performance" (in the particular sense defined in linguistic anthropology - cf. Bauman and Briggs, 1990) - provides a basis both for authority and for the coordination of activities, through the building of what Diné CARE members called "trust".

This approach to the construction of authority is not simply a vestige of some vanishing "tribal" mode of existence. Oral interaction plays a significant role in "modern" institutional settings as well. The key difference between the Navajo approach and the Western approach to documentation is perhaps primarily a matter of emphasis. Researchers have shown how orality can be embedded in - and integral to the continued operation of - numerous rationalized settings (e.g., Suchman, 1983; Giddens, 1990; Cicourel, 1990). Documentation and codified procedures can be continuously circumvented and abrogated in Western society, but still often retain a critical sense of importance as an "objective" record which binds social participants to a prior interactional outcome. For Navajo people, articulation work hinges less on representational artifacts which transcend situational particulars, and depends more on interpersonal trust, continuously and repeatedly constructed in locally situated interaction.

Conclusion

Discussions of hegemony in the social sciences often focus on how modern modalities of power reproduce the social order by forcing people to think in the terms which the dominant system lays down, thereby assuring its perpetuation even by those who oppose it. This point of view probably underestimates the ability of social actors to finesse and negotiate meanings, and to deconstruct dominant discursive practices (Bauman and Briggs, 1990). In spite of all the troubles described above, Diné CARE members displayed far more creativity and ingenuity in assimilating and reframing technical discourses, documentary practices, and technology than most discussions of hegemony seem to acknowledge is possible. Unfortunately, space does not permit a detailed discussion of the ways in which Diné CARE members managed various foreign practices, but a few examples may help to illustrate the point. With regards to funding, for instance, the visibility and outspokenness of Diné CARE's treasurer, as well as the prominence of the organization in the news during 1993 and 1994, allowed her to make extensive contact with potential funders. She skillfully leveraged this exposure to encourage personal site visits by funders - thereby changing significantly the way many organizations approached the funding of local work. Not surprisingly Diné CARE made enemies of many urban groups by attempting to knock them out of their (often lucrative) mediating positions during this time.

Sometimes infrastructure problems were addressed through simple technological solutions, such as the acquisition of fairly inexpensive telephone equipment which allowed multiple voice messages at a single location, Diné CARE members without phones could at least be contacted by voice mail by outsiders who often had no idea about the infrastructure problems on the Reservation.

In the production and manipulation of documents, or other text based communication, Diné CARE members displayed considerable differences from their non-Indian counterparts. Some of these differences I offer only tentatively, as issues of familiarity with various technologies may have played some role. Among these, Diné CARE members displayed a significantly lower tendency to use faxed paper documents, or modem-transferred electronic documents as mutable, shared workspaces than the non-Indian associates with whom they worked. Instead, Diné CARE members were far more likely to follow up on a transmission of a document with a personal phone call, in which their reactions to the text were discussed. This may be partially explainable as an issue of familiarity with technology, as their likelihood of editing and retransmitting such documents did slightly increase over the course of a year. However, even at the end of a year, a significant difference remained. This seems evidence of the preference for oral interaction discussed above. The tremendous phone bills which most members had each month seem to testify to this as well.

In spite of this "interpretive flexibility" however, Diné CARE's experience suggests that relations of dominance may be reinforced purely because marginalized groups must adopt foreign discursive practices in order to make their voices heard at all. Members of Diné CARE were fully conscious of how foreign practices were inappropriate for the framing and organization of their work, but they were nonetheless forced into adopting them to access support. This presented them with a constant source of tension in their organization, which they regarded as always becoming either too hierarchic or too bureaucratic, not by the will of any of its members, but rather as the result of interactions mediated by technologies and representational artifacts that were imposed on them from outside.

For designers interested in facilitating cooperation across increasingly heterogeneous networks of participants, or for the more general technological goals of "empowerment" and "democratization", such considerations may be of value. What may seem "natural" or "transparent" in "our" designs may embody practices which make technology a means of perpetuating relations of power rather than a force for liberation.

Acknowledgments

This research was supported in part by a grant from the National Science Foundation (SBR-9300310). I would like to thank Jane Hill and three anonymous reviewers for comments on an earlier draft of this paper.

References

Adler, P. and T. Winograd (1992) *Usability: Turning technologies into tools.* Oxford: Oxford University Press.

Anderson, R.J. (1994) "Representations and requirements: The value of ethnography in system design." *Human-Computer Interaction* 9: 151-182.

Bauman, R. and C. Briggs (1990) "Poetics and performance as critical perspectives on language and social life." *Annual Review of Anthropology* 19: 59-88.

Brown, J. S. and P. Duguid (1994) "Borderline issues: Social and material aspects of design." *Human-Computer Interaction* 9: 3-36.

Churchill, W., ed. (1983) *Marxism and Native Americans.* Boston: South End Press.

Cicourel, A. (1990) "The integration of distributed knowledge in collaborative medical diagnosis." In *Intellectual teamwork: Social and technological foundations of cooperative work,* ed. Jolene Galegher, Robert Kraut, and Carmen Egido. Hillsdale, NJ: Erlbaum. Pp. 221-242.

Clement, A. (1990) "Cooperative support for computer work: A social perspective on the empowering of end users." *Proceedings of the 2nd conference on CSCW, October 7-10, Los Angeles, CA.* New York: ACM.

Edwards, J.R. (1989) *A history of financial accounting.* New York: Routledge

Epstein, M.J. (1978) *The effect of scientific management on the development of the standard cost system.* New York: Arno Press.

Foucault, M. (1973) *The Archaeology of knowledge.* New York: Pantheon Books.

Foucault, M. (1977) *Discipline and punish: The birth of the prison.* New York: Pantheon.

George, J., R. Kling and S. Iacono (1989) "The role of training and support in desktop computing." *PPRO*, UC Irvine, 1989.

Giddens, A. (1990) *The Consequences of Modernity.* Palo Alto, CA: Stanford University Press.

Goodwin, C. (1994) "Professional vision." *American Anthropologist* 96(3): 606-633.

Gramsci, A. (1992) *Prison Notebooks.* New York: Col.umbia University Press.

Greenbaum, J. (1993) "A design of one's own: Towards participatory design in the United States." In Schuler, Douglas and Aki Namioka (eds.) pp. 75-103.

Habermas, J. (1984) *A Theory of Communicative Action*. Boston: Beacon Press

Hutchins, E. (1995) *Cognition in the wild.* Cambridge, MA: MIT.

Hymes, D. (1974 (1964)) "Toward ethnographies of communication." In Dell H. Hymes (ed.) *Foundations of sociolinguistics*. Philadelphia: University of Pennsylvania Press.

Kling, R. (1980) Social analyses of computing: Theoretical perspectives in recent empirical research. *Computing surveys* 12(1) 61-110.

LaDuke, W. (1983) "From the natural to the synthetic and back again." In Churchill, (ed.) pp. iv-xxiii.

Lave, J. and E. Wenger (1990) *Situated learning: Legitimate peripheral participation.* New York: Cambridge University Press.

Luff, P., C. Heath and D. Greatbatch (1992) "Tasks-in-interaction: paper and screen based documentation in collaborative activity." *CSCW '92 Proceedings, Toronto, October 31 to November 4, 1992.* New York: ACM.

Mitchell, T. (1990) "Everyday metaphors of power." *Theory and Society* 19: 545-577.

Norman, D. and S. Draper (1986) *User centered system design: New perspectives in human-computer interaction.* Hillsdale, NJ: Erlbaum.

Panko, R. (1988) *End user computing: Management, applications and technology.* New York: Wiley.

Philips, S. U. (1983) *The invisible culture*. New York: Longman.

Schmidt, K. and L. Bannon (1992) "Taking CSCW seriously: supporting articulation work." *CSCW* 1(1): 7-40.

Schuler, D. and A. Namioka, eds. (1993) *Participatory design: Principles and practices.* Hillsdale, NJ: Erlbaum.

Scollon, R. and S. Scollon (1981) *Narrative, literacy and face in interethnic communication.* Austin: University of Texas Press.

Seltzer, M. (1992) *Bodies and Machines.* New York: Routledge.

Suchman, L. (1983) "Office procedures as practical action: Models of work and system design." *ACM Transactions on Office Information Systems* 1(4): 320-328.

Suchman, Lucy (1987) *Plans and Situated Actions.* New York: Cambridge University Press.

Proceedings of the Fourth European Conference on Computer-Supported Cooperative Work,
September 10–14, Stockholm, Sweden
H. Marmolin, Y. Sundblad, and K. Schmidt (Editors)

Reconsidering the Virtual Workplace: Flexible Support for Collaborative Activity

Christian Heath
King's College, London and Rank Xerox Research Centre (EuroPARC)

Paul Luff
University of Surrey and King's College, London

Abigail Sellen
Rank Xerox Research Centre (EuroPARC) and The MRC Applied Psychology Unit, Cambridge

Abstract: Despite the substantial corpus of research concerned with the design and development of media space, the virtual workplace has failed to achieve its early promise. In this paper, we suggest that a number of problems which have arisen with the design and deployment of media space, derive from their impoverished concept of collaborative work. Drawing from our own studies of video connectivity, coupled with analyses of work and interaction in real-world settings, we consider ways in which we might reconfigure media space in order to provide more satisfactory support for collaboration in organisational environments.

> [The future of the telephone will mean]...nothing less than a reorganisation of society — a state of things in which every individual, however secluded, will have at call every other individual in the community, to the saving of no end of social and business complications, of needless goings to and fro, of disappointments, delays, and a countless host of great and little evils and annoyances which go so far under present conditions to make life laborious and unsatisfactory. (Scientific American, 1880 p.16)

> That's a funny kind of thing, in which each new object becomes the occasion for seeing again what we see anywhere; seeing people's nastinesses or goodnesses and all the rest, when they do this initially technical job of talking over the phone. The technical apparatus is, then, being made at home with the rest of our world. And that's a thing that's routinely being done, and it's the source for the failures of technocratic dreams that if only we introduced some fantastic new communication machine the world will be transformed. Where what happens is that the object is made at home in the world that has whatever organisation it already has.
> (Sacks, 1972 [1992] p. 548)

1. Introduction

In recent years we have witnessed the emergence of a growing body of research concerned with 'media space'. Both in Europe and North America, a number of laboratories have established audio-visual and computing networks which allowed individuals in distinct physical locations to communicate with each other both visually and vocally. So, for example, at PARC a video window was established which provided scientists with audio-visual access to a common area in a related laboratory in Portland (Olson and Bly, 1991). A similar videowindow facility was established at Bellcore (Fish, et al., 1990). Elsewhere, at EuroPARC in Cambridge, and at the University of Toronto, audio-visual infrastructures were developed which allowed individuals to scan and search various offices, form links colleagues based in other locations, and establish long term connections, often called 'office shares' (Gaver, et al., 1992; Mantei, et al., 1991).

In many cases these technologies were deployed in order to encourage informal communication between personnel and enhance collaborative work. It was hoped that these new technologies could go 'beyond being there' (Hollan and Stornetta, 1992). These various media spaces became increasingly sophisticated as additional facilities were added. For example, individuals were provided with the possibility of receiving multiple images of different domains so that could remain 'aware' of colleagues throughout the workplace, and, in some cases, auditory signals were added which could warn people of upcoming events and encounters (Dourish and Bly, 1992). Despite the extraordinary effort which has been directed towards research in media space, the energy and excitement seems to be on the wane, and wc arc still no nearer to actually deploying a usable and used media space within a 'real world' organisational environment.

In this paper we wish to suggest that the growing concern with media spaces to provide a 'working' environment derives from underlying assumptions or presuppositions concerning interaction and collaboration within the workplace. In particular, the principle concern in media space research with supporting (mediated) face-to-face communication, has inadvertently undermined its ability to reliably support collaborative work. Our growing recognition of the shortcomings of media space and the need to rethink the domain it aims to support, derives from a wide range of research concerning the nature of collaborative work. This includes:

- Naturalistic observations of the use of a media space (EuroPARC's in-house system; Heath and Luff, 1992b).
- Naturalistic studies of work, interaction, and technology in a range of organisational settings (Greatbatch, et al., 1993; Heath and Luff, 1992a; Heath, et al., 1995; Luff and Heath, 1993).
- Experimental studies aimed at extending the design of media spaces by providing multiple views of the remote space (Gaver, et al., 1993; Heath, et al., in press).

By drawing on this work, and the work of others, we consider the problems with the ways media spaces are currently conceived and configured. In considering these problems, we focus on the prevalence of the face-to-face view as the basis for most existing systems. Finally, we briefly consider an alternative conception of collaborative work and outline its implications for media space technologies.

2. The Informal Turn

With the best of intentions, one of the motivations which drove the development of media space within a number of laboratories derived from the growing recognition that the informal organisation of the workplace was an important if not critical aspect of collaborative work. It was argued in particular that 'informal sociability', passing conversations and the like provided the gel to the organisation, and the means through which decisions are made and work gets done. In the scientific domain it was suggested that some of the most innovative ideas and work derived from informal conversations which happened to arise around the work place, often in areas such as lunch rooms, coffee lounges or common rooms (cf. Fish, et al., 1990; Kraut, et al., 1990). At EuroPARC, for example, where the office building straddles three floors and inevitably reduces the possibility for informal contact between particular scientists, it was felt that an audio-visual infrastructure could provide a virtual environment which allows personnel to be 'aware' of each other, and provided opportunities for 'unmotivated encounters'; that is chance meetings and conversations. At EuroPARC, various devices were built into the media space to facilitate awareness and informal contact, whilst of course being careful to preserve a sense of privacy amongst the personnel. A similar emphasis on 'informal sociability' permeated the development of other media spaces, not surprisingly at PARC, but also at Bellcore, the University of Toronto, and to a lesser extent perhaps at Hewlett Packard (UK) (Abel, 1990; Gale, 1994; Gaver, et al., 1992; Kraut, et al., 1990; Mantei, et al., 1991).

It was an inspired and sophisticated decision to deploy a technology within the workplace to support the informal rather than formal organisation. At EuroPARC, individuals were provided with cameras and monitors in their offices and within public domains which, through a complex computing infrastructure, supported awareness, context, and conversation. It was assumed correctly, that most users would simply place the camera and monitor on their desk close to their workstation, and thereby be able to see and establish contact with colleagues. At EuroPARC and elsewhere, it was largely taken for granted that the access that one would like of the other(s) was to see their face, their head and shoulders. In consequence, in almost in media spaces, it has become the practice to provide 'users' with a (mediated) face to face view of each other. In some cases, it was assumed that if users need an alternative view, then they could negotiate a shift in the position of the camera and monitor and physically re-site the equipment.[1]

It is interesting to note that the location of camera and monitor in their respective domains were treated as largely unproblematic in most media spaces. Indeed, despite the emphasis on peripheral awareness and sensitivity, it was assumed that a head and shoulders view of the other would provide the relevant information. The forms of access that the user required once they had established contact was given less emphasis, so that, for example, the idea that another might be engaged in object focused task, like making notes on a paper pad, did not feature as important for the design. In part, this relative lack of concern with task-focused collaboration may have derived from the decision to support informal sociability where one would not properly assume it being relevant to provide access to the working domain and the wider environment of the person with whom one is conversing. It seems then, that the concern with providing support for sociability and (mediated) face-to-face communication throughout a variety of media spaces may help to explain why such sophisticated technological environments have largely failed to support individuals' access to each others activities and working domains.

It would be an exaggeration to suggest that the commitment to support sociability is solely responsible for the relative failure of media spaces. Nonetheless, it is the case that, despite the desire to engender new forms of human sociability, there is little evidence to suggest that media spaces, throughout the various organisational environments in which they have been deployed, have served to establish new interpersonal relations and relationships. Moreover, given the restricted access that they provide to users, the media spaces with which we are closely familiar have not generally provided an environment for collaborative work. Indeed, in the cases where individuals do, for example, try to write to paper together using the media space, or provide advice on the use of new software, the inability to see and share objects and shift ones views of each other domains causes frustration and difficulty for those involved. The evidence suggests that media spaces are instead used as a new form of communication for personnel in more 'formal' settings (e.g. in video-conferences), when they are already known to each other, or to demonstrate to others the nature of existing interpersonal relationships (Kantarijev and Harper, 1994). The technology therefore has served as a resource for those who already know each other, but rarely led to new forms of collaboration or 'sociability'.

There are, of course, some examples where media space has provided individuals with a useful environment in which talk to each other, share ideas and undertake collaboration. At EuroPARC for example, two scientists established an 'office share', an open video connection, through which they maintained contact, conversed and worked together (Dourish, et al., 1994). It is interesting to note that

---

1 An interesting exception to this is Bill Buxton's 'fly-on-the wall' camera at the University of Toronto which is designed specifically for the purpose of glancing and is positioned above the office door.

an 'informal' set of practices emerged between the two scientists to enable them to cope with some the limitations of the technology. For example, they soon learned to differentiate looking at the camera to establish mutual gaze, as opposed to looking directly at the other in the monitor, so as to deal with the distortions that are necessarily introduced when a camera is placed above or to one side of the monitor. They also learned to cope with the problems which emerged when it only appeared that they may be alone, since part of each others' office were out of range of the respective cameras. In general however, at EuroPARC as with other media spaces, the infrastructure did not give rise to new forms of sociability or interpersonal relationship, and it was relatively rare for individuals to collaborate with each other in the virtual workplace.

3. Support for focused, collaborative work

Whilst media spaces are undeniably an innovative and exciting concept that have done much to advance the interconnection of audio-visual and computing technologies, they have largely provided 'users' with conventional (mediated) face to face views with which to work together. Indeed, even in the more sophisticated examples of media spaces, we find that users are provided with access to each other which does not differ significantly from the arrangements found with conventional video-phone and video-conferencing technologies. It is assumed, or presupposed, that single view is adequate and that the most important view of the other for a range of purposes, is a head and shoulder, face to face image. Most commercial video-phones and video-conferencing equipment, for example, provide this as the built-in view. It is assumed that if users wish to discuss any 'physical' object such as a document, then this can be adequately supported either by exchanging documentation prior to establishing video-mediated contact or by switching over to an alternative 'document view'. In such cases, participants necessarily lose sight of each other.

There are of course one or two important exceptions. These tend to be restricted to prototypes in research laboratories. For example a number of researchers have begun to provide users with shared work space as well as audio-visual link through which they can collaboratively work on text or diagrams (Olson, et al., 1990; Smith, et al., 1989). However, even in these more innovative cases, the audio-visual infrastructure is primarily designed to provide a face-to-face view rather than to allow participants to vary their access to each other with respect to ongoing demands of the tasks in which they are engaged.

Whilst it might be thought that in cases of focused collaborative work such as meetings, it is unnecessary to provide individuals with anything more than a head and shoulders view of each other, it is not at all clear that even in these relatively restricted and formally organised applications, that the conventional media space is satisfactory. For example, the remote participant(s) are often presented on a fairly small monitor (14" or so). The image is perceived 'en bloc', and distorts our ability to discriminate the relative weighting of the other's conduct, so that for example, gestural activity and even major bodily rearrangements, pass unnoticed to the remote participant(s) (Heath and Luff, 1992b). Moreover, the image does not appear to provide participants with the ability to monitor the other on the periphery of their visual field, outside the direct line of their regard. They sometimes notice gross changes in the image, as when someone sits down or places a hand over the camera, but relatively small changes in the other's comportment, which subtly display changes in the ways in which they are participating in the activity at hand, pass unnoticed to the remote 'user'. These 'problems' are exacerbated by video configurations which preclude one participant seeing the other in relation to their activity or local environment, so that, for example, an individual's engagement in a document, or happenings within their office, are hidden to the remote participant. Focused collaboration, like other forms of interaction, rests upon people's ability to remain 'peripherally aware' of the other and to be sensitive to actions and events outside the direct like of their regard. Media space, and its predominant concern with providing (mediated) face to face views, undermines the ordinary resources upon which individuals rely in working together and coordinating their activities with each other.

Almost all media space therefore, like more conventional video-conferencing and video-phone facilities, provide 'users' with a restricted and severely delimited choice of views. The problem is not simply that media space tends to provide (mediated) face to face views, but rather that it is assumed that access between participants does not need to vary with respect to ongoing and shifting demands of a particular task or activity. It is this static and inflexible notion of collaborative activity which has inadvertently hindered media space research, and undermined its ability to provide a useful environment to enable people to work, or even socialise with each other. In consequence, it is difficult to imagine that current media space research constitutes the first brave steps towards 'beyond being there', rather people are provided with a poor and inadequate approximation of co-presence in which it is difficult to accomplish even the most simple collaborative tasks.

4. Working Together

Whilst there are significant technological constraints which currently shape the ways in which we might develop media space, we would like to suggest that many of the difficulties which arise with the deployment of current systems derive more from the assumptions which inform their design, than the limitations of the technology. It is not simply that we have misconceived the activities we are attempting to support, but rather that media space research has been informed by an impoverished conception of interaction and collaboration. This may be a consequence of conflating the organisation of informal conversation with the demands and complexities of focused, cooperative work. Or it may be that we have sought a compromise between technical practicalities and the demands of collaboration. In any case, the inadequacies and limitations of offering a single and fixed, face-to-face view become even more apparent when we consider the organisation of collaborative work in more conventional, organisational environments.

We believe that examining the ways in which people ordinarily work together can direct our attention towards requirements for more satisfactory systems. This is not to suggest that the design of innovative systems should simply be based on the status quo, or be shaped to support current working practices, but rather that in developing new technologies we need to take into account the complexity of even the most mundane tasks, and the richness of the skills and competencies utilised by participants in doing what they do. A more thorough understanding of how people do what they do in organisational life, and in particular accomplishing collaborative work, can provide resources not only to evaluate our ideas and concepts, but to envisage more radical solutions to conventional problems.

In this light, alongside our research on media space, we undertook a series of interrelated, naturalistic studies concerned with the organisation of work, interaction and technology in a variety of organisational environments such as control rooms (Heath and Luff, 1992a), medical consultations (Greatbatch, et al., 1993), architectural practices (Luff and Heath, 1993) and news agencies (Heath, et al., 1995). Whilst the settings encompass a broad range of tasks and technologies, there are some findings which generalise. These can be summarised as follows:

- Cooperative work involves the ongoing and seamless transition between individual and collaborative tasks, where personnel are simultaneously participating in multiple, interrelated activities.
- An individual's ability to contribute to the activities of others and fulfil their own responsibilities relies upon peripheral awareness and monitoring; in this way information can be gleaned from the concurrent activities of others within the "local milieu", and actions and activities can be implicitly coordinated with the emergent tasks of others.
- Much of the interaction through which individuals, produce, interpret and coordinate actions and activities within co-present working environments is accomplished using various objects and artefacts, including paper and screen-based documents, telephones, and the like. The participants' activities are mediated and rendered visible through these objects and artefacts.
- Both focused and unfocused collaboration is largely accomplished not through direct face-to-face interaction, but through alignment towards the focal area of the activity, such as a document, where individuals coordinate their actions with others through peripheral monitoring of the others involvement in the activity "at hand". For example, much collaboration is undertaken side by side where the individuals are continuously sustaining a

shared focus on an aspect of a screen or paper-based document, such as a section of an architectural drawing.

- Collaborative work relies upon individuals subtly and continuously adjusting their access to each others' activities to enable them to establish and sustain differential forms of co-participation in the tasks "at hand".

These observations stand in marked contrast to the support that media space provides for collaborative work. It becomes increasingly apparent, when you examine work and collaboration in more conventional environments, that the inflexible and restrictive views characteristic of even the most sophisticated media spaces, provide impoverished settings in which to work together. This is not to suggest that media space research should simply attempt to 'replace' co-present working environments, such ambitions are way beyond our current thinking and capabilities. Rather, we can learn a great deal concerning the requirements for the virtual office by considering how people work together and collaborate in more conventional settings. A more rigorous understanding of more conventional collaborative work, can not only provide resources with which to recognise how, in building technologies we are (inadvertently) changing the ways in which people work together, but also with ways in which demarcate what needs to be supported and what can be left to one side (at least for time being). Such understanding might also help us deploy these advanced technologies.

5. Preliminary designs: the MTV Studies

Perhaps the most important lesson for the design of media space, drawn from studies of collaborative work in more conventional environments, is the ways in which participants utilise and rely upon their ability to continually shape their access to each other and the activities in which they are engaged. It is not simply that a face-to-face orientation is inappropriate for the accomplishment of certain types of cooperative task, but rather that face-to-face is just one amongst a variety of orientations that participants rely upon in working together.[2] In thinking, therefore, of developing a virtual environment to support collaborative work, it is necessary to explore ways of providing users not simply with alternative views of the other, their work space and their local environment, but with ways of flexibly and even 'seamlessly' varying their access to each other.

Actually building a media space that fulfils these requirements is not straightforward. It is not only difficult to provide individuals with flexible access to each other's, and their respective settings, but in so doing one can exacerbate problems which haunt even the most basic media space, namely the perspectival incongruities of the different participants. Nonetheless, we believe that it is only by

2 Adopting an alternative orientation for video that focuses on the activity at hand may alleviate some problems associated with face-to-face views (Nardi, et al., 1993). However, such a proposal still restricts participants to a single view with no suggestions on how to implement more variable forms of accessibility.

building and evaluating technologies 'in use', no matter how simple, that the benefits and problems of alternative configurations can be uncovered.

In collaboration with our colleague Bill Gaver, our first attempts at reconfiguring media space began with a series of experiments at EuroPARC called the MTV (Multiple Target Video) experiments. The purpose of the experiments was to explore ways of offering users an expanded view of the remote space. We did this by wiring up two offices at EuroPARC to simulate what might happen in a distributed work situation.

In the first experiment (MTV I), we provided participants with an environment which offered four different views. These views consisted of: a conventional face-to-face view; a 'desktop' camera to focus on the details of any activities on the work surface; a wider 'in-context' view providing an image of the co-participant in relation to their work; and a "bird's eye" view giving access to the periphery of a colleague's environment (Figure 1). Participants were also given a single monitor to view their co-participant, and could change their view on the remote site by turning a simple rotary switch. Thus, each participant could select for display on their monitor only one view at a time, doing so by sometimes momentarily passing through other views. To give information concerning which view their colleague was connected to, each participant was also given a 'feedback monitor' showing which view one's co-participant had currently selected of them.

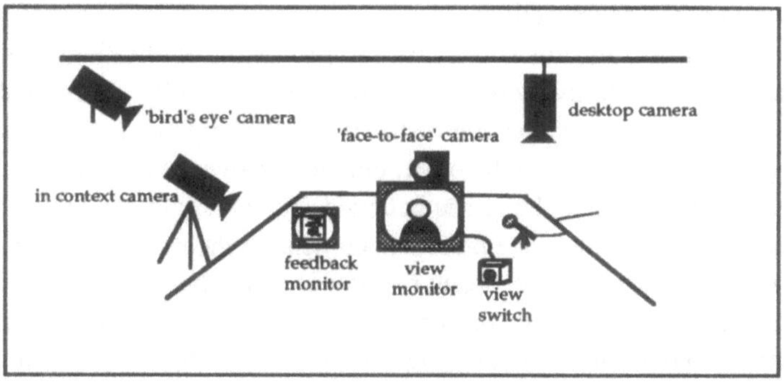

Figure 1. Configuration of the MTV I system using multiple cameras and a single monitor for each participant.

Pairs of users were asked to perform two experimental tasks. In the first, participants were each asked to draw the other's office. In the second, they were asked to carry out a collaborative design exercise where they had asymmetrical resources; one could manipulate a model to present possible solutions whilst the other drew the design. The results of these experiments, (described more fully in Gaver, et al., 1993), revealed how little the face-to-face view was used in the accomplishment of either task. Instead, participants mainly switched between the in-context, model, desk and bird's eye views. Given the nature of the design task it is perhaps not surprising that most participants who were doing the drawing focused on the view showing most details of the model. On the other hand, the participants in the offices with the model appeared to utilise the in-context and bird's eye cameras for allowing them to assess their colleague's orientation and to make sense of particular aspects of visual conduct, for example, gestures pointing to objects. Finally, some participants appeared to take advantage of the different views to track their colleagues as they moved around the room.

However the system generated difficulties for the participants. These difficulties arise in the use of any media space, but become increasingly severe when you provide individuals with the ability to select between alternative views of each other, and their respective domains. Whilst participants presuppose that their own activity and domain is visible to the other, they discover, that within the developing course of the interaction, their conduct and their local environment may not be accessible, or inaccessible in the ways in which they have assumed. They presuppose a 'reciprocity of perspective' or 'interchangeability of standpoint' (cf. Schutz 1962, and Cicourel 1972), organise their conduct with respect to such assumptions, only to find that establishing and sustaining a mutually compatible frame of reference can prove deeply problematic. In MTV I, whilst we increased the relative access that participants had to each other (and their respective domains), we exacerbated the difficulties in participants knowing what was available to the other, and what the other was currently able to see. In consequence, the experiment reveals numerous instances in which the subjects are attempting to clarify and reconcile each other's perspective.

These difficulties are not solved by the provision of the feedback monitor; indeed users did not intuitively realise that the smaller 'vanity' monitor showed the other's view of themselves, despite instructions. Participants presupposed that an object or gesture was visible to the other, only to discover that it was unavailable or not available in the way that he or she believed. For example, it was quite common for one participant to point to the other's document on their monitor in an attempt to refer to something, when the feedback monitor showed that such gestures could not possibly be seen by the other. At other times participants expressed uncertainty about what the other could see, and together, pairs of subjects often had difficulty not only determining what each other could see, but actually attempting to align their 'perspectives' with each other in order to establish, if only temporally, a mutually compatible frame of reference.

In the second experiment (MTV II), we attempted to address some of these difficulties by providing a more stable configuration which allow access both to the other and the workspace. Rather than providing access to the various views via a switch, each participant was provided with several monitors, so that all the views from the cameras were simultaneously available. The monitors provided three views: a face-to-face view, a 'desktop' view and an 'in-context' view; the latter giving access to the periphery of the colleague's environment (see Figure 2). The three monitors were arranged in each rooms in a similar fashion with the face-to-face monitor and camera positioned in the middle. This meant that a orientation towards the face-to-face view would also appear to a colleague as a reorientation away from their in-context or desktop view, and *vice versa.* As both participants had access to all views simultaneously, there was no need for a feedback monitor. The tasks the users were asked to perform were the same as those used in MTV I

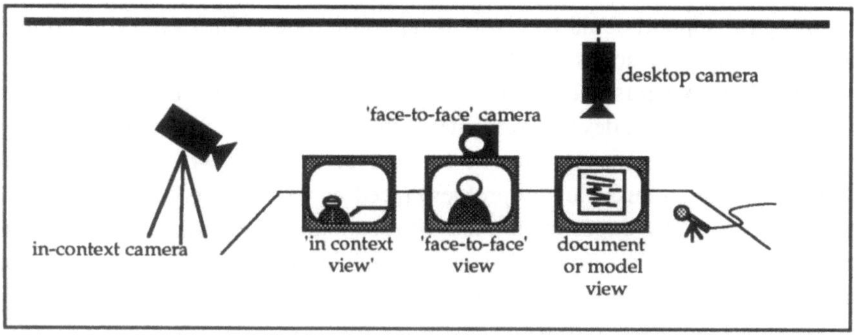

Figure 2. The configuration of the MTV II system using multiple cameras and multiple monitors for each participant.

Although preliminary observations reveal that participants used all three views and 'switched' views more frequently than they did in MTV I, as in the first experiment, participants mainly focused on the view displaying the most details of the model or the drawings. Participants glanced at the face-to-face view more frequently than in MTV I, but only for short durations, appearing to utilise the view, sometimes with the in-context view, to assess their colleague's involvement in the ongoing activity.

A further brief trial was carried out which provided a closer side-by-side orientation, mimicking that found in co-present environments. While the results were inconclusive, it appeared that the participants in this trial were particularly sensitive to this repositioning, perhaps due of the increased access it gave to the colleague's orientation to their activity.

The simultaneous availability of views appeared to increase the ease with which participants could flexibly vary their access to the remote space and did not require them breaking from the activity 'at hand' to switch the view. However, despite having similar access to their colleague's domain and this access remaining stable, limitations remained. As with MTV I, separate, fixed cameras failed to offer complete access to the remote space, there being gaps in the views offered. Moreover, participants still had little access to the actual document or artefact on which their colleague was focused. Perhaps more importantly, participants still encountered difficulties ascertaining what aspects of their own conduct and environment were visible to their colleagues. Although the co-participants had available, at the same time, similar views, and were also able to simultaneously monitor shifts in colleagues' shifts in orientation, there are still instances in which participants attempt to reconcile each other's perspective.

6. Flexible Access for Collaborative Work

By observing the use of both conventional media spaces and experimental configurations, it is possible to envisage ways in which more advanced technological support could be given to support remote collaboration. Noting that access to a remote space is problematic even when participants are provided with multiple fixed cameras and monitors, it may be worth considering more mobile solutions, for example, developing systems that allow a participant to 'rove' around a colleague's remote environment (cf. Gaver et al. 1994). However, such solutions do not address the key problem faced by participants in media spaces or subjects in the MTV experiments, that of reconciling their own perspective with their co-participant's. Instead, systems that automatically track a person's movements in order to provide images of a colleague's domain may well exacerbate the problems facing a colleague when trying to establish a mutual frame of reference. An alternative approach would be investigate how our understanding of collaborative work could suggest requirements for 'virtual environments'.

For example, our studies of work in real-world settings have revealed a resilience of the paper document that is perhaps surprising in the light of the various sophisticated computational facilities that are available (Luff, et al., 1992). Much collaborative work is mediated and rendered visible through objects and artefacts, including both paper and screen-based documents, where individuals co-ordinate their actions through peripheral monitoring of the other's involvement in the activity "at hand". Such flexible forms of collaboration are not supported by those current CSCW systems that simply place various facilities on the screen of the workstation and allow participants to refer to and operate on electronic copies of a shared document.

With its emphasis on providing computational support within current work spaces and existing artefacts, like documents, many of these concerns do appear to be shared by those exploring the possibilities for 'ubiquitous computing' and 'augmented reality' (e.g. Weiser, 1991). One direction these efforts have taken has been to explore the possibilities of extending work surfaces so that, for example, electronic documents can also be manipulated on them (Wellner, 1992). Although, the size and orientation of innovations, such as the DigitalDesk, do appear to provide resources for supporting the alignments to artefact-focused collaborative activity found in real-world settings they currently, as yet, provide no explicit support even for co-present collaboration. The attempts at supporting remote collaboration, by projecting images of co-participants through the work surface, for example, appear to have largely ignored the orientations through which collaborations through which collaboration is ordinarily accomplished (Ishii and Kobayashi, 1992; Tang and Minneman, 1991b). Thus, it may not be surprising that providing co-participants with a face-to-face view of a colleague whilst they engage in focused collaborative work, has been found to be intrusive and inflexible, (Ishii personal communication).

What it may be useful to consider is how to support different forms of, and orientations to, collaborative work, allowing co-participants not only to move seamlessly between individual and collaborative activities (cf. Ishii, 1990), but also to allow co-participants to adjust their own access to another's activity. So, for example, one could explore how to allow for the many ways in which individuals can be aligned to a focal area of an activity and for transitions between these orientations to be made easily. In order to explore these requirements in more detail and to suggest ways in which they could be integrated into a common design, it is perhaps worthwhile envisaging a more concrete example of a system to support more flexible access to collaborative work.

At present, in collaboration with David Travis of the Centre for Human Communication at British Telecom, and with Bill Buxton of the University of Toronto, we are developing a system that aims to support different orientations to focused collaborative work. This system consists of two prototype video desks and is a preliminary attempt at providing the variable access into another's domain by integrating the capabilities of video, computer and digital tablet technologies.

As with MTV II experiments, the requirement for the system to support variable access into a remote space can be met by providing co-participants with multiple views from multiple cameras, these views displaying the co-participant and the co-participant's in the context of their work. However, it is important for co-participants to be able to make fine adjustments to the positioning and orientations of cameras and monitors in order to tailor the environment to the demands of particular activities. Providing multiple views simultaneously and allowing some flexibility in their placement also makes it feasible to reconfigure desk to support other kinds of collaborative arrangements, for example, between several users at several remote sites, or with several users at a particular site. However, in these configurations participants have less variety and flexibility in their access to their colleagues. In order to reduce the problems of separating cameras from the image, the views are provided by 'through the screen', adjustable cameras (cf. the 'Hydra' system Sellen, 1992; Sellen, et al., 1992). A feedback monitor being available for each view to give participants access to the views their colleagues can see. Moreover, each different view is accompanied by an audio speaker for sound from the appropriate camera, thus providing a further resource for participants to monitor the orientation and participation of their colleagues. Most importantly, perhaps, the views will be configured in such a way to support the alignments most commonly found when individuals engage in collaborative activities; not only is it possible to present one view at the side of the user (to support side-by-side collaboration) but also the appropriate orientation of the image will be displayed (i.e. with the relevant height-width ratio).

In order to support greater access to the focus of any activity 'at hand' it is necessary to allow for the manipulation of both paper and electronic documents so that co-participants can have resources collaboratively to refer to, discuss and manipulate. Although electronic documents can be transmitted in the conventional way, to support more flexible forms of collaboration a more sophisticated approach is required. This could be accomplished by integrating camera and projection technologies so that paper documents are scanned from, and electronic documents are projected to, the work surface (cf. 'DigitalDesk', Wellner 1992) However, a simpler solution that does not require complex calibration of the document could be adopted that supports some mobility of the paper document. This requires that the relative position of the document and the camera be kept fixed.

The importance of providing access to both paper and electronic documents is further revealed when considering the requirements for providing participants to establish and sustain different forms of participation to collaborative activities. In particular, the need to provide users with the ability to see each other and to be able to change orientation to the other, there is also the requirement to see each other in relation to the relevant documents and artefacts (cf. Tang and Minneman, 1991a). In part, this can be achieved by viewing, or 'peripherally monitoring', the side-by-side view of the co-participant. However, access through video allows for another possibility - displaying the images of gestures as they pass over the document so that a co-participant can see details of visual conduct, such as gestures like pointing, in relation to a remote document, whether it be electronic or paper.

An implementation of the above environment is currently being developed and, needless to say, there are many technological issues to be overcome in its design; not least coping satisfactorily with the problem of multiple images of participants, artefacts and gestures. The particular system description above aims to be a more concrete way of illustrating the requirements that have been derived from our studies and experiments. What is important is the requirements not only provide participants with different forms of access to another's domain and activities, but also bring closer the ways tasks and interaction are supported; support that has largely been considered distinct within CSCW.

7. Discussion

It is perhaps an understandable ambition that in designing new technology we hope conventional ways of working will be replaced by more efficient and innovative practices, relieving us of past incumbencies and burdens. In the case of media space there is little evidence to suggest, however, that we likely to achieve our brave new world. We are now perhaps at a stage where we need to reconsider both the technology and the activities that we are attempting to support.

In this paper we have attempted to show how the design of media space has been founded on limited, if not mistaken, assumptions regarding both the nature of collaborative work and the ways in which technology can be deployed to facilitate informal interaction in organisational environments. In identifying some properties of work and collaboration in more conventional environments in order to inform the requirements for innovative systems, we are not suggesting that new technology should simply support current social organisation (though that would be indeed an extraordinary achievement), but rather that an understanding of even the most simple, collaborative activities reveals the richness and complexity of working together, and that our systems should not impoverish what individuals do in their day to day working lives. We should at least attempt to support some basic aspects of collaborative activity, and unless we can, it is unlikely, even with most persuasive marketing strategy, that our heart felt innovations will have a significant impact on the organisation of work. In the case at hand, it remains to be seen to what extent the system we are currently developing comes even a small way to actually provide individuals with a useful environment in which to work together. It is only through building, deploying, and evaluating the prototypes that we can begin to identify their limitations and possibilities.

Ethnographic studies of workplace activities might not only serve to identify some properties of collaborative work which could inform the requirements of complex systems, but also provide resources though which we can begin to reconfigure key concepts in CSCW and HCI. As we have suggested elsewhere (see for example Heath and Luff 1992, and Heath et al. forthcoming) we need to develop an understanding of concepts such as 'task', 'collaboration' and 'user' which charts a course through the potentially polarised distinctions of the 'individual and the group', the 'cognitive and the social', HCI and CSCW. A glance at the details of workplace activities, reveal ways in which 'tasks' are embedded in interaction, 'users' include a range of individuals who may not be directly involved with the system, and participants are seamlessly and continuously moving between the individual and the collaborative as they mutually accomplish the 'business at hand'. A more thorough going reconsideration of many of the key concepts in HCI and CSCW in terms of an understanding of the workplace is not only of theoretical importance, but of practical significance to the ways in which we think about design and technological support for collaborative activity. Indeed, such theoretical respecifications and the burgeoning body of empirical findings concerning workplace activities, might not only provide the resources for developing more 'suitable' technologies for conventional organisational environments, but also inform the design of more innovative and exciting systems for collaboration and communication.

Acknowledgements

We would like to thank Bill Buxton, Paul Dourish, Bill Gaver, David Greatbatch, Richard Harper and David Travis for discussions concerning the work reported in this paper. The research is jointly supported by BT Research Laboratories, Rank Xerox Research Centre (EuroPARC) and the EU RACE MITS Project (R2094).

References

Abel, M. J. (1990). Experiences in an Exploratory Distributed Organization, in *Intellectual Teamwork: The Social and Technological Foundations of Cooperative Work*, Kraut, R. E., Galegher, J. and Egido, C. (eds.), pp 489-510. Hillsdale, New Jersey.: Lawrence Erlbaum Associates.

Cicourel, A. (1972) *Cognitive Sociology*. Harmondsworth, England: Penguin

Dourish, P., Adler, A., Bellotti, V. and Henderson, H. (1994). *Your Place or Mine? Learning from Long-Term Use of Video Communication*. Working Paper, Rank Xerox EuroPARC Cambridge.

Dourish, P. and Bly, S. (1992). 'Portholes: Awareness in a distributed work group', in *Proceedings of CHI '92*, 3-7 May, pp.

Fish, R. S., Kraut, R. E. and Chalfonte, B. L. (1990). 'The videowindow system in informal communication', in *Proceedings of CSCW '90*, 7 - 10 October, pp. 1-11.

Gale, S. (1994). Desktop Video Conferencing: Technical Advances and Evaluation Issues, in *Computer-Supported Cooperative Work: The multimedia and networking paradigm*, Scrivener, S. A. R. (eds.), pp 81-104. Aldershot: Avebury Technical.

Gaver, W. W., Moran, T., Maclean, A., Lovstrand, L., Dourish, P., Carter, K. A. and Buxton, W. (1992). 'Realizing a video environment: EuroPARC's RAVE system', in *Proceedings of CHI 92*, 3 - 7 May, pp. 27-35.

Gaver, W. W., Sellen, A., Heath, C. C. and Luff, P. (1993). 'One is not enough: Multiple Views in a Media Space', in *Proceedings of INTERCHI '93*, April 24 - 29, pp. 335-341.

Gaver, W. W., Smets, G., & Overbeeke, K. (1994). *A virtual window on media space*. Unpublished manuscript.

Greatbatch, D., Luff, P., Heath, C. C. and Campion, P. (1993). Interpersonal Communication and Human-Computer Interaction: an examination of the use of computers in medical consultations, *Interacting With Computers*. **5**: (2), 193-216.

Heath, C. C. and Luff, P. (1992a). Collaboration and control: Crisis Management and Multimedia Technology in London Underground Line Control Rooms, *CSCW Journal*. **1**: (1-2), 69-94.

Heath, C. C. and Luff, P. (1992b). Media Space and Communicative Asymmetries: Preliminary Observations of Video Mediated Interaction, *Human-Computer Interaction*. **7**: 315-346.

Heath, C. C., Luff, P. and Nicholls, G. M. (1995). 'The Collaborative Production of the Document: Context, Genre and the Borderline in Design', in *Proceedings of International Workshop on the Design of Cooperative Systems (COOP'95)*

Heath, C.C., Jirotka, M.., Luff, P. & J. Hindmarsh (Forthcoming) Unpacking Collaboration: The Interactional Organisation of Trading in a City Dealing Room. *Journal of Computer Supported Cooperative Work*.

Heath, C. C., Luff, P. and Sellen, A. (in press). Reconfiguring Media Space, in *The Information SuperHighway: Multimedia Drivers*, Emmott, S. and Travis, D. (eds.), pp London and New York: Academic Press.

Hollan, J. and Stornetta, S. (1992). 'Beyond Being There', in *Proceedings of CHI '92*, 3 - 7 May, pp. 119-125.

Ishii, H. (1990). 'TeamWorkStation: Towards a Seamless Shared Workspace', in *Proceedings of CSCW '90*, 7th -10th October, pp. 13-26.

Ishii, H. and Kobayashi, M. (1992). 'Clearface: a seamless medium for sharing drawing and conversation with eye contact', in *Proceedings of CHI 92*, 3-7 May, pp. 525-532.

Kantarijev, C. K. and Harper, R. (1994). *Portable Portholes Pads: An investigation into the Use of a Ubicomp Device to Support the Sociality of Work.* Technical (Draft), Xerox PARC and Rank Xerox Cambridge EuroPARC.

Kraut, R., Egido, C. J. and Galegher, J. (1990). Patterns of contact and communication in scientific research collaborations, in *Intellectual Teamwork: Social and Technological Foundations of Cooperative Work*, Galegher, J., Kraut, R. E. and Egido, C. (eds.), pp 149-173. New Jersey: Lawrence Erlbaum Associates.

Luff, P. and Heath, C. C. (1993). System use and social organisation: observations on human computer interaction in an architectural practice, in *Technology in Working Order*, Button, G. (eds.), pp 184-210. London: Routledge.

Luff, P., Heath, C. C. and Greatbatch, D. (1992). 'Tasks-in-interaction: Paper and screen based documentation in collaborative activity', in *Proceedings of CSCW '92*, Oct. 31 - Nov. 4, pp. 163-170.

Mantei, M., Baecker, R., Sellen, A., Buxton, W., Milligan, T. and Wellman, B. (1991). 'Experiences in the Use of a Media Space', in *Proceedings of CHI '91*, April-May, pp. 203-8.

Nardi, B. A., Schwartz, H., Kuchinsky, A., Leichner, R., Whitakker, S. and Sclabassi, R. (1993). 'Turning Away from Talking Heads: The Use of Video-as-Data in Neurosurgery', in *Proceedings of INTERCHI'93*, 24th-29th April, pp. 327-334.

Olson, J. S., Olson, G. M., Mack, L. A. and Wellner, P. (1990). 'Concurrent editing: the group interface', in *Proceedings of Interact '90 - Third IFIP Conference on Human-Computer Interaction*, 27th - 30th August, pp. 835-840.

Olson, M. H. and Bly, S. A. (1991). The Portland Experience: a report on a distributed research group, *International Journal of Man-Machine Studies*. **34**: 211-228.

Sacks, H. (1972 [1992]). Lecture 3, Spring 1972, in *Lectures on Conversation: Volume II*, Schegloff, E. A. (eds.), pp 542-553. Oxford: Blackwell.

Schutz, A. (1962) *The Problem of Social Reality: Collected Papers 1.* (edited by M. Natanson) New York: Academic Press

Scientific American, (1880). *The Future of the Telephone*, Jan. 10.

Sellen, A. (1992). 'Speech Patterns in video-mediated conversations', in *Proceedings of CHI '92*, 3-7 May, pp. 49-59.

Sellen, A., Buxton, W. and Arnott, J. (1992). *Using spatial cues to improve desktop conferencing. Presented at CHI'92.* Monterey, Ca.: Dynamic Graphics Project, Computer Research Institute, University of Toronto.

Smith, R. B., O' Shea, T., O' Malley, C. and Taylor, J. S. (1989). 'Preliminary experiments with a distributed, multi-media problem solving environment', in *Proceedings of First European Conference on Computer Supported Cooperative Work*, Sept. 13-15, pp. 19-35.

Tang, J. C. and Minneman, S. L. (1991a). VideoDraw: A Video Interface for Collaborative Drawing, *ACM Transactions on Information Systems*. **9**,: (2), 170-184.

Tang, J. C. and Minneman, S. L. (1991b). 'VideoWhiteboard: Video Shadows to Support Remote Collaboration', in *Proceedings of CHI' 91*, April-May, pp. 315-322.

Weiser, M. (1991). The Computer for the 21st Century, *Scientific American*. September 1991:

Wellner, P. (1992). *Interacting With Paper on the DigitalDesk.* Rank Xerox EuroPARC and University of Cambridge Computer Laboratory.

Proceedings of the Fourth European Conference on Computer-Supported Cooperative Work,
September 10–14, Stockholm, Sweden
H. Marmolin, Y. Sundblad, and K. Schmidt (Editors)

Contact: Support for Distributed Cooperative Writing

Andrew Kirby
Computing Department, Lancaster University, Lancaster

Tom Rodden
Computing Department, Lancaster University, Lancaster

Abstract: This paper presents a novel system to support the activities of distributed cooperative writing. The system builds upon the results from previous studies of cooperative work, and on a set of short focused studies of cooperative authoring to outline a framework and system to meet the requirements of cooperating authors. The system provides facilities to represent the decomposition of the writing task and assignment of responsibilities. In addition, a series of monitoring facilities is provided which allows authors to coordinate their activities in the construction of documents.

Introduction

Cooperative writing has represented a considerable proportion of research in CSCW and has featured prominently in the literature. In general, work on cooperative authoring has focused on the development of editors intended to support real-time cooperative editing, Grove (Ellis et al., 1991), ShrEdit (Killey 1990) and so on, or on studies of the authoring process (Beck 1993, Beck et al., 1993, Posner 1993, Rimmershaw 1992, Sharples ed 1993). While studies consider the overall strategies and activities involved in the construction and development of documents the current generation of editors focuses on the very detailed set of activities required in the construction of typewritten documents.

As a result of this distinction these two activities often appear to take place in isolation from each other and reported studies of cooperative writing are seldom directly connected to the construction of dedicated cooperative editors. In fact, empirical based arguments are often presented against the narrow scope of dedicated editors :

> "support for writing should embrace the entire process from registering the task to supporting a finished manuscript" (Sharples and Pemberton 1990).

Studies of writing do not dismiss or detract from real-time cooperative editors such as Grove (Ellis et al., 1991) or authoring editors like PREP (Neuwirth et al., 1990). Rather they suggest that such editors have a role to play in the wider process of planning and constructing a paper.

The intention of this paper is to examine the development of a cooperative application that directly builds upon the results of existing studies of cooperative work. We take as the starting point in informing our work studies undertaken by (Beck 1993, Posner et al., 1993, Sharples ed 1993). This corpus of empirical material has been complemented by a series of short focused studies of cooperative authoring in an academic environment.

Contact, aims to support the activities of cooperative writing across a community of geographically disparate authors. The focus of support is on the provision of facilities for the decomposition of the writing activity, the assignment of responsibilities and the monitoring of progress. The system makes use of widely available facilities to provide this support to authors within their own environments.

The Needs of Cooperative Writing

In this section we seek to outline the needs of cooperative writing that have driven the construction of Contact. These needs have been gathered from existing studies of cooperative writing across a number of domains. In particular three principal sets of studies have been used to inform our requirements :

- Research Issues in the study of Cooperative Writing (Sharples ed 1993)
- Informed Opportunism (Beck et al., 1993)
- How people write together (Posner et al., 1993)

These studies have been complemented by a short local study of cooperative authoring. The study was conducted at Lancaster University and involved interviewing members of an academic department. These interviewees were drawn from several disciplines and research groups. In general, interviewees were familiar with the other authors and some had often worked with the others on one or more papers.

Interviewees were located in the same building and had regular contact with some of the other interviewees due to the proximity of their offices. In addition, interviewees were also involved in producing collaborative documents with remote participants in the UK and Europe. Interviews were conducted in an informal manner, with an audio tape to record the conversation that took place. The aim of the study was to get a feel for the collaborative processes that the interviewees had taken part in, and not to ascertain any specific data on a particular model or method of work.

Interviewees were asked to focus on the last or most memorable collaborative paper production that they had participated on. The papers discussed included:

- A journal article that was written for a tight deadline, in response to the acceptance of an abstract that was submitted.
- A paper that involved two of the interviewees, and a third collaborator based in Germany.
- A paper for a conference written locally by two of the interviewees who were seldom together in the department.

The mix of papers discussed also covered those working within the same interest or research area, those asked to collaborate due to specialised knowledge from another area, collaborators who had worked together frequently and those collaborators who had not worked together before.

Rather than focus on the particular details of the study we wish to consider the requirements we feel have emerged to drive our software development. In the following sections we consider these requirements in terms of previous studies and of our own short local study.

These recommendations highlight some of the features a system intended to support the dynamic and flexible nature of collaborative writing should have. They are intended to complement the collaborative writing process when supported by electronic tools. In particular, the dynamic, unpredictable and flexible nature of the collaborative writing process is the key factor that will need to be addressed by useful collaborative tools. Consequently any support must allow for considerable flexibility and for considerable control to rest with the user of any supporting systems. This desired flexibility is reflected in many of the existing studies of cooperative work including (Rimmershaw 1992) and (Beck et al., 1993). In the development of our system we wish to focus on two dominant themes which emerge from the investigation of cooperative writing.

Support for coordinating activity

The need for co-authors to coordinate their activities is central to the process of collectively writing documents. For example, (Beck 1993) outlines the need to provide support for coordination which is flexible and open to interpretation by authors. A number of significant points are stressed in the support of coordination:

- The need to integrate with standard platforms given the commitment of users to existing facilities.
- The need to communicate changes across a community of authors.
- The need to provide author information to allow users to infer the impact and consequences of change.

Authors of previous studies also highlight the importance of social control in the development of co-authored documents and the continual change and re-negotiation that this implies. As a consequence, many authors highlight the need for lightweight support.

> " We therefore believe that rather than provide generic co-author roles for tools to support, designers might usefully seek to support co-authors exchange of information to help them make their own judgements about appropriate contributions" (Beck et al., 1993, page 246)

The need for an awareness of the activities of others on which to base the development of a document is also reflected in our experiences of studying co-authoring. During the authoring processes studied, there would be periods of time when collaborators could not have regular and easily arranged meetings. This was due to the remote location of the collaborators or the absence of collaborators from their usual place of work. During this time each of the collaborators were expected to carry out work according to their responsibilities in order to be ready to communicate the results of this work to other collaborators. This often led to unease among others who were uncertain how other parts of the document were progressing. As one author expressed "you are reliant upon other people producing their sections."

The need for an awareness of different authors' progress was also reflected in terms of the need to keep the work of the group synchronised. As one author put it " working with busy people .. it is hard not to go badly out of synch .. I hold back, waiting for others to complete their work." Trying to minimise this problem requires some form of management of the different components being worked upon by separate authors. It would be of direct benefit to provide other collaborators with information about the current state of the co-authoring process. This should include:

- When different components may be expected and which have been completed.
- Information to allow a collaborator who has been away from the project to catch up on current progress.

This information promotes a group awareness of the state of the process. Inferences drawn from this information may highlight problems as they occur and support the manual reassigning of responsibilities.

Support for the allocation of responsibility

Our second major theme focuses on the need to allow cooperating authors to divide the task of writing a document into smaller, more manageable chunks. This support needs to recognise the flexible nature evident in a division of labour and that often this division is open to continued re-negotiation. One consequence of this division is that the allocation of work to different users needs to be sufficiently lightweight to allow work to be continually reallocated at low cost.

The need for a flexible approach to the allocation of work requires a careful consideration of the nature of plans and planning. The need to consider the flexibility of plans in cooperative writing is essential. A number of different strategies have been identified in previous studies for partitioning and coordinating writing including what (Sharples ed 1993) calls sequential, reciprocal and parallel. Similar models were suggested by (Thompson 1967) and seen to be employed by groups in studies by (Sharples 1992, Rimmershaw 1992, Kaye 1993 and Posner et al., 1993).

However, the extent to which these models exist in isolation and are followed completely is open to question. As (Beck 1993) states when discussing a detailed study of collaborative writing:

> " A view is emerging from the data of the experience of collaborative writing as a process which is dynamically renegotiatied." (Beck 1993, page 111)

The need for this flexibility is reflected within the short studies we undertook. However, a clear role existed for the representation of the allocation of sections of the document to users. This representation was either explicit and resulted from a focused effort on planning or implicitly assumed by members of a group. Both the explicit and implicit allocations were reflected by the members of our study. For example, one group stated “we had a meeting to discuss the structure of the document and assign tasks” while another claimed “we each just knew what sections we had to write.”

In all of the recorded collaborative writing experiences some form of outline plan was used to divide the work among the collaborators, to provide a set of goals to be achieved by individuals or to describe the steps that must be taken to complete the writing process. These were interpreted quite loosely and often the status of the work against the plan was inferred from considerable knowledge of the individuals involved.

The use of explicit plans detailing which responsibilities each individual had were most commonly used when the group was remotely located. In developing support for such planned activity we need to make available responsibilities throughout the writing process. However, the enforcement or imposition of a plan is inherently social, and support must take account of the dynamic nature of the writing process and be flexible enough to allow frequent changes in line with the changes of group membership and individuals' capabilities to achieve their assigned tasks.

The Contact Approach

The core of our approach is the development of mechanisms that make visible the current allocation of responsibility and the activities that need to be coordinated across a group. Our starting point is the electronic context within which the actions involved in cooperative writing take place. Rather than consider the representation of these activities abstractly we wish to focus on the ways in which the endeavour of cooperative writing is manifest electronically among the community of users. The cooperative writing of documents involves a number of heterogeneous tools which are used in tandem to manipulate stored artifacts. When the group is distributed these often exist across a wide variety of machines and much of the effort of cooperative writing involves understanding and managing the ways in which a document is spread across these different electronic stores. For example, to write a bibliography for a paper an author will interact with several tools to generate the text of the bibliography. Constructing the bibliography may also require knowledge of which authors are responsible for constituent parts of a document and where these are located. Often remote information stores cannot be directly accessed and users need some form of version system to control the exchange of replicated document copies. Active contexts for a project are formed by aggregating all the resources of local contexts for each user. Users may form the local active context by associating local resources with the writing project. Alternatively these associations maybe given to them from a centralised server.

In line with previous approaches we seek to develop techniques which allow actions involved in cooperative activity to be monitored or recorded (Beck 1993, Kreifelts et al., 1991, Sarin et al., 1991, Trigg et al., 1986). The increased access to component parts of documents will reduce the need for version control. Members of the group may use the information concerning the interactions with stored information to make inferences about the overall state of the activity. From the initiation of the activity, as soon as an interaction occurs with any of the resources in the activity context the state of the activity could be inferred to be started. A period of sustained interactions with the resources within the context could indicate that the action was being performed or executed. If after such a period there was then a period of inactivity with any of the resources, then perhaps the action has been completed or halted, unable to be completed. It is clear that the captured interactions do indicate information about how the activity is being performed or conducted, and that some inferences can be drawn about the state of an individual activity based upon these captured interactions.

The actions on shared objects also serve as an overall indicator of the state of the document development process across its lifetime. From its planned inception until the first recorded interaction with a component, the development of a document remains initiated, but not started. When the first interaction occurs the process starts and while interactions occur then the process can be inferred to be under execution, until all interactions cease, when the action may be deemed complete or finished. This is obviously a simplified view of the nature of interactions over time, and the process of starting and completing can be considerably more complex. The point to make is that many of these subtleties are subject to the particular circumstances and can be inferred by the community involved in the cooperative development of the document.

In addition to publicising the interactions with shared resources, the available attributes of the resources can be used to infer information about the state of the shared endeavour. In particular we wish to initially focus on the existing attributes of electronic files such as size, owner, and write time. Each of these attributes offers the possibility of inferring different information about the state of the cooperative activity. For example, a file's last write time indicates the last time any modifications were made to the file. This may allow a user to determine within the context of cooperative development if a component has altered in some significant way.

Each of these attributes can be used only within a given context and users may wish to view particular attributes as significant and may wish to be informed when these attributes alter. For example, within our small scale field studies one user commented "I know that he takes care and time to construct what he wishes to say but when he does he writes incredibly quickly and it seldom needs much editing". This use could make considerable use of the size attribute of a file to indicate when his colleague had begun writing his component.

Similarly within a given context users may introduce measures to estimate the overall level of completion of an activity and these measures can be checked against the current document. For example, we found that members of a writing group often used word count as a rough guide to the level of completeness of component parts. A document meeting agreed measures may indicate that the activity is nearing completion. The use of these measures can be used in conjunction with the level of interaction to add weight to any inference.

Our principle aim is to provide the mechanisms to enable the capture of this interaction and the value of attributes with shared resources. We achieve this by making the resources used in the construction of a shared document active. To encourage heterogeneity we have chosen to adopt a low tech approach and have restricted the scope of the resources. In particular, we endeavour to make only the electronic files representing the data resources, and the results of commands and tools used to manipulate these publicly available. In adopting our minimalist approach we do not consider the internal effects of tools on the structure and content of documents since this will require the general use of a common editor. A number of authors highlight the many benefits of a single system approach and highlight the advantages of technologies such as Hypertext to represent the structure of documents. For example, SEPIA (Haake et al., 1992) offers sophisticated internal support for representing the cooperative structure of documents.

Our philosophy is to provide support for the heterogeneous collection of editors which our user community has invested in. In this respect our aims are similar to those of the MESSIE developers (Sasse et al., 1993). However, we focus on more readily available common access to shared components making up the document under construction. The core of our approach rest with three inter-related components:

- A decomposition tool wich assigns portions of a writing activity to shared information resources.
- A framework which monitors interaction with shared objects and propagates these across the user community.
- An association facility which links the action of specific tools on objects with events significant to the user community.

These different components work in tandem to provide lightweight monitoring support across a community of users.

The Developed System

The basis of our approach is the development of mechanisms which promote a shared awareness of a common electronic context within which the work is taking place. A set of assumptions about the supporting environment which constitutes the electronic context are critical to the systems development. These assumptions include:

- Each of the users involved in the cooperative endeavour has regular access to a computer environment for conduction of the work.
- The computer environments used will normally be distributed across a range of diverse machine types.
- Users will have access to at least EMail facilities as a means of remote electronic communication.
- Any developed system needs to be used alongside existing systems or provide mechanisms to allow integration with existing systems.

Support is provided through a toolkit which supports the propagation of effects on shared objects. To allow the toolkit to operate across a diverse range of platforms a set of shared resources are made commonly available. These include the files and tools that are the subject of interest, and the object data for the toolkit. The toolkit data is accessed through an object interface that allows for extendibility and the future inclusion of a database to store toolkit data. The interaction monitors within the environment are the principle mechanisms by which interaction with the resources is captured. These communicate the captured data to the toolkit managers, locally and when at a remote site through any available TCP/IP distributed communications platforms.

The toolkit managers are process objects responsible for the maintenance of data in the system, the control of active contexts. They also provide the interface for applications wishing to use the Contact platform. The current toolkit contains the following components:

- *A Project Editor* responsible for the initialisation of the project, maintenance of the project group membership and members' data. It provides an interface allowing other applications to initiate a new project.
- *A Component Editor* responsible for the list of resources making up the context. Like the project editor it offers an interface to allow applications to edit project components and their active contexts.
- *A Report Object* responsible for communicating the interactions monitored by watching agents to a server message object. The report object ensures that routing occurs to the correct message object, and also provides a damping effect for multiple interactions with resources that occur over a very short period.
- *A Message Agent* responsible for communication and data passing between the remotely located elements of the system. The message agent is independent of any supporting distributed platform. Communication is via a dedicated communication object that uses its own protocol to communicate with the message agent on top of the underlying platform. This allows a communications object to be written for the actual platform that is in use or available between the remotely located areas of the collaboration.

A writing project in the system is represented by a decomposition list where the activity of writing is divided into different components. The system allows particular users to become responsible for components within the project. This form of rough outlining and allocation of responsibilities figured significantly in the development of documents we observed and it is widely reported in the writing literature. This approach has also been used to present activity based systems, for example the Task Manger (Kreilfelts at el., 1993). In addition to assigning responsibilities we also allow local electronic resources to be associated with parts of the project. Normally, this takes the form of a file containing a portion of the document. In addition, we allow users to make public commands invoked on these objects. In the case of UNIX platforms this includes commands to spell and count words in a file.

The active context within the system is supported and maintained by three distinct system elements, the "local objects", "server objects" and a set of user interfaces. Local objects are located on work site machines, and their primary purpose is to maintain the associations that describe members' working contexts. For each component of the project the local user has responsibility, two lists are maintained, one listing the associated files and the other the associated commands.

Server objects focus on distributing details of the project and recording the captured interactions from local objects. They also maintain data describing the collection of components in each project, and the membership of the writing project. It is here that the associations between members and components are maintained. At present two forms of user interface to the system have been developed, an X Windows interface, and a World Wide Web interface.

Server Objects and Data

Any project in the system consists of the collection of components created for that project; the membership of the project and some optional data, such as a deadline for completion of the project. This information is held in a project record, and the project editor is responsible for any amendments to existing projects, or for creating new projects. It also contains a message object which is responsible for distributing any amendments or new component records to local message objects.

The Context server objects are responsible for initiating component parts of the project and recording the reported interactions from component's active contexts. Figure 1 shows the objects located at an Active Context Server. Only the Message Server object is persistent, the others are invoked as needed.

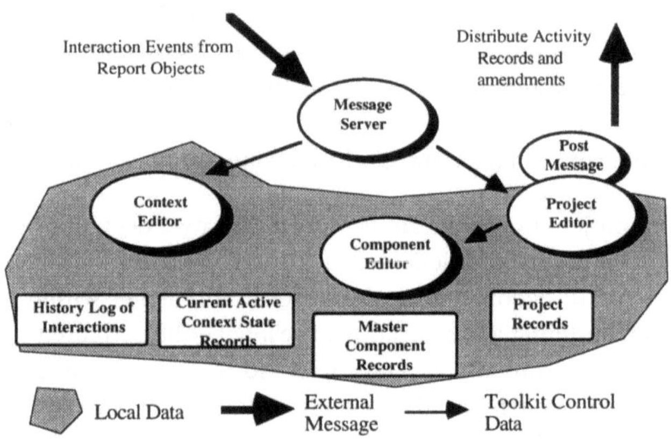

Figure 1 The Active Context Server Objects.

The Message Server is responsible for accepting all interaction events, decoding the source message and passing the data to the Context Editor. It also decodes information about changes in the component records from remote locations and passes these to the project editor.

The Context Editor is responsible for maintaining the two Active context records, the History Log and the Current Active Context Record. The History Log is an archive of event interactions that have taken place. The current active context record provides an overview of the resources within a particular component's active context. It displays the resources associated with a component along with additional information such as the last time an interaction took place. The record also maintains state to indicate which resources in an active context have been used since the last time the record was viewed. The context editor also provides an interface allowing the records to be viewed by other applications.

The use of message objects both for sending and receiving information between the local and server domains is motivated by the need to support the different platforms and operating systems members may use. The message object is independant of any supporting distributed platform. This is achieved by making use of individual specific communications objects, each communications object is written for a specific distributed communications platform or media.

Local Objects and Data

Four principal objects are used at local sites to support the system as shown in Figure 2. The Local Message Receiver and Watch Control Objects are persistent processes, while the Report Object and Component Editor are invoked as required. Local data consists of a record for each component that the member is responsible for, and two local lists specifying the files and commands that are part of the working context.

The Local Message Receiver is responsible for accepting and decoding messages from the project server. These messages are usually amendments to the component information and any required updates are carried out. In addition the component editor allows access to the local component information and the list of resources making up the active context. The Watch Control Object is responsible for creating and destroying watch objects. Watch Objects are created to monitor individual resources, and report when interactions occur or the resource is used. Our initial implementation has focused on UNIX and two types of watch object exist at the moment, one to detect alterations to files, and the other to register commands invoked upon files.

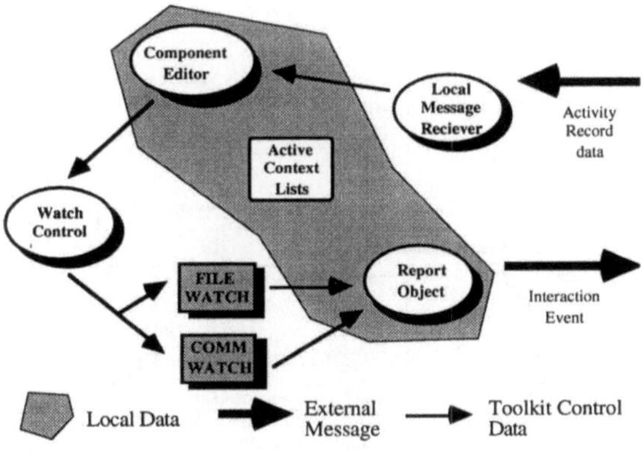

Figure 2 Showing the Local Objects and the interactions between Local Objects.

The Report Object is responsible for communicating the interactions monitored by the Watch Objects to the project server. The Report Object is used to communicate with the project server rather than allow direct communication from Watch Objects. As a result, only one Watch Object is required per resource, as multiple associations are handled by the Report Object. It also provides a damping effect for multiple interactions with resources that occur over very short time periods, where one interaction notification is sent rather than several.

One of the key design goals for Local Objects was to allow for multiple platforms or operating systems to be supported. Consequently, the Report Object, Component Editor and Watch Control Objects make no direct calls to the underlying operating system. Any system dependant code has been structured within a set of library functions called *sysutils*. This allows us to write a set of sysutils for each platform that the system may be placed on, and limit changes to the above objects. The File Watch and command Watch Objects are platform specific as they rely upon interrogating detailed operating system resources. To aid portability Watch Objects can be developed for different platforms. We have developed UNIX Watch Objects and are currently constructing watch objects for Macintosh platforms.

The System in Use

To demonstrate how the Contact system can be used we will describe a simple scenario based upon the generation of this paper. We will present a series of snapshots of web pages presented by the Contact system during the lifetime of the project. The web interface allows us to promote ubiquitous and heterogeneous access to the system.

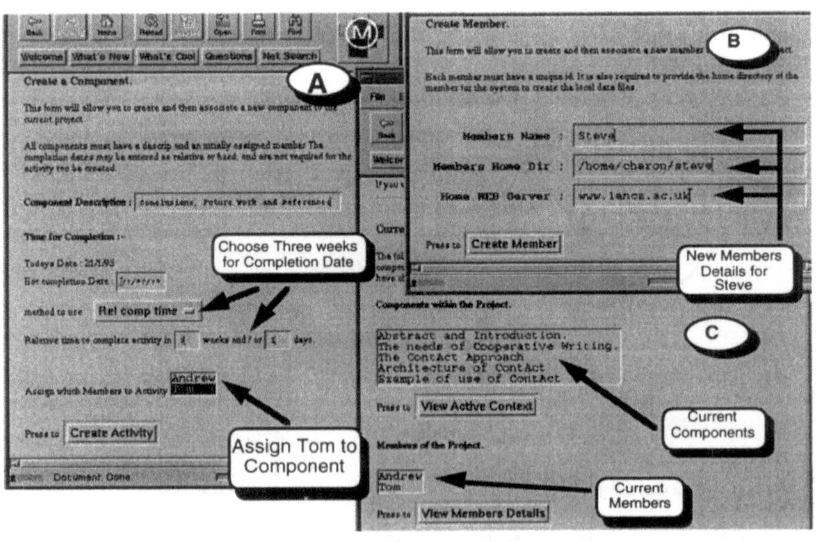

Figure 3 Snapshot 1, the addition of a new member and component to the project.

The Project involves the writing of a conference paper describing the system and its design goals. The initial task is therefore to initiate a project, called *Contact: Support for Distributed Cooperative Writing*. There are two members in the group, Andrew and Tom. After requesting Contact to initiate a new project, it is possible to start the decomposition of the writing process into components. The details of the two initial members, Andrew and Tom are entered using form interface **(B)** shown in Figure 3. The initial data allows Contact to create Local Object data so that local active context lists can be created. The initial components of the project represent the various sections of the document to be written. At the time of snapshot 1 five components have been created and assigned between Andrew and Tom (shown in form **(C)**). At this point it is decided that another person is required to help with the project, as Tom is often difficult to find. Form **(B)** shows the creation of a new member associated with the project called Steve. In form **(A)** Tom also creates another component, *Conclusions, Related Work and References*, with an initial completion target date of 3 weeks.

As each component is created, Contact will pass a component record to the Local Objects of each responsible member. At each members local site, they may assign whichever files and commands they will use for each component. Tom assigns the file ContactDraft.1 and his choice of editor Xedit to the component *Conclusions, Related Work and References.* Similarly each of the other users assign whichever resources they will be using.

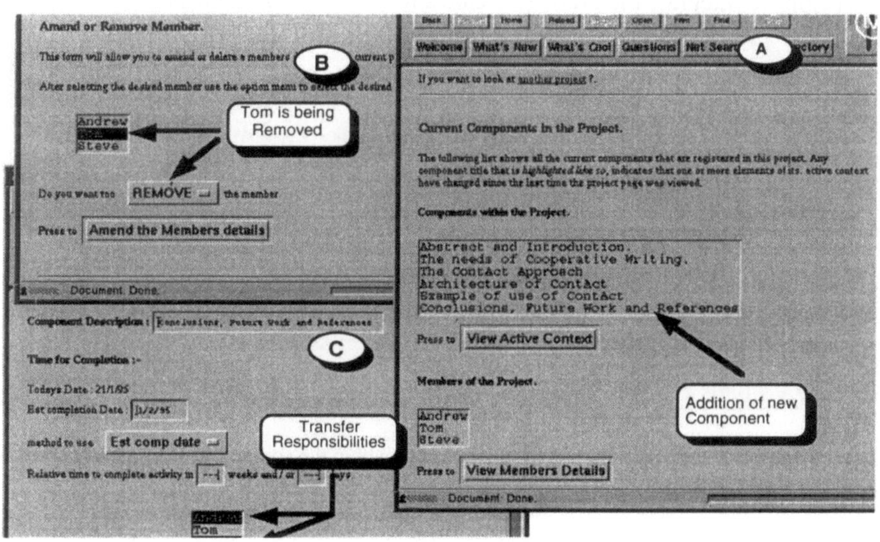

Figure 4 Snapshot 2 showing the transfer of responsibilities between members.

The project then proceeds until Tom is called away. At this point because the component *Conclusions, Related Work and References,* has not been completed there is a need to reassign responsibility to others in the group. In snapshot 2, Fig 4. Tom decides to remove himself from the project, and can be seen doing this in form **(B).** The current components within the project are displayed in form **(A)**, and the reassignment of responsibilities is conducted in form **(C).** The re-assignment can be performed by any of the members either accepting responsibility, or by Tom giving responsibility to another member. Since the deadline for the completion of the project is nearing, both Andrew and Steve are given responsibility. Negotiation of responsibilities is assumed to take place socially and is not driven by the system.

It is decided that Andrew should continue working on the file ContactDraft.1 and a new copy, ContactDraft.2 will be used by Steve. Andrew associates the spell command with the active context as he nears completion of ContactDraft.1 and he begins to proof check the document. Steve is waiting on Andrew to complete his work before integrating the two drafts with the references file he has written. He knows from previous experiences of working with Andrew that once the spell command has been used successfully on ContactDraft.1 that Andrew will probably have completed his work. Steve consults the current active context state for component *Conclusions, Related Work and References,* shown in Fig 5, until he notices that the spell command has been used, but no changes were made to the file ContactDraft.1. Steve infers that the draft is complete, confirms this with Andrew and begins to integrate the drafts to create a final version of the paper.

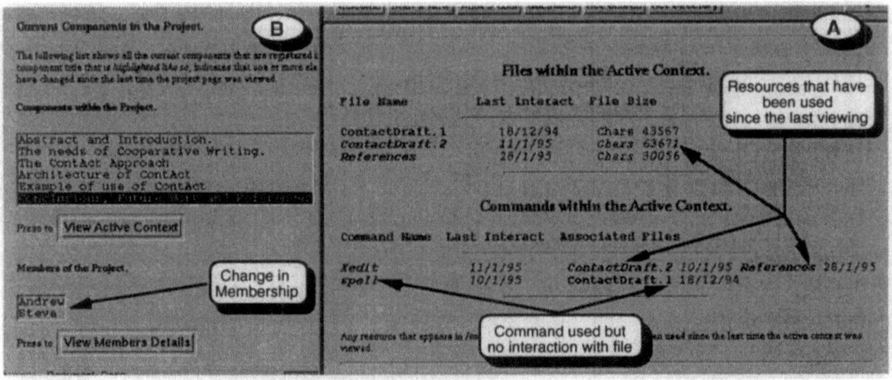

Figure 5 Snapshot 3 showing the use of the resources within the component *Conclusions, Related Work and References.*

Conclusions and Future Work

We have identified and attempted to address some of the issues raised in studies of cooperative authoring. In particular we have focused on providing a lightweight framework within which members of a collaborative authoring project can decompose the writing task, and freely assign responsibilities for the tasks in a flexible and unconstrained manner. We also provide users with a facility to construct an active context for the project. This context is composed of the electronic resources used by members of the group in the process of completing their work. By interrogating this active context we allow users to draw inferences on the state of any component activity within the project. This offers a greater degree of "author information" and increases the possibility for coordination between the members.

A study of the implementation and use of our system will provide us with more empirical data on the nature and characteristics of cooperative writing. However, at this point we already believe that the use of Contact may be beneficial in other domains. In highly distributed project environments, where many sub-components are in use at any time, Contact will allow a supervisor to monitor which sub-components are used or accessed. In any highly versioned situation, Contact may also make users aware if old or abandoned versions are still being used. One of the main design features of the Contact toolkit was to allow its use with third party software. We are particularly interested in its use with Workflow systems and shared object servers.

At present the Contact system is fairly passive, its use of the web relies on users interrogating active contexts and drawing conclusions based upon the latest set of interactions. We wish to make the toolkit more proactive, so that a user can be informed when a specified state has arisen. For example the user may request to be informed when a component's file has reached a set word length, or a particular editor has been used in conjunction with two files. To enable this we are developing trigger mechanisms for the Contact server that will notify users when particular interaction patterns have occurred. As part of this endeavour we are exploring how to modify the Web server to make it more active and to allow greater integration and functionality with Contact.

References

Beck, E.E. (1993) A survey of Experiences of Collaborative Writing. In Computer supported Collaborative Writing, ed. M Sharples, London: Springer-Verlag.

Beck, E.E. and M.E. Bellotti. (1993) Informed Opportunism as Strategy: Supporting Coordination in Distributed Collaborative Writing. In ECSCW 93, Milan Italy, pp 233-247.

Ellis, C.A. , S.J. Gibbs, and G.L. Rein. (1991) Groupware: Some Issues and Experiences. Communications of the ACM 34 (1): pp 38-58.

Haake, J.M. and B. Wilson. (1992) Supporting Collaborative Writing of Hyperdocuments in SEPIA. In CSCW 92, Toronto Canada, pp 138-147.

Kaye, A.R. (1993) Computer Networking for Development of Distance Education courses. In *Computer Supported Collaborative Writing.*, ed. M. Sharples, London: Springer-Verlag.

Killey, L. (1990) ShrEdit 1.0: A shared editor for macintosh. Cognitive science and Machine Intelligence Laboratory, University of Michigan, 1990.

Kriefelts, T., E. Hinrichs and G. Woetzel. (1993) Sharing To-Do lists with a Distributed Task Manager. In ECSCW 93, Milan Italy, pp 31-46.

Kreifelts, T., U. Pankoke-Babatz, and F. Victor. (1991) A Model for the Coordination of Cooperative Activities. In Proceedings of the International Workshop on CSCW, Berlin, pp 85-100.

Leland, M.D.P. , R.S. Fish, and R.E. Kraut. (1988) Collaborative Document Production using Quilt. In CSCW 1988, Portland Oregeon, pp 206-215.

Miles, V.C., J.C. McCarthy, A.J Dix, M.D. Harrison, and A.F. Monk. (1993) Reviewing Designs for a Synchronous-Asynchronous Group Editing Environment. In Computer supported Collaborative Writing, ed. M Sharples, London: Springer-Verlag.

Neuwirth, C.M. , D.S. Kaufer, R. Chandok, and J.H. Morris. (1990) Issues in the Design of computer support for co-authoring and commenting. In CSCW 90, pp 183-195.

Posner, I.R. and R.M. Baecker. (1993) How people Write Together. In Readings in Groupware and Computer Supported Cooperative Work., ed. R.M. Baecker, pp 239-250. Morgan Kaufmann.

Rimmershaw, R. (1992) Technologies of Collaboration. In Computers and writing: Issues and Implementations, ed. M. Sharples, Dordrecht: Kluwer.

Sarin, S.K., Abbott, K.R., and McCarthy, D.R. (1991) A process model and system for supporting collaborative work. In COOCS 91, pp 213-224.

Sasse, M.A. and M.J. Handley. (1993) Support for Collabortive Authoring via Email : The MESSIE Environment. In *ECSCW 95, Milan Italy*, pp 249-264.

Sharples, M. (1992) Adding a little structure to collaborative writing. In CSCW in practice: An introduction and Case Studies, ed. D Diaper and C Sanger, London: Springer-Verlag.

Sharples, M. ed. (1993) Computer supported Collaborative Writing. London: Springer-Verlag.

Sharples and Pemberton (1990). Starting from the writer: guidelines for the design of user centred document processors. Computer Assisted Language Learning 2, pp 37-57.

Thompson, J.D. (1967) *Organisations in Action.* New York: McGraw-Hill.

Trigg, R.H., L.A. Suchman, and F.G. Halasz. (1986) Supporting collaboration in NoteCards. In CSCW 86, Austin Texas, pp 153-163.

Proceedings of the Fourth European Conference on Computer-Supported Cooperative Work,
September 10–14, Stockholm, Sweden
H. Marmolin, Y. Sundblad, and K. Schmidt (Editors)

CSCW for Strategic Management in Swiss Enterprises: an Empirical Study

Christian Sauter

Othmar Morger

Thomas Mühlherr

Andrew Hutchison

Stephanie Teufel
Department of Computer Science, University of Zurich, Switzerland

This paper presents the results of an empirical study into the current usage of groupware in strategic management and the potential of Computer Supported Cooperative Work (CSCW) for the top management in large-scale Swiss business enterprises. For this purpose we conducted a survey amongst 168 organisations.

1 Introduction

The study presented in this paper is part of the STRATUM project (Sauter et al., 1995, Teufel, 1993). The overall goal of STRATUM is to develop tools to support cooperative work in the strategic management of business enterprises.

As new technology is developed to support cooperative work (so-called groupware) it is important to understand how that technology can best be applied to help users accomplish their work. A clear understanding of group work, as prerequisite for design or redesign of adequate groupware, is included in research frameworks that many research groups have developed (Krcmar, 1991, Mühlherr et al., 1994).

Following the concept of such a research framework, we first have to analyse strategic management groups in order to get an adequate understanding of the nature of their group work. In order to do so, we formulated the following research questions:

- What is the *current usage of groupware* for strategic management in the largest business enterprises in Switzerland?
- What is the *potential of CSCW for top management* in the largest business enterprises in Switzerland?

Since CSCW as an identifiable field emerged in the middle of the 1980s, most work has been done in the development of groupware prototypes. A wide spectrum of systems has been developed (e.g. group decision support systems, electronic meeting systems, electronic bulletin boards) and there has been growing interest in investigating information technology to support the type of group decision making closely associated with management tasks.

Only a few systems are directly related to the field of strategic management or top management although some of the tasks supported are encompassed in strategic management. Some prototypes or commercial products have been evaluated in case studies with top management groups, e.g. (Tyran et al., 1992). Some empirical studies have investigated the application of specific tools (Seward et al., 1993, Sheffield et al., 1993). Further research has been done in developing theoretical groupware methods, and concepts more or less related to the field of strategic management. However, only a few studies have explored top management from the viewpoint of group work (Reder et al., 1990), and none of them has looked at the application of groupware for strategic management in the sense of our perspective. In order to obtain answers to our research questions, we therefore conducted an empirical study (Morger et al., 1995).

In the next Section we will present the background to our study. First we introduce strategic management as we see it from the viewpoint of our work. Next we give a short overview of CSCW, or groupware respectively, in order to convey a clear understanding of the terms we use for different types of groupware. In Section 3 we present the research methodology used in this study. In Section 4 we report our results. We first present the current usage of groupware in strategic management and then show results which give us information about the potential of CSCW for top management. In Section 5 we present some conclusions and remarks regarding further work.

2 Background to the Empirical Study

Strategic management. Strategic management is generally defined as the development and control of the long-term evolution of an enterprise. Strategic management can be viewed from three perspectives (Rühli, 1991):

(1) The manner in which strategic management is *instituted.*

(2) Strategic management as a *process*.

(3) Strategic management as an *instrument*.

If we interpret strategic management as *instituted* in an organisation, we have to describe the group of persons performing strategic management - in other words, the strategic actors (Wilson, 1994). Strategic actors are the people in a business enterprise who are directly involved in the strategic management process. The people with direct responsibility for this process are the board of directors and upper management. In the following we will use the term *top management* as a synonym for strategic actors. Note that top management needs assistance from staff.

Strategic management as a *process* involves four basic elements (Wheelen et al., 1992): (1) environmental scanning, (2) strategy formulation, (3) strategy implementation, and (4) evaluation and control (see Figure 1).

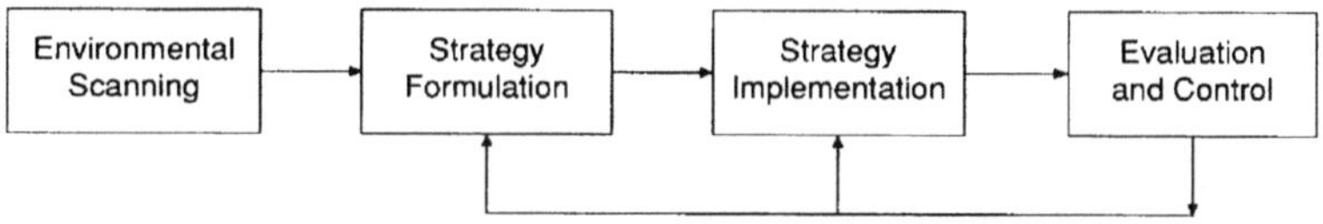

Figure 1. Strategic management process (source: (Wheelen et al., 1992))

Such simple descriptive models are developed in order to illustrate a phenomenon that is very complex in reality. We can assume that many business processes exist in reality, primarily for operational and tactical purposes. At the same time these processes are the necessary basis of specific phases of the strategic management process. For this reason we cannot clearly demarcate strategic processes from operational processes (Mintzberg, 1994, Rühli, 1991).

To perform tasks related to the basic elements of the strategic management process one can use a large variety of *instruments*. We distinguish instruments that support *generic tasks* of top management from instruments used for *specialised tasks* related to the basic elements of the strategic management process. Instruments used for generic tasks are those which support different processes of interaction between people (typical tools are e-mail or electronic meeting systems); instruments used for specific tasks might be, for example, tools for financial budgeting or project planning.

CSCW. The research field CSCW has the overall goal of improving efficiency and effectiveness of group work through the usage of groupware. Groupware applications are based on different technologies (e.g. video, telecommunication, data base management systems). Such applications support a set of functions (e.g. mailing, shared writing) using textual, visual and audio media types. For classifying applications, one can take a schema like the time-space-matrix (Grudin, 1994). For *our purposes*, the *functions* of groupware are the most important characteristics. A classification schema which we derived in (Sauter et al., 1994) represents this.

Groupware tries to support groups by providing functions for communication, coordination and cooperation. Within this triangular framework we have placed typical group applications, corresponding to their functions. In addition to this, we have classified each application type into a *system class* corresponding to its application concept (see Figure 2). This classification schema allows groupware to be placed, corresponding to its focus of supported functions.

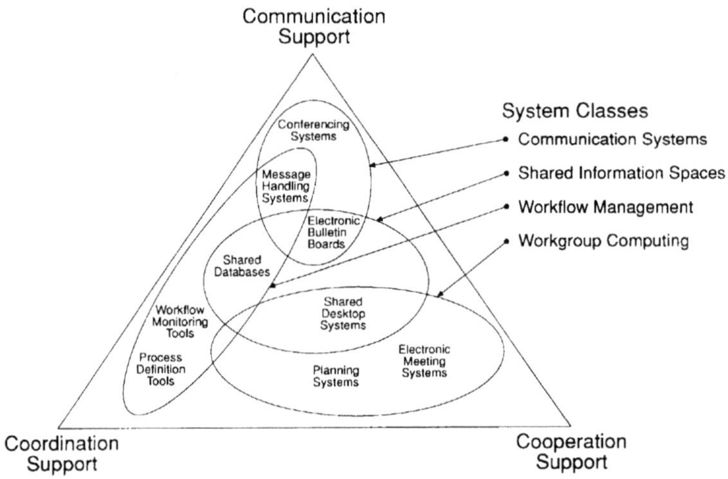

Figure 2. Functional classification schema for groupware (adopted from (Sauter et al., 1994))

We used this schema as the basis for designing our empirical study. For clarification we provide a short description of each system class and a few examples (for a detailed description see e.g. (Teufel et al., 1995)).

Communication Systems. Typical groupware applications which focus on supporting communication are message handling systems (e-mail, voice mail, video mail) and conferencing systems (computer conferences, audio conferences, video conferences). We assign such systems to the class of communication systems. The application concept for communication systems is the separation of communication partners according to time and/or place.

Shared Information Spaces. Groupware such as electronic bulletin boards allows implicit communication between several persons. Such forms of communication can be realised through any form of shared information spaces. Systems of this kind can take on both functions for communication (e.g. electronic bulletin boards) and functions for coordination and cooperation (e.g. in the case of a shared project data management system or a group calendar application).

Workflow Management. Groupware that we place in the system class workflow management has as its priority the support of coordination functions. Coordination functions are specified on the basis of permanent organisational rules with the help of process definition tools. Monitoring tools should enable workflow participants to obtain information concerning different aspects of the business process. Application concepts for this systems class are group tasks that are well structured and have a high frequency of repetition (e.g. customer order processing).

Workgroup Computing. Into the field of workgroup computing fall complex tasks with middle to low frequency of repetition that have to be fulfilled in cooperative groups. With respect to the supported functions, the focus of workgroup computing systems lies in the field of cooperative processes, which means goal-oriented working together. Important representatives of this system class are electronic meeting systems, or group decision support systems respectively, planning systems and shared desktop systems (e.g. shared drawing).

3 Research Methodology

3.1 Contextual Issues

For our purposes we found analytical methods to be inappropriate. With the help of analytical methods one wants to be able to formulate statements about a domain by testing hypotheses. Prerequisites for this are the ability for demarcation and well-known determinants of the domain. As we pointed out in Section 2.1, strategic management is a very complex phenomenon with interdependent relationships to operative processes. In order to explore the domain in a broad manner we therefore applied a *descriptive* method.

Letters inviting participation and questionnaires were mailed in September 1994 with the reply deadline set as the middle of November 1994. Processing and analysis have been in progress since November 1994.

3.2 Subject and Method of Investigation

The subject of the investigation, as described, is strategic management in large-scale Swiss business enterprises. As we suggested in Section 2.1, one can assume that strategic management is performed by top management. For this reason we decided to target the top management.

As the method for data collection, we decided to use a standardised questionnaire. The questionnaire consisted of four parts with 17 questions and several sub-questions, so that the evaluation of about 300 answers was possible. Most questions were qualitative questions. We utilised the resulting data through frequency counts. In some cases we extended those results with mean values (mode and median). In cases of quantitative questions we got back interval scaled data (e.g. percentage distribution). We utilised this data through calculating arithmetic means and standard deviations.

3.3 Selection of the sample

The domain of the survey was business enterprises in Switzerland. For the selection of business enterprises we considered two criteria: *sector of industry* and *scale of the enterprise*. We assumed that the topic of CSCW in strategic management was not limited to specific sectors of industry and thus included all sectors (manufacturing, trading, services, banking and insurance).

Typical problems of strategic management are characterised by high complexity and low frequency of repetition (Schoemaker, 1993). For such problems in particular, group work is appropriate. We assumed the following: the bigger the enterprise the more complex the problems of strategic management; the more the need for group work; and the more the need for groupware. We therefore decided to restrict our survey to large-scale enterprises.

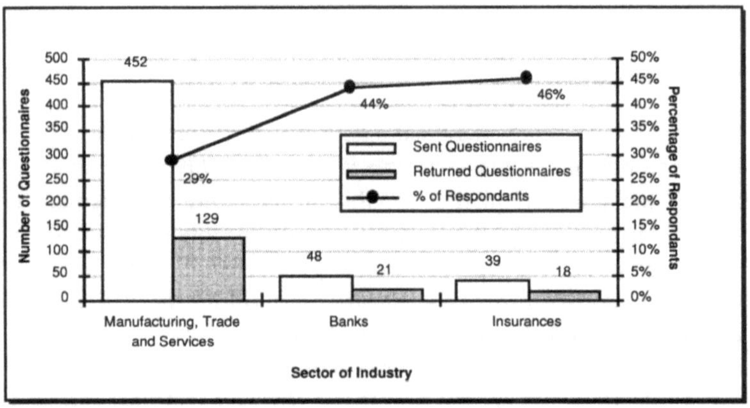

Figure 3. Distribution of the sample and percentage of respondants for each sector

For the selection of enterprises we took the following criteria:

- *turnover* for manufacturing, trade and services: ≥ US $ 125 million
- *total assets* for banks: ≥ US $ 1,5 billion
- *gross premium income* for insurance companies: ≥ US $ 75 million

As a result of the selection process we got 539 business enterprises. In order to achieve representative statements about the domain of the survey, we decided to include all 539 enterprises in our inquiry. We addressed the questionnaire to the CEO or a member of the Senior Management Group, or where possible to the person, responsible for the IS department or IS function. The response rate to our survey was 31% (168 returned questionnaires). In addition to the response we got 46 letters or phone-calls from enterprises which could not participate in the survey for various reasons. Figure 3 shows the distribution of the sample, with percentage of respondants for each sector of industry.

4 Results of the Survey

In the following we present some of the results of the empirical study. First, we give an overview of the usage of groupware in strategic management according to our classification schema. Second, the potential of CSCW for top management is explored.

4.1 Current Usage of Groupware in Strategic Management

Our first objective was to establish whether computer support for top management is provided. The results were that 57% of the respondants said that they personally use computers to support strategic tasks, 40% said they use no computer and 3% gave no statement.

As pointed out in Section 2.1, one can distinguish instruments supporting *generic tasks* from instruments supporting *specialised tasks*. Generic tasks are communication, coordination and cooperation. Specialised tasks are all tasks which have to be fulfilled within the basic elements of the strategic management process (e.g. market analysis in the process element of environmental scanning). In the following Sections we will first present the survey results related to generic support, then those pertaining to specialised support.

4.1.1 Usage of Systems Providing Support for Generic Tasks

As a basis for exploring the usage of systems providing support for generic tasks, we took our classification schema for groupware as shown in Section 2.2. First we asked about each application type: its availability or whether or not it is planned. Second we asked these top managers how they estimate the importance of each type of system if available.

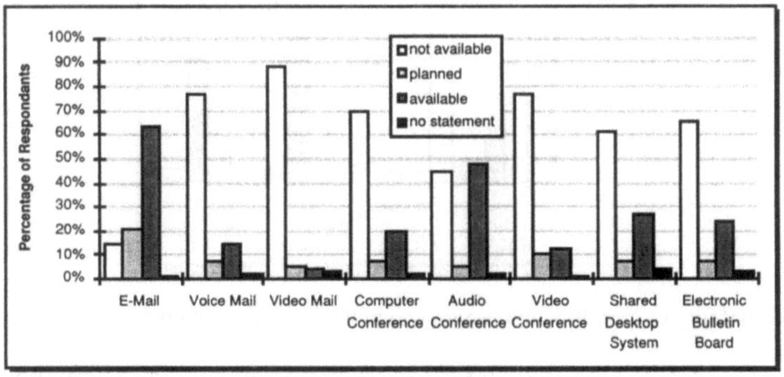

Figure 4. Availability of communication systems and shared information spaces

Figures 4 and 5 show the results for system classes *communication systems* and *shared information spaces*. The most commonly available communication systems can be seen to be electronic mail and audio conferencing. More than a quarter of the respondants indicated that shared desktop systems are currently available. It is interesting to note that while nearly 50% of the respondants have access to audio conferencing, more than 60% of this group consider it to be an unimportant communication medium. Otherwise over 70% considered e-mail as an important or very important communication medium. The high importance and availability that has been attributed to e-mail, together with other results not reported here for economy of space, indicate an impending shift in guiding employees more and more by e-mail then by oral or other written directives. Furthermore it is interesting to see that shared desktop systems ha... high rating of importance with respect to the other systems while video mail seems to have no importance at all.

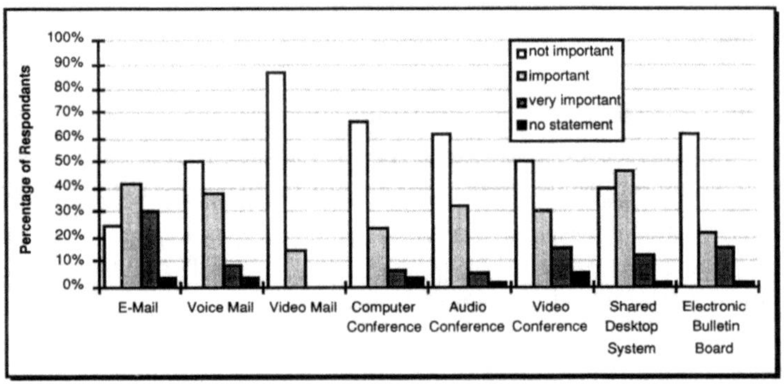

Figure 5. Importance of communication systems and shared information spaces (where available)

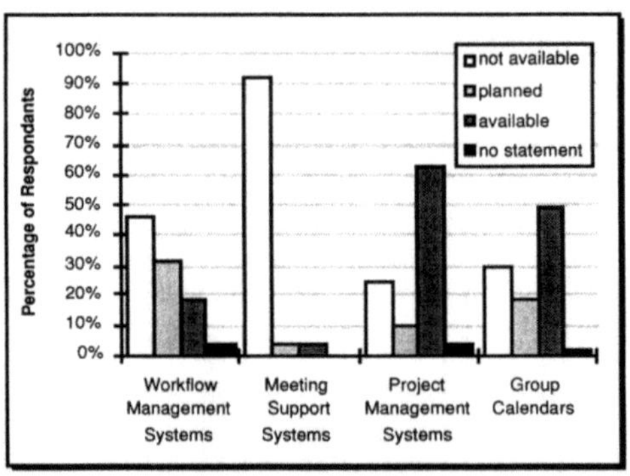

Figure 6. Availability of workflow management and workgroup computing

Figures 6 and 7 show the availability and importance of workflow management and workgroup computing systems. Project management systems are the most commonly available type of system. This was followed by the availability of group calendars. The absence of meeting support systems clearly demonstrates that this type of system has not yet penetrated any of the business sectors. It is evident from the ratings of importance of these systems, that group calendars are considered more important then project management systems, even though group calendars are less available. It is also surprising that even amongst the few who do have meeting support systems, these were seen by a majority to be unimportant. Furthermore it is remarkable that over 30% of the respondants plan to appy workflow management systems in top management, although management systems particularly support group tasks of high frequency of repetition.

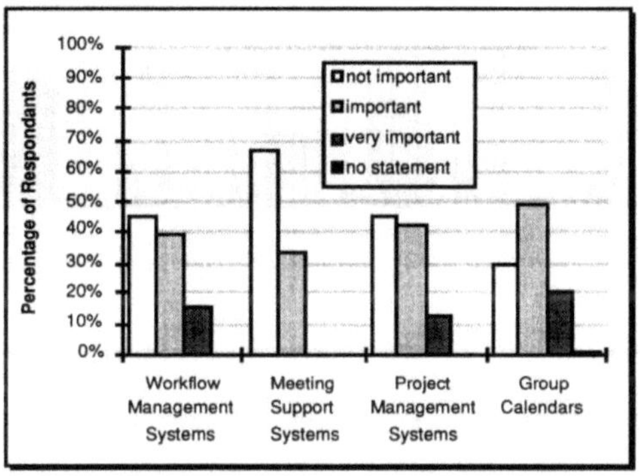

Figure 7. Importance of workflow management and workgroup computing (where available)

4.1.2 Usage of Systems Providing Support for Specialised Tasks

For exploring the availability and usage of systems providing support for specialised tasks, we presented some typical tasks in the questionnaire, according to basic elements of the strategic management process (see Figure 1). Respondants had the opportunity to add tasks or systems respectively. We assumed that most available applications would not support groups. We therefore asked explicitly whether group support is given or not.

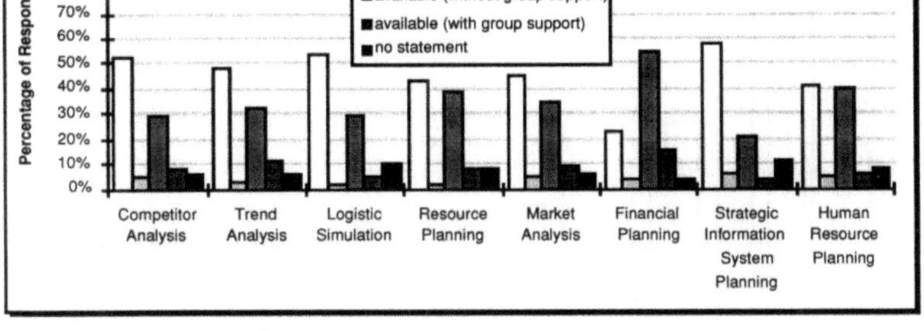

Figure 8. Availability of systems providing support for specialised tasks

Figures 8 and 9 show the availability and usage of systems providing support for specialised tasks. The most commonly available systems for specialised tasks are those for financial planning which are also often or very often applied in 97% of respondants. Unsurprisingly, most of these (and the other specialised systems reported) are available without group support.

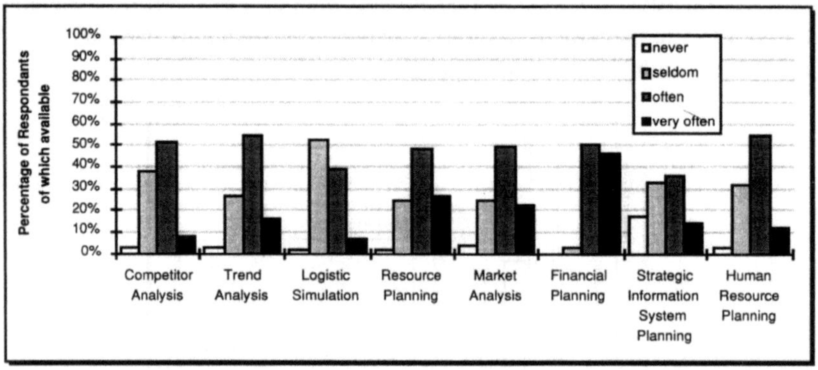

Figure 9. Usage of systems providing support for specialised tasks (where available)

4.2 Potential of CSCW for Top Management

As our second research question we explored the potential of CSCW for top management. We therefore asked top managers, according to the three perspectives of strategic management (Section 2.1), about the general organisational, procedural and instrumental aspects of their environment. Empirical studies show that top managers spend most of their time in meetings (Kurke et al., 1983) and we attempted to verify this by collecting detailed data about the meetings of top management. In the following sections we will present related results.

4.2.1 Organisational Aspects

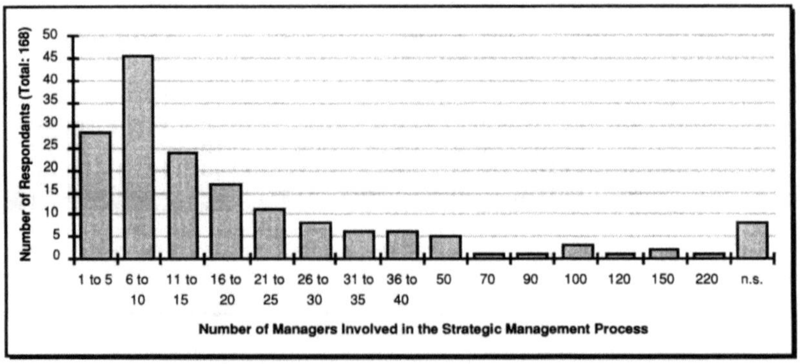

Figure 10. Number of managers regularly involved in the strategic management process

One of the questions asked of survey respondants was the number of managers who are involved in the strategic management *process* on a regular basis. Clearly the level of involvement can vary, but on average these were the number of participants collaborating in the performance of strategic management. The results of this question are very valuable when considering computer support for the cooperative process of strategic management, since they reveal the average number of participants which such a system should provide for. It can be seen that involvement of 6 to 10 persons was true for the majority of respondants (see Figure 10).

Figure 11 shows that although participation in the strategic management process is in the range described above, *strategic decision making* is most often carried out by three managers together. We also see that strategic decisions are generally performed by up to 10 persons while more than 10 persons are the exception. Considering these results we assume, that functions such as those for voting (often integrated in electronic meeting systems), which directly support the decision process of a group, are not appropriate for strategic decision makers such as those surveyed.

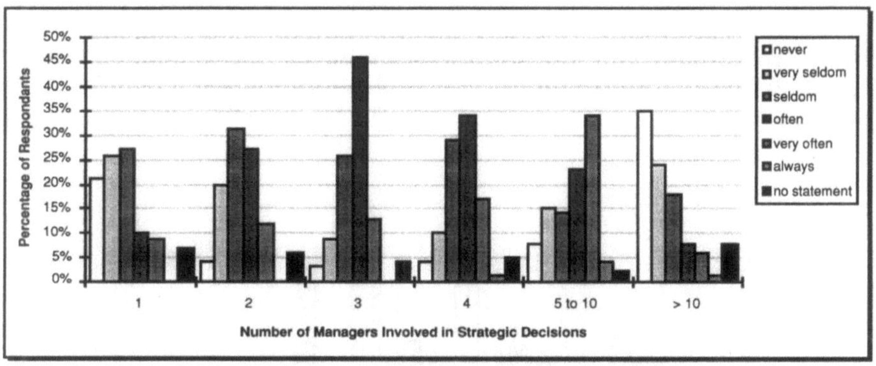

Figure 11. Number of managers regularly involved in strategic decisions

4.2.2 Communication of Top Managers

As we pointed out in Section 2.2 support of communication is an important domain of groupware. Therefore, we collected detailed data about communication patterns of top management.

Figure 12 shows the average mean, the median and the modus of time spent on communication with different partners of top management. The results show that the average mean of time spent on communication, ranges from 22% (within top management) up to 28% (top management with staff). In most cases top management communicates not mainly within top management (as we assumed) but also with representatives from all management levels in nearly the same frequency.

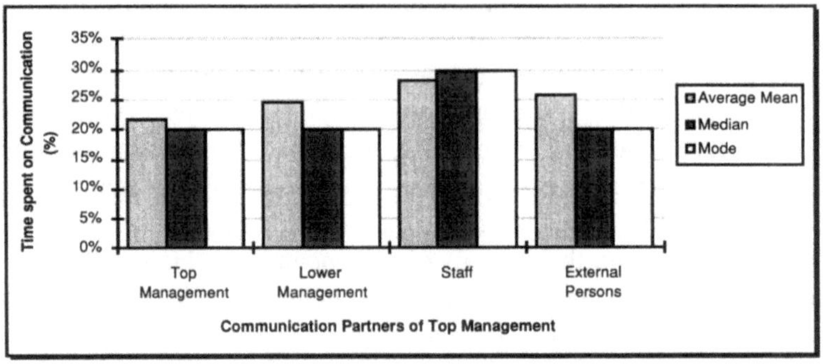

Figure 12. Distribution of communication with different communication partners

Figure 13 shows the average mean of usage of different communication mediums according to the different communication partners of top management. Unsurprisingly face-to-face communication dominates as the medium of communication between top management and the other groups within the enterprise. 10% of top management's communication is done via electronic mediums (both within top management, with lower management and with staff; about 4% with external persons). Remarkable is the dominance of textual communication with external persons.

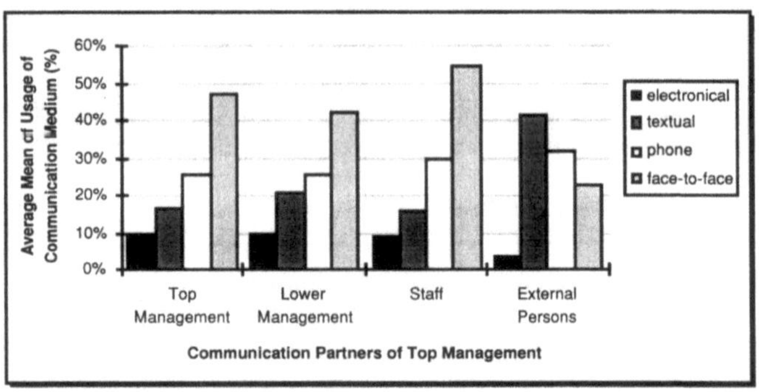

Figure 13. Communication of top management

Analysing the results shown in Figures 12 and 13, we discover that communication of top management is synchronous in most cases. We assume that there is a large potential for substituting or supporting traditional synchronous mediums for communication with groupware (e.g. e-mail or electronic bulletin boards). We also assume that groupware which is appropriate for support of the textual communications of top management with external persons has great potential.

4.2.3 Meetings in Top Management

Results of empirical studies (Kurke et al., 1983) looking at the activities of top or middle management, show that managers spent most of their time in meetings. Our survey confirmed those results (see Figure 14). Considering all respondants, the average percentage of working time spent in meetings was 41%. The median was 40% and the mode was 50%. We also distinguished between planned and unplanned meetings. The average mean for planned meetings was 75% (unplanned 25%). Both the median and the mode of planned meetings were 80% (20% unplanned).

In order to assess the potential of electronic meeting systems in strategic management, we were also interested in the number of participants in meetings and the duration of meetings. Figure 15 shows the results for planned meetings. We found that in most cases a maximum number of 10 persons took part in meetings. In addition we discovered that the duration of meetings ranged mostly between one and four hours.

To determine how satisfied top managers are with their meeting patterns, we asked the question: "Are you satisfied with meetings as they are now?" From our point of view it was remarkable to see that about 70% of top management are satisfied or very satisfied with meetings. Therefore, we were not surprised about the answers to the following question: "Would you appreciate the application of an Electronic Meeting System?" (Results: 25% *yes*, 31% *no*, 38% *don't know*, 6% *no answer*).

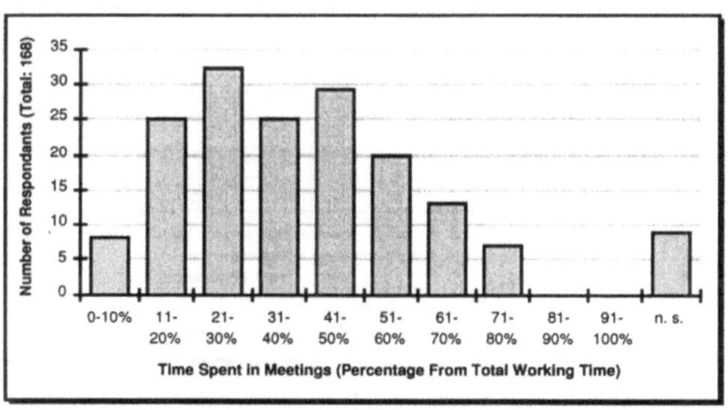

Figure 14. Time spent in meetings (% from total working time)

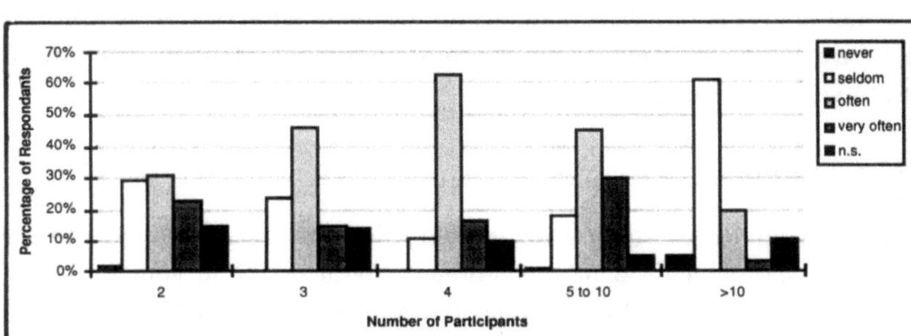

Figure 15. Number of participants in planned meetings

Considering the results shown in Section 4.1.1 (only a few enterprises do have electronic meeting systems (EMS); most of those who have an EMS found them unimportant; only 7 enterprises plan to install an EMS) and the results shown in this section (most of top managers are satisfied with current meetings; only 25% would appreciate the application of EMS) we assume little potential for EMS in the strategic management of large-scale Swiss business enterprises.

4.2.4 Trends in CSCW from the viewpoint of top management

To explore trends in CSCW for top management we asked respondants about the usefulness of CSCW in general; their assessment about trends in general; and for specific domains where they believe CSCW could be applied.

First we asked: "How do you assess general trends for CSCW in strategic management?" 76% of respondants said that they expect increasing application of CSCW; 0% expect a downward tendency in the application of CSCW; 20% expect no changes; and 7% gave no answer.

Second we asked: "Do you think CSCW is useful in strategic management?" The majority of respondants (76%) said that CSCW is useful (14% *it is not useful*, 10% *no statement*).

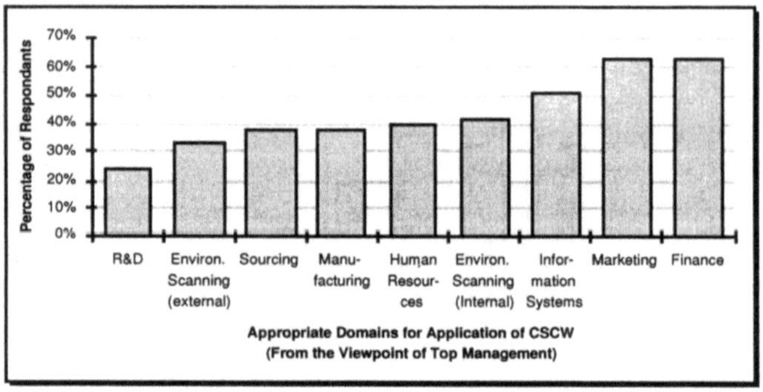

Figure 16. Appropriate domains for the application of CSCW

Those respondants who considered CSCW in strategic management as useful, were asked to give appropriate domains for the application of CSCW. Information systems, marketing and finance are the most appropriate domains from the viewpoint of top management (see Figure 16).

4.4 Limitations

The participation in our study was voluntary. For this reason we have to keep in mind that respondants and nonrespondants could differ in some investigated characteristics. In view of this situation, and considering that our response rate was 31 % (168 out of 539 returned questionnaires), there is a possibility of skewed results. We assume however, that our data represents a random sample of the investigated domain and therefore believe that our study can be seen as representative.

5 Conclusions and Further Work

In this paper we presented results and preliminary interpretations of an empirical study. The study was conducted in order to gain a clear understanding of group work for the purpose of supporting strategic management in the most effective manner. The study was part of the project STRATUM, the overall goal of which is to develop tools to support cooperative work especially in the strategic management of business enterprises. Two research questions were formulated in order to investigate the current usage of groupware in strategic management as well as to reveal the potential for CSCW usage by top management in Switzerland. The most interesting preliminary results are:

- Looking at groupware supporting generic tasks, we found that the most available and important system class providing functions for communication is e-mail. It was interesting to see that over 30% of respondants plan to apply workflow management systems which mainly provide functions for coordination.
- Looking at the class of workgroup computing systems, we found that group calendars and project management systems in particular, are commonly available and also assessed as important from the viewpoint of top management.
- The results of questions asked about groupware supporting specialised tasks show that a large number of different systems are available. Most of these systems do not support group functions.

In summary we can say, that we now have a good overview about the current usage and potential of CSCW in strategic management and of how top management assesses groupware in general. Further results gave us detailed knowledge about different organisational aspects of top management (e.g. the number of managers regularly involved in the strategic management process or in strategic decisions respectively). We also collected detailed data about the communication patterns of top management and in particular about meetings.

Further work must thus be done in completing the analysis, the interpretations and in drawing conclusions through cross relations. In addition we plan to investigate qualitative statements further, through the use of case studies.

Acknowledgments

We would like to thank Prof. Dr. K. Bauknecht for the support that made this work possible. This research was partially financed by the Swiss National Science Foundation.

References

Grudin J. (1994): "Computer-Supported Cooperative Work: History and Focus", IEEE Computer, vol. 27, no. 5, 1994, pp. 19-26.

Krcmar H. (1991): Computer Supported Cooperative Work - State of the Art, Lehrstuhl für Wirtschaftsinformatik, Universität Hohenheim, Stuttgart, Germany, Working Paper no. 20.

Kurke L. B., Aldrich H. E. (1983): "Mintzberg was right!: A replication and extension of the nature of managerial work", Management Science, no. 8, 1983, pp. 975-984.

Mintzberg H. (1994): "The Fall and Rise of Strategic Planning", Harvard Business Review, no. Jan. - Feb., 1994, pp. 107-114.

Morger O., Sauter C., Mühlherr T., Teufel S., Bauknecht K. (1995): Computerunterstützte Gruppenarbeit im strategischen Management schweizerischer Grossunternehmen: eine empirische Untersuchung, Institut für Informatik der Univ. Zürich, Institutsbericht no. 95.14.

Mühlherr T., Sauter C. (1994): Überblick über den Stand der Entwicklung im Gebiet Computerunterstütztes kooperatives Arbeiten, Institut für Informatik der Universität Zürich, Institutsbericht no. 94.19.

Reder S., Schwab R. G. (1990): "The Temporal Structure of Cooperative Activity", in: Bikson T. (ed.) Proceedings of the CSCW'90, Los Angeles, CA, ACM Press, 1990, pp. 303-316.

Rühli E. (1991): "Strategische Unternehmungsführung heute", in: Rühli E. (ed.) Strategisches Management in schweizerischen Industrieunternehmungen, Haupt, Bern, 1991, pp. 13-56.

Sauter C., Mühlherr T., Teufel S. (1994): "Sozio-kulturelle Auswirkungen von Groupware - Ein Ansatz zur Adaption und Operationalisierung eines sozialpsychologischen Modells für die Gestaltung und den Einsatz von Groupware", in: Rauch W. et al. (eds.): Proceedings des 4. Int. Symposiums for Information Science, Graz, Uni.-Verlag Konstanz, 1994, pp. 517-526.

Sauter C., Mühlherr T., Teufel S. (1995): Forschungsprojekt Stratum: Strategisches Management - Methoden, Techniken und Werkzeuge zur Unterstützung kooperativer Aufgaben, Informatik Forschung und Entwicklung, vol. 10, 1995, to be published.

Schoemaker P. J. (1993): "Strategic Decisions in Organisations: Rational and Behavioral Views", Journal of Management Studies, vol. 30, no. 1, 1993, pp. 107-129.

Seward R. R., Diaper D., Sanger C. (1993): "The Pod: A Purpose-built Environment to Support Group Working", in: Diaper D., Sanger C. (eds.): CSCW in Practice: an Introduction and Case Studies, Springer, London, 1993, pp. 151-161.

Sheffield J., Gallupe B. (1993): "Using Electronic Meeting Technology to Support Economic Policy Development in New Zealand: Short-Term Results", Journal of Management Information Systems, vol. 10, no. 3, 1993, pp. 97-116.

Teufel S. (1993): "Unterstützung der kooperativen Aufgaben innerhalb des Informationsmanagements", in: Kirn S. et al. (eds.): Workshop: Unterstützung organisatorischer Prozesse durch CSCW, Arbeitsberichte des Institut für Wirtschaftsinformatik, Universität Münster, Münster, FRG, 1993, pp. 21-35.

Teufel S., Sauter C., Mühlherr T., Bauknecht K. (1995): Computerunterstützung für die Gruppenarbeit, Addison-Wesley, Bonn, forthcoming.

Tyran C. K., Dennis A. R., Vogel D. R., Nunamaker J. F. J. (1992): "The Application of Electronic Meeting Technology to Support Strategic Management", MIS Quarterly, vol. 16, no. 3, 1992, pp. 313-334.

Wheelen T. L., Hunger D. J. (1992): Strategic management and business policy, Addison-Wesley, Amsterdam.

Wilson F. A. (1994): "Computer support for strategic organizational decision-making", Journal of Strategic Information Systems, vol. 3, no. 4, 1994, pp. 289-298.

Proceedings of the Fourth European Conference on Computer-Supported Cooperative Work,
September 10–14, Stockholm, Sweden
H. Marmolin, Y. Sundblad, and K. Schmidt (Editors)

Medium versus mechanism: Supporting collaboration through customisation

Richard Bentley
German National Research Centre for Computer Science (GMD FIT.CSCW)

Paul Dourish
Rank Xerox Research Centre, Cambridge Laboratory (EuroPARC) and Department of Computer Science, University College, London

Abstract: The study of cooperative work as a socially-situated activity has led to a focus on providing 'mechanisms' that more closely resonate with existing work practice. In this paper we challenge this approach and suggest the flexibly organised nature of work is better supported when systems provide a 'medium' which can be tailored to suit each participant's needs and organised around the detail of their work. This orientation towards 'medium' rather than 'mechanism' has consequences for cooperative system design, highlighting a need to allow participants to adapt details of policy currently embedded in the heart of the systems we build. We describe an approach which allows users to perform such 'deep customisation' through direct manipulation of user interface representations.

Introduction

A principal tenet of CSCW is that systems intended to support cooperative work should be sensitive to the context in which they will be used. A number of recent studies of cooperative work have highlighted a disparity between descriptions of the working context as given in job description manuals, process-oriented accounts, and so on, and the *actual* pattern of use, which is often far more flexible and contingent on particular knowledge, skills and local decision making (see Anderson *et al.* 1989, for example). These observations have led to general agreement across the CSCW community on the desirability of a better understanding of the way in which work is carried out in groups, in order to inform the development of more effective cooperative systems.

One interpretation of this is a need for better representations and models of group work to enable development of systems that resonate more closely with actual work practice. Models such as the Milan Conversation Model (De Michelis and Grasso 1994), for example, are intended to provide representations of cooperation at a level of detail suitable for the needs of system design. However there are a number of problems with this approach, as a gulf exists between the kinds of information required by system designers and that provided by methods of analysis that purport to capture actual working context (Sommerville *et al.* 1994). It has been suggested that this gulf can be overcome by adapting methods of analysis such as ethnography to better meet the needs of designers (Hughes *et al.* 1994); however others contend that by adapting methods in this way, many of the benefits in terms of provision of contextualised, situated accounts are lost in the compromise (Anderson 1994).

We believe that these modelling problems, and the resulting debates, are artefacts of an inappropriate focus of design activity and reflect a narrow interpretation of the notion of 'computer support' for cooperative work. In this paper we are concerned with an alternative approach; one which does not regard the creation of ever more intricate and more detailed representations of group work as the main route towards more effective cooperative systems. Rather, our approach promotes the view of a cooperative system as one whose behaviour can be adapted through high-level customisation to meet the needs of its users, and that effective 'support' arises from precisely this openness and flexibility. We characterise this distinction as a contrast between systems which provide 'mechanisms' to structure collaboration, and those that provide a 'medium' which can be shaped by the users rather than the technology, in and through which collaboration occurs.

The context for this discussion is a project at GMD which is developing a simple shared workspace system to provide basic facilities for cooperative work across the Internet. Our focus in this paper is the development of the client interface which allows users to cooperate through a representation of a shared space, and more specifically on the general issues which underpin its design. Motivated by the different requirements that users may have for interacting with a shared workspace, we have developed a client prototype which supports customisation of underlying system behaviour through high-level user interface manipulation.

The rest of the paper is structured as follows. The next section presents in more detail our distinction between a system-as-medium and system-as-mechanism, and suggests a need for participants to configure systems to meet their requirements for support. We then show how this configuration requires a much 'deeper' notion of customisation than is evident with most tailorable systems, and the problems that this poses in terms of the 'language' with which customisation requirements are expressed. We describe a possible solution that allows participants to express their requirements *incrementally* using high-level customisation operations, and illustrate this approach with examples from our shared workspace client. We conclude by highlighting the general implications of our approach for the development of CSCW system architectures.

Medium versus mechanism

The distinction between medium and mechanism is concerned with the notion of 'support' a system provides for cooperative work, and specifically how the support required for individual participants and activities is derived. Although the concept of a system-as-mechanism has previously been equated with systems that are built around some social model of interaction (Greenberg 1991), we argue that the distinction is rather concerned with how such models structure the activities of the users, both *within* and *around* the system. This is reflected in the extent to which systems can be 're-purposed' to support activities that they were not designed for, and to provide support in a manner not envisaged by their designers.

System-as-medium and system-as-mechanism

A good example of a system that provides a medium for cooperation rather than a mechanism is electronic mail. Email applications are (by far) the most successful CSCW technologies developed to date, despite (or perhaps because of) the fact that they are amongst the simplest to design and implement. A characteristic of email use reported in a number of studies is the extent to which email supports different users' requirements, including the kind of information sent and received, frequency of reading email, different methods of notification of new mail and so on. Sproull and Kiesler (1991), for example, discussing the introduction of email systems into large organisations, show how users adapted the technology to their particular needs and exploited the opportunities which it introduced in ways not envisaged by management. So how does an email system provide support for such a wide range of potential activities and behaviours?

Consider the ways that email systems can be configured to save copies of your mail. For incoming mail, most mail programs provide options for saving mail in a special folder or file, storing in a default file for mail which has been read, leaving it in the 'spool' file and dumping it to the printer. In the same way most mailers offer a number of options for saving copies of outgoing mail, such as storing in a file, carbon copying to your spool file and so on. The decision to file a copy of a mail message, and which method to use, is contingent on many factors including (and this is just a small sample), who the mail is from (or to), what it is about, your attitude to email communication - whether it is communication 'in writing' or more 'verbal' - and even such issues as the trust you have in the system's reliability.

Email provides a *medium* for action because it can be adapted to support participants' specific requirements, contingent on any of the above factors and more besides. It provides a framework within which activity can take place, rather than structuring activities themselves. Whether to save a copy of a mail and which option to use are decisions for the user alone; the system does not attempt to determine what should be done with each mail message, but simply does what it is told. It is hard to imagine how another arrangement could be successful—after all, how could an email program know that I will find a particular message humorous and save it to my 'funnies' folder?

This may not seem so startling an observation, but it highlights a key issue to do with the extent and use of *representations* in computer systems in general and in cooperative systems in particular. An electronic mail system has no representation of the activities it is supporting, how the users' interactions relate to those activities, or what the requirements of those activities might be, but provides a service which can be adapted to the needs of each participant. We will return to this question of computational representations later in this section.

The alternative to providing an adaptable medium is characterised by a focus on providing mechanisms which directly regulate and manage participants' activity. In theory, participants are then free to concentrate on aspects of the task which require their attention, and the responsibility for the accomplishment of work is shared by the participants and the computer system. The key to this division of labour is the formalised description of 'regularities' in participants' activity; regularities which provide opportunities for automation of elements of work that would otherwise be performed by participants themselves.

An example of this approach is given by the class of Workflow systems[1] which aim to separate task *performance* from task *coordination*. Regularisations in the patterns of participants' activities are encoded in 'working processes', allowing the system to take over elements of coordination so that participants can concentrate on aspects of the activity, the performance of individual tasks, requiring their particular attention. This approach, then, is characterised by the *mechanisms* embodied in the system for the achievement of aspects (specifically, coordination aspects) of the supported activity. The problems arise when users wish to step outside the regularised patterns of behaviour which the mechanisms prescribe.

Structure, representation and 'support' for cooperative work

On the surface this distinction between medium and mechanism might be seen as one of *structure*, or the extent to which interaction is guided and/or constrained by policies embedded within the system. In this sense, email systems provide little in the way of structure, while for Workflow applications this structure is implicit in the goals of the technology. However, interaction with any computer system is structured in some sense, and it is not the existence of such structure which is at issue here, but rather the methods by which it is derived, employed, and how it can be manipulated to support different user requirements.

---

1 "Workflow" is a wide-ranging term; we use it here only in the broadest sense

Mackay (1990) reports on a study of the Information Lens system (Malone *et al.* 1987), which supports filtering of *semi-structured* email messages on the basis of user-specified rules. She describes how some users working with a version of the system exploited a little-used debugging feature to allow them to filter their mail for archiving purposes *after* they had read it—a use of the system not envisaged by its designers, who assumed that the value of the system lay in filtering messages *before* they got to the user. It is interesting to note that after this 'feature' was made more explicit in the following release of the software, a number of users who had rejected the technology as unsuitable for their methods of working then adopted the system and found it useful (Mackay, 1990).

This example shows that even highly-structured systems can be re-purposed to support activities not considered by their designers. A system's ability to adapt to different user requirements is determined by the ease with which the structures and policies embedded in the system can be customised. Customisation in this sense implies not only the ability to mould and manipulate structures within the system, but also the ability to appropriate them and use them in new ways; support for customisation is support for innovation. This position echoes the arguments of Greenberg (1991) who suggests that we should be developing 'personalizable' groupware, which can be adapted to the needs of individual users. Contrast this with the idea of a system which governs its behaviour according to some model or representation of its users' working contexts, where the objective of the representation is to enforce roles and commitments to ensure the group is 'efficient and effective' (Greenberg 1991).

The modelling of working context and its representation to govern the behaviour of cooperative systems is a central focus in current CSCW research. There are a number of reasons to doubt that this approach, which we have referred to as an attempt to provide 'mechanism' rather than 'medium', will be successful. We have already alluded to the problem of describing contextualised cooperative activities at a level of abstraction suitable for system design. In addition, a focus on existing work context would seem to inhibit the exploration of more innovative approaches to supporting cooperation, and also preclude innovation in the way that users employ systems to support their activities (as was seen to be a factor that influenced the successful adoption of the Information Lens system).

It is crucial to recognise that the forms of group support which are embodied in a cooperative system affect not only the establishment of working behaviour *within* the system (those defined within the systems' terms), but also those *around* it. It is frequently the behaviours around rather than within the system which are important determinants of its acceptability. In a study of a collaborative text editor, Dourish and Bellotti (1992) emphasise the way in which 'shared feedback' within a shared workspace—essentially a 'non-structure' in comparison to more formalised models of collaborative writing—is key to the emergence of a range of coordinating mechanisms by writing groups. Not only do the coordination activities of these groups arise around, rather than within, the shared system, but, arguably, it would have been much more difficult for such naturalistic coordination to occur had mechanisms been directly embodied in the tool.

The question of medium and mechanism is really one of representation—what is to be represented in the system, and how are the representations going to be used. We have tried to show that it is not necessary that a cooperative system has access to a representation of the activities it is supporting in order to provide 'support'. This should be obvious from the non-computational domain. For example, a piece of paper does not have access to a model of the writing process yet it still supports that activity. Not only does it support writing, with the requirements of different styles, smooth transition between writing and drawing, concurrent and serial access and so on, but it can also be used to soak up spilt coffee. As with the email example discussed earlier, the lack of embedded representations allows great flexibility in supporting different styles and behaviours.

This should by no means be interpreted as an argument *against* representation. After all, representation and formalisation lie at the heart of computational design. There is however a great deal of variability in how computational representations are *interpreted* in supporting human activity. The danger is that we may be seduced by the representational qualities of software systems and begin to confuse the representations for the activities they represent. This confusion between reality and representation lies at the heart of debates in the CSCW community such as that highlighted by Suchman and Winograd (Suchman 1993, Winograd 1993). Our proposal here embodies an attempt to view computational representations in CSCW systems as objects of, rather than proxies for, user activity.

So one motivation behind the call for a better understanding of the way that group work is actually carried out is to allow development of systems that more closely resonate with existing work practice. We agree that such an understanding is indeed essential for the development of more effective systems, but that the value of this understanding is in revealing the flexibility required by groups of participants with different individual requirements for support, rather than in yielding up ever-more-detailed fare for representation. This position places the emphasis on developing systems which users can adapt to meet their requirements, rather than systems that constrain interaction to some model of how they perform their work—manipulating representations instead of being manipulated by them.

Customising system behaviour

Our focus on medium rather than mechanism has suggested an approach to the design of cooperative systems that places the emphasis on customisation rather than rigid structures and policies governing system behaviour. Details of individuals' working contexts, which determine their requirements for system support, are so contingent on factors like individual, local and organisational knowledge, as well as the tasks being supported and personal preferences, that trying to model these factors at a level suitable for system design is unlikely to be successful. Indeed, the very variability of these factors, and their highly individual nature, suggests that we should take an alternative approach rooted in the recognition of open-ended variation, rather than an attempt to close it under some fixed representation.

Customisation is often advocated for systems which must support users with different working practices, levels of expertise and personal preferences. However, although many systems provide facilities for tailoring of *surface* interface features, few allow aspects of *deeper* system behaviour to be customised at the point of use. The conventional wisdom is that this separation of surface and deep—interface and application—is a good thing, both for developers and users. In particular, details of implementation decisions made within a system—the policies which determine how distributed data is managed in a collaborative application, or how information regarding user activities is made public—should be hidden from users who are focused on carrying out their work. The realities are that such 'low-level' policy decisions have important consequences for how users do their work—Greenberg and Marwood (1994), for example, show how different methods of concurrency control have a major impact on the interaction that can be supported by a system.

It is these details of system policy or behaviour that we have argued should be flexible and open to customisation, rather than hidden under some representation of the activities the system is supporting. In traditional systems however there is a *gulf* between the ability to customise aspects of process and functionality as opposed to interface and presentation. If possible at all, the former usually requires much more knowledge of system internals and the ability to express customisation requirements in a programming language. We examine the characteristics of this 'customisation gulf' below, before discussing an approach which attempts to bridge this gulf and provide support for both surface and deep system customisation.

The customisation gulf

The gulf between surface and deep customisation in most current systems reflects the separation in system architectures between interface and application functionality (Dourish 1995a). This gulf is an artefact of software engineering practice which does not reflect the customisation requirements of systems' users. An example of surface or interface customisation is the option provided by some word processors to switch between menus with an abridged and the full command set, where the list of commands available with each option is pre-defined by the system developer. An example of deep customisation is the ability to integrate the word processor with a foreign language translation program, when this operation was not pre-programmed by the system developer.

Although many systems are advertised as being highly-customisable, very few support flexible mechanisms for deep customisation. For example, some systems extend the idea of selection from different menu sets to allow users to change menu labels, key bindings, menu composition and even to create 'macros', so that one keystroke or menu selection causes execution of multiple commands. In all these cases however the user is constrained to using the functions the system developer has provided, and cannot customise the actual behaviour of the system. Indeed, in a study of word processor and spreadsheet packages, Oppermann (1994) states "few packages offer options for redefining their current functionality in such a way that a task- and user-specific adaptation can be achieved" (page 18).

A deeper model of customisation is provided by systems whose functionality is *parameterised*; that is, users can configure system behaviour by selecting from lists of alternative functions. However, rather than a smooth progression in the level of complexity and the degree of expertise required to perform customisation operations with such systems, there is often a 'steep incline' to be climbed before the user can isolate the functions that should be modified and appropriate values for parameters (Maclean *et al.* 1990). The 'parameters of interaction' provided by a version of the PREP collaborative editor (Neuwirth *et al.* 1994), for example, allow users to set parameters to control frequency of update propagation, granularity of updates and so on. This greater flexibility is however bought at the cost of increased expertise required of the user in knowing how these functions relate to the system behaviour, and how to set them to serve the requirements of the current working context.

This increased expertise is partly explained by the shift in the *language* through which customisation is performed. Basic macros begin to form such a language by providing the facility to *compose* or combine existing operations to form new ones, and more complex extension facilities add other linguistic features such as conditional operations and iterators. To customise surface features, users can often use techniques such as demonstration or menu selection that are part of the usual operating language for the system. Deeper customisation, however, must typically be performed in a different language which is oriented more towards the system developer than the application user, and a step function is often involved in acquiring the skills to begin to express customisation requirements in this language. This is particularly true for systems which allow users to extend system behaviour by creating new functions or modifying existing ones, often via an *Application Programmer Interface* (API), which open up the levels of customisation involved at the cost of the reusability of existing system components.

The customisation gulf is therefore characterised by two inter-related problems. The first one is the *level of customisation* possible, and with most systems this lies above the functionality of the application, rather than within it. The second problem is the *language of customisation*, and traditional systems provide limited facilities to express customisation requirements using the skills users already have, requiring the learning of new languages to describe new system behaviours. Both of these problems combine to give users no way to reach into the system and customise the way in which functionality (and not simply the interface to the functionality) relates to their accomplishment of work.

Incremental customisation

Issues of level and language of customisation form a barrier to users wishing to customise the behaviour of their systems. Studies carried out in the HCI community have shown that users are often unwilling to invest the time and effort required to surmount this barrier and acquire customisation knowledge, even if acquiring such skills would allow them to accomplish their work more easily (Carroll and Rosson 1987, for example). These observations have led some to suggest that users should be guided and encouraged in adopting a more exploratory approach (Oppermann 1994), and a 'tailoring culture' should be established which encourages users to share their expertise and results of customisation operations (Maclean *et al.* 1990). Trigg and Bødker (1994) observe that in some organisations such a tailoring culture is actively promoted by assigning responsibilities for customisation and establishing procedures to discuss proposed modifications.

The establishment of a tailoring culture does not require users to become skilled system designers, as there will inevitably be differences in users' willingness and abilities to acquire new skills. However it is important that users are aware of the possibilities for change which exist with their systems, to allow them to express their needs to more skilled customisers (Maclean *et al.* 1990). The barrier formed by separation of surface and deep system details, and use of different languages to customise features of each, inhibits users from even envisaging what can be done to tailor their environments, regardless of whether or not they themselves perform the customisation. This suggests that an approach is required that explicitly recognises that users need to customise, or envisage customisation of, both surface and deep system details, and that the separation currently enforced by different customisation languages is not a useful one.

In effect this calls for a more *incremental* approach to customisation, where users can express their requirements for support as much as possible using the skills they already possess. This is a similar technique to the support in more advanced word processors which allow customisation of menu contents using direct manipulation techniques, but here we are discussing its application to details of deeper system behaviour and not just the surface user interface. More complex customisations which cannot be performed using the same language should require a minimal increase in the level of expertise required. This should then reduce the size of the customisation gulf, both in terms of the language and level of customisation, and equate increases in tailoring power with proportionate increases in knowledge and skill required.

At the lowest level it may be possible to support customisation of some aspects of system behaviour through high-level user interface tailoring. An example of this is provided by the MEAD system (Bentley *et al.* 1993) which supports construction of different *User Displays* (UDs) of information from a shared space. With MEAD it is possible to develop a multi-user interface for a shared information system that allows users to select the UD representations which suit their requirements, and to switch between UDs as these requirements change. Although MEAD only supports selection of UDs from a developer-specified list, the customisation possibilities go beyond surface tailoring to aspects of system behaviour.

Underlying MEAD is an event service which distributes notifications of changes in the shared information space to interface clients. It maintains a list of the kinds of updates each client is interested in, and uses this list to selectively propagate updates to clients that should be informed. When users select alternative UDs to represent information from the shared space, the client automatically informs the notification service of the change in its interests to ensure it can maintain consistency between UDs and shared information. Thus MEAD supports limited customisation of the notification policy embedded in the system, but without requiring users to do extra work or learn a new customisation language.

So this approach begins to address issues of deeper customisation, and does not make the usual distinction between user interface adaptation and changes in system behaviour. Customisation is not a separate activity from normal interaction with the system, but rather users express their requirements for support from the system in terms of the information displays they require, and in doing so adapt the details of deep system policy with regard to update notification. What MEAD doesn't support is the ability to go beyond adapting the kinds of event notifications that users are interested in to more flexible strategies for configuring event granularity, different representations of events, event importance and so on.

To support incremental customisation requires techniques which allow users to move up the 'customisation curve', gaining more customisation power at the cost of a minimal increase in complexity. The next section describes a system to illustrate this incremental approach, showing how the basic language of system interaction is enhanced with facilities to customise details of system behaviour.

Incremental customisation in the BSCW client

The Basic Support for Cooperative Work (BSCW) project at GMD is concerned with the development of a simple shared workspace system that runs on top of the Internet. Our target user population is the academic research community as a whole, and specifically academics involved in large research projects. Such projects often consist of a number of project partners who have different organisational concerns, computing infrastructures and so on, but have a requirement to share information and work collaboratively.

The BSCW client is an application program which allows users to interact with a shared workspace. It provides basic functionality such as browsing the contents of a workspace, adding and removing documents, examining change histories and so on. The volume of information that can be stored in a shared workspace is large; for example, each document in the workspace can have associated annotations, version information, creator/modifier details, current status and so on. It is not practical to display all this information at the same time to every user; moreover, it is not useful to do so, as each user may have different reasons for interacting with the workspace at any point in time, and much of the information it contains may not be relevant to the current working context.

To address this problem the client prototype supports incremental customisation of the policies which determine the visualisation, interaction and change notification properties of the shared workspace. Thus, rather than using some representation of users' activities (such as 'roles') to determine their requirements for support, the client provides facilities which allow users to adapt system behaviour to reflect the requirements of their current working contexts. The aim is to provide a medium for cooperation which can be customised as much as possible using skills users already possess. This approach is illustrated below.

Customising system policy with Attachments

User customisation of the workspace is performed by associating *Attachments* with basic representations of workspace artefacts (figure 1). An Attachment carries with it (customisable) methods which adapt the visualisation, interaction and notification policies associated with items in the workspace for an individual user. In figure 1, for example, two users have tailored their representations of a simple workspace by associating different Attachments with a document called *ECSCWpaper*. User Paul is currently responsible for editing the next draft of the document, and Dik wants to proof-read it when Paul has finished editing. The different Attachments associated with the document reflect the different orientations of the users to the workspace. Paul, possibly trying to locate text from an old draft, has placed an Attachment over the document allowing him to open previous versions by clicking on their names, while Dik has added an Attachment to show who is currently editing the document.

In this example, the system reveals information to the users in response to their customisation operations, and allows them to perform different actions (such as opening a previous version). The system does not have a representation of the two users' activities, which they have negotiated externally and can re-negotiate at any time (if the authors decide a further draft is needed, for example). The process of customisation through addition, removal and tailoring of Attachments is therefore an ongoing one, reflecting the fluid and highly dynamic manner in which roles and responsibilities are negotiated in group work (Anderson *et al.* 1989).

In addition to visualisation and interaction details, associating Attachments with workspace artefacts may customise the underlying notification service. This service uses an expression of each users' interests in a similar manner to the MEAD system discussed above to select the events to be propagated, the method of propagation to use, and how events are represented at the user interface. In figure 1 the addition of the *current editors* Attachment registers an interest for Dik in changes to the set of editors for ECSCWpaper. When Paul finishes editing, his name will be removed from the Attachment, providing feedback on his activities. This feedback is generated within the context of the workspace and the context of users' activities, as the interests users hold are derived from the adaptations they make to suit their individual situations. Thus Attachments are not just 'views' but carry with them relevant interest patterns and behaviours.

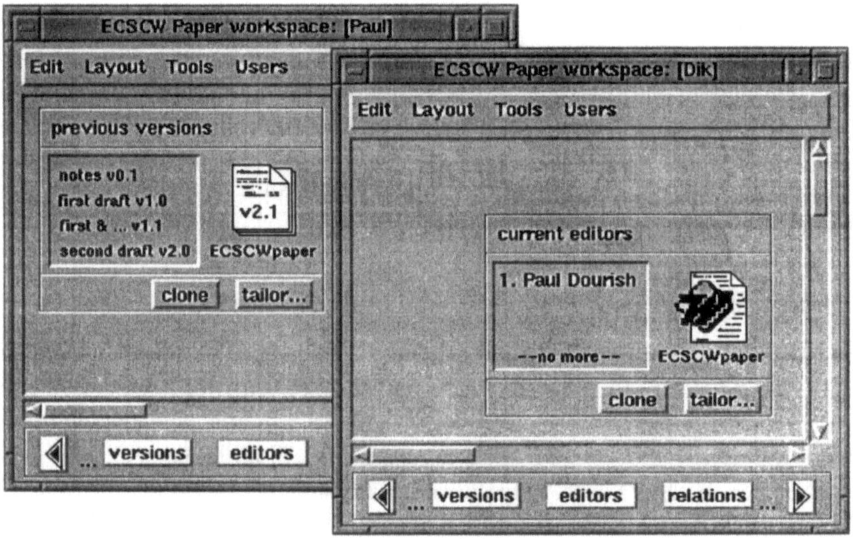

Figure 1 Alternate representations of a shared workspace using Attachments

The basic customisation of a shared workspace offered by adding and removing Attachments does not enforce a separation between surface interface features and deeper aspects of system behaviour. In addition to addressing some issues of *level* at which customisation is supported, users customise their workspaces using the same *language* of customisation, as association and removal of Attachments are part of the ordinary language for interacting with the client. However, interacting with a workspace using only pre-specified Attachments has limitations. For example, the indication of an interest in a workspace artefact may not be enough; users may hold many such interests at any one time, but their requirements for event notification may vary, depending on the relevance and importance of events for their working contexts. Thus there is a need to support customisation of details of the Attachments themselves.

Moving up the customisation curve: Customising Attachments

The bottom of the customisation curve is characterised by association of pre-defined Attachments with representations of workspace artefacts. A number of Attachments have been developed in the first version of the workspace client like those described above. In addition, the client provides a range of facilities for customising details of the basic Attachments to give users more flexibility in expressing their requirements for support from the system. Each of these methods requires slightly more skill on the part of the customiser, but brings with it a proportionate increase in the power available to perform customisation operations.

The emphasis here is on providing facilities for flexible customisation of system behaviour at the point of use that build incrementally on knowledge and skills that users already have. The techniques that have been implemented are described below in order of increasing customisation power.

- *Sharing Attachments*: The importance of customisation as a cooperative activity has been highlighted by a number of studies (Mackay 1990, Trigg and Bødker 1994). To support cooperative customisation it is possible to add Attachments to the shared workspace for others to retrieve and use. Thus users can share the expertise they have acquired with the system, and others become familiar with the possibilities for customisation offered. This is similar to the strategy used by Maclean *et al.* (1990) to exchange 'Buttons' by email, but here the Attachments are treated just like other information in the workspace, and can be added and retrieved in just the same way as other documents. Therefore users do not have to acquire new skills in order to share the Attachments developed by others.

- *Tuning Attachment properties*: To customise existing Attachments requires a slight increase in knowledge about their construction. Attachments consist of a number of methods that comprise the visualisation, interaction and notification properties of each Attachment component. Each component is similar to the concept of an *Icon Region* in Iconographer (Gray *et al.* 1990), but unlike Iconographer each property can be configured without programming. In figure 1, for example, it is possible to customise the notification properties of the *current editors* Attachment to provide audio feedback, put up a dialogue box, send an email and so on when someone finishes editing a workspace item. These can be combined—a 'finish editing' event might remove the editor's name and sound a chime, to bring the event to a user's attention even if the current orientation is not to the workspace. This example of event notification emphasises our focus on medium rather than mechanism. Rather than derive 'importance' or 'relevance' of events from some representation of activity, users can configure the system to provide notifications that are suitable. This is similar to the approach of Khronika (Lövstrand 1991), which supports a range of flexible practices by a focus on information rather than action (Dourish *et al.* 1993).

- *Composing Attachments*: Attachments can be associated with other Attachments to create composites. The model we use is that each Attachment has an empty *slot* which will represent the workspace artefact it is associated with. In figure 1 for example the slots of both the Attachments shown are occupied by the workspace artefact called ECSCWpaper. As Attachments are workspace artefacts just like any other (can be added and retrieved from the workspace and so on), they can occupy slots in the same way as representations of documents.[2]

- *Editing Attachments and creating new events*: It is possible to create new kinds of Attachments or re-configure properties of existing Attachments using a graphical Attachment editor. This supports definition of simple components which present information from a workspace, perform actions when sequences of interactions are recognised, and can re-configure when represented information changes. We are currently developing this tool to support more powerful visualisations and interaction techniques, one of which is the ability to create new kinds of events, more descriptive and oriented towards the activities users are performing. Most notification services tend to propagate events oriented more towards the system, as information such as 'file added', 'user logged in' and so on is easy to capture. However, if users can define new events, conditions under which they are generated, and means to represent them in the user interface, it is not necessary that these are described in system-oriented terms (as with, for example, the 'pub-call' event provided by the Khronika system—Lövstrand 1991). This approach is consistent with our emphasis on the system as a medium to support activities without representations of what those activities might be.

Thus the shared workspace client supports incremental customisation of surface and deep system features with a range of techniques. These techniques provide greater flexibility and power without the common 'step function' in terms of the expertise required to perform more complex customisation operations. The techniques show one way in which a deeper model of customisation can be provided which utilises existing skills and integrates customisation behaviour as part of normal interaction with the system.

Conclusions

Much effort in CSCW development has been aimed at creating detailed models of collaborative activity which can be used as the basis for computational design. The application of such models, however, has often been highly problematic. In this paper we have outlined an alternative approach which emphasises a CSCW system as a *medium* through which collaborative work occurs, rather than an embodiment of *mechanisms* representing perceived regularities in collaborative activity. This perspective, recognising the emergence of patterns of collaborative behaviour both

---

2 It is not possible or appropriate to go into detail in this paper. In brief, we use standard object-oriented techniques to send messages to representations of workspace objects, which either ignore the messages or re-configure their presentation, interaction and/or dynamic properties. As the Attachments are also workspace objects, they can respond to these messages, allowing them to be occupants of slots in other Attachments.

within and *around* technology, necessitates an examination of the ways in which customisation and adaptation are supported in CSCW systems.

We have pointed to a gulf in many current systems between the customisation of surface features and deeper functionality. This 'customisation gulf' forms a barrier to the forms of emergent, adaptive behaviour which we advocate. However, the use of incremental techniques provide a means for effective deep customisation through the manipulation of high-level interface components, as illustrated by the prototype client for the BSCW system currently under development at GMD.

Customisation is not simply a method for individuals to adapt technology to meet their own needs; it is, fundamentally, a means by which users can *construct* their working patterns, individually or as groups, from the basic materials provided. We believe that facilities of this sort are critical in CSCW, and motivate re-consideration of how systems are developed. In particular, this focus highlights a need for more *open* system architectures (Dourish 1995b), where details of deep system policy are 'visible, accessible and tailorable' at the point of use (Bentley 1994). One approach to providing such architectures which builds on the use of reflective, 'meta-level' architectures for CSCW system construction is described by Dourish (1995b). In general, however, we look towards the use of customisation techniques as more effective than explicit representation in bridging between the expertise of social science and the needs of computational design.

Acknowledgements

The prototype of the BSCW client was implemented by Markus Wasserschaff. The authors would also like to thank David England and Thilo Horstmann for fruitful discussions about many of the issues dealt with in this paper.

References

Anderson, R., Hughes, J. and Sharrock, W. (1989): *Working for Profit: The Social Organisation of Calculability in an Entrepreneurial Firm*, Aldershot, Avebury, 1989.

Anderson, R. (1994): Representations and requirements: The value of ethnography in system design, in *Human-Computer Interaction*, 9, 1994, pp 151-182.

Bentley, R., Rodden, T., Sawyer, I. and Sommerville, I. (1993): Architectural support for cooperative multi-user interfaces, in *IEEE Computer*, 27(5), May 1994, pp 37-46.

Bentley, R. (1994): *Supporting Multi-user Interface Development for Cooperative Systems*, PhD thesis, Computing Department, Lancaster University, June 1994. Available by anonymous FTP from Lancaster University at "ftp://ftp.comp.lancs.ac.uk/pub/reports/ThesisRB.ps.Z"

Carroll, J. and Rosson, M. (1987): Paradox of the active user, in J. M. Carroll (ed), *Interfacing Thought*, MIT Press, 1987, pp 80-111.

De Michelis, G. and Grasso, M. A. (1994): Situating conversations within the Language/Action perspective: The Milan Conversation Model, in *Proceedings of CSCW'94*, Chapel Hill, ACM Press, 22-26 Oct. 1994, pp 89-100.

Dourish, P. (1995a): Accounting for system behaviour: Representation, reflection and resourceful action, to appear in *Proceedings of Computers in Context (CIC'95)*, Aarhus, Denmark, 14-18 Aug. 1995.

Dourish, P. (1995b): Developing a reflective model of collaborative systems, to appear in *ACM Transactions on Computer-Human Interaction*, 1995 (in press).

Dourish, P. and Bellotti, V. (1992): Awareness and coordination in shared workspaces, in *Proceedings of CSCW'92*, Toronto, ACM Press, 31 Oct.-4 Nov. 1992, pp 107-114.

Dourish, P., Bellotti, V., Mackay, W. and Ma, C. (1993): Information and context: Lessons from a study of two shared information systems, in *Proceedings of COOCS'93*, Milpetas, California, 1-4 Nov. 1993, pp 42-51.

Gray, P., Waite, K. and Draper, S. (1990): Do-it-yourself iconic displays: Reconfigurable iconic representations of application objects, in *Proceedings of INTERACT'90*, 1990, pp 639-644.

Greenberg, S. (1991): Personalizable groupware: Accommodating individual roles and group differences, in *Proceedings of ECSCW'91*, Amsterdam, Kluwer Academic Publishers, Sept. 1991, pp 17-31.

Greenberg, S. and Marwood, D. (1994): Real time groupware as a distributed system: Concurrency control and its effect on the interface, in *Proceedings of CSCW'94*, Chapel Hill, ACM Press, 22-26 Oct. 1994, pp 207-217.

Hughes, J., King, V., Rodden, T. and Andersen, H. (1994): Moving out from the control room: Ethnography in system design, in *Proceedings of CSCW'94*, Chapel Hill, ACM Press, 22-26 Oct. 1994, pp 429-439.

Lövstrand, L. (1991): Being selectively aware with the Khronika system, in *Proceedings of ECSCW'91*, Amsterdam, Kluwer Academic Publishers, Sept. 1991, pp 17-31.

Mackay, W. (1990): Patterns of sharing customizable software, in *Proceedings of CSCW'90*, Los Angeles, ACM Press, 7-10 Oct. 1990, pp 209-221.

Maclean, A., Carter, K., Lövstrand, L. and Moran, T. (1990): User-tailorable systems: Pressing the issues with Buttons, in *Proceedings of CHI'90*, Seattle, ACM Press, 1-5 April 1990, pp 175-182.

Malone, T., Grant, K., Turbak, R., Brobst, S. and Cohen, M. (1987): Intelligent information-sharing systems, in *Communications of the ACM*, 30, 1987, pp 484-497.

Neuwirth, C., Kaufer, D., Chandhok, R. and Morris, J. (1994): Computer support for distributed collaborative writing: Defining parameters of interaction, in *Proceedings of CSCW'94*, Chapel Hill, ACM Press, 22-26 Oct. 1994, pp 145-152.

Opperman, R. and Simm, H. (1994): Adaptability: User-initiated individualization, in R. Oppermann (ed), *Adaptive User Support*, Lawrence Earlbaum, 1994.

Sommerville, I., Bentley, R., Rodden, T. and Sawyer, P. (1994): Cooperative systems design, in *The Computer Journal*, 37(5), 1994.

Sproull, L. and Kiesler, S. (1991): *Connections: New Ways of Working in the Networked Organisation*, MIT Press, Cambridge, Mass., 1991.

Suchman, L. (1993): Do categories have politics? The language/action perspective reconsidered, in *Computer-Supported Cooperative Work*, 2(3), 1993, pp 177–90.

Trigg, R. and Bødker, S. (1994): From implementation to design: Tailoring and the emergence of systematization in CSCW, in *Proceedings of CSCW'94*, Chapel Hill, ACM Press, 22-26 Oct. 1994, pp 45-54.

Winograd, T. (1993): Categories, disciplines and social coordination, in *Computer-Supported Cooperative Work*, 2(3), 1993, pp 191–198.

Proceedings of the Fourth European Conference on Computer-Supported Cooperative Work,
September 10–14, Stockholm, Sweden
H. Marmolin, Y. Sundblad, and K. Schmidt (Editors)

The Session Capture and Replay Paradigm for Asynchronous Collaboration

Nelson R. Manohar and Atul Prakash
Department of Electrical Engineering and Computer Science
University of Michigan, Ann Arbor, MI 48109-2122, USA.
E-mail: {nelsonr,aprakash}@eecs.umich.edu

In this paper, we describe a paradigm and its associated collaboration artifact to allow flexible support for asynchronous collaboration. Under this paradigm, a user session with an application's user interface is encapsulated into a data artifact, referred to as a *session object*. Users collaborate by annotating, by modifying, and by a back-and-forth exchange of these session objects. Each session object is composed of several data streams that encapsulate audio annotations and user interactions with the application. The replay of a session object is accomplished by dispatching these data streams to the application for re-execution. Re-execution of these streams is kept synchronized to maintain faithfulness to the original recording. The basic mechanisms allow a participant who misses a session with an application to catch up on the activities that occurred during the session. This paper presents the paradigm, its applications, its design, and our preliminary experience with its use.

Introduction

Many approaches to computer supported collaboration have been centered around synchronous collaboration [5, 6, 10]. In synchronous collaboration, users of a multi-user application first find a common time and then work in a WYSIWIS (What You See Is What I See) collaborative session. However, a synchronous mode of collaboration can often be too imposing on the schedule of the participants. It requires that users be able to find a common time to work together but, in many cases, that is not easy.

Several systems for the support of asynchronous collaboration provide ways to model the interactions among users and the evolution of collaboration repositories [8, 11, 15]. In this paper, we present a complimentary paradigm for

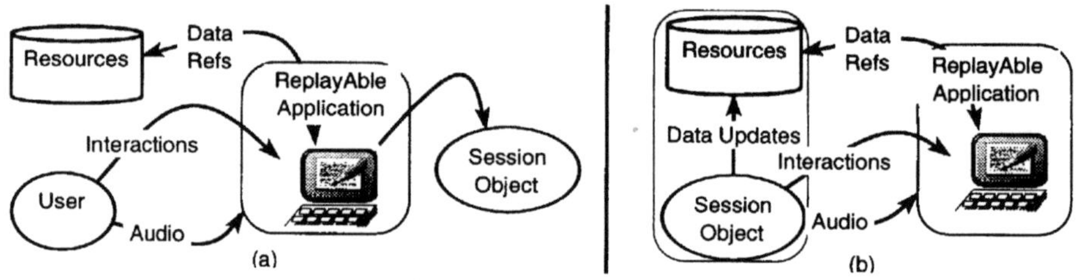

Figure 1. Capture and replay of an interactive session.

asynchronous collaboration that allows users to record and replay an interactive session with an application. We refer to this paradigm as **WYSNIWIST** (*What You See Now Is What I Saw Then*) [12]. The paradigm introduces an associated data artifact, the *session object*, used to capture the collaborative session. Figure 1 shows a high level view of the capture and replay of an interactive session with an application. During the capture of the session, user interactions with the application, audio annotations, and resource references (e.g., fonts, files, environment) are recorded into a session object (Figure 1a). The replay of the session uses the data stored in the session object to recreate the look and feel of the original session (Figure 1b).

Our replay approach is application-dependent. During replay, input events are re-executed (as opposed to a passive replay form such as a series of screen dumps). The re-execution approach to session replay exhibits benefits that are of particular interest in collaborative work. First, if a participant misses a collaborative session, our approach allows the participant to replay the session, catch up with the team, and if desired, continue further work. Second, because input events are recorded, session objects are typically small in size and thus easier to exchange among collaborators. Finally, because the application is re-executing the original session, the highest possible fidelity of replay is achieved, which for some domains may be essential.

The rest of the paper is organized as follows. First, we illustrate some applications of the paradigm. Next, we present the goals of our design. Then, we discuss related work. Next, we describe how session objects are modeled. Then, we discuss the design issues in building a system to support the paradigm. Next, we describe the implementation of a prototype. Finally, we discuss our experiences with its use and present some concluding remarks.

Examples

The next examples illustrate how different asynchronous collaboration scenarios could benefit from both the paradigm and its artifact.

Using the paradigm to support synchronous collaboration

Our work was originally motivated by the UARC[1] project, a collaboratory experiment among domain scientists in a wide-area network [4]. The domain of research among the scientists is space science. From the use of the current version of the UARC system over the past year, it has become clear that all domain scientists are not always able to be present at all times on their workstations to observe the data arriving from the various remote instruments. One reason is that the scientists are often working from different time-zones — the geographical distribution of scientists spans from Denmark to California. Secondly, because the space phenomena being observed are often not well-understood, it is not known *apriori* when interesting data will be observed. Providing support for some form of session capture and for allowing scientists to exchange annotated session recordings should facilitate *both* asynchronous and synchronous collaboration among them.

Using the artifact as an exchangeable document part

Consider a code walkthrough. It consists of a reader, a moderator, a clerk, and several reviewers. Often, reviewers have different areas of expertise. In fact, most of the time, a synchronous collaboration of reviewers with disjoint areas of expertise is both unnecessary and, in some cases, impractical. The feasibility of a synchronous collaboration approach was shown in the ICICLE system [2]. Although, there are some benefits to holding such a meeting, providing an asynchronous collaboration mode also seems appropriate.

Under our paradigm, the reader role becomes a baseline recording. Each reviewer independently walkthroughs over the code. Reviewers work asynchronously and edit, splice, and annotate segments of the baseline recording with their interactions and annotations.

It is well known that code walkthroughs are not only used for detecting errors. Indeed, they are also intended to share knowledge and to bring people on-board. Since a recorded walkthrough session captures both actions as well as annotations, and it can be replayed at any time, the session object therefore becomes on-line, *live* documentation of system validation.

Goals

The following are our goals in designing a system that makes an effective use of the paradigm:

- The replay of a session object must be consistent with the original session. This translates to the need to provide a synchronized replay of the data

[1] Upper Atmospheric Research Collaboratory

streams and to the need to maintain a consistent view of referenced resource inputs.

- Users must be able to successfully manipulate the artifacts in ways that capture and lead to collaboration. As has been the experience with the use of email for collaboration among a group, we expect that the users will need features such as the ability to exchange, edit, browse, and interact with session recordings. Some of the features above are similar to those found in the VCR metaphor.
- It is desirable for users to be able to statically browse session contents for events of interest. For instance, a user-interface analyst might be interested in browsing through the recording to determine when a particular command was typed or when the mouse was dragged.

Finally, the following conditions are assumed to maintain the determinism of the replay: the application performs deterministic computations; the state and events that affect the computation can be captured; and the same application is used for record and replay.

Related Work

Our work is related to work in screen capture, and pseudo-servers, collaboration-aware systems, conversation systems, and multimedia replay systems.

Screen recorders, such as WATCHME (for NEXTs), work at the screen level, intercepting and recording screen updates (or even screen dumps). Updates from *all* applications are captured, as opposed to those from a specific application. Because these approaches maintain the external look of the screen, interaction with the underlying application or its artifacts is not possible.

X pseudo-servers such as SHAREDX and XTV [1, 3] intercept events sent by applications being shared to the window server. These systems are primarily targeted for synchronous work. However, if these events are recorded and the state of the window server captured, this approach, in principle, allows the events to be replayed for specific applications. While our approach does not need to reconstruct the interface, these approaches must reconstruct it using low-level updates. Furthermore, replay is limited to only those events that go through the window server.

Our approach is based on the **exchange and refinement** of a work-in-progress by group members. Several other systems also support this paradigm, such as CONVERSATIONBUILDER [9] and STRUDEL [16]. These systems work by first defining a shared object and then formalizing a protocol that defines and limits the transactions that modify this object. In both cases, the shared object is an argumentative tree. In these systems, interactions are usually in reference to some data artifacts. Our paradigm introduces a new data artifact, which can be used to enrich intra-task descriptions on these systems.

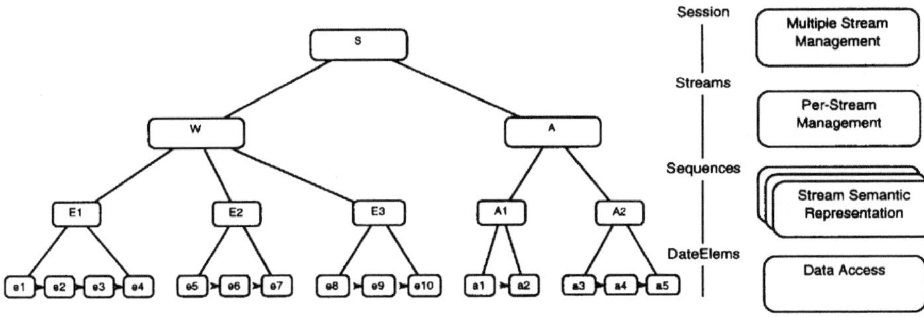

Figure 2. The object hierarchy (a) and corresponding abstraction layers (b).

Collaborative writing systems such as QUILT [7] and PREP [14] support the idea of allowing users to work asynchronously through annotations added to a document. Our approach builds on those ideas but, in our case, the artifact being annotated is a software-based recording of interactions with an application. Annotations can be made by gesturing (e.g., telepointing), text, and audio.

Modeling of Session Objects

The session object encapsulates all the information needed to replay a recording and is the building block of this paradigm. The session object is composed of multiple stream objects, such as the streams for audio and window events. Each stream is composed of sequences of data elements, where data elements represent the lowest-level of granularity at which events are captured. For audio, data elements correspond to audio frames. For window stream, the data elements typically correspond to events such as MOUSEDOWN, MOUSEUP, etc. Each object class provides functionality which is used to build services for its parent object class in the hierarchy. Figure 2 shows the correspondence of the abstraction layers and the object hierarchy.

The SESSION ABSTRACTION LAYER provides services for the management of multiple streams. For example, it provides inter-stream synchronization services. The next layer, the STREAM ABSTRACTION LAYER provides per-stream management services. For example, it provides adaptive stream scheduling services to adapt to each stream's performance requirements. Its services distinguish between two classes of streams: *annotation* and *functional* streams. An annotation stream contains annotation events. A functional stream updates the state of the application. The window stream (W) is typically a functional stream, whereas the audio stream is usually an annotation stream. The following layer, the SEQUENCE ABSTRACTION LAYER provides efficient sequence-based access to data element objects. This layer groups low-level events into logical units that must be executed as an atomic unit. Consider the following two window events, MOUSEDOWN immediately followed by a MOUSEUP. In this case, this layer abstracts these as $E_1 = \left(\texttt{MouseDown MouseUp} \right)$, that is, a MOUSECLICK sequence. The DATA ELEMENT ABSTRACTION LAYER, the lowest layer, provides transparent access to data element objects. These data elements can reside in local disk, remote repositories or be already in memory. Regardless, this layer provides transparent access services to the sequence abstraction layer.

Design

Session objects are similar to video recordings. Both are composed of temporal multimedia streams, both can be used for describing processes, and in both recorded segments can be edited, copied, and exchanged to fit user needs. With the help of the VCR metaphor we hope to facilitate the discussion of the features of the paradigm.

Recording a Session

A session with an application can be modeled as interactions with the application and its data resources. To capture the session, we record these interactions. To increase its information content, we also simultaneously record voice annotations. For each of these streams, a per-stream sampling module is provided to efficiently record the events. In capturing interactions, we considered the following issues. Interactions could be captured by means of recording either (1) user-level operations over the application, (2) window events, or (3) display updates. User-level operations (e.g., OPEN, PRINT, QUIT commands) are at a more abstract level than window events, but require extensive work in making existing applications replayable. Furthermore, certain operations such as gestures using mouse movements are typically not captured. Both approaches (2) and (3) allow capturing of mouse-movements used for gesturing or for indicating hesitation on the use of a feature of the application. We however decided to record window events, rather than display updates. While the use of display updates is application-independent and requires less sophisticated synchronization schemes, it has the disadvantages of a larger session object size, the inability to query the contents of a session object, and the inability to interact with a session object — features of collaborative interest which are possible with the use of window events. Although we are currently exploring approach (2) (window events), we feel, however, that a complete system would give the user the option to also record display updates.

Replay support using approach (2) requires capturing the state of the application. We require that the application provides functions to record and reset its state. To record a session, the toolkit calls back the application to tell it

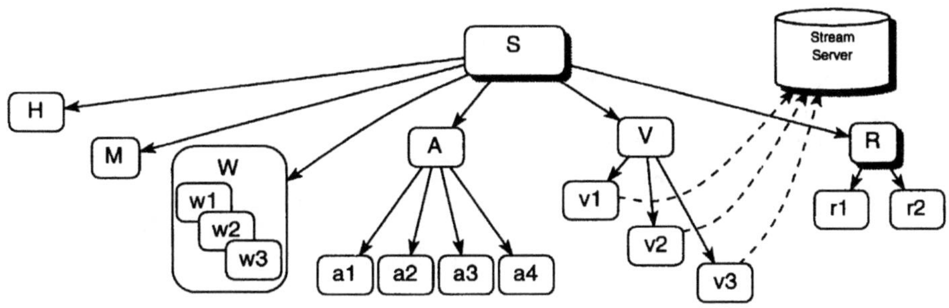

Figure 3. Storage representation of recorded sessions.

to capture its state. Resource references (e.g., environment, files etc.) must also be faithfully reproduced during replay. This problem is addressed in the Section on Replaying a Session.

Each stream is represented as a tuple containing the stream's initial state and its events. For example, the initial state of the window stream contains the state of every object of every window. This is accomplished by periodically sending a write message to the root parent object of every window in the display hierarchy. We use S_t to denote the state checkpoint at time t.

Storage and Access of Sessions

Session objects are persistent objects and must be stored on disk. However, in order to be exchanged and be used over time, we need to provide: (1) an editable representation for them and (2) efficient access to them.

To address (1), we opted for a file-based representation for session objects, as shown in Fig. 3. A session object is stored as a directory S. To illustrate this representation, suppose that S consists of a window stream (W), an audio stream (A), and a shared video stream (V). It is composed of a session header file H, a measurements file M containing the data needed to support synchronized replay of the session, a header file for each stream (W, A, V), and a resource directory R. Each stream maps to a file. However, the stream data may be stored directly in the header file (as for W), indirectly as references to persistent objects (as for A), or as proxy references to shared objects (as for V).

Streams typically have different access requirements. To address (2), the use of this file-based representation allowed us to tailor access strategies to each stream's requirements. To amortize read access costs, we used prefetching of events. To amortize write access costs, we used buffering of events. These techniques were optimized so as to balance the overhead for disk-accesses vs. the available time for stream-execution. Note that access and execution tasks execute and compete for the same resources within the same CPU.

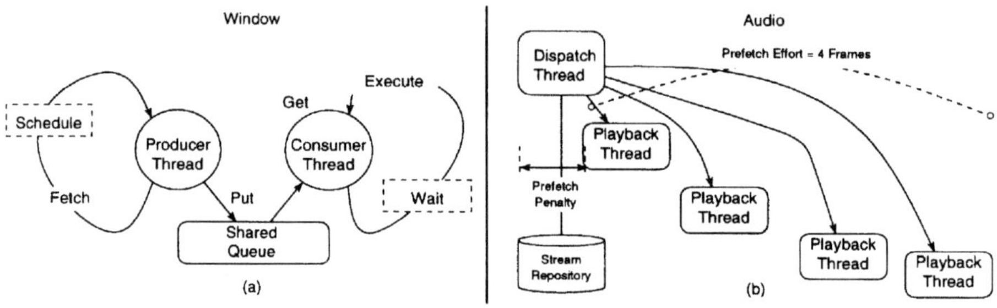

Figure 4. Thread models for replay of the window event stream (a) and for the replay of the continuous audio stream (b).

Replaying a Session

To ensure a faithful replay, we addressed the following questions:

- *Is there a need for synchronization?* Yes. Early on, our experiments showed that both streams (audio and window) had different susceptibilities to load conditions and that their rate of progress was dependent on the current load. Therefore, the ability to dynamically adjust the speed of replay of streams is desirable.

- *How to synchronize different streams?* We decided to test several different protocols for synchronizing audio and window streams. Two way protocols, which maintain relative synchronization between the two streams at the cost of their occasional re-synching, led to audio discontinuities, and were deemed untolerable by users. Consequently, we designed a one-way inter-stream synchronization scheme that synchronized slave streams to a master stream. The scheduling of events from a slave (window) stream was periodically adjusted to synchronize to its master (audio) stream.

- *Is an adaptive synchronization protocol needed?* Yes. The variances due to CPU availability, DMA access, thread overheads, disk access, reliability of timing services, etc., affected the scheduling of both window and audio streams. Our results in [13] showed that an adaptive protocol that attempts to compensate for varying load generally performs better across all load conditions.

Streams execute as cooperating thread tasks in a single CPU. The infrastructure provides two generic thread models. Figure 4(a) shows the thread model used to replay window events. On the average, during the sampling of the window stream, between 10 to 30 window events per second are generated by the user. However, during replay, these events must now be produced *and* consumed by the application itself. Therefore, a producer and consumer thread pair is used. The producer thread prefetches events from disk and puts them in the shared queue at intervals determined by the differences between event time-stamps as well as the protocol used for multi-stream synchronization. The consumer thread gets events from the shared queue and dispatches them to the window system for event replay. Figure 4(b) shows the thread model used to replay audio frames on the NEXTs. Read access for the audio stream relies on a parametrized disk-prefetching of audio frames.

The replay also introduces problems with the handling of resource references (e.g., fonts, files, devices, etc.) made during the recording of a session [3]. On the replay platform, referenced resources may be unavailable and, even worse, if available, may not be in the same functional state. To address the unavailability problem, resource references are classified as being public or private. Public resources are assumed to be widely available across platforms. Private resources need to be made available to replay platforms. To address the state problem, resource references are also classified as being stateful or stateless. Stateless resources are made available only when classified as private resources. Stateful resources must be available under a consistent state to replay platforms. A session recording also contains a *resource requirements list* and a *resource shipping list*. The resource requirements list indicates which resources are referenced by a session. The resource shipping list indicates which, how, and where resources referenced by a session should be accessed. These lists are provided at replay time to ensure a correct replay of the recording.

Editing of Sessions

The editing problem comprises recording new streams over a baseline recording, copying and pasting stream segments, extending a session with additional interactions and annotations, and the like. However, the editing problem is a difficult one and remains open. We are currently exploring some preliminary approaches to this problem.

On a VCR, streams are functionally independent and editing is typically done on a per-stream basis. We take a similar approach. However, in the case of session recordings, editing can only be done between well-defined points across all streams. Suppose that we want to dub-over a segment of the window stream. Conceptually, this is equivalent to replace some stream segment modeled by some events $[e_i, .., e_{i+k}]$ with a new set of events $[e'_i, .., e'_{i+n}]$. However, we must address the following two constraints. First, editing must preserve the synchronization that exists between streams. Secondly, since streams are not stateless — events have to be executed in the correct state — editing must preserve correctness of replay.

To maintain the correspondence that exists between streams, editing must be performed with identical sampling and synchronization schemes as in the original recording. To ensure correctness of replay, a stateless execution boundary is needed. One strategy is to allow only editing to start from a state checkpoint. The efficiency of this editing strategy depends on how apart the state

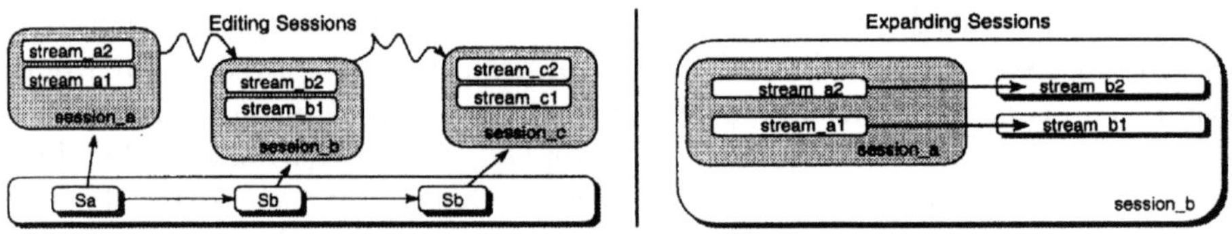

Figure 5. Editing (a) and expanding (b) session objects.

checkpoints are from each other. Note, however, that if the replay is based on display updates instead (previously discussed in the Section on Replaying a Session), editing of a session becomes much simpler since the streams are now stateless.

Figure 5 shows two of the potential ways of editing sessions. Figure 5a models editing of a session through concatenation of previously recorded session segments, s_a, s_b, and s_c. Figure 5b models a session s_b that extends a previously recorded session s_a with additional interactions and annotations.

Browsing a Session

Use of the VCR metaphor seems appropriate for doing simple sequential search of a recording. A VCR has two modes of forward search: fast forward and fast replay. A VCR easily performs any of these operations because it is based on a stateless model. In our case, streams are associated with a state but we show next how these operations can still be done efficiently. Say we want to fast forward from a current event e_i to event e_n. We can not just randomly index to that event because: (1) event e_n may have some causal dependency with a previous event in the sequence; (2) event e_n may not provide a clean execution boundary across all streams.

There are two solutions to these problems: (a) replay all events in the sequence $< e_i, ..., e_n >$, but at a faster (perhaps variable) rate or (b) jump to the last state checkpoint S_t prior to e_n and then apply the sequence of events $S_t + < e_j, ..., e_n >$. Solution (a) (i.e., fast replay) is reasonable when the forward distance is small. Solution (b) (i.e., restartable replay) is appropriate when the forward distance is large. Note that in general, variable speed replay relies on strong synchronization support, requiring the scaling of the rate at which events are to be dispatched while maintaining the relative synchronization between streams (or requiring the disabling of replay of some of the streams such as audio).

Backward replay can be implemented if every event has an inverse or undo operator. For many streams (e.g., discrete streams), the ability to execute the stream in backward order is likely to be difficult. In such cases, backward replay may have limited or no feasibility.

Interacting with Sessions

Interactions with a recorded session can be performed at two granularities: (1) between recorded sessions and (2) within a recorded session. Suppose that session s_1 results in the drawing of a layout and session s_2 results in the formatting and printing of a layout. A user may wish to replay session s_1, add some final touches to the layout, and then print it by means of session s_2. This is an example of between-type interactions. Interactions within a session are possible through the use of the resource reference list. In this case, users parametrize and modify resources referenced to by a session to fit their needs and requirements (e.g., printing a different file than that printed in the original recording by replacing the file resource).

Other Features

Users, such as interface analysts, may want to browse a session recording for interesting events.

Static browsing of the session contents is a feature that does not have a simple match in the VCR model. Consider a window stream segment corresponding to having a user click on a window, position the cursor and then start typing the word "*password*". Such a content can be potentially retrieved from the window stream without having to replay the session. Knowledge discovery tools can be created to examine and peruse repositories of these digital recordings.

Users also need a way to efficiently exchange session objects. Resources referenced by a session must be faithfully forwarded or equivalenced during replay. Mailing of a session S (recall example in Fig. 3) reduces to the problem of mailing of directories. The mailing of a shared stream, such as V, is straightforward, by means of using relative referencing to the repository R. The resource reference lists and resource shipping lists are used here to ship resources.

Implementation

We implemented an object-oriented prototype toolkit for NEXT workstations under the Mach Operating System. The toolkit provides the REPLAYABLE object class. The REPLAYABLE class provides applications with transparent access to the infrastructure services. A MACDRAW-like object oriented drawing application and a text editor application were retrofitted with the toolkit. REPLAYABLE applications access the paradigm features through menus and windows added to the application. The session controller window provided by the prototype to each REPLAYABLE application is shown in Fig. 6. The infrastructure allows applications to: (1) re-execute window events (e.g., ges-

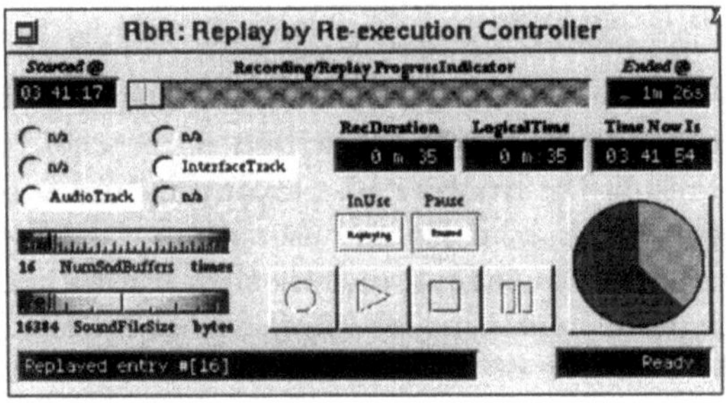

Figure 6. View of the REPLAYABLE application controller.

turing, typing, moving windows), (2) record voice-annotations, (3) provide synchronized replay of these streams, and (4) to replay selected streams.

The infrastructure provides a *logical time system* (LTS) to support time-stamping of events. It also provides efficient, disk-based, read and write of streams. Finally, it provides per-stream scheduling and inter-stream synchronization protocols to support faithful replay of streams.

The prototype currently supports two streams: a *discrete stream* (i.e., window events) and a *continuous stream* (i.e., audio). Each stream is dispatched to a separate processor. The window event stream is dispatched to the CPU — which is subject to arbitrary load conditions. The audio stream is dispatched to the DSP — assumed to be dedicated. These components (application, streams, DSP, CPU, infrastructure services, disk, and data paths) are shown in Fig. 7. Side (a) shows the record-time view and side (b) shows the replay-time view of the prototype.

We designed an adaptive synchronization protocol that attempts to: (1) maintain statistical control over inter-stream asynchrony, and (2) update a weighted history forecast formulation to determine the presence of a significant trend in the asynchrony history. The adaptive behavior of the protocol works as follows. If the current asynchrony is large enough, the past asynchrony history is examined to determine the presence of a trend in the asynchrony. If such a trend exists, the window stream schedule is either compressed or expanded — thus increasing or decreasing the relative replay speed of the window stream, respectively.

Experience

Our experience with the prototype shows several results. The duration of most recorded sessions tends to be of the order of a few minutes, typically 2 to 4 minutes in our experience. To capture a session of about 4 minutes, the size of our compressed document artifact was only $1.7MB$. Note that capturing the

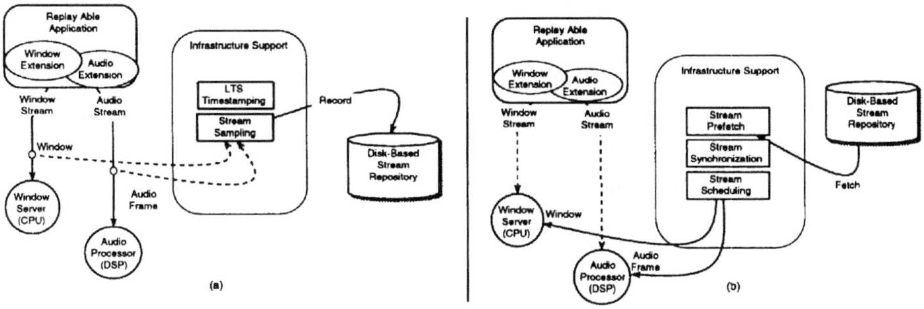

Figure 7. Application model for record (a) and replay (b) of window and audio streams.

document artifact	artifact size (MBytes)	fidelity of replay
digital audio and video	16 MBytes (4 fps, MPEG compressed)	$(1024x1024 \rightarrow 320x240)$ pixels, lossy
session object	1.7 MBytes	$(1024x1024 \rightarrow 1024x1024)$ pixels, lossless

Table I. Comparison of data artifacts for session capture and replay. The session objects document artifact has small size and lossless fidelity of replay.

same session using digital video and audio required at least $16MB$ of storage. These results are summarized in Table I.

While users tolerated some inter-stream asynchrony — up to 1 or even 2 seconds was acceptable — most users did not tolerate audio discontinuities. We found that our adaptive synchronization protocol [13] provided acceptable performance across all load conditions. The average asynchrony μ_{async} for this protocol was about half the mean duration of the scheduling interval used. The standard deviation of the asynchrony σ_{async} for the protocol was also about one third the mean scheduling interval duration. These parameters could be lowered by using smaller scheduling intervals (and thus, smaller audio frame sizes), but then the audio quality was found to deteriorate on the NEXTs because of the increased thread scheduling overheads. Both parameters μ_{async} and σ_{async} were stable across all load conditions.

Maintaining data as separate streams was a good design choice for record, storage, and access. Both streams had substantially different characteristics. The window stream had a 10 : 1 compression ratio. The stream had a variable event density between 10 to 30 events per second. For the audio stream it was possible to achieve a 2 : 1 compression ratio but only by the use of the audio-specific compression software. We found that to handle access overheads for the audio stream, it was best to amortize the overhead over several frames.

The access overheads of the prototype averaged about 2%.

There are basically three important parameters that determine access overheads for the audio stream: (1) the audio frame size; (2) the number of audio frames that are written to disk at one time during recording; and (3) the number of audio frames that are prefetched from disk at one time during playback. We summarize the appropriate values found for these parameters next. Audio frame sizes of 16 KB were found to work best on our platform. Since the NeXTs use threads to dispatch audio frames, using smaller frame sizes made thread scheduling overheads appreciable, so as to affect the quality of audio playback. Using much larger values did not cause significant additional improvements in performance. Writing 2 frames at a time (32 KB of data) to the disk at a time led to the best amortization of the disk penalty hit during recordings. Prefetching 4 frames at a time (64 KB of data) was found to give the best amortization of the disk penalty hit during playback.

Experience with the prototype also made us aware of the potential for the following further uses of the paradigm.

Using the paradigm to capture collaboration content

In a recently funded NSF project, we plan to support the type of collaboration that occurs between a radiologist and a doctor over radiographs to diagnose a patient's medical problem. Doctors and radiologists often have very busy schedules. So the ability to collaborate asynchronously is needed. We would like a radiologist or a doctor to be able to record a session in which they are interacting with one or more images, pointing to specific areas of interest, using audio to explain their understanding or raise questions about regions of interest in the images, and adding text or graphical annotations. They can collaborate by exchanging such recordings. Such digital, high resolution session recordings will not only help to capture radiologists' *diagnostic conclusions*, but also their *diagnostic process*. This is important because in many instances how the diagnosis was reached is as important as the diagnosis itself.

Using the artifact as an active process description

Consider the use of tutorials. Tutorials typically illustrate how to perform a task — i.e., a process instance. One step further than tutorials is the idea of process capture. The goal of process capture is encapsulate the use and description of a task. Unlike tutorial documents, the paradigm's artifact allows one to encapsulate an *active* — rather than passive — description of a process. That is, rather than just illustrating a task, the session artifact re-executes the task and thus leaves the underlying application in a state that allows its user to continue interacting with the application.

Using the artifact for process analysis

Consider the task of building a user interface using a graphical interface builder. By recording the GUI building session, we obtain both: 1) an active document that captures the rationale of why the objects were placed in a given arrangement; and 2) a tutorial that shows and reconstructs the resulting layout and connections. A collection or library of such active artifacts has reuse and knowledge-capture value to organizations. Therefore, means to modify, interact, and browse these session artifacts are needed. This can be regarded as a *digital library* of process descriptions — active artifacts. By supplying own context data to a generic artifact, users may be able to transform a generic process description to a process instance.

Conclusions

In this paper, we presented a new paradigm and its associated collaboration artifact for the support of asynchronous collaboration. The paradigm and its underlying synchronization infrastructure allow users to capture interactive sessions with an application into data artifacts, i.e., the session objects. Unlike other data artifacts, session objects are active objects. Session objects can be manipulated, replayed, interacted with, and analyzed to fit the needs of collaborators. Sessions objects are represented by temporal streams, kept synchronized during the replay of the session. Furthermore, this new data artifact introduced by the paradigm can also be used to enrich the artifact-base of existing collaboration systems, so as to capture intra-task descriptions in both asynchronous and synchronous collaborative systems.

Our goals for the near future are (1) to support efficient recordings of sessions that involve interactions with image and video artifacts and (2) to use the paradigm to support asynchronous collaboration among radiologists and doctors at the University of Michigan hospitals.

Acknowledgements

We would like to thank all the UARC project members, in particular, Amit Mathur and Hyong Shim. This work has been supported in part by the University of Michigan's Rackham Merit Fellowship and by the National Science Foundation under the Grant ECS-94-22701 and under the Cooperative Agreement IRI-9216848.

References

[1] H.M. Abdel-Wahab, S. Guan, and J. Nievergelt. Shared workspaces for group collaboration: An experiment using Internet and Unix inter-process communication. *IEEE Communications Magazine*, pages 10–16, November 1988.

[2] L. Brothers, V. Sembugamoorthy, and M. Muller. ICICLE: Groupware for code inspection. In *Proceedings of the Second Conference on Computer-Supported Cooperative Work*, pages 169–181, October 1990.

[3] G. Chung, K. Jeffay, and H. Adbel-Wahab. Dynamic participation in computer-based conferencing system. *Journal of Computer Communications*, 17(1):7–16, January 1994.

[4] C. R. Clauer, J. D. Kelly, T. J. Rosenberg, C. E. Rasmussen, P. Stauning, E. Friis-Christensen, R. J. Niciejewski, T. L. Killeen, S. B. Mende, Y. Zambre, T. E. Weymouth, A. Prakash, G. M. Olson S. E. McDaniel, T. A. Finholt, and D. E. Atkins. A new project to support scientific collaboration electronically. *EOS Transactions on American Geophysical Union*, 75, June 28 1994.

[5] C. Ellis, S.J. Gibbs, and G. Rein. Design and use of a group editor. In G. Cockton, editor, *Engineering for Human-Computer Interaction*, pages 13–25. North-Holland, Amsterdam, September 1988.

[6] C.A. Ellis, S.J. Gibbs, and G.L. Rein. Groupware: Some issues and experiences. *Communications of the ACM*, pages 38–51, January 1991.

[7] R. Fish, R. Kraut, M. Leland, and M. Cohen. Quilt: A collaborative tool for cooperative writing. In *Proceedings of ACM SIGOIS Conference*, pages 30–37, 1988.

[8] V. Goldberg, M. Safran, and E. Shapiro. Active Mail: A framework for implementing groupware. In *Proceedings of the Fourth Conference on Computer-Supported Cooperative Work*, pages 75–83, Toronto, Canada, October 1992.

[9] S. Kaplan, W. Tolone, D. Bogia, and C. Bignoli. Flexible, active support for collaborative work with ConversationBuilder. In *Proceedings of the Fourth Conference on Computer-Supported Cooperative Work*, pages 378–385, Toronto, Canada, October 1992.

[10] M. Knister and A. Prakash. DistEdit: A distributed toolkit for supporting multiple group editors. In *Proceedings of the Third Conference on Computer-Supported Cooperative Work*, pages 343–355, Los Angeles, California, October 1990.

[11] K.Y. Lai, T.W. Malone, and K.C. Yu. Object Lens: A "spreadsheet" for cooperative work. *ACM Transactions on Office and Information Systems*, 6(4):332–353, 1988.

[12] N.R. Manohar and A. Prakash. Replay by re-execution: a paradigm for asynchronous collaboration via record and replay of interactive multimedia streams. *ACM SIGOIS Bulletin*, 15(2):32–34, December 1994.

[13] N.R. Manohar and A. Prakash. Dealing with timing variability in the playback of interactive session recordings. In *submitted to: Proceedings of ACM Multimedia '95*, San Francisco, CA, USA, November 1995.

[14] C.M. Neuwirth, D.S. Kaufer, R. Chandhok, and J.H. Morris. Issues in the design of computer support for co-authoring and commenting. In *Proceedings of the Third Conference on Computer-Supported Cooperative Work*, pages 183–195, Los Angeles, California, October 1990.

[15] C.M. Neuwirth, D.S. Kaufer, J. Morris, and R. Chandhok. Flexible diff-ing in a collaborative writing system. In *Proceedings of the Fourth Conference on Computer-Supported Cooperative Work*, pages 147–154, Toronto, Canada, October 1992.

[16] A. Sheperd, N. Mayer, and A. Kuchinsky. Strudel: An extensible electronic conversation toolkit. In *Proceedings of the Second Conference on Computer-Supported Cooperative Work*, October 1990.

Proceedings of the Fourth European Conference on Computer-Supported Cooperative Work,
September 10–14, Stockholm, Sweden
H. Marmolin, Y. Sundblad, and K. Schmidt (Editors)

Virtual Reality Tele-conferencing: Implementation and Experience

Chris Greenhalgh
Department of Computer Science, The University of Nottingham, UK.

Steve Benford
Department of Computer Science, The University of Nottingham, UK.

This paper describes the implementation of and early experiences with a virtual reality tele-conferencing system called MASSIVE. This system includes a full realisation of the spatial model of interaction and its concepts of aura, awareness, focus, nimbus and adapters as was presented at ECSCW'93. This model supports users in interacting over ad-hoc combinations of audio, graphical and textual media through both 3-D and 2-D interfaces. Observations arising from the use of MASSIVE to support laboratory meetings are discussed; these include the need to support richer peripheral awareness, the need to improve the sensitivity of navigation, problems with lack of engagement between users, the need to support varying degrees of presence and problems arising from different perceptions of space between 2-D and 3-D users. Possible solutions to these problems are proposed.

1. Introduction

We describe the implementation of and initial experiences with a virtual reality based tele-conferencing system called MASSIVE in which communication between participants is controlled by movement within a shared virtual space. Specific design goals of this system include:

- MULTIPLE PARTICIPANTS: supporting groups of several participants at different locations in undertaking real time communication with one another.
- MUTLI-MEDIA: allowing these participants to communicate over different media. In particular, the system should support aural, visual and textual communication.
- HETEROGENEITY: allowing users with radically different interface equip-

ment to communicate within a common space. At the extreme, users of high end VR systems should be able to interact with users of, say, VT-100 character based terminals.

- SPATIAL MEDIATION: to support spatially mediated conversation management as opposed to traditional floor control. More specifically, a user's perception of others across different media should be governed by spatial factors such as their relative positions and orientations (e.g. people get louder as you move or turn towards them and vice versa).
- BALANCE OF POWER: there should be a balance of power between speakers and listeners so that (taking the audio medium as an example) speakers can try to influence who can hear them, e.g. by interrupting, and listeners can control who they are hearing.
- VARIED MEETING SCENARIOS: supporting a range of meeting scenarios ranging from face-to-face conversations to lectures and presentations;
- SIMULTANEOUS MEETINGS: allowing many simultaneous meetings to occur with the possibility for users to move between them.
- WIDE AREA: operating over wide area networks.
- SCALE: being capable of scaling to similar numbers of participants as are involved in every-day cooperative activities (e.g. tens or hundreds).

We propose that by meeting all of these goals we will eventually be able create more flexible, natural, open and scalable tele-conferencing systems than are currently available.

At the heart of our system lies the spatial model of interaction which was introduced at ECSCW'93 along with some early concept demonstrators. This paper describes a full implementation of this model and presents some initial observations arising from its use.

2. A brief overview of the spatial model

We begin by very briefly summarising the spatial model of interaction. Full details are given in the ECSCW'93 paper [Benford, 93]. The aim of the model is to support the flexible management of communication in densely populated virtual spaces. The model assumes the existence of some shared spatial frame of reference which is populated by human and other agents which communicate over combinations of different media.

The first component of the model, *aura*, addresses the problem of limiting the number of connections between the occupants of a densely populated space. In its simplest form, an aura is a subspace which scopes the presence of an object in a given medium. A connection between two objects is not made in this medium until the relevant auras collide (e.g. we cannot see each other until our visual auras collide or see each other until aural auras collide).

The concepts of *awareness*, *focus* and *nimbus* control the information passing across a connection once it has been established. An object may have different awareness of each connected object in each medium. Awareness is quantifiable and may range continuously from full, through peripheral to none. Having a low awareness of another object results in little information being received from it and a high awareness results in more detailed information. Thus, awareness provides a way of expressing desired quality of service across different connections. Awareness is medium specific and is interpreted differently for each medium (e.g. it may be mapped onto volume for an audio connection).

Mutual awareness need not be symmetrical and is controlled through focus and nimbus. Nimbus represents the transmitter's control over how information is propagated to other objects while focus represents the receiver's control. Focus and nimbus are typically expressed in terms of the spatial relationship of the objects (i.e. they are spatial fields), although they might also involve other attributes. Thus, the more object B is within object A's focus the more A is aware of B and the more A is within B's nimbus, also the more A is aware of B. More specifically, A's awareness of B in some medium M is a combination of A's focus in M and B's nimbus in M.

Finally, aura, focus and nimbus, and hence awareness, might be altered by various adapter objects. Adapters might represent communication tools such podia (aura and nimbus amplifiers), or boundaries (e.g. windows which attenuate audio awareness but not visual awareness), or other kinds of object; they provide a degree of extensibility to the model.

3. MASSIVE functionality

Our system is called MASSIVE (Model, Architecture and System for Spatial Interaction in Virtual Environments!). This section provides a user's view of MASSIVE's functionality.

Within any given instantiation of the system the MASSIVE universe is structured as a set of virtual worlds connected via portals. Each world defines a disjoint and infinitely large virtual space which may be inhabited by many concurrent users. Portals allow users to jump from one world to another.

Users can interact with one another over combinations of graphics, audio and text media. The graphics interface renders objects visible in a 3-D space and allows users to navigate this space with a full six degrees of freedom. The audio interface allows users to hear objects and supports both real-time conversation and playback of pre-programmed sounds. The text interface provides a MUD-like view of the world via a window (or map) which looks down onto an infinite 2-D plane across which user moves (similar in style to the UNIX games Rogue and Nethack). Text users are embodied using a few text characters and may interact by typing text messages to one another or by "emoting" (e.g. smile, grimace etc.).

A key feature of MASSIVE is that these three kinds of interface may be arbitrarily combined according to the capabilities of a user's terminal equipment. Thus, at one extreme, the user of a sophisticated graphics workstation may simultaneously run the graphics, audio and text clients, the latter being slaved to the graphics client in order to provide a map facility and to allow interaction with non-audio users. At the other extreme, the user of a dumb terminal (e.g. a VT-100) may run the text client alone. It is also possible to combine the text and audio clients without the graphics client and so on.

In order to allow interaction between these different clients a text user may export a graphics body into the graphics medium even though they cannot see it themselves. Similarly, a graphics user may export a text body into the text medium. In other words, text users can be embodied in the graphics medium and graphics users can be embodied in the text medium. MASSIVE uses a dynamic brokering mechanism (described below) to determine whether objects have any media in common whenever they meet in space (i.e. on aura collision). The net effect is that users of radically different equipment may interact, albeit in a limited way, within a common virtual world; for example, text users may appear as slow-speaking, slow moving flatlanders to graphics users.

All media (i.e. graphics, text and audio) are driven by the spatial model. Specifically:

- audio awareness levels are mapped onto volume; this means that audio interaction is sensitive to both the distance between and the relative orientations of the objects involved. This is observable in general conversation and also forms the basis of the "audio gallery" where users wander round a selection of audio-exhibits which play audio samples.
- graphics awareness levels are compared against threshold values to select one from a number of alternative object appearances according to the observer's location and orientation. This is typically used to display an object in more detail as awareness of it increases, although arbitrary changes are possible.
- the display of text messages is governed by levels of awareness as shown in table I, below; this lists awareness levels (values between 0 and 1) and the effects they have on the display of text messages.

Awareness	Level	Example Text Display
0.0-0.2	none	
0.2-0.4	presence	Chris at 0,0
0.4-0.6	events	"Chris says something"
0.6-0.8	peripheral	"(Chris says hi!)"
0.8-1.0	full	"Chris says hi!"

Table I: example levels of awareness for the text medium

Aura, focus and nimbus are attached to the user's current position and are therefore manipulated by moving about. Thus, turning towards another person may bring them more into ones focus or nimbus. In addition, users may explicitly manipulate awareness by choosing between three general settings for focus and nimbus:

- normal - provides conical focus and nimbus regions projecting out from the user which allows for full awareness of a few objects and peripheral awareness of other objects;
- narrow - a smaller aura and a thinner cone for focus and nimbus which enables private conversation (maximum awareness only occurs when two users are directly face to face, and there is little peripheral awareness);
- wide - a spherical region intended for general all round awareness (this nullifies the directional effects of focus and nimbus).

Users may also dynamically alter both the range and conical angle of focus and nimbus (aura is automatically updated when this happens). Thus, it is possible to arbitrarily widen and narrow focus and nimbus and to telescope them in and out to any desired range.

Four adapter objects have also been implemented:-

- A podium which extends the auras and nimbi of its users to cover a wider area, allowing them to address a crowd of other users;
- A conference table which replaces its users' normal auras, foci and nimbi with a new ones which span the table.
- A text to speech translator which converts messages in the text medium to synthesised speech in the audio medium (implemented using a public domain text to speech package).
- A text to graphics translator which displays messages received through the text medium on a "board" object in the graphics medium.

These adapters are themselves driven by the spatial model so that they only become active when a user gets sufficiently close to them. For example, a text interface user approaching the text-to-speech adapter will cause the adapter to activate and to automatically begin translating their text messages and re-transmitting them in the audio medium, enabling nearby audio users to hear them. Consequently, many users can use them simultaneously and can jostle around them to negotiate access.

A user's embodiment determines how they appear to other users. Each user may specify their own graphics embodiment in a personal configuration file using a simple geometry description format. In addition, we provide some default graphics embodiments intended to convey the communication capabilities of the users they represent (which is an important issue in a heterogeneous environment). For example, an audio user has ears, a non-immersive (and hence monoscopic) user has a single eye and a text user has the letter "T" embossed on their head. The aim of such embodiments is to provide other users with the necessary basic communication cues to decide how to address them. The basic shape of graphics embodiments is also intended to convey orientation in a simple and efficient manner. Graphics embodiments may be labelled with the name of the user they represent in order to aid identification. Finally, users may emote to one another by switching between different bodies by using key strokes.

Text embodiments consist of a single character (the first letter of the person's chosen name) along with a short line which indicates the direction in which this person is currently facing.

Users may define any number of worlds containing simple graphics scenery and other objects. These worlds may be interconnected in any configuration via portals. An important aspect of MASSIVE is that in multi-site use across wide area networks each site may define its own local worlds; portals can then be used to allow users to move between sites in a transparent manner. Thus, each MASSIVE site can define its own conferencing environment as well as connecting to the broader "universe" of MASSIVE worlds across wide area networks.

We complete this overview of MASSIVE's functionality with two sets of screen-shots.

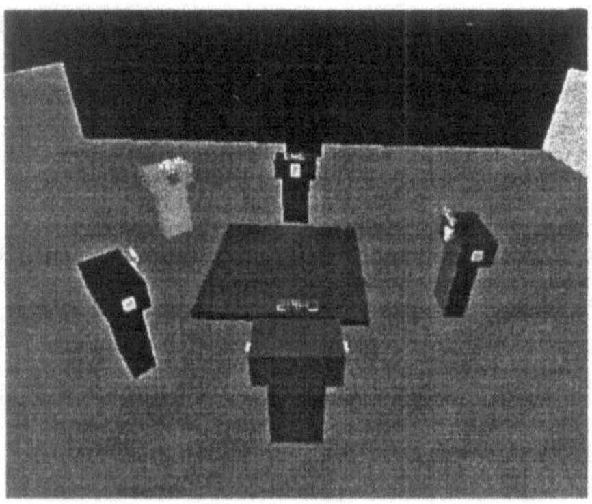

1 (a) perspective view

1 (b) bird's eye view

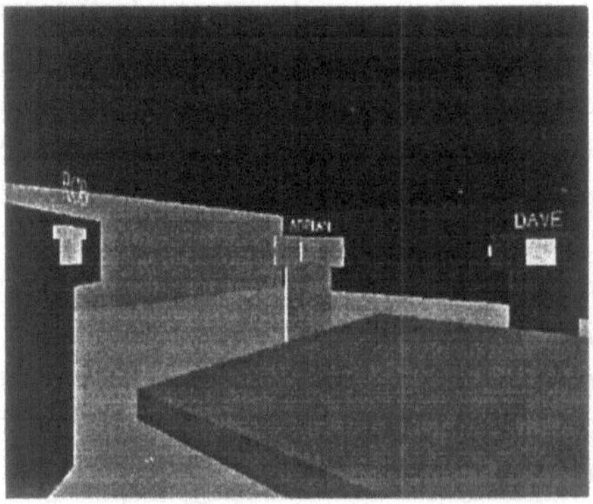

1 (c) eye-level view

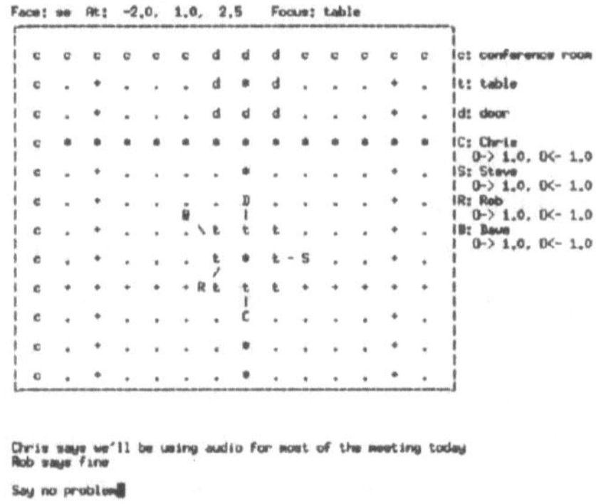

1 (d) text user's view

Figure 1: Five meeting participants around the "table" adapter

Figure 1 shows a meeting in progress involving five participants who are using the conference table adapter. Figure 1 (a) provides a perspective view of the scene and figure 1 (b) a birds-eye view (obtaining different views has been made possible by the recent viewpoint extensions described in section 5.2 below). Figure 1 (c) shows the default eye-level view that participants normally experience from inside their bodies. Finally, figure 1 (d) shows a text user's view of the same scene. Note the use of simple characters to represent the conference table, walls, door and users in the text view (see the key at the right of the image). Also note the display of mutual awareness levels for users of whom we are currently aware ('O->" denotes our awareness of them, while "O<-" denotes their awareness of us). The area at the bottom of the image shows the on-going text conversation.

Figure 2 shows the same five participants using the text-to-graphics board adapter. When a user stands sufficiently close to the board and enters a message in a text client as in figure 2 (d), their message is automatically displayed on the board for graphics users to see as in figures 2 (a) to (c). Remember, graphics users can also run supplementary text clients as well.

2 (a) front perspective

2 (b) rear perspective

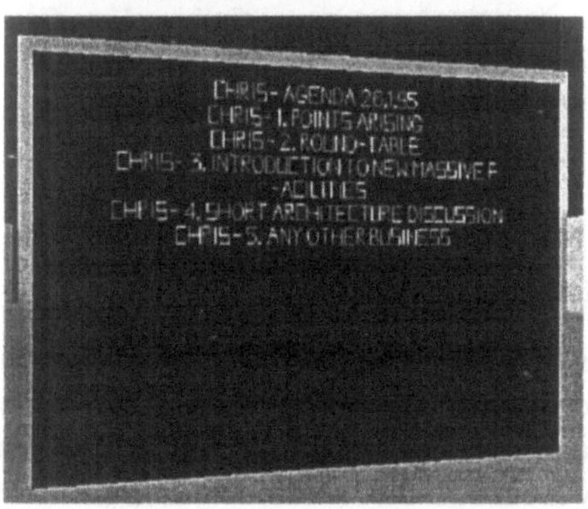

2 (c) close up of the board

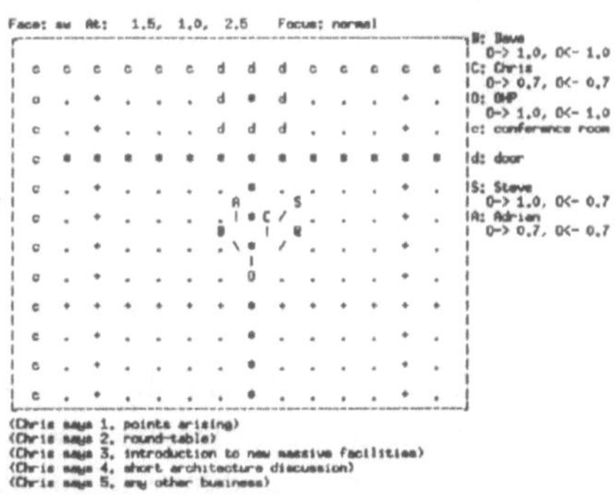

2 (d) text user's view

Figure 2: Five meeting participants using the "board" text to graphics adapter

4. MASSIVE Implementation

This section briefly describes some of the implementation techniques that have been introduced in order to provide the functionality described in the last section. In particular, we discuss the implementation of aura, focus, nimbus and adapters.

4.1. Auras and spatial trading

Interaction between objects only becomes possible if two conditions are met. First, it must be established that the objects involved support some at least one compatible medium. Second, these objects must become sufficiently proximate in order for their auras to collide. These two pre-conditions are reflected in the concept of *spatial trading*. Spatial trading combines the virtual reality technique of collision detection with the distributed systems concept of trading (e.g. [Van der Linden, 92]), or request brokering as it is sometimes called. To explain how spatial trading operates we follow the sequence of events which occurs when two objects enter a MASSIVE virtual world, move towards each other and begin to interact. This process is summarised in figure 3.

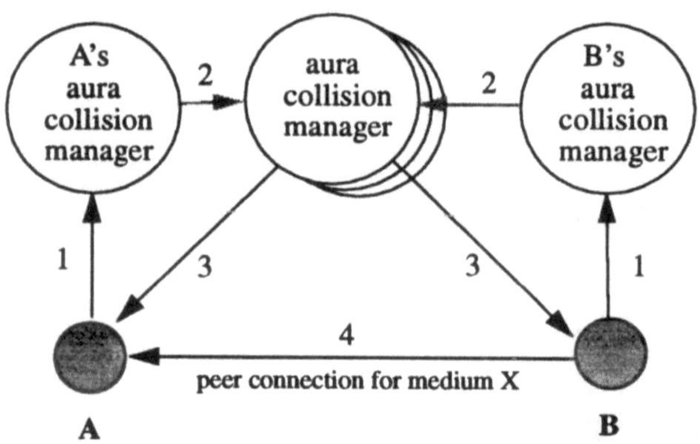

1. object declares its world and media to the local aura collision manager.

2. local aura manager passes the object on to the appropriate aura collision manager for that world.

3. aura collision manager detects collisions and passes out mutual interface references to peer objects.

4. peer objects exchange information via media controlled by awareness.

Figure 3: Objects involved in spatial trading

On entering a world, an object contacts the local spatial trader, called the *aura collision manager*, and declares the world which it wishes to join and the media which it supports. The address of this aura collision manager is the only information that an object requires in order to enter any local or linked world. An aura collision manager is responsible for detecting aura collisions for each declared medium in one or more worlds. Each aura manager has a partial locally-configured list of other aura managers and the worlds which they manage. Thus objects may be passed from one aura manager to another when they change worlds. A second object subsequently entering the world will go through the same procedure of declaring its world and media to its local aura collision manager and being passed on to the appropriate aura collision manager for that world.

Each aura collision manager monitors the auras of all objects known to it. Upon detecting an aura collision (within any given world and medium) the aura collision manager passes out mutual addresses to the objects involved, enabling them to establish a peer connection.

Notice how MASSIVE's implementation of spatial trading meets the goals of heterogeneity and scaleability. Heterogeneity is realised through the aura collision manager effectively registering all media and worlds currently active. This enables MASSIVE to dynamically cope with hitherto unseen media. Scaleability is supported by distributing the responsibility for detecting aura collisions between multiple aura collision managers, thereby avoiding excessive centralisation.

4.2. Focus and nimbus

Once connected through spatial trading the calculation of mutual awareness levels is the responsibility of the peer objects themselves. This is achieved through a simple peer protocol which allows any pair of objects to exchange information describing their positions and orientations and values of focus and nimbus. The communication protocol for each medium (e.g. graphics, audio or text) is derived by extending this basic peer protocol to handle additional medium-specific information (e.g. transmission of audio data in the case of the audio medium).

In the current implementation objects are described by a point location in space; focus and nimbus are described by mathematical functions which yield an awareness value in the range 0 (minimum) to 1 (maximum). Our current awareness function, which is used to combine focus and nimbus to give overall awareness, is multiplicative. I.e. focus and nimbus values are simply multiplied together to give awareness. This gives equal control to the observer and the observed, and is "subtractive" in nature - i.e. either party can force zero (no) awareness, but neither party can force awareness against the other's "wishes."

Our current focus and nimbus function has been designed to be general purpose so that, by changing the values of a few key parameters, a wide range foci and nimbi can be obtained. These parameters can be used to control the behaviour of focus and nimbus with respect to both the relative positions and orientations of objects. Thus, our three focus and nimbus settings and different adapters can all be realised by simply changing the values of a few key parameters while still using the same basic function code (see below). Figure 4 summarises our general focus/nimbus function using a polar coordinate model.

The left of the diagram shows how focus and nimbus are divided into three conical regions: a foreground region in which they take a maximum value; a background region in which they take some minimum value; and a transition region in which they change linearly from the foreground to the background value. The right of the diagram shows how the values of focus and nimbus depend on distance from an object and are again divided into three regions: they take the maximum value up to an initial radius; they then decay linearly to a cut off value at a second radius; beyond this, they tail off according to an inverse square law. Table II summarises the parameters which can therefore be used to control focus and nimbus.

4.3. Adapters

There are two issues to be dealt with when implementing adapter objects: how to trigger the use of an adapter and how to realise its effect on aura, focus, nimbus and awareness. Both of these issues are addressed through the introduction of a separate adapter medium. Adapters exist in their own medium, complete with its own aura, focus and nimbus. Any object wishing to use an adapter must therefore support this medium so that as the object moves about it will connect to adapters as a result of aura collisions in the adapter medium. When an object's awareness of an adapter crosses some threshold level the adapter is triggered. This mechanism enables several people to use an adapter simultaneously and also allows adapters to exhibit their own spatial properties (e.g. implementing a highly directional microphone).

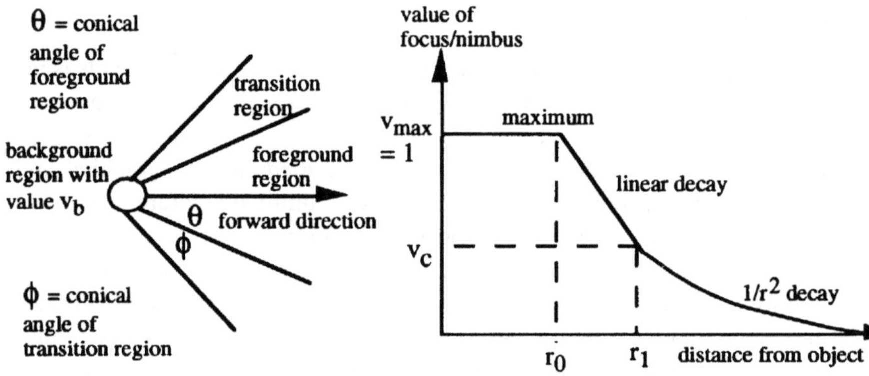

Figure 4: focus and nimbus function used by MASSIVE

name	meaning
θ	conical angle of foreground region
ϕ	conical angle of transition region
v_b	focus/nimbus value of background region
r_0	radius of extent of maximum value
r_1	radius of extent of linear transition
v_c	cut off value for linear transition

Table II: parameters affecting focus and nimbus

When triggered by an object, an adapter passes a new set of focus/nimbus parameters back to the object via the adapter medium. These new parameters replace the object's current aura, focus and nimbus parameters. Thus, an adapter may extend the range of focus or nimbus, may change their shape (i.e. conical angle) or may alter the way in which they fade to the background level. When an object subsequently moves away from an adaptor so that it is no longer triggered the object restores its original focus, nimbus and aura parameters.

Having discussed some key aspects of MASSIVE's implementation, we now turn our attention to some initial reflections arising from the implementation and early piloting activities.

5. Initial experiences

In this section we present some initial reflections on MASSIVE arising from recent experience. In particular, we reflect on two recent events: a laboratory meeting over the local area network in our own laboratory and a five site meeting between The University of Nottingham (UK), Lancaster University (UK), GMD (Germany), The Swedish Institute of Computer Science - SICS (Sweden) and the Royal Institute of Technology - KTH (Sweden), spanning three countries.

The laboratory meeting involved six participants connected over a single segment of Ethernet and lasted for half an hour. The hardware configuration was two SGI Indigo2s, a SUN 10 ZX and two SGI Indys, so that each participant was capable of using the audio, graphical and textual media. All but two of the participants were in physically separate rooms and even these two had their backs to each other and were using headphones. The six participants included the developer of MASSIVE, four users who had previously been involved in demonstrations and one novice user. The task was to conduct our weekly laboratory meeting, involving a round table presentation from each person followed by a loosely chaired free discussion. The view of one of the participants was captured on video and participants were asked to quickly write down their own reflections after the meeting's close.

The five site distributed meeting involved eight participants, three at Nottingham, one at Lancaster, two at SICS, one at KTH and one at GMD, and lasted for an hour and a half. All of the participants were audio/graphical. Each person was in a physically isolated space. Once again, the proceedings were videoed and participants were encouraged to write down their own observations.

The following informal observations constitute a rough and ready summary of what happened. Their main purpose is to identify some of the immediate and major issues that should be addressed in order to progress virtual reality tele-conferencing to a more useful state. Where appropriate we propose possible solutions.

5.1. It works!

First it must be stated that, technically at least, it works. It was straight-forward to install the software at each site onto standard machines via FTP and we would be confident of doing this at other sites. Configuring the wide area meeting took a little time and there were some minor teething problems, but nothing serious. It was not necessary to book time on networks or schedule conference calls. The meeting was open to as many participants as wanted to join at each site and people could come and go as they pleased.

Second, it was fun. The participants clearly enjoyed themselves and there were several light hearted moments (particularly involving the text-to-speech translator).

Third, the machines and the network coped, albeit under strain at times. Sometimes the graphics slowed down and the audio broke up (problems of packet based audio), but most of the time people could communicate.

The experience uncovered some interesting issues.

5.2. Limited peripheral awareness

A key goal of MASSIVE is providing the ability to separate what is immediate from what is peripheral. However, in the graphics medium, the current field of view seems to be too limited to provide a powerful sense of periphery at the edges of ones field of vision (although periphery in terms of distance *is* experienced). The screen based view has a default field of view of 64 degrees and although this can be widened (a parameter can be set in the graphics client code) larger fields of view introduce serious perspective distortion. Our current headmounted display, a Virtual Research EyeGen 3, has a field of view of width 40-50 degrees (although this wasn't used in the trial meetings). It is possible to buy headmounts with wider fields, but usually at the cost of lower resolution. Thus, in neither the screen based nor the immersive modes can we achieve anywhere near our real-world field of view of about 150 degrees width. The clearest indication of this problem was the difficulty experienced by participants in the, usually simple, act of forming a circle at the start of the laboratory meeting.

Our immediate solution to this problem has been to provide users with a choice of new 'camera angles' from which to view the world, coupled with the ability to zoom in and out on each of them. In addition to the normal 'in-body' view, users may now adopt a perspective view over the shoulder, a birds eye view, a front on view looking at themselves and side views. They may also adopt multiple simultaneous viewpoints which track one another (e.g. simultaneous in-body and birds eye views). In addition, given MASSIVE's flexible distributed architecture, it is easy to dynamically attach these additional viewpoints to other people, not just to oneself. Thus, one might view the world through someone else's eyes. In turn, this poses the question of how and when to configure different combinations of viewpoints. One approach might be to extend adapter objects towards being more general configuration management tools. For example, in addition to adapting my aura, focus and nimbus, the conference table adapter described above might automatically provide me with an additional birds eye view of the table while I am seated at it.

5.3.Navigation difficulties

There were numerous examples of people experiencing problems moving about, one of the most common being a tendency to fall backwards into portals through which one has just emerged. There was an obvious difference between novice and more experienced users which suggests a significant learning curve, but even experienced users still encountered problems. At a finer level of detail, current interaction techniques for moving one's virtual head and body appear too unwieldy to support rapid movement. This is particularly true when using a mouse to drive the screen based interface. When combined with a limited field of view this hampers the ability to use gaze direction or even body position to negotiate turn taking in conversation (see below). The use of magnetic tracking devices attached to the user's head may speed up interaction, but current devices still suffer from noticeable lag. The solution seems to lie in the development and use of better tracking devices and more "exotic" controls for screen based systems.

5.4. Lack of engagement

There were a number of breakdowns in the conversation, including several cases of participants being unsure as to whether they had been heard. Although there were some examples of back channels, these were generally few and far between. There might be several causes for this, including the lack of consistent audio quality and hence lack of confidence in being heard as well as considerable variability of microphone sensitivity. However, we suspect that there may be more general problems with engaging other users. In particular, even though the current graphics medium allows one to tell at a glance who is present in the current conversational group and who is approaching and leaving, lack of fine detail such as precise gaze direction make it hard to tell who is directly attending at any moment in time. Lack of visual feedback as to when people are speaking may be another factor here.

Immediate steps might involve improving the quality and reliability of the audio channel as well as the consistency of microphones and other audio hardware. Longer term work might involve analysing and reproducing key aspects of facial expressions such as eye-tracking and mouth movement as in the work of [Ohya, 93] and [Thalmann,93]. A small step has already been taken in this direction with the addition of a simple graphics mouth to the default MASSIVE embodiment which appears when the user speaks. Alternatively, one could consider texture mapping real time video onto embodiments as in the "Talking Heads" of [Brand, 87].

5.5. Degree of presence

Several times during the meetings, it became clear that the inhabitants of various embodiments had become involved in external activities and were not fully present. The most extreme case involved one user blatantly ignoring another even though they were being directly addressed. The problem here seems to involve conveying the degree of presence of different participants. This relates to the above problem of engagement and might be at least partially addressed through the same mechanisms (i.e. reproduction of dynamic user information such as facial expressions). However, one might also allow users to explicitly switch their body between different degrees of presence. In such cases, uninhabited bodies might act as markers or contact points for alerting their owners and inviting them to communicate (i.e. one would "prod" a body in order to grab the attention of its owner). Using the spatial model, one could construct a body which alerted its user only when directly addressed and which otherwise monitored background conversation (perhaps recording it).

5.6. Different perceptions of space

A more surprising observation concerns inter-working between 3-D graphics users and 2-D text users. Although they are mutually visible within a common space, their perception of that space seems quite different. In particular, the "texties" seem to lack any notion of personal space and tend to stand directly in front of others or even walk straight through them. In contrast, graphics users tend to maintain a reasonable distance from others. The problem may be that the graphics field of view is much more limited than the textual one (which is 360 degrees) so that the graphics users are forced to stand back in order to obtain a decent view. On the other hand, it may be that the graphics view is sufficiently rich for people to more easily associate the embodiments they see with other people and so feel compelled to behave in a socially polite manner in contrast to the text users. Either way, there appear to be some deeper issues involved when users with radically different interfaces interact in a common space.

6. Conclusions

This paper has described a prototype virtual reality based tele-conferencing system called MASSIVE. We begin our conclusions by considering how the implementation of MASSIVE meets the general design goals listed in the introduction.

- MULTIPLE PARTICIPANTS: the system demonstrably supports groups of at least six concurrent users.
- MUTLI-MEDIA: communication is possible in audio, visual and textual media.
- HETEROGENEITY: these three media can be arbitrarily combined accord-

ing to a user's terminal equipment and requirements. Furthermore, users may be embodied in media which they cannot display themselves (thus, text and graphics users can communicate). The concept of spatial trading has been introduced whereby the communication capabilities of users are dynamically matched whenever they become sufficiently proximate. Finally, text to speech and text to graphics translator adapter objects have been provided to further enhance cross-medium communication.

- SPATIAL MEDIATION: the implementation of the spatial model of interaction means that users' perceptions of one another in any given medium are sensitive to their relative positions and orientations; this is done with the intention of replacing traditional conference floor-control with a more autonomous and natural form of mediation.
- BALANCE OF POWER: conversation is influenced through movement, and everyone is free to move as they want at any time. Furthermore, support for both focus and nimbus means that the transmitter and receiver can both influence how any given utterance is eventually perceived. Adapter objects such as the podium alter this power balance without destroying it.
- VARIED MEETING SCENARIOS: in its most basic mode the system supports face-to-face conversation. However, the use of narrow focus and nimbus settings and also the conference table allow for more private discussions within a shared space. Similarly, the podium supports presentations and lectures to larger groups. So different worlds can be configured to support different meeting styles and sizes by including different adapters and scenery.
- SIMULTANEOUS MEETINGS: these are supported at several levels of granularity. First, different meetings may be held at the same time but in different worlds. Second, several meetings may be held in the same world at the same time, separated by simple partitions or just by distance. If these meetings are far apart they will be completely oblivious to one another; if they are close some mutual awareness may spill over (e.g. participants in one meeting may be able to see that the other meeting is happening without being able to hear what is being said). Participants are free to move between meetings at any time.
- WIDE AREA: Operation over wide area networks has been successfully demonstrated. This is encouraged by allowing each site to construct and master their own worlds locally, and then to connect them to remote ones via portals (similar to the way information is published on the World Wide Web).
- SCALE: The implementation of aura and spatial trading enhances the scaleability of system by removing the necessity for an object to maintain connections to all others objects all of the time. Providing multiple worlds also aids scaling. Finally, in a more pragmatic sense, the heterogeneous nature of MASSIVE encourages greater participation in worlds by allowing as many users as possible to participate using a wide range of technologies.

We are pleased to report that, from a technical perspective, the system works and has been used to hold multi-site meetings over wide area networks. However, several key issues have been identified that require further consideration including providing richer peripheral awareness, supporting easier and more rapid navigation, resolving problems with engagement, conveying varying degrees of presence and reconciling differences in perception between 2-D and 3-D users. These issues provide an agenda for future research along with the general problem of redesigning MASSIVE to support far greater numbers of users than at present.

To conclude, the MASSIVE system represents an early attempt to develop a collaborative virtual environment for tele-conferencing. We argue that, in spite of a number of challenges that have arisen, MASSIVE demonstrates the potential of such environments to go beyond our current tele-conferencing and shared space environments towards more flexible, natural and scalable future systems.

Acknowledgements

This work has been sponsored by the UK's Engineering and Physical Sciences Research Council (EPSRC) through their PhD studentship programme and by the Commission of the European Communities (CEC) through their ESPRIT Basic Research Programme.We would also like to thank Lennart Fahlén and John Bowers for their work on the spatial model. We would also like to thank Adrian Bullock, Rob Ingram, Dave Snowdon and Ok Ki Lee of the University of Nottingham; Andy Colbourne, Gareth Smith and Tom Rodden of Lancaster University; Lannart Fahlén of SICS; Kai-Mikael J-Aro of KTH; John Bowers of the University of Manchester; Mel Slater and Rob Kooper of QMW; and Dave England of GMD for volunteering to be cybernauts (we did consider using dogs, monkeys and rats at first, but they were too smart to volunteer ;-)).

References

[Benford, 93] Benford, S. and Fahlén,L., A Spatial Model of Interaction for Large Virtual Environments, In Proc. ECSCW'93 - Third European Conference on Computer Supported Cooperative Work, Milano, September, 1993, Kluwer Academic Publishers.

[Brand, 87] Brand, S., The Medialab - Inventing the future at MIT, Viking Penguin, 1987, ISBN 0-670-81442-3, p. 91-93.

[Carlsson, 93] Carlsson, C., and Hagsand, O., DIVE - A Platform for Multi-User Virtual Environments, Computer & Graphics, Vol 17, No. 6, 1993, pp. 663-669.

[Ohya, 93] Ohya, J., Kitamura, Y., Takemura, H., Kishino, F., Terashima, N., Real-time Reproduction of 3D Human Images in Virtual Space Teleconferencing, in Proc.VRAIS'93, IEEE, Seattle Washington September, 1993, pp. 408-414.

[Thalmann, 93] Thalmann, D., Using Virtual Reality Techniques in the Animation Process, in Virtual Reality Systems, Earnshaw, R.A., Gigante, M.A and Jones, H. (eds), Academic Press, 1993, ISBN 0-12-227748-1.

[Van der Linden, 92] Van Der Linden, R.J., and Sventek, J.S., The ANSA Trading Service, in IEEE Distributed Processing Technical Committee Newsletter, Vol 14, No 1, (Special Issue on Naming Facilities in Internet Environments and Distributed Systems), pp 28-34, June 1992.

Proceedings of the Fourth European Conference on Computer-Supported Cooperative Work,
September 10–14, Stockholm, Sweden
H. Marmolin, Y. Sundblad, and K. Schmidt (Editors)

Can the GestureCam be a Surrogate?

Hideaki Kuzuoka, Gen Ishimoda, Yushi Nishimura
Institute of Engineering Mechanics, University of Tsukuba, Japan

Ryutaro Suzuki, Kimio Kondo
National Institute of Multimedia Education, Ministry of Education, Japan

The GestureCam is a remote-controlled actuator onto which a small camera and laser pointer are mounted. The term "GestureCam System" includes other user interfaces which control the GestureCam, such as the master actuator and the touch-sensitive CRT. We expect the system to act as the surrogate of a remote person. In order to clarify advantages and problems of the GestureCam system, we conducted some experiments. As a result of those experiments, we found that the GestureCam has the ability to support gaze awareness and remote finger pointing. We also found, however, that the system has some problems which need to be refined.

INTRODUCTION

When we collaborate, we share not only the papers which may be on a desk, but often three-dimensional (3-D) objects dispersed in 3-D space as well. Since 1987, the authors have been working on a video communication system which supports remote collaboration in a 3-D environment (Kuzuoka, 1992 and Kuzuoka et al., 1994). Through our research, we discovered some of the problems of previous video communication systems.

- **Problem of Static Cameras**
  In "The Affordances of Media Spaces for Collaboration," Gaver points out that "camera and microphones are stationary or only moved re-

motely, preventing perceptual exploration (Gaver, 1992)." Remote control cameras seem to be effective in dealing with this problem. We wish to clarify the type of remote control camera that is required for effective video communication.

- **Problem of Gaze Awareness**
  Gaze awareness is known to be an important factor in predicting a person's interest. ClearBoard (Ishii et al., 1992) is one of the most effective systems available which supports gaze awareness for shared drawing tasks. Since the system is static, however, gaze awareness of the objects in the 3-D environment cannot be supported.

- **Problem of Remote Pointing**
  With existing video-mediated communication systems, it is hard to point at an object at a remote site. Gaver (Gaver, 1992) wrote that "we can reach into other peoples' views, almost literally grasping their attention and directing it to oneself or to a relevant direction." In current media space, however, "one can't gesture within a shared space because of the barrier presented by monitor screens."

  VideoDraw (Tang & Minneman, 1990), ClearBoard and Double DigitalDesk (Wellner, 1993) use superimposed real hand images, [1] and this method is known to be very effective. Since the cameras are static, however, only objects on the drawing surface can be pointed at.

We are interested in determining the types of technology which effectively solve the above-mentioned problems. This paper describes what we learned from our experiments using the GestureCam system.

GestureCam System

The GestureCam system was developed to support communication between an instructor and an operator. An instructor is able to give instructions remotely to an operator on how to accomplish a given task. Although the system was described in a previous paper (Kuzuoka et al., 1994), we will briefly describe it again here.

GestureCam

The GestureCam is an actuator with three degrees of freedom of movement. A small finger-sized camera and a laser pointer are mounted on the actuator. The GestureCam is controlled remotely by an instructor, and the instructor can look around a remote site freely. The laser pointer is used to point at a certain object in the same way that a finger points.

[1] In the case of the Double Digital Desk, hand images were projected down onto the desk.

Because the GestureCam moves in front of the operator and is highly visible, operators can involuntarily sense its motion with their peripheral vision. Therefore, it is expected that the GestureCam supports remote gaze awareness, and operators can predict that an instructor may point inside his or her field of view. In this way, the laser pointer helps define the area which is being pointed at. This feature of the GestureCam is expected to support smooth communication in 3D environments.

Interfaces to Control the GestureCam

In this paper, "GestureCam" refers to the remotely-controlled camera actuator. The term "GestureCam system" includes the user interface which controls the GestureCam. Currently two types of user interface have been developed to control the GestureCam.

Master Actuator The master actuator is identical to the GestureCam, but a camera and laser pointer are not mounted onto it. The instructor changes the position of the master actuator with his/her hand; then, the GestureCam mimics the movements of the master actuator until it ends up in the same position as the master actuator.

Touch-Sensitive CRT A touch-sensitive CRT is also used in the system to control the GestureCam and to superimpose annotations on the video image.

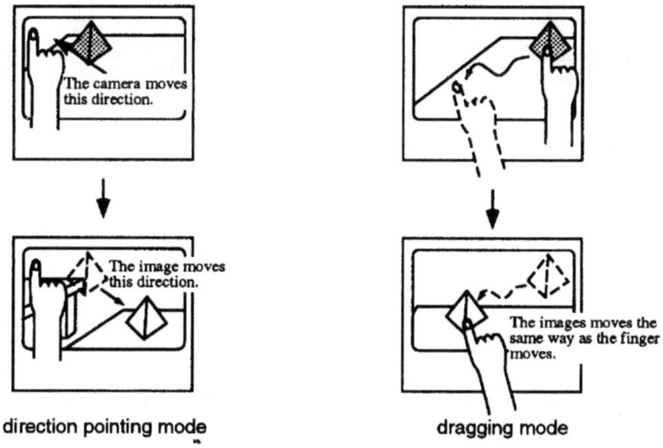

Figure 1. Controlling modes of the touch panel.

Two control modes of the GestureCam (e.g. direction pointing mode, and dragging mode) were tested (Fig. 1): the direction pointing mode and the dragging mode. In the direction pointing mode, a user touches the screen and the camera moves toward the spot that was touched. The speed and the direction in which the camera moves is defined by the distance and direction from the center of the display to where the user points to. In the dragging mode, a user changes the image on the display by "dragging" a finger across the display.

Using a touch sensitive CRT, it was also possible to superimpose drawings on a displayed image. Instructors could use their finger to draw lines and write annotations. The superimposed image that is created can then be seen by both the instructor and the operator. Thus, it was possible for the instructor to specify an object or remote position in two ways: either by using the laser pointer on the GestureCam, or by using superimposed drawings(Fig. 2).

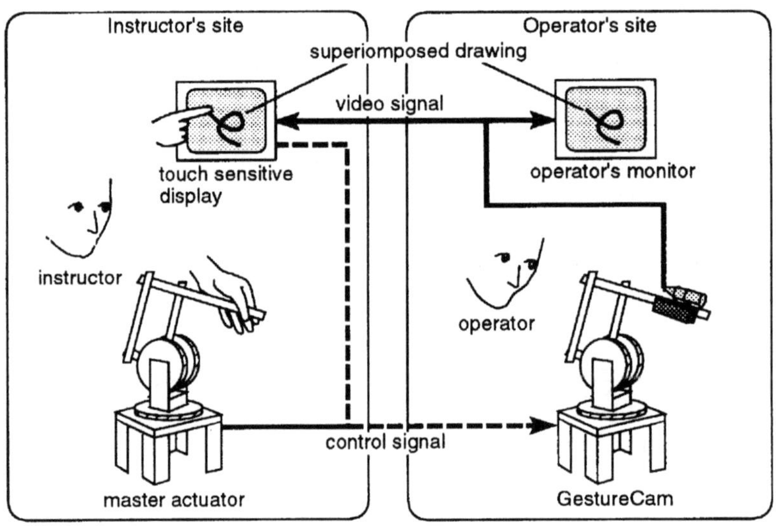

Figure 2. An example configuration of the GestureCam system.

Expected Advantages of the GestureCam System

We anticipate the possibility of the GestureCam acting as a surrogate (Sellen & Buxton, 1992) instructor. That is, we expect the GestureCam to be able to function as the instructor's head, eyes, and finger. In order to evaluate that possibility, we wished to investigate the following points:

- Can the instructor control the GestureCam easily enough so that he/she can look around and point at an object as he/she wishes?

- Can the operator detect the GestureCam's motion and the GestureCam's (e.g. instructor's) gaze naturally?
- Is the laser pointer an effective way to point at an object? How good or bad is the laser pointer compared to the superimposed drawings?

Predictability Experiment Without Communication

By conducting the experiment described in this section, we wished to determine the ability of the GestureCam in supporting gaze awareness.

Task The GestureCam and the small liquid crystal display (LCD) were set in front of the operator. An image from the GestureCam's camera was shown on the LCD. A cross was superimposed at the center of the display (Fig. 3). At first, the operator closed his/her eyes. While he/she was closed his/her eyes, the instructor controlled the GestureCam so that the cross overlapped a pre-defined object in the room. The operator then opened their eyes when the instructor said "yes" to so indicate. Immediately after the operator opened their eyes, he/she tried to find the real object corresponding to the object indicated on the LCD. When the operator found the object, he/she said "yes". The time between the instructor's "yes" and the operator's "yes" was measured.

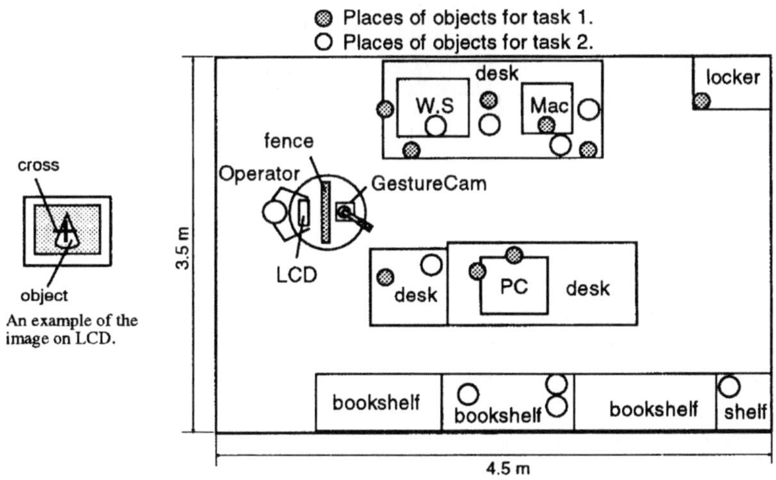

Figure 3. An overview of the predictability experiment.

Fourteen subjects served as operators, and each subject performed two test runs. In the first run (case 1), the operator could see the GestureCam. In the second run (case 2), a small fence was placed between the operator and the GestureCam so that the operator could not see the GestureCam. Two types of tasks (task 1 and 2) were used: seven subjects (group 1) were given task 1 as case 1 and task 2 as case 2. The other seven subjects (group 2) were given the tasks in the reverse order(Table I). We did this to alleviate the effects of the experience.

Table I. Visibility of the GestureCam in the predictability experiment.

	task 1	task 2
group 1	visible (case 1)	invisible (case 2)
group 2	invisible (case 2)	visible (case 1)

Result Figure 4 shows the average time and the standard deviation to find an object. It was statistically significant that operators could find objects faster when the GestureCam was visible. (t=4.6).

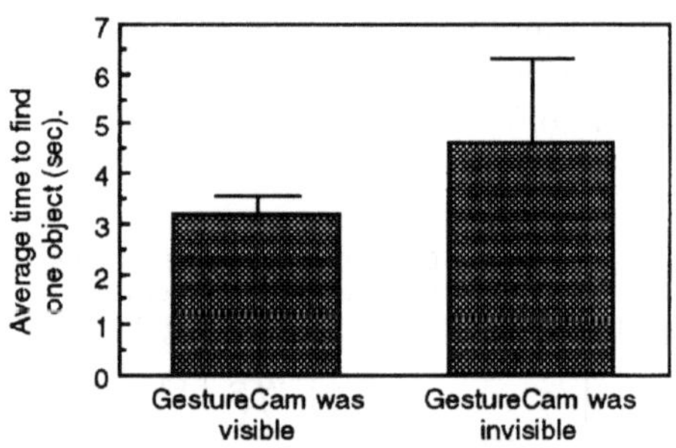

Figure 4. Average time to find one object.

From the results shown, we can assume that the positioning of the GestureCam helped operators find an object faster. According to the interviews with test subjects, the GestureCam was most effective when the object shown was relatively large in proportion to the background in the display to a degree where that background was not seen very well. Also, the GestureCam was most effective when the object was not in the field of view of the operator.

REMOTE INSTRUCTION EXPERIMENTS

In the two experiments described in this section, the instructor gave instructions on some tasks remotely to the operator. The goal of these experiments is to determine the advantages and problems of the current GestureCam system. In order to achieve this, the instructor gave instructions to the operator under various realistic communication conditions.

Experiment 1

In experiment 1, the instructor and the operator were separated by approximately 50 kilometers. The ETS-V communication satellite was used to transmit voice and video and a telephone line was used for computer communication. The transmission delay for the satellite was slightly less than one second. In order to identify as many problems as possible, our research staff acted as instructors and attempted to use GestureCam's functions in an aggressive manner. The operators were university students in the engineering department.

During the test sessions, the instructors asked operators to make an electronic circuit and observe its output with an oscilloscope. Initially, the equipment was placed at various locations and the operators were asked to retrieve them and position them as they wished. The instructors had to instruct the students on such tasks as how to connect the power supply and how to operate the oscilloscope (Fig. 5).

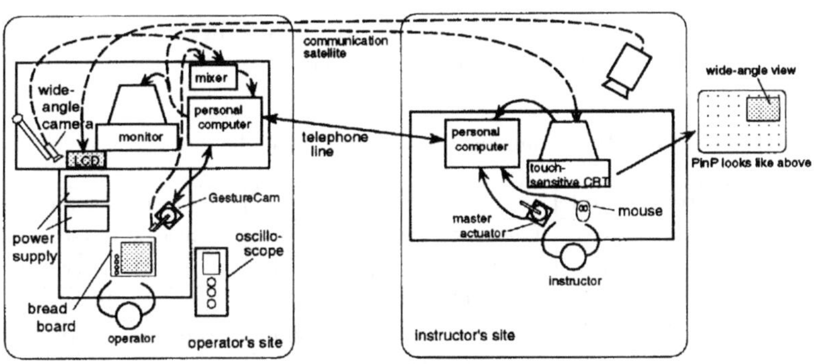

Figure 5. An overview of experiment 1.

There were various parameters for the user interface. To control the GestureCam, either the master actuator or a touch-sensitive CRT could be used. When the touch-sensitive CRT was used, only the dragging mode was available to specify the GestureCam's movement. In addition to the GestureCam, a wide angle camera attached to a cantilevered desk lamp provided an additional view. When the GestureCam was used, an image from the wide-angle camera could be displayed within a smaller area on the monitor. We refer to that image as "picture in picture," or "PinP." When the GestureCam was not used, the image from the wide-angle camera was displayed on the entire screen. Due to limitations of the system, when the master actuator was used to control the GestureCam, only one of either the laser pointer or superimposed mouse cursor could be used to specify positions.

When the touch-sensitive CRT was used, both the laser pointer and superimposed drawings could be used. When only the wide-angle camera was used, only superimposed drawings could be used; in this situation, the instructor could also verbally ask the operator to change the camera's direction during the session. During every session, the instructor's image was also transmitted via satellite and displayed on a small LCD at the operator's site. Table II shows the conditions of communication for each session. The first and the second sessions had identical conditions.

Six subjects served as the operator, and each session lasted between 30 and 50 minutes. After the experiments, the subjects were interviewed and their comments have been compiled as part of the Appendix.

In order to study the subjects' activities, we recorded the number of times the GestureCam was controlled and the number of the times that the operator followed it's motion, i.e. the operator changed his/her head direction or gaze according the motion of the GestureCam. Table III shows the number of GestureCam movements and the number of times that the operator followed those motions. Table IV shows the method instructors used when he/she specified positions. "Verbal" refers to the fact that the instructors did not use one word directions such as "this" or "that" in specifiying positions, but that more descriptive verbal expressions were used.

Table II. The conditions of communication for experiment 1.

session	control method	camera view	pointing method
1-1	master slave	GestureCam+PinP wide	mouse cursor+laser
1-2	master slave	GestureCam+PinP wide	mouse cursor+laser
1-3	master slave	GestureCam	laser
1-4	touch CRT	GestureCam+PinP wide	superimp. drawing+laser
1-5	touch CRT	GestureCam	superimp. drawing+laser
1-6	–	wide camera	superimp. drawing

As table III shows, the instructors moved the GestureCam many times during the sessions. It is worth noting that when the GestureCam was not used in session 6, the instructor of the session stated that he felt it to be an inconvenience.

Experiment 2

In order to study the effectiveness of the GestureCam System on novice users, a further experiment was conducted in which both instructors and operators were not comprised of our research staff. This time, the instructor and the operator

Table III. The number of GestureCam's motions and the number of times that the operator followed those motions in experiment 1.

session	GestureCam's motion	Operator followed GestureCam
1-1	63	32
1-2	62	unknown
1-3	106	45
1-4	37	7
1-5	25	5
1-6	–	–

Table IV. Frequency of activities according to methods of pointing for experiment 1.

session	verbal	laser	superimpose
1-1	23	17	0
1-2	29	4	7
1-3	32	15	–
1-4	25	1	45
1-5	17	3	18
1-6	21	–	18

were situated in close enough proximity that the video signals were transmitted through an NTSC video cable. As a result, there were no transmission delays. The task was to connect some video equipment (TV camera and device A, B, and C in Fig. 6) and to operate them. This task was much simpler than that given in experiment 1, and each session lasted between 3 and 9 minutes. The participants also had more flexible communication conditions.

In this experiment, there were also various parameters for the user interface. To control the GestureCam, either the master actuator or the touch-sensitive CRT was used. When the touch-sensitive CRT was used, the instructor could choose from either of these modes: the direction pointing mode or the dragging mode.

Normally, both the laser pointer and superimposed drawings could be used and the instructor could choose either method during instruction. In the case of sessions 1 and 2, however, the operator's monitor was turned off and the instructor could not use superimposed drawings.

Table V shows the parameters of communication for experiment 2. Table VI shows the number of the GestureCam's motions and the number of times that the operator followed those motions. Table VII shows the method instructors used when he/she specified positions. After the experiments, the subjects were interviewed about the usability of the system, and again, these comments are chronicled in the Appendix.

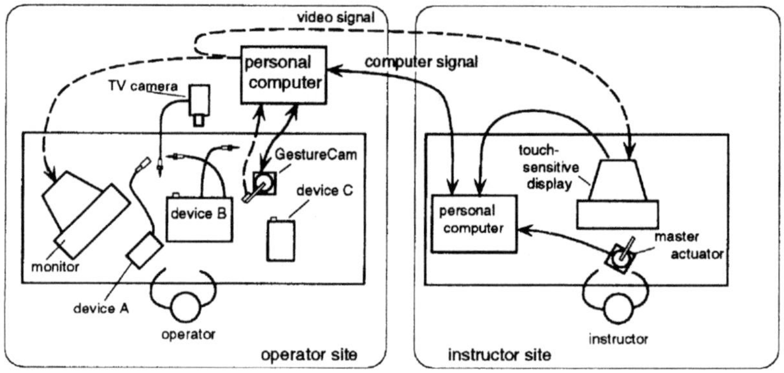

Figure 6. An overview of experiment 2

Table V. Conditions of Communication for Experiment 2.

session	control method	operator's monitor	pointing method
2-1	master slave	no	laser
2-2	master slave	no	laser
2-3	master slave	yes	superimp. drawing+laser
2-4	master slave	yes	superimp. drawing+laser
2-5	touch CRT	yes	superimp. drawing+laser
2-6	touch CRT	yes	superimp. drawing+laser

As Table VI shows, the instructors moved the GestureCam many times during the sessions of experiment 2. It is clear from the results of both experiments 1 and 2 that the remote-control camera is effective for these kinds of tasks.

DISCUSSION

Controllability of the GestureCam

Although the remote-control camera is useful for both experiments 1 and 2, handling the currently existing master actuator seems to require some skill. This was demonstrated by the fact that when the instructor wanted to turn the GestureCam approximately 180 degrees, or when the instructor wished to look downward or at an object close to the GestureCam, the instructor had to hold the master actuator in an uncomfortable, unnatural way. In order to deal with this problem, the mechanism needs more degrees of freedom to enable it to explore 3D space. Although the master actuator's structure does not

Table VI. The number of the GestureCam's motions and the number of times that the operator followed the GestureCam's motions for experiment 2.

session	GestureCam's motion	Operator followed GestureCam
2-1	10	8
2-2	17	12
2-3	13	1
2-4	13	4
2-5	11	5
2-6	16	2

Table VII. Frequency of activities according to methods of pointing for experiment 2

session	verbal	laser	superimpose
2-1	1	9	–
2-2	4	15	–
2-3	2	11	0
2-4	2	6	4
2-5	0	2	7
2-6	6	7	2

necessarily have to be identical to that of the GestureCam, a new structure that will enable the instructor to conveniently look around him/her approximately 360 degrees is required.

When the instructor controlled the laser pointer with the master actuator, many instructors claimed that the fine control of the pointing position was difficult. Generally, as the instructor of 2-2 stated, the touch-sensitive CRT was preferable for fine control functions such as pointing to an object with the laser pointer, and the master-actuator was preferred for functions requiring less control. When the touch-sensitive CRT was used, however, some instructors often lost sense of which direction the GestureCam was looking at. Therefore, when they wished to look at an object which was not within the field of view of the camera, they did not know which way to look and how much to turn the GestureCam.

From these results, we noticed both the advantages and disadvantages of the current master actuator and the touch-sensitive CRT. We therefore plan to use the master actuator and touch-sensitive CRT simultaneously. If the master actuator were to be equipped with a motor, the GestureCam and the master-actuator would move in unison when the instructor used the touch-sensitive CRT, and the instructor would be able to determine the GestureCam's position by that of the the master actuator.

Position and Direction Specifications

Once the instructor was able to point at a certain object, the operator liked the laser pointer because it can do so directly; it is an especially potentially useful device when an object is relatively small and when one object among similar objects should be specified. TableVII shows that when the superimposed mode was not available (session2-1 and 2-2), instructors used the laser pointer many times and verbal expressions did not increase substantially. This result indicates that the laser pointer was useful to some extent. The problem of the laser pointer, however, lies in the controllability of its positions, which is less than desirable; one instructor also noted that the laser spot was too small to point at a small object. Furthermore, when there was a delay in transmission such as in experiment 1, the instructors tended to use more verbal expressions to express their instructions, rather than relying on the laser pointer(Table IV).

With our prototype, it was faster to point at an object by the use of superimposed drawings than by using the laser pointer. This was one of the main reasons why instructors preferred the superimposed drawing mode. If the control of the laser pointer's position can be fine-tuned to where it becomes much easier and faster to use, it will probably be used more often. Another advantage of superimposed drawings was its expressive ability. For example, by drawing a circle around an object, the instructor could specify the whole equipment and not simply a button on it. Also, the instructor could express directions by drawing arrows.

To incorporate both the expressive ability of the superimposed drawing method, and the direct pointing capability of the laser pointer, one of the solutions may be to employ a laser drawing facility and draw directly onto the object. Small mechanisms for laser drawings, however, would have to be developed.

Different Orientation Towards the Shared Object

When superimposed drawings were used to point at an object or to show direction, some communication problems were observed due to the different orientations toward the shared object.

When the laser pointer was used, since the pointer pointed directly at the real object, this type of problem was not observed. In contrast, however, the laser pointer cannot express directional information; laser drawings would be useful in alleviating this problem.

Predictability

In experiment 2, when the operator's monitor was turned off (session 2-1 and 2-2), the operator often looked at the GestureCam. Furthermore, the operators of session 2-1 and 2-2 said they looked at the GestureCam's motion. Thus, we can assume that the GestureCam was regarded as the surrogate of the instructor's eyes in that it has shown its ability to support gaze awareness. When the operator's monitor was turned on, however, the operator looked mostly at the monitor to ascertain the instructor's view. When the instructor kept the laser pointer turned on, some operators looked at the laser spot but not at the GestureCam while it was moving.

From this observation, the operators apparently preferred a more precise information of the instructor's view, such as that which was obtained from the operator's monitor or the laser spot. We do not feel, however, that the GestureCam is entirely irrelevant. The GestureCam was most likely seen through peripheral vision, and provided some help in locating the real object. Furthermore, the GestureCam was used for confirmation (2-5-ope), especially when it moved a lot (2-4-ope). For the time being, the best solution is to prepare the GestureCam and the operator's monitor at the same time.

If the GestureCam could be controlled faster and more accurately, an operator might look at the GestureCam more, but further studies must be conducted to confirm this. On the other hand, if the monitor can be mounted on the GestureCam in such a way that it does not cause a difference in orientation between the instructor and operator, the monitor would also be an effective way to support gaze awareness. One possibility is to mount a Liquid Crystal Display (LCD) on the GestureCam.

Usefulness of Wide-Angle Cameras

When the wide-angle camera was not used, instructors sometimes faced difficulties in locating an object which was out of the camera's view. In addition, when the master actuator was not used, although the camera moved continuously, the instructor did not know which direction the GestureCam was looking at.

The wide-angle camera seems to be effective in alleviating these problems. However, even though this method can save transmission bandwidth, the PinP is unfortunately obtrusive. If possible, the wide angle view should be displayed on a separate screen. If that is not possible because of insufficient transmission bandwidth, (in experiment 1, only one channel was available for video transmission), the system should allow an instructor to be able to turn the PinP on and off at will. One instructor suggested that the wide-angle view's refresh rate can be lower than the GestureCam's view. If this is true, it may save even more of the video transmission capacity.

Face View

Gaver wrote that tasks such as those presented in this paper do not require a substantial face-to-face view, but he also pointed out that it does not mean that a face-to-face view is entirely unnecessary. In experiment 1, when the instructors did not say anything for a while, many operators looked at the LCD. During these times, the operators did not necessarily want to look at the instructor's face, but they wanted to see what the instructor was doing. Thus, it may be preferable to include the work area of the instructor and not only the instructor in the view.

CONCLUSIONS

For the GestureCam to become a surrogate of the instructor, smooth control of the mechanism appears to be very important in supporting communication. Thus, the user interface should be considered both from instructor's side and the operator's side. The following items should be considered:

- A remote-control camera is more effective than a static camera in supporting 3D tasks. One of the most important factors in improving the effectiveness of the GestureCam, however, is to create a faster and more accurate control of the mechanism. If this factor is not at a satisfactory level, users will tend to rely more on verbal expressions rather than controlling the GestureCam.

- It seems that both the GestureCam's motion and monitor could support gaze awareness. Also, it seems that both the master actuator and touch-sensitive CRT have advantages over controlling the GestureCam and specifying positions; however, even though it is common knowledge to groupware researchers, we recognize that each person has his/her own preference. Thus, we will refine the system so that users can choose and change to any interface as they wish. In other words, we will try to support the seamlessness of tools (Stefik & Brown, 1989).

Appendix

Following are the opinions expressed about the controllability of the GestureCam. Their opinions are numbered in this manner: "1-3-ope". The first number is the experiment number. The Second number is the session number of each experiment. The third word indicates who stated the opinion. "ins" stands for instructor, "ope" stands for operator, and "obs" stands for an observer who is part of our research staff. The observers' opinions are based on their observation of each session.

Controllability of the GestureCam

- **1-3-ins** "Since fine control of the GestureCam was not easy, it was not easy to point at a small object with the laser pointer."

- **1-4-obs** "When I turned the GestureCam almost 180 degrees using the touch-sensitive CRT, it took a longer time than to use the master actuator."
- **1-5-ins** "I sometimes did not know the GestureCam's posture."
- **1-6-ins** "Even though the wide-angle camera was used, the static camera is inconvenient and it is troublesome to ask the operator to move the camera."
- **2-1-ope** "It was irritating to wait for the laser spot to point at an object."
- **2-2-ins** "It was hard to point at a place close to the GestureCam, and low places. For controlling the laser pointer, I like the dragging mode of the touch-sensitive CRT the best. To look around, or to look for an object, the master actuator was better."
- **2-4-ins** "There was no problem in controlling the master actuator, but the laser spot was too small to point at a small object."
- **2-6-ins** (He used the master actuator after the session and said,) "I can control the GestureCam easily because I could imagine its posture."

Position and Direction Specifications

- **1-4-ins** "It is easier to use superimposed drawings than the laser pointer to point at an object."
- **1-4-ope** "Both superimposed drawings and the laser pointer have their merits."
- **1-4-obs** "Mostly superimposed drawings were used to show direction."
- **2-1-ope** "The laser pointer is convenient for pointing at small objects."
- **2-2-ins** "The laser pointer is convenient for pointing at one object among similar objects."
- **2-4-ins** "The superimposed drawing was convenient for specifying bigger objects."
- **2-4-ope** "I prefer the laser pointer over superimposed drawings."
- **2-6-ins** "I prefer superimposed drawings because I can point at an object faster."

Different Orientation Towards the Shared Object

- **1-1-ope** "When I compared the object in the monitor to the real object, they looked as if they were different objects."
- **1-6-ope** "When I was told something like 'On the screen, right direction,' it was not easy to understand which direction in the real world."
- **2-6-ins** "Because orientation towards the object was different between the operator and the GestureCam, I sometimes had difficulties in giving instructions."
- **2-6-ope** "When I saw superimposed drawings, I got confused because the orientation towards the object was different. In this respect, the laser pointer was better."

Predictability

- **1-2-obs** "When the instructor looked at the oscilloscope with the GestureCam, the operator also looked at it even though the instructor said nothing."
- **2-2-ope** "The GestureCam's motion helped me find a specified object."
- **2-3-ope** "When there was the operator's monitor, I felt like I could look at the work space from the instructor's point of view. The combination of the operator's monitor and the laser pointer was good."
- **2-4-ope** "The operator's monitor helped me find a certain position. I only looked at the GestureCam when it moved a lot."
- **2-5-ope** "I seldom looked at the GestureCam, but I was usually looking at the operator's monitor. Even though the laser was pointing at an object, I looked at the monitor first, then I looked at the laser spot. I looked at the GestureCam just to confirm if the position was right."

Usefulness of the Wide-Angle Camera

- **1-3-ins** " Maybe the wide-angle view does not have to be a live video."
- **1-4-ins** "Although the wide-angle view was convenient, PinP screen was too large and become an obstacle."
- **1-5-ins** "When there was no wide-angle view, it was much easier to see the monitor, but I often felt that I needed wide angle view."

Face View

- **1-4-ope** "It is good that I could see the instructor."
- **2-4-ope** "I was irritated when the instructor did not say anything."

References

Gaver, W. (1992): " The Affordances of Media Spaces for Collaboration". In *Proc. of CSCW'92*, 1992, pp. 17–24.

Ishii, H., Kobayashi, M. and Groudin, J. (1992): "Integration of Inter-Personal Space and Shared Workspace: ClearBoard Design and Experiments". In *Proc. of CSCW'92*, 1992, pp. 33–42.

Kuzuoka, H. (1992): "Spatial Workspace Collaboration: A SharedView Video Support System for Remote Collaboration Capability". In *Proc. of CHI'92*, 1992, pp. 533–540.

Kuzuoka, H., Kosuge, T. and Tanaka, M. (1994): "GestureCam: A Video Communication System for Sympathetic Remote Collaboration". In *Proc. of CSCW'94*, 1994, pp. 35–43.

Sellen, A. and Buxton, W. (1992): "Using Spatial Cues to Improve Videoconferencing". In *Proceedings of CHI'92*, 1992, pp. 651–652.

Stefik, M. and Brown, J. (1989): "Toward Portable Ideas". In Margrethe H. Olson, editor, *Technological Support for Work Group Collaboration*, pp. 147–165. Lawrence Erlbaum Associates, Inc.

Tang, J. and Minneman, S. (1990): "VIDEO DRAW: A VIDEO INTERFACE FOR COLLABORATIVE DRAWING". In *Proc. of CHI'90*, 1990, pp. 313–320.

Wellner, P. (1993): "The DigitalDesk: Supporting Computer-based Interaction with Paper Documents". In *Proc. of Imagina*, 1993, pp. 110–119.

Proceedings of the Fourth European Conference on Computer-Supported Cooperative Work,
September 10–14, Stockholm, Sweden
H. Marmolin, Y. Sundblad, and K. Schmidt (Editors)

The Use of Hypermedia in Group Problem Solving: An Evaluation of the DOLPHIN Electronic Meeting Room Environment

Gloria Mark, Jörg M. Haake, Norbert A. Streitz
IPSI - Integrated Publication and Information Systems Institute
GMD - German National Research Center for Computer Science
Dolivostr. 15, D - 64293 Darmstadt, Germany
{mark, haake, streitz}@darmstadt.gmd.de

Abstract

In this paper, we report on an empirical evaluation of selected aspects of DOLPHIN, a meeting room environment of computers networked with an electronic whiteboard. Our results show that in a face-to-face meeting, the use of DOLPHIN's hypermedia functionality changed the nature of the product and the way groups worked, compared to using only electronic whiteboard functionality. Groups organized their ideas into network, rather than pure hierarchical, structures. These were more deeply elaborated, contained more ideas, and had more relationships between the ideas. The problem solutions were also judged to be more original. Groups were more likely to use a top-down planning strategy, and to exhibit a different temporal work pattern. The results suggest that work groups can benefit from using hypermedia in problem solving.

1 Introduction

The design of DOLPHIN is grounded in a conceptual framework which tries to bring together the research areas of CSCW and hypermedia. While a wide range of collaborative work can benefit from the approach taken, one can characterize our starting point as support for document-based activities, i.e., work where documents are either produced or are used as means during group work.

In our approach, we use the notion of "documents" in a very general and comprehensive way. Documents are not only traditional memos, letters, articles, or books, but they also include sets of scribbles and drawings on a whiteboard or an overhead transparency, and collections of information items which can contain multimedia elements (pictures, audio, video) which are usually available in electronic formats. In general, we consider documents to be hypermedia documents. This implies the possibility of employing nonlinear network structures of complex relationships (links) of information components (nodes) as it is defined by the concept of hypertext (Nielsen, 1995). We consider hypermedia as the subject matter to be created and used as well as a medium facilitating computer-supported cooperative work (Streitz, 1994). Defining relationships between different tasks, coordinating and assigning tasks to different group members, commenting and communicating on the progress of parts of the overall work activities, and much more, can be represented as hypermedia structures. At the same time, this information can be linked to the (hyper)documents which are created and used in the course of group activities.

From a CSCW perspective, we currently focus on the support for face-to-face meetings and their equivalents facilitated by telecooperation techniques resulting in distributed "virtual meetings". Observing the central role of public displays as they are provided by overhead projectors and whiteboards in face-to-face meetings, we investigate what kind of added value could be provided by using an electronic, i.e. a computer controlled, whiteboard. Another line of research for computer support in face-to-face meetings focuses on providing a computer to every participant in the room. Using common application software, each participant can actively enter, edit, and use information while sitting in the meeting room. Our approach is based on recognizing that a combination of these two scenarios is needed, i.e., an interactive electronic whiteboard *and* computers for each participant. As group activities are dynamic, rather than static, their support requires a high degree of flexibility. Flexibility can be provided in many ways. It is our view that hypermedia systems are able to provide this flexibility and serve as an ideal basis for building the next generation of cooperative information systems.

From a hypermedia perspective, flexibility translates into investigating which class of hypermedia structures should be provided for supporting group work. A prominent aspect is the modularity and inherent annotation capability of hypermedia structures. Hypermedia allows for flexible decomposition, restructuring, and reuse of components in a dynamic fashion. Decomposition can be used for domain structuring as well as for structuring the division of labour in the group. Another aspect of flexibility refers to the degree to which a system is able to provide a wide range of structures in accordance with the requirements of the tasks, their coexistence and means for transformation (Haake et al., 1994). Combining these requirements, we propose to provide a basic node-link hypermedia model for structure representation. In addition to and coexistent with, we support more informal ways of communication by "free form" scribbling, drawing, gesturing, etc. as is the case on (electronic) whiteboards. Since DOLPHIN is a cooperative hypermedia system, this range of flexible structures can be used by each group member simultaneously at the workstation and/or at the public electronic whiteboard. DOLPHIN's collaboration functionality provides shared workspaces between all group members with an additional distinction between private and public workspaces (Streitz et al., 1994).

The evaluation of DOLPHIN is concerned with a unique combination (to our knowledge) of physical setting and cooperative hypermedia functionality. Nevertheless, we can relate our approach to forerunners in the development of relevant technologies. Due to space limitations, we cannot discuss these systems in detail. These include CSCW environments such as CoLab (Stefik et al., 1987), the Capture Lab (Mantei, 1988) and the NICK project (Rein & Ellis, 1989). A recent example meeting our criteria of an electronic whiteboard is the LiveBoard (Elrod et al., 1992), in combination with appropriate software, e.g., Tivoli (Pedersen et al., 1993). Software supporting cooperative activities include GroupSystems (Nunamaker et al., 1991) and ShrEdit (McGuffin & Olson, 1992). We can also include systems primarily used in telecooperation situations, e.g., ClearBoard (Ishii et al., 1993), cooperative hypermedia systems, e.g., DHM (Grønbaek et al., 1994), SEPIA (Streitz et al., 1992), or collaboration in distributed design (Marmolin et al., 1991).

2 Motivation and goals for the evaluation experiment

In order to obtain relevant feedback for the revision of the current design of DOLPHIN, we planned an evaluation experiment addressing basic design decisions, especially related to the support of group problem solving. Since we consider the role of hypermedia structures to be highly relevant for the design of CSCW systems, we focused the experiment on the effects of adding hypermedia functionality to what can be considered to be standard on an electronic whiteboard. We chose to study the effect of adding a 'simple' node-link model (see section 3). This is motivated by our focus on supporting processes especially in the early phases of group problem solving such as problem exploration, idea generation, information structuring, and adding/reducing information elements.

We propose that the use of hypermedia structures is beneficial because it provides multiple ways and parallel views of a problem representation. Psychological evidence suggests that the quality or accuracy of the problem solution is dependent on the appropriateness of the external problem representation (Newell, 1980, Schwartz, 1971, Streitz, 1985) and that the problem solving process is facilitated by opportunities for multiple views and representations of the problem structure (Gick & Holyoak, 1983, Mayer & Greeno, 1975). We investigated whether DOLPHIN's hypermedia functionality compared to DOLPHIN without hypermedia functionality could yield a different problem representation in terms of how information is structured. This resulted in two conditions of the experiment: our implementation of more or less standard electronic whiteboard functionality vs. this functionality in combination with additional hypermedia structure functionality. We concentrated on the early phases of group problem solving.

In the context of this experiment, this led us to address the following questions which again determined our choice of dependent variables and measures.

1. *Hypermedia document creation: for groups as well as for individuals?*

While there is evidence that users with much experience can create very extensive hypermedia documents over time (Landow, 1989, Schuler et al., 1995), it is not yet clear whether users without much experience and situated in a face-to-face meeting can also portray their ideas in a hypermedia format within a reasonable training time. This might become even more critical if the composition of the group is more or less ad hoc as it might happen, e.g., in a business environment.

2. *Does hypermedia facilitate the formation and elaboration of relationships?*

The hypermedia functionality of creating nodes and links enables users to form multiple connections between concepts, i.e., many-to-many mappings. We would expect that this functionality would facilitate the creation of a network structure which we define as a structure containing at least one concept with multiple connections to other concepts. We would expect this as opposed to a pure hierarchical structure with superordinates at the highest level and subordinate concepts at lower levels (no cross-hierarchical connections). On the other hand, we expect that using a standard electronic whiteboard where links are not provided as a system feature (although subjects can handdraw arrows to express relationships) would not necessarily lead one to create a network structure.

Based on the property that hypermedia node structures can be used to elaborate ideas by using nested nodes (each containing content), we expect that this functionality would lead groups using hypermedia structures to elaborate their ideas more, creating subsequently deeper levels containing new information compared to groups using only a flat electronic drawing surface. There might also be a tradeoff between depth and breadth. The nested nodes, along with the link functionality should result in more ideas associated with a superordinate concept compared to a nonhypermedia information structure.

3. *How does hypermedia influence strategy and memory?*

We expect that the role of hypermedia in group problem solving will also be reflected in the strategies used and in the retention of information. Working with hypermedia may lead groups to fundamentally change their planning strategy when organizing ideas.

According to the depth of processing view of memory (Craik & Lockhart, 1972), information that is more deeply processed should be reflected in a better memory of the information. Therefore, we expect that the decision-making process of turning information into nodes should result in deeper processing of the information, and would be reflected in a better memory of the ideas compared to groups not using hypermedia structures. In addition, we expect that the higher the level of the hyperdocument structure, the better would be the memory of the information at that level due to repeated exposure, importance of information, and strength of association (Wingfield & Byrnes, 1981).

4. *How does hypermedia structuring influence group participation?*

The possibilities of decomposition by using hypermedia structures can be used for the distribution of tasks among group members and for parallel work and may affect group participation. We expect that different decision making occurs when organizing information into a hypermedia structure and it may be reflected in differences in group participation, such as speaking or system use.

3 The DOLPHIN System

3.1 Hypermedia functionality

DOLPHIN provides scribbles, text, nodes and links. A scribble is freehand writing or drawing, such as exclamation marks, Figures like boxes, circles, arrows, tables, etc. A text is a string of ASCII characters.

DOLPHIN documents begin with a top node corresponding to the highest level of the document. Nodes consist of a title and a content. The content of a node can contain scribbles, text, and links to other nodes. A content of a node is displayed in a DOLPHIN window. DOLPHIN provides operations for creating, editing, selecting, moving, copying, pasting and deleting scribbles, text, nodes and links.

Links connect different nodes. DOLPHIN supports two kinds of links: inter-node links for navigational purposes and intra-node links as a kind of graphical representation of relationships between nodes. Inter-node links start in the content of a node and end in the content of another node. They are displayed in the source content by a node representative for the destination node (thus, functioning as anchors). Following the inter-node link leads to the content of the destination node and displays it in a new DOLPHIN window. Users can create such a link either by creating a new node and including its representative in the currently displayed content, or, they can copy an already existing node representative and paste it into a different content. In hypermedia systems, these links are usually called embedded links. With inter-node links users can create hierarchical as well as non-hierarchical structures between nodes. Intra-node links connect two nodes contained in the same content. Users can create these links between any two node representatives in the same content. These links present themselves as directed arrows. In hypermedia systems, they are usually called node-to-node links.

Using the above types of objects and operations, users may create different structures, ranging from hierarchically nested structures, i.e. each node at a higher level of the hierarchy contains the nodes of the next lower level (thus forming tree-like structures) to nonlinear structures where nodes are included in the content of several other nodes (thus constituting nonlinear graph structures). Users can also create graphical arrangements of objects in each node's content (see Figure 1).

The pen-based user interface of DOLPHIN provides gestures for creating, deleting, moving, and selecting objects and for opening a node's content. An always visible menu with buttons for cut-copy-paste operations, closing DOLPHIN windows, and erasing scribbles is provided by DOLPHIN windows.

These objects are mapped onto a general hypermedia data model provided by an underlying cooperative hypermedia server. Each object includes their content and additional presentation attributes (e.g., size, color, position). Further technical information can be found in Streitz et al. (1994) and Haake et al. (1994).

3.2 Cooperative editing and viewing functionality

When working with DOLPHIN, users can share the content of a node, thus using it as a public workspace which displays all nodes, links, text and scribbles at that level. They can also decide to work in different nodes, thus each using a private workspace. Within a shared workspace, DOLPHIN supports concurrent operations performed by different users. Shared access and active update/synchronization of concurrent DOLPHIN windows displaying the same node's content are provided by DOLPHIN's cooperative hypermedia server. All changes to the DOLPHIN hypermedia document are reflected in the hypermedia server and made persistent.

4 Method of the Experiment

4.1 Setting

In our electronic meeting room (the OCEAN Lab), groups are seated around a rectangular table with a large interactive, electronic whiteboard facing them on one end of the table. While other scenarios are possible (cf. Streitz et al., 1994), in this experiment, DOLPHIN was used only to support two usages: as a pen-based single user system on an electronic whiteboard and as a multi-user application shared between an electronic whiteboard and networked computers.

In this particular experiment, we used a SUN-based Xerox Liveboard (Elrod et al., 1992) as the hardware basis for the electronic whiteboard and two SUN Sparc-2 workstations with 17" color monitors mounted into the meeting table. One subject worked on the Liveboard, visible to everybody. Two subjects used the workstations while still being able to see and talk to the others. The public workspace on the Liveboard could also be presented on the workstations. For the public displays, we provide a relaxed WYSIWIS functionality (What You See Is What I See; Stefik et al., 1987), which means that users could scroll and resize their windows independently. The provision of workstations to two subjects allowed them to work in parallel in a "private workspace" (similar to taking individual notes on paper or looking at separate documents, etc.).

4.2 The evaluation infrastructure

During the experiment, various data have been recorded. Screendumps were taken from every workstation and the Liveboard every 15 seconds by a snapshot program. The total view of the meeting room was videotaped. The final state of the meeting document was automatically captured in DOLPHIN's cooperative hypermedia server. After the meeting, the document structure was reconstructed on a piece of paper and coded. An observer took notes during the meeting.

To be able to evaluate concurrent activities of several users using the computers provided in the meeting room, a specialized evaluation tool has been developed. The screenshots from the workstations and the Liveboard plus the videotape were digitized into Quicktime movies on a Macintosh computer. The evaluation tool can present all four digital video streams concurrently on the Macintosh. One may choose to play one or all of the four streams available, resize the active video window, hear the sound in parallel to the video, and synchronize the screen content of all participants. By playing the video streams backwards or forwards, one can observe how the meetings developed. This tool was especially valuable for analyzing the groups' strategies during the meetings.

4.3 Design

In order to isolate the effects of using hypermedia structures, a between-subjects design was used. Subjects worked in groups of three, with eight groups per condition. Groups were assigned to two conditions which correspond to two different functionalities of the DOLPHIN system:

Nonhypermedia structures (N-Condition). Subjects were trained only in the nonhypermedia structures which employs the standard electronic whiteboard functionality. Here, DOLPHIN offers scribbles with the pen (and mouse) and typed text using a keyboard. These are objects which can be created, selected, moved, and deleted. Subjects could work only in one window, but could scroll to any area of the window and could scroll to different views independently from each other if they preferred.

Hypermedia structures (H-Condition). Subjects were trained both in the nonhypermedia structures of DOLPHIN (see above) as well as in the hypermedia structures of the system: for nodes and links the operations included creation, selection, opening (of nodes), deletion, and movement. Subjects were also shown how to create nonlinear structures by copying and pasting nodes and links.

4.4 Subjects

The experiment took place during an eight-week period in Fall of 1994. A total of 48 subjects were mainly recruited from students of the Technical University in Darmstadt, while eight of them were recruited from the staff of GMD-IPSI, most of whom had received their university degree within three years. Subjects were assigned to conditions so that students and staff were randomly distributed among the groups. Subjects were not paid. No significant differences were found in subjects' computer experience, or age, between the conditions.

4.5 Procedure

Subjects first received a 40-minute training session on the system functionality. In both conditions, subjects were shown an example of a network structure on the

Liveboard as a possible information structure that one can create with the DOLPHIN system. In the N-Condition, the structure was created with handwritten words and arrows; in the H-Condition, the same structure was created with nodes and links. Afterwards, subjects worked on a 20-minute practice exercise.

After training, groups were instructed to spend the first 20 minutes in brainstorming and were read standard instructions for this task (Osborne, 1957). Subjects then were told to spend 40 minutes structuring and developing their brainstormed ideas. In both conditions, subjects were told that they could order their ideas into categories or graphical arrangements. In addition, subjects in the H-Condition were told that they could use nodes and links to structure their ideas. It was emphasized that subjects in both conditions could structure their ideas any way they preferred, using their own strategy, and were not bound to any particular format. Subjects could choose to work in any style they wanted: together, separately, or varying their styles. Directly after the experiment, subjects were given a memory test and then filled out a questionnaire in order for us to survey users' work group experience, opinions of the system, and to receive suggestions.

4.6 Task

It was decided that the task should meet the following requirements: 1) it should have the potential to allow subjects to generate a wide range of ideas, 2) its solution should be able to comfortably assume both the form of a nonhypermedia and hypermedia structure, 3) it should have a realistic purpose to increase motivation, and 4) it should be complex enough that its solution could take advantage of DOLPHIN's electronic capabilities in both experimental conditions.

Subjects were told to design a "library of the future" for the city of Darmstadt, Germany. They were to prepare a proposal for the city, which did not have to be in the form of a finished text document. The instructions stated that the citizens of Darmstadt would be the main users, cost was not to be a factor, financing should be left out, and ideas were to be generated without consideration of their feasibility, i.e. that current technology did not have to exist to realize their ideas.

4.7 Measures

The choice of our measures was guided by the hypotheses that we earlier developed addressing hypermedia use:

Relationship between ideas: The information structures produced by both conditions were categorized into network, pure hierarchical, and other.

Elaboration of superordinate concepts: We counted the number of levels (depth) in the documents in both conditions. Depth of the document is defined as the deepest pathway that one can reach beginning from the highest level of the document. In the H-condition it was the top node, and in the N-condition it was the highest level which in all cases was identifiable by some graphical marker such as an underline or enumeration. We also measured breadth, defined as the number of superordinate concepts at the highest level of the document.

Ideas connected to superordinate pathway: We counted the average number of ideas following intra- and inter-node links along each superordinate pathway.

Changes of ideas from brainstorming to information structuring. We counted how many ideas were generated during brainstorming and the net number of ideas the group ended up with after structuring the ideas, after additions and deletions. Each node was counted as one idea, and details in parentheses were included as part of the same idea.

Quality of documents. We asked two experts, a linguist, and a sociologist specializing in conversation patterns, to judge the documents along four dimensions. *Logic of local structure* was a measure of the logical relationship of elements within separate parts of the document (nodes in the hypermedia document, and clusters in the nonhypermedia document); *logic of global structure* was a measure of the logical relationship between separate parts of the document; *originality of solution* was a measure of how inventive/unusual were the ideas, the general approach to the solution, and the framework that the ideas were presented in; and *comprehensiveness* was a measure of how multifaceted the document was.

Group Strategy. Using the evaluation tool, groups' strategies were categorized as: primarily top-down (all/most of the superordinate concepts are set up initially; subordinate concepts are then categorized under them), depth-first (one superordinate concept was set up, developed with subordinate concepts, and then the process repeated for each superordinate), primarily bottom-up (subordinate concepts are first grouped, and then superordinate concepts assigned), and mixed (a mixture of the preceding strategies).

Memory of information. Directly after the experiment, subjects were given 15 minutes to try to reconstruct with paper and pencil the ideas and structure which they had just created.

The effect of hypermedia structuring on group processes was measured by:

Group participation. The length of time in seconds of speaking and of system use by each group member was coded from the videotapes.

Group satisfaction. Satisfaction was measured in the questionnaires.

4.8 Coding

For all dependent measures that we report, with the exception of group participation, coding was done by two separate coders, with percentage agreement exceeding 89% (this value occurred with quality of documents). For group participation, we used one coder, since the coder had to simply observe start and end times of talking and typing, and we felt that this was an objective measure that could be done competently by one coder. Where there was any question about the data, the data was checked by a second coder.

5 Results

Relationship between ideas. It was expected that groups in the H-Condition would be more likely to create a network structure than a pure hierarchical structure.

This was indeed the case: 6 out of 8 groups in the H-Condition created a network structure using intra-node links whereas 7 out of 8 groups in the N-Condition created a pure hierarchical structure (chi-square$_{(1)}$ = 6.36, p<.025).

Figure 1 shows a network structure created by an N-group. When H-groups did create a pure hierarchical structure, in one case they created a two-level (superordinate and subordinate) hierarchy, and in one case, they created multiple levels (four). Figure 2 shows an example of a network structure created by an H-group. When N-groups created a pure hierarchical structure, in six cases they created a two-level hierarchy, and in only one case did they employ three levels .

Elaboration of ideas. It was expected that subjects in the H-Condition would be more likely to create structures having deeper levels. H-groups did create structures having deeper levels and the result was highly significant (mean$_H$=3.5 levels, s.d.=.76, mean$_N$=2.25 levels, s.d.=.46 t(14)=3.99, p<.001). However, no significant difference was found in the breadth of the structures: (mean$_H$=4.5 concepts, s.d.=1.85, mean$_N$=5.4 concepts, s.d.=.74).

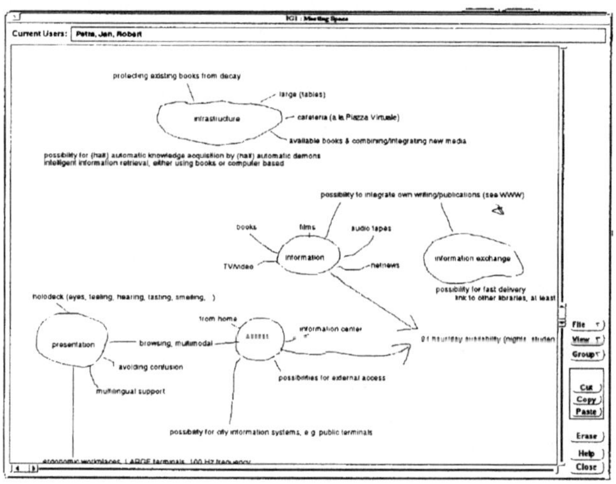

Figure 1: Example of a network structure created by an N-Group (translated from German).

Ideas connected to superordinate pathway. It was also expected that more ideas would be associated with each superordinate concept in the H-Condition. Compared to the N-Condition, a strong trend showed that the information structures of groups in the H-Condition had, on the average, double the number of subordinate ideas connected to each superordinate concept, (mean$_H$=13.26 ideas, s.d.=10.08, mean$_N$=6.60 ideas, s.d.=2.70, t(14)=1.81, p<.09).

Ideas connected to superordinate pathway. It was also expected that more ideas would be associated with each superordinate concept in the H-Condition. Compared to the N-Condition, a strong trend showed that the information structures of groups in the H-Condition had, on the average, double the number of subordinate ideas connected to each superordinate concept, (mean$_H$=13.26 ideas, s.d.=10.08, mean$_N$=6.60 ideas, s.d.=2.70, t(14)=1.81, p<.09).

Changes of ideas from brainstorming to information structuring. More ideas were generated by the H-Condition than the N-Condition during brainstorming, but the difference did not reach significance. However, the difference increased in value over the duration of the experiment as a result of adding and deleting ideas leading to a difference which now approached significance ($mean_H$=48 ideas, s.d.=9.35, $mean_N$=38.25 ideas, s.d.=10.90, t(14)=1.92, p<.08).

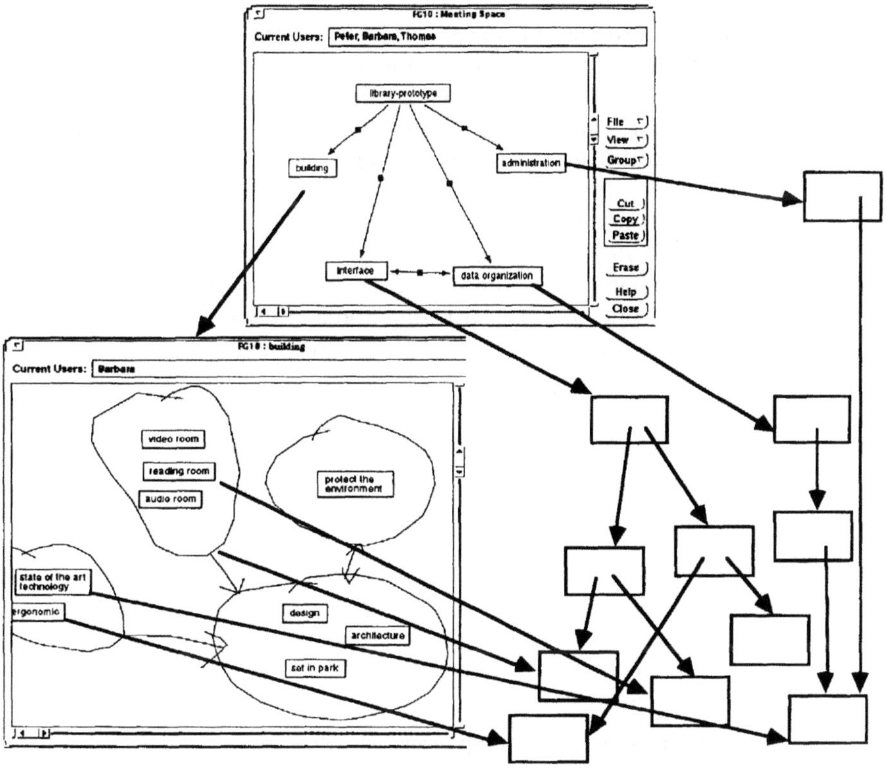

Figure 2: Results of a H-Group (translated from German). This Figure shows the content of the top node and one of the subordinate nodes. Due to lack of space we used a graphical representation of the rest of the document's structure. Here, empty rectangles denote nodes and fat arrows denote inter-node links.

Quality of documents. No difference was found by the expert coders in their judgment of the logic of local structures, logic of global structure, or comprehensiveness. However, documents from the H-Condition were judged as being significantly more original in their solution (t(14)=2.16, p<.05).

Quality of documents. No difference was found by the expert coders in their judgment of the logic of local structures, logic of global structure, or comprehensiveness. However, documents from the H-Condition were judged as being significantly more original in their solution (t(14)=2.16, p<.05).

Group strategy. The type of strategy used in structuring the information was compared between conditions. Six out of eight groups in the H-Condition used a primarily top-down strategy. In contrast, groups in the N-Condition were found to be more likely to use a depth-first strategy (5 out of 8 groups). For the statistical test, a top-down vs. non top-down strategy was compared and the results show a significant difference in top-down strategy use (chi-square$_{(1)}$=4, $p<.05$).

Memory of information. We expected that a higher proportion of ideas in the H-Condition would be remembered than in the N-Condition. Surprisingly, the contrary turned out to be the case: subjects in the N-Condition actually remembered significantly more ideas (mean$_H$=49%, s.d.=7%, mean$_N$=64%, s.d.=7%, $t(13)=4.11$, $p<.001$). One outlying value from the H-Condition had to be eliminated. However, subjects in both conditions remembered the same proportion of superordinate concepts (mean$_H$=86%, s.d.=19%, mean$_N$=86%, s.d.=16%). We also expected that for the H-Condition, the memory of information would increase with the document level. The results confirmed this: subjects remembered 79% of the information on the first level of the document, 42% on all intermediate levels (combined for the analysis), and 31% on the bottom level of every branch in the structure. Some of the H-groups reconstructed the information structure as a network structure in the memory tests.

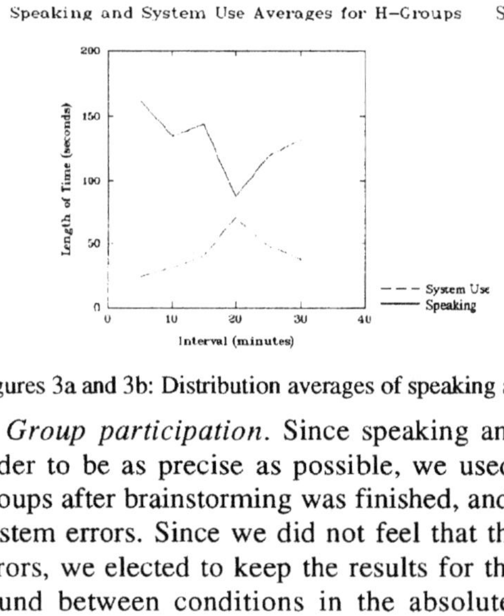

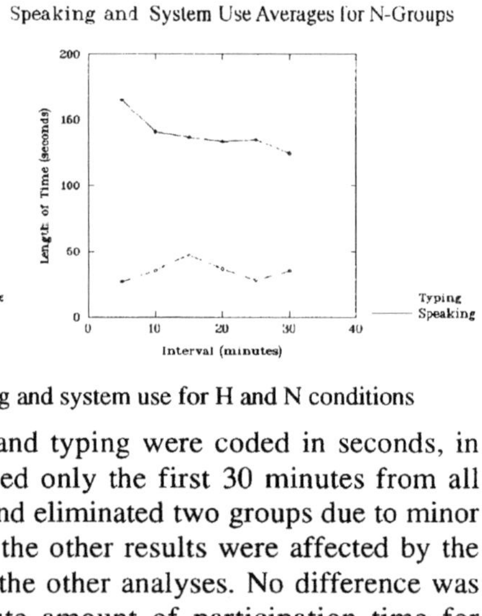

Figures 3a and 3b: Distribution averages of speaking and system use for H and N conditions

Group participation. Since speaking and typing were coded in seconds, in order to be as precise as possible, we used only the first 30 minutes from all groups after brainstorming was finished, and eliminated two groups due to minor system errors. Since we did not feel that the other results were affected by the errors, we elected to keep the results for the other analyses. No difference was found between conditions in the absolute amount of participation time for speaking or system use. However, we did find interesting results when speaking and system use were plotted in five minute intervals. Figures 3a and 3b show the averages for both conditions, for speaking and system use. For the H-groups, speaking decreases and system use increases in one of the five minute intervals, generally occurring around 20 minutes into the structuring task (Figure 3a). In contrast, the amount of speaking and system use in the N-groups generally follows a uniform distribution (Figure 3b). One sees the correspondence between the dip and peak in the group averages for the H-groups but no clear correspondence appears in the curves for the N-group averages.

Group satisfaction. N-groups reported higher satisfaction working in their groups than H-groups ($t(14)=2.22$, $p<.03$).

6 Interpretation of results and future work

6.1 Interpretation of results

Based on the group protocols, combined with the quanititative measures, a common thread appears to emerge to bind together some of the results of the H-groups. We argue that the hypermedia functionality of creating nodes, adding content, and linking nodes affects the group process, strategy, and the nature of the documents produced. This capability is in contrast to working on a 2-D "flat" working surface. We now address the four questions raised earlier in Section 2.

Hypermedia document creation: for groups as well as for individuals?

We found that with a reasonable training period all the groups were able to use the hypermedia structures without difficulty. Despite the fact that a nonlinear structure was not a requirement of the information structuring, six out of the eight H-groups created a nonlinear structure using inter-node links, showing that groups understood the concept of nonlinearity. One N-group also created a nonlinear structure using handdrawn arrows (see Figure 1).

Does hypermedia facilitate the formation and elaboration of relationships?

H-groups produced documents with more relationships and deeper elaborations of concepts, which confirmed our expectation. Hypermedia use resulted in documents with more levels of depth, and with a greater number of ideas associated with the superordinate concepts. The functionality of creating nodes could explain the deeper levels because of the availability of sorting information into separate nodes and the ease of its access. Adopting a metaphor of a book, one group proposed putting the superordinate ideas on the first "page" and then putting the subordinate ideas on a second "page". The greater number of ideas associated with the superordinate concepts follows as a result of the deeper levels since they generally led to wider branches at a lower level in the tree structure.

Groups who used hypermedia were more likely to create network, rather than pure hierarchical structures, and included more ideas in the structures as well. In addition, their ideas and problem approach were judged by experts to be more original. In a similar argument to the availability of the node structure, the prevalence of the network structures could have been due to the availability of the link function, as opposed to the N-condition, where groups must hand-draw arrows in order to indicate a relationship. Links were also used to create unexpected relationships. One group used links between the superordinates to establish a "higher" and "lower" level of superordinates, although they were all contained on the same page.

The claim that the complexity of relationships produced using hypermedia may facilitate problem solving can also be explained by considering some of the models developed in cognitive psychology. Anderson (1983) claims that memory is organized as a network structure and that the spread of activation among associated concepts is an automatic process. This view is consistent with the facilitation of a hypertext-based network representation and problem solving.

How does hypermedia influence strategy and memory?

H-groups were more likely to use a top-down strategy whereas N-groups tended to develop one superordinate concept at a time. One explanation could be that H-groups knew that they had unlimited space in depth, which could be considered as a "third dimension" by creating and nesting nodes many levels down. Thus, they could plan the top level knowing they would have room for as many subordinate concepts as they needed. Some of the H-groups referred to creating and opening nodes as a space-keeping device which supports this notion. In one group, one member suggested that they put the brainstorming results in a new node, as a "notebook", to create a free page to plan the superordinate concepts. After the group had decided on the superordinate concepts, one member proposed that they create "subordinate" nodes.

A memory test revealed the N-groups to recall more of the total information than the H-groups, against our expectations. The N-groups could have recalled more information because they viewed all of the information a longer amount of time compared to the H-groups who kept changing the information on their screen by opening and closing different nodes. However, although H-groups viewed the superordinate concepts for less time, they recalled them as well as the N-groups.

How does hypermedia influence group participation and satisfaction?

The speaking and system use over time of the H-groups show a trend for a different temporal work pattern than for the N-groups. Temporal patterning in groups is described as involving sets of complex activities including work flow coordination, matching time allocation to tasks, and synchronization of group members (McGrath, 1993) as well as involving conversation patterns (Mark, 1992). Whereas N-groups distribute their speaking and system use generally equally throughout the meeting, H-groups tend to work in a more uneven pattern.

The five-minute interval where system use increases in the H-groups appears to be related to the use of the top-down strategy. Many of the H-groups had one member who proposed a plan of action which appears to have been a catalyst for the group to take action. Speaking declined and system use increased as a result of the group carrying out this plan. There was some variability however, concerning the proposals, such as whether a proposal was acted upon immediately or discussed, or the number of proposals concerning the action. In five of the groups, the proposal was for the group to divide into subgroups and work in parallel, and in one group the proposal was for collective work. For example, in group H1, one member proposed that now that they have the superordinates, they begin to divide up the subpoints. During the peak in system use, one member worked on the Liveboard to turn the superordinates into nodes and created the network structure by linking the superordinates. After a five-minute period, speaking increased due to discussing details of how the subordinates should be categorized. In group H3, the members decided to contrast an electronic with a conventional library. One member proposed that they break up into subgroups.

One subgroup could work on the conventional, and the other on the electronic. The group then divided up, and this work pattern is reflected in the system use peak. Group H5, after reviewing their brainstormed ideas, decided to divide the ideas up into three work areas: building, offerings, and organization. One member proposed that they begin sorting the ideas into these three areas (corresponding to the three group members), and the group divided up to begin working, again reflecting this system use peak. Group H7 proposed to divide up into two subgroups--one responsible for technology, and the other responsible for the building. However, the group began to work on technology and the building, but did so publicly using the Liveboard, ignoring the proposal for parallel work. Again, this action is reflected in the system use peak. In group H4, a member proposed that the group now work independently. Each group member chose a superordinate to develop and the system use peak reflects the time when members first began to work separately.

Thus, a summary of a typical group process using the hypermedia functionality can be described as follows. Groups used a top-down strategy, and spent the first part of the organizing session planning what superordinate concepts to create. Then, a proposal was made for the group to divide up the superordinate concepts and work on them individually, which the members then did (four of the groups worked in parallel at this point; two of the groups performed the sorting operation publicly). The peak in system use and dip in speaking seems to reflect this action. After an initial period of elaborating the superordinates, the group began to discuss new points, generally clarification, e.g. verifying what the other subgroup had done, or under which superordinate a particular idea would be more appropriate.

H-groups reported a lower satisfaction working in the group than N-groups. In the questionnaire, H-groups reported that DOLPHIN was significantly harder to use than the N-groups ($p<.05$), a result not surprising considering the added functionality of the hypermedia, and which could partially explain their lower satisfaction. The lower group satisfaction in the H-condition is consistent with other results found when groups use a new technology (McLeod, 1992; Olson et al., 1993). Using the electronic whiteboard may be analogous to using familiar markers on a whiteboard, and this may have resulted in higher satisfaction for N-groups. We assume that overcoming an initial period of getting familiar with a new technology would lead to higher satisfaction. Despite their lower satisfaction, however, H-groups produced a more original and elaborate product.

6.2 Comparisons to other studies and future work

Our results suggest that when groups use hypermedia in problem solving, they change their habits, i.e., creating more deeply elaborated and more network-oriented problem representations. Our N-condition is similar to Tivoli (Pedersen et al., 1993). Therefore, it seems plausible to expect similar differences in group process and product if DOLPHIN use were to be compared to Tivoli use.

Some studies have addressed the impact of technology on groups in face-to-face meetings (e.g. for a meta-analysis see McLeod, 1992; or for the impact of a simple collaborative editor ShrEdit, see Olson et al. 1993). We feel that our study extends this direction by looking at finer distinctions between groups who use different forms of technology. Although in the NICK experiment (Rein & Ellis, 1989), the use of an electronic blackboard was contrasted with the use of networked workstations (resulting in more group exchange and group focus with higher group product ratings for the electronic blackboard condition), we looked at the combined effect of Liveboard with networked workstations. The studies we know of fall short in terms of comparing the impact of different kinds of software as we did by examining the added value of providing hypermedia functionality.

Complementing this work on early phases, we plan to investigate later phases of problem solving, as well as medium range and longterm collaboration, public vs. private work, and hypermedia as a "medium" for coordination. We plan to do this in more realistic situations, e.g., in the business domain. Our results suggest research opportunities for the future development of DOLPHIN. For example, in the redesign of DOLPHIN we want to include new support for orientation and navigation in the hypermedia structures. In another direction, we will investigate the use of DOLPHIN to include "virtual meetings" by coupling remote meeting rooms and external experts via ATM-based networks (Streitz et al., 1994).

Acknowledgments

The authors would like to thank the following people for their invaluable help and support: Jörg Geißler, Petra Rexroth, Chris Neuwirth, Matthias Will, Elke Teich, Adelheit Stein, Wiebke Möhr, Ajit Bapat, and finally Lutz Kirchner, Christian Schuckmann, and Jan Schümmer.

References

Anderson, J. (1983). *The Architecture of Cognition.* Cambridge: Harvard University Press.

Craik, F., Lockhart, R. (1972). Levels of processing: a framework for memory research. *Journal of Verbal Learning and Verbal Behavior, 11*, 671-684.

Elrod, S. et al. (1992). Liveboard: a large interactive display supporting group meetings, presentations and remote collaboration. *Proc. of the CHI'92 Conf., Monterey,*, pp. 599-607.

Gick, M., Holyoak, K. (1983). Schema induction and analogical transfer. *Cognitive Psychology., 15*, 1 - 38.

Grønbaek, K., Hem, J., Madsen, O., Sloth, L. (1994) Cooperative hypermedia systems: A Dexter-based architecture. *Communications of the ACM, 37 (2)*: 64-74.

Haake, J., Neuwirth, C., Streitz, N. (1994). Coexistence and transformation of informal and formal structures: Requirements for more flexible hypermedia systems. *Proc. of ACM European Conference on Hypermedia Technology (ECHT'94).* Edinburgh, pp. 1-12.

Ishii, H., Kobayashi, M. Grudin, J. (1993). Integration of interpersonal space and shared workspace. *ACM Transactions on Information Systems*, Special issue on CSCW. T. Malone & N. Streitz (Eds.), *11(4)*, 349-375.

Landow, G. (1989). Hypertext in literary education, criticism, and scholarship. *Computers and the Humanities*, 23, 173 - 198.

Mantei, M. (1988). Capturing the Capture Lab Concepts: A case study in th design of computer-supported meeting rooms. *Proc. of the ACM Conf. on CSCW '88, Portland,* 257-268.

Mark, G. (1992). *The generation of idea proposals: an illustration in a negotiation setting.* Behavioral Decision-Making Research in Management Conference, UC, Berkeley. EDS Center for Advanced Research Technical Report.

Marmolin, H., Sundblad, Y., Pehrson, B. (1991). An analysis of design and collaboration in a distributed environment *Proc. 2. European Conference on CSCW, Amsterdam.* pp. 147-162.

Mayer, R, Greeno, J. (1975). Effects of meaningfulness and organization on problem solving and computability judgements. *Memory & Cognition, 3,* 356 - 362.

McGrath, J. E. (1993). Time, interaction, and performance (TIP). In R. Baecker (Ed.), *Groupware and Computer-Supported Cooperative Work,* San Mateo: Morgan Kaufman, pp. 116-129.

McGuffin, L. & Olson, G. M. (1992). *ShrEdit: A Shared Electronic Workspace.* Technical Report No. 45, University of Michigan, Cognitive Sciences and Machine Intelligence Lab, 1992.

McLeod, P. (1992). An assessment of the experimental literature on electronic support of group work. *Human Computer Interaction, 7,* 257 - 280.

Newell, A. (1980). Reasoning, problem solving, and decision processes: The problem space as the fundamental category. In R. Nickerson (Ed.), *Attention and Performance VIII.*. Erlbaum.

Nielsen, J. (1995). *Multimedia and Hypertext: The Internet and Beyond. NY:* Academic Press.

Nunamaker, J.F. et al. (1991). Electronic meeting systems to support group work. *Communications of the ACM, 34(7)*:40-61.

Olson, J., Olson, G., Storrosten,M., Carter, M. (1993). Groupwork close up: A comparison of the group design process with and without a simple group editor. *ACM Transactions on Information Systems,* Special issue on CSCW, T. Malone & N. Streitz (Eds.). *11(4)*:321-348.

Pedersen, E., McCall, K., Moran, T., Halasz, F. (1993). Tivoli: An electronic whiteboard for informal workgroup meetings, *Proc. of the InterCHI'93 Conf., Amsterdam,* pp. 391-398.

Rein , G. L., Ellis, C. A. (1989). The Nick experiment reinterpreted: Implications for developers and evaluators of groupware. *Office: Technology and People, 5(1)*:47-75.

Osborn, A. F. (1957). *Applied Imagination.* New York: Charles Schribner's Sons.

Schuler, W., Hannemann, J., Streitz, N. (Eds.) (1995). *Designing User Interfaces for Hypermedia.* Heidelberg: Springer.

Schwartz, S. (1971). Modes of representation and problem solving: Well evolved is half solved. *Journal of Experimental Psychology, 91,* 347 - 350.

Stefik, M. et al. (1987). Beyond the chalkboard: computer support for collaboration and problem solving in meetings. *Communications of the ACM, 30(1),* 32-47.

Streitz, N. (1994). Putting objects to work: Hypermedia as the subject matter and the medium for computer-supported cooperative work. In M. Tokoro & R. Pareschi (Eds.), *Object-Oriented Programming.* (ECOOP'94). Lecture Notes in Computer Science. Springer, pp. 183-193.

Streitz, N., Geißler, J. Haake, J., Hol, J. (1994). DOLPHIN: Integrated meeting support across Liveboards, local and remote desktop environments. *Proc. of the ACM Conf. on Computer-Supported Cooperative Work (CSCW'94)* Chapel Hill, pp. 345 - 358.

Streitz, N., Haake, J., Hannemann, J., Lemke, A., Schuler, W., Schütt, H., Thüring, M. (1992). SEPIA: A cooperative hypermedia authoring environment. *Proc. of the 4th ACM European Conf. on Hypertext (ECHT'92),* Milan, pp. 11-22.

Streitz, N. (1985). *Subjektive Wissensrepräsentationen als Determinanten kognitiver Prozesse.* Doctoral Dissertation. Technical University of Aachen.

Wingfield, A., Byrnes, D. (1981). *The psychology of human memory.* NY: Academic Press.

Proceedings of the Fourth European Conference on Computer-Supported Cooperative Work,
September 10–14, Stockholm, Sweden
H. Marmolin, Y. Sundblad, and K. Schmidt (Editors)

The Parting of the Ways: Divergence, Data Management and Collaborative Work

Paul Dourish
Rank Xerox Research Centre, Cambridge Laboratory (EuroPARC) and Dept of Computer Science, University College, London (dourish@europarc.xerox.com).

Abstract: Systems coordinating distributed collaborative work must manage user data distributed over a network. The strong consistency algorithms which designers have typically borrowed from the distributed systems community are often unsuited to the particular needs of CSCW. Here, I outline an alternative approach based on divergence and synchronisation between parallel streams of activity. From a CSCW perspective, this strategy offers three primary advantages. First, it is scalable, allowing smooth transitions from highly interactive collaboration to more extended, "asynchronous" styles of work. Second, it supports "multi-synchronous" work, in which parties work independently in parallel. Third, it directly supports observed patterns of opportunistic activities in collaborative working.

Introduction: Distributed Data Management

Collaborative applications coordinate activities which may be distributed in time and/or space. Distributed in time, activities may take place at different times but are coordinated to achieve a unified effect (such as the production of a document). Distributed in space, activities may take place on different computers perhaps linked by a data network. So, collaborative applications, are heir to a set of design problems which have arisen in the development of distributed computing systems (or just "distributed systems"), concerning distributed data management.

This paper considers strategies to meet the conflicting demands placed on collaborative applications, in presenting users with a single, uniform data "space".

We are primarily concerned here with "user data"; that is, largely the computational representations of artefacts which are manipulated directly by the system's users. So, in a collaborative writing system, user data would include the representation of the document, or of users' activities over that document.

Distribution criteria include: *availability*—users should be able to gain access to data when they need it; *transparency*—users should not have to worry about the details of distribution; *consistency*—users should see identical (or, at least, consistent) views of shared data, even though they may be working at different places or different times; and *responsiveness*—data management should not interfere with the system's interactive response.

However, these place conflicting demands on an implementation. For example, *availability* can be enhanced by maintaining multiple copies of the data on different network nodes,. Unfortunately, this approach conflicts with *consistency*, since two users can make incompatible changes to two copies of the same piece of data. Various strategies can avoid or resolve these conflicts, but these, in turn, endanger *transparent* operation, by introducing more ways in which users can be exposed to the consequences and details of data distribution. Different systems have different requirements, and differently prioritise these criteria.

This paper concerns the relationship between distributed data management and applications supporting specifically collaborative work. I will argue that traditional mechanisms which we might adopt from distributed systems are frequently ill-suited to the needs of collaborative systems. I will outline an alternative approach and show how it addresses problems in effectively supporting collaborative systems in an open and flexible way. First, though, I will outline some current approaches to the problems of distributed data management, and in doing so, set out some issues, parameters and terminology[1].

Distributed Data and Collaborative Work

Our starting point is to examine the design issues behind existing strategies.

Distribution

The first set of design decisions concern the mechanisms which determine where a particular data structure will reside in the system at any given time—data *distribution*. The distinction between *centralised* and *replicated* approaches, has long been a concern for CSCW developers (Ahuja et al, 1990; Lauwers, 1990; Greenberg et al, 1992). Centralisation concentrates data at one point in the system; clients communicate with this central point to retrieve or update information, so "consistency" is trivial since there is only one copy of a data item

---

[1] At this point, I beg the indulgence of more technical readers. In a spirit of fairness, I'll beg the indulgence of non-technical readers later on.

at any time. Replication allows multiple copies of data structures, which improves availability, but complicates consistency management.

Management

The critical question for any distribution strategy, however, is how consistency can be maintained in the face of the simultaneous activity of multiple users

Often this is a "non-problem". Many applications do not require absolute consistency in user data. For instance, in a "shared whiteboard", absolute consistency is rarely a concern and the system would be unlikely to attempt to rigorously maintain data integrity. However, in more structured applications, consistency can be vital. The inconsistency acceptable on a shared whiteboard is unacceptable in a spreadsheet.

Inconsistency generally arises through misorderings in applying changes to user data at different sites. User actions arise independently at different points in the network, and are then propagated to other users. This distributed activity introduces timing problems; events may arrive at different nodes in different, unpredictable sequences. To maintain consistency, the system must ensure that each client sees the result of these changes applied *in a consistent order*.

In a centralised system, since everyone sees the single copy of any data item, they see the same changes arise; there is a single, network-wide consistent ordering of events. Only one event can be processed at a time, so changes which arrive at the "same" time will be processed separately, in some specific (if arbitrary) order. So, centralised data storage inherently introduces a *serialisation* of change events, which, while potentially unpredictable, maintains consistency.

Replicated systems can also achieve consistency through global serialisation. The simplest approach is *data locking*. Since only one client at a time can hold the lock on an specific item, simultaneous changes are prohibited and consistency is maintained. Locks operate at different granularities, from the whole document down to individual objects or insertion points, but their role remains the same—to avoid inconsistency by preventing simultaneous action on data items.

Many floor control policies can be seen as locks on the entire workspace, restricting activity to one individual at a time. This is *input multiplexing*—reducing multiple input channels (one or more per individual) to a single channel (the input channel to the workspace). Mechanisms such as baton-passing and round-robin divide access between participants so that only one has control at any point. That participant holds a lock on the entire workspace; no-one else can contribute until she loses her "lock", and so consistency is maintained.

Managing Divergence

The variety of data management strategies is testament to the fact that no single approach is applicable in all cases. In part, this is simply due to the considerable variation in the needs of CSCW systems. In addition, it is because the choice of management strategies has strong implications for the interface and for the nature of collaborative interaction in a CSCW system (e.g. Greenberg and Marwood (1994)). Collaborative systems differ crucially from other distributed systems in that not only the application, but also the interface, is distributed. The trade-offs between availability, transparency, consistency and responsiveness must be made with this in mind, and so design must be constantly mindful of the way in which application distribution and interface distribution are mutually influential.

These issues are particularly important when building a CSCW toolkit, which will be used to create a wide range of applications. The toolkit designer is even more distant from end-users than is the developer of individual applications; and so it becomes critical to understand the implications of distributed data strategies for particular usage situations. Here, we need to find a general characterisation of distributed data management in CSCW.

Inconsistency Avoidance and Streams of Activity

We begin with a simple but crucial observation; that most approaches to data management in CSCW deal with *inconsistency avoidance* rather than *consistency management*. Rather than working to achieve data consistency, they erect barriers to prevent inconsistency arising in the first place. This is a distributed systems approach; the system manages the action of the separate components to avoid inconsistency. Applying this strategy to collaborative work is problematic. Our distributed entities are users, not programs; and they're less prepared to accept the imposition of global mechanisms to constrain their activity!

Since inconsistency arises through the simultaneous execution of conflicting operations, the simplest approach to avoiding inconsistency is to avoid simultaneous action over individual data items. This approach attempts to define *single, global stream of activity* over the data space. Asynchronous access achieves this, by sharing one stream between multiple participants, one at a time. Floor control policies and locking mechanisms do likewise, at a finer granularity.

The alternative approach explored here abandons this attempt to construct a single stream of activity out of multi-user activity. Instead, it begins with a picture of *multiple, simultaneous streams of activity*, and then looks to *manage divergence* between these streams. Divergence occurs when two streams have different views of the data state. This could arise through simultaneous execution of conflicting operations; or through a lag in propagating compatible operations.

Since this general view does not imply any particular number of parallel streams of activity, it encompasses the traditional views outlined earlier; they correspond to the special case of just one stream. Divergence between multiple streams of activity is the *more general case*; it subsumes attempts to maintain a single thread of control. This generality is critical to the design of a toolkit.

This paper explores divergence in pursuit of a generic, specialisable model of distributed data management. By *generic*, I mean that this model describes, in general terms, a range of distribution strategies which can be used in CSCW systems. By *specialisable*, I mean that any particular example can be operationally described as a refinement of the general model. The model is not simply a tool for the analytic description of CSCW architectures and implementations; it can also be used to generate and implement new ones. It has been developed as part of Prospero, a toolkit for CSCW application design using explicit specialisable models as a basis for highly flexible, open-ended design (Dourish, 1995a); and its framework is the basis for creating data management strategies in CSCW applications.

Divergence

So, first, we regard collaborative activity as the progress of *multiple, simultaneous* streams of activity. Second, we view inconsistency as *divergence* between these streams' views of data. Hence, we see distributed data management in terms of the *re-synchronisation* of divergent streams of activity. As collaboration progresses, the streams continually split and merge, diverge and synchronise. At synchronisation, they re-establish a common view of the data; further activity will cause them to diverge again, necessitating further synchronisation later.

Divergence and Versioning

This view of continual divergence and synchronisation is similar to that of versioning systems, which maintain a historical record of the versions of some object which have existed over time. They typically allow multiple versions of an object to exist at once, and in some, multiple versions can be simultaneously active. GMD's CoVer (Haake and Haake, 1993) uses a version system to manage the cooperative work. ; however, it emphasises the creation and management of parallel versions rather than the subsequent integration of different versions (divergent streams). Munson and Dewan (1994) provide a framework organised around version merging, but, again, they primarily emphasise versioning and merging within a context of "asynchronous" work, rather than as a more general approach to distributed data management. I want to consider the wider use of divergence as a general strategy (discussed in more detail below).

Divergence and Operational Transformation

An alternative technique which has been employed effectively in a number of collaborative systems is operational transformation (Ellis and Gibbs, 1989; Beaudoiun-Lafon and Karsenty, 1992). Operational transformation employs a model of multiple streams, and uses a transformation matrix to *transform* records of remote operations before applying them locally, using information about the different contexts in which the operations arose. Clearly, this approach is much closer to the divergence model advocated here, but there are two principal differences. First, just as versioning approaches have typically emphasised *asynchronous* activity, operational transformation has typically emphasised *synchronous*; as will be discussed, Prospero's model attempts to be more general. Second, operational transformation relies upon the transformation matrix to resolve conflicts (easier in the tightly-coupled, synchronous domain); whereas Prospero employs a more general notion of synchronisation which potentially offers a much wider scale of applicability.

Much of what's critical about the divergence view is what it *doesn't* say, because those areas of openness are the keys to the specialisable nature of the model. So far, nothing has been said about the defined units of activity, or what constitutes a "stream"; nothing has been said about the granularity of "divergence" per se and how it is recognised; and nothing has been said about the timescale on which divergence and resynchronisation takes place. In fact, this openness is critical to the particular advantages of divergence for CSCW.

Divergence and Replicated Databases

Replicated database research has also addressed questions of divergence. In a replicated database, multiple copies of all or part of the database are maintained in parallel, to increase availability. This is discussed in detail elsewhere (Dourish, 1995b), but an outline is appropriate here.

In database work, consistency is normally maintained by supporting the transaction model, which decomposes database activity into a sequence of transactions. Transactions group related operations for atomic execution; since transactions execution is all-or-nothing, consistency can be maintained. In replicated databases, research focuses on the detection of transaction conflicts and on finding an execution order which avoids potential conflicts. Various approaches can be used to sustain the transaction model under replication. For instance, distributed conflict detection can be used to generate the consistent serialisation globally, rather than individually at each replication point; or rollback techniques can be used as an optimistic concurrency model, so that conflicting transactions can be undone and reexecuted later.

These techniques place the detection, avoidance and management of conflicts *within* the database itself; unlike this proposal, the application is typically not involved in the conflict management process. This is generally true when collaborative applications are based on database technology. However, there are times when this model must break down. In Lotus Notes, for example, users interact directly with document databases replicated amongst different sites but largely disconnected from each other, and so conflicts can occur during periods of simultaneous work (as here). However, in these cases, Notes merely flags the conflict and carries on, rather than providing any means for conflict resolution. Replicated databases deal with some problems which divergence raises; however, they generally do not directly exploit divergence to support multi-user activity.

Capitalising on Divergence

Divergence-based data management in CSCW offers three particular advantages over other techniques. First, it is highly scalable, supporting inter-application communication from periods of milliseconds to periods of weeks or more. Second, it opens up direct CSCW support for an area of application use—one I term *multi-synchronous*—which are supported poorly or not-at-all by existing approaches. Third, it directly supports common patterns of working activity based on observational studies which are at odds with the models embodied in most systems today.

Scalability

Scalability refers to graceful operation across some dimension of system design. In particular, the scalable dimension here is the pace of interaction (Dix, 1992); or, more technically, its relationship to the period of synchronisation.

The period of synchronisation is the regularity with which two streams are synchronised, and hence the length of time that two streams will remain divergent. When the period is very small, then synchronisation happens frequently, and therefore the degree of divergence is typically very small before the streams are synchronised and achieve a consistent view of the data store. When individuals use a collaborative system with a very small period of synchronisation, their view of the shared workspace is highly consistent, since synchronisation takes place often relative to their actions. This essentially characterises "real-time" or synchronous groupware, in which users work "simultaneously" in some shared space which communicates the effects of each user's actions to all participants "as they happen". The synchronous element arises from precisely the way in which the delay between divergence(an action taking place) and synchronisation (the action being propagated to other participants) is small. This is one end of the "pace of interaction" dimension.

At the other end, synchronisation takes place much less frequently in comparison to the actions of the users. There is considerably more divergence, arising from different sorts of activities which take place between synchronisation points. When the period of synchronisation is measured in hours, days or weeks, we approach what is traditionally thought of as "asynchronous" interaction. A (well-worn) example might be the collaborative authoring of an academic paper, in which authors take turns revising drafts of individual sections or of the entire paper over a long period, passing the emerging document between them.

Within the CSCW community, these sorts of asynchronous interactions have generally been seen and presented as being quite different from real-time or synchronous interactions; "synchronous *or* asynchronous" has been a distinction made in both design and analysis. However, by looking at them in terms of *synchronisation* rather than *synchrony*, we can see them as two aspects of the same form of activity, with different *periods* of synchronisation. Being highly scalable across this dimension, the divergence approach provides the basis of a toolkit which generalises across this distinction.

Multi-Synchronous Applications

We can exploit a divergence-based view of distributed data management to go further than standard "synchronous" and "asynchronous" views of collaboration.

Standard techniques attempt to maintain the illusion of a single stream of activity within the collaborative workspace. We know, however, that groups don't work that way; it's much more common to have a whole range of simultaneous activities, possibly on different levels. Consider the collaboratively-authored paper again. In the absence of restrictions introduced by particular technologies or applications, individuals do not rigorously partition their activity in time, with all activity concentrated in one place at a time; that is, they do not work in the strongly asynchronous style, one at a time, that many collaborative systems embody. A more familiar scenario would see the authors each take a copy of the current draft and work on them in parallel—at home, in the office, on the plane or wherever. Here we have simultaneous work by a number of individuals and subsequent *integration* of those separate activities; not synchronous, or asynchronous, but *multi-synchronous* work.

Multiple, parallel streams of activity is a natural way to support this familiar pattern of collaborative work. Working activities proceed in parallel (multiple streams of activity), during which time the participants are "disconnected" (divergence occurs); and periodically their individual efforts will be integrated (synchronisation) to achieve a consistent state and progress group activity.

Here, we're concerned with the *nature* of synchronisation, discussed in more detail subsequently. At this stage, the details of synchronisation in a variety of cases are not of prime importance; examples will be considered in more depth later on. For the moment, however, what's important is to recognise the support for multi-synchronous working within this model of distributed data management.

Supporting Opportunistic Work

Divergence does not simply support a different working style; it's also a means to *more naturally* support the other styles to which CSCW has traditionally addressed itself. In studies of collaborative authoring, Beck and Bellotti (1993) highlighted the opportunistic way in which much activity was performed. In particular, they pointed to the ways in which opportunistic action on the parts of individual collaborators often went *against* pre-defined roles, responsibilities or plans. Individuals acted in response to specific circumstances; while the plans and strategies formed *one* guide to their actions, they were by no means the only factors at work, and in each of their case studies, they observed occasions on which agreements about who would do what and when were broken. Critically, these broken agreements are neither unusual nor problematic; this opportunistic activity is part of the natural process of collaboration. (Suchman (1987) has, of course, made similar telling observations about the status of plans as resources for action rather than as rigorous constraints upon it.)

So, we must be wary of introducing technology which inappropriately reifies plans and use pre-formed strategies to organise collaborative activity since observational studies show that they are opportunistically broken in the course of an activity. Turn-taking floor control policies, or partitioning a workspace into separate regions accessible to different individuals, are examples of technological approaches which structure user interaction around plans of this sort. Once again, this contrasts the particular needs of CSCW systems with traditional distributed systems, and shows that a distributed *interface* is an important consideration. To support the sort of opportunistic working described by Beck and Bellotti, then, our technology must relax rules about exclusion and partitioning; exactly the rules which have been employed to maintain the fiction of the single stream of activity.

So the same sorts of mechanisms which were described earlier as supporting multi-synchronous collaboration have, in fact, a wider range of applicability; they support a more naturalistic means of *making asynchronous collaboration work.* Divergence is a direct consequence of these ways of working; and so a model of distributed data management based on a pattern of repeated divergence and synchronisation fits well with support for a wide range of working styles.

Constraining Divergence: Consistency Guarantees

There is still a problem which must be addressed if we hope to use divergence as a strategy for *building* CSCW systems rather than simply talking about them. At any given point, how can we maintain reasonable expectation that synchronisation will be possible? If two streams diverge arbitrarily, how can we be sure that a consistent view can be constructed later?

Syntactic and Semantic Consistency

The answer has two components. The first lies in the very general nature of "synchronisation". The notion of synchronisation is in not meant to imply that consistency can be achieved automatically. Certainly, it *may* be possible in many cases—particularly where divergence is slight, or activity over the data is highly structured—to resolve divergence by automatic mechanisms; but this automation is not central to the model. In other cases, conflict resolution may require human intervention. However, we can make a distinction between *semantic* and *syntactic* consistency. By "semantic" consistency, I mean that the data is internally "consistent" and "appropriate for its intended use". By "syntactic" consistency, I mean merely that two streams see the same view of the data, even if that view doesn't necessarily make sense in context.

Consider collaborative writing again. Simple changes in formatting, text insertion, and so forth can be automatically integrated and so synchronisation is largely automatic. Others, however, require human intervention. For instance, if two authors have completely changed the same paragraph, then clearly the authors should be responsible for deciding which paragraph text should be used, and how the conflict can be resolved. So human intervention is required to achieve semantic consistency; but a different form of consistency—syntactic—can be achieved without human intervention. The system can apply the same approach which collaborative authors might well employ when out-of-touch with each other; preserving *both* texts, along with some marker that "this choice remains to be resolved". This approach is *aggregation*—the combination of unresolvable data elements to form a single larger unit. Aggregation achieves syntactic consistency, which retains the property we require at the system level—that the two streams share a view of the user data. It allows the two individuals involved to be able to continue working for the moment, although they will have to come back and sort out the problem later, together.

So, by maintaining semantic consistency when possible, resorting to syntactic consistency when necessary, and potentially using weak techniques such as aggregation, we can achieve a *working* level of consistency under a variety of circumstances. However, we can do more to help ensure that this works smoothly.

Consistency Guarantees

The second aspect of our solution is technological.

Clearly, we can be more confident about achieving consistency if we have some idea of what type of divergence is likely to occur. The longer the periods of divergence, the less sure we can be about this, and hence about achieving consistency. If we knew in advance what sort of actions were likely to occur on a stream before the next point of synchronisation, we could make some kind of guarantee of the degree of consistency which can be achieved.

In Prospero, consistency guarantees explicitly represent these interactions. Before divergence, one stream can "describe" the likely actions which will occur during the period of divergence. For instance, if a user has opened a document for reading only, then it's likely that no changes will be made. Alternatively, it may be possible to say that the expected changes are all structural, rather than affecting the content, or that the user will only add information but not delete any. In exchange for this, the client can receive a statement of the level of synchronisation which can likely be achieved at the next synchronisation point—a consistency guarantee. Again, these are explicit computational artefacts in Prospero. Essentially, the guarantee says, "if only actions of those sorts occur, given other declarations of expected activities in other streams, this level of consistency should be achievable when synchronisation occurs."

Consistency guarantees are a more general mechanism than traditional locks, although they share certain properties. Consistency guarantees are used to manage simultaneous action (rather than to avoid it, like locks); and as a result, they embody more limited guarantees of later consistency (while locks guarantee absolute consistency). However, they share the principle of providing information about activities in advance, in exchange for guarantees of later consistency. We wish to avoid the problems of locking described above, such as poor support for opportunistic working. So in Prospero, the client can break its "promise" about expected behaviour, in which case the system will no longer be held to its guarantee. If the client, or the user, performs actions which were not part of its declaration, then perhaps only some weaker form of consistency can be achieved.

Consistency guarantees are a way to manage expectations, but not to enforce activity. Space is too limited here to go into the full details of this approach and the way in which it is embodied in Prospero; and in later sections, I will pass over the relationship between divergence, synchronisation and consistency guarantees. A fuller discussion is presented elsewhere (Dourish, 1995b).

Divergence in Prospero

We can now look at how divergence work in practice. Prospero is a CSCW toolkit written in Common Lisp which has been designed to provide application developers with a great deal of flexibility in tailoring the toolkit's components and strategies to the needs of specific applications or usage situations. It employs computational reflection (Smith, 1984) and open implementation (Kiczales, 1992) to open up the implementation and allow application developers—the toolkit's users—principled access to internal aspects of the toolkit. This approach exploits specialisable generic models of the sort outlined here. In Prospero, the divergence/synchronisation patterns form a framework within which particular distribution mechanisms are implemented. This is encoded in an object-oriented class hierarchy; new strategies are developed by specialisation.

Here, I will present examples to illustrate the use of the divergence mechanism in Prospero and show how divergence supports a wide range of application strategies. The examples take the form of code fragments[2] illustrating the framework's specialisation to the needs of particular applications. After presenting these examples, I'll step back to consider the structure of the framework itself. Some points should be noted. First, the examples have been considerably simplified to illustrate the main points in the space available. In particular, the interaction between divergence management and consistency guarantees has been

[2] At this point, and as promised, I beg the indulgence of *non*-technical readers. However, the structure of the code fragments is more important than their detail.

omitted. Second, these examples operate on three levels at once, and it's critical to a conceptual understanding that these are kept separate. The first is that of the example applications used to illustrate the ideas; the second is the use of programming structures to realise these applications, and the third (most important) level is the use of divergence to provide a programming framework. Since the examples have been structured to highlight this third level, liberties have been taken with application requirements and efficient programming.

Example: Shdr

Shdr is a simple replicated shared whiteboard application, designed outside the divergence framework. Actions are performed on the user's own copy of the data, and are recorded in a buffer of activity records. Periodically, buffers are sent to other participants using a simple high-level protocol. The update frequency varies, but generally the history is be transmitted multiple times per second.

```
(defmethod perform-local-action :after ((action <edit-action>))
  (add-action-to-stream action *my-stream*))

(defmethod add-action-to-stream ((action <edit-action>) (stream <stream>))
  (push action (stream-actions stream)))

(defmethod add-action-to-stream :after (action (stream <bounded-stream>))
  (if (full-p stream)
     (synchronise stream (stream-remote stream))))

(defmethod synchronise ((stream <bounded-stream>) (remote <remote-stream>))
  (dolist (action (reverse (stream-actions stream)))
    (propagate-action-to-stream action remote))
  (stream-reset stream))

(defmethod propagate-action-to-stream (action (stream <remote-stream>))
  (remote-call (stream-host stream) incorporate-action action))
```

Figure 1: Mapping shdr's strategy into the Prospero framework.

We can reconstruct shdr's approach in the divergence framework (figure 1). Local actions create divergence from a shared view of the whiteboard until synchronisation, when history records are exchanged. Each user's actions are associated with a particular stream, where they are recorded until synchronisation.

User actions are explicitly represented within a class hierarchy rooted in the abstract class `<action>`. Different actions are instances of its subclasses. Here, we use the subclass `<edit-action>` for actions which have an effect on the data store (such as making or erasing a mark, but not cursor movement).

Activity streams are also explicitly represented, under the abstract class `<stream>`. Two subclasses of `<stream>` are used here. The first, `<remote-`

`stream>`, represents the streams of other users; the second, `<bounded-stream>`, is a particular kind of local stream with specialised behaviours, particular to the way that shdr manages user data. A `<bounded-stream>` accumulates local actions and periodically flushes them to other participants.

We define shdr's strategy in Prospero by writing specific methods on a generic function framework[3] which in turn describes the general model that Prospero embodies. These are the hooks onto which specialised behaviour can be hung. For instance, the generic function `perform-local-action`, which Prospero uses to operate on the local copy of user data, is a place to "attach" the association of user actions with a specific stream. This is defined for `<edit-action>` operations, rather than all `<action>` operations, since only the actions which cause a change in the data store contribute to divergence. Next, the test for whether a bounded stream is "full" and needs to be synchronised is made after any new action record is stored there, and so the after-method we define for `add-action-to-stream` specialises on `<bounded-stream>` rather than `<stream>`, so it applies only to bounded streams.

```
(defmethod add-action-to-stream ((action <edit-action>) stream)
   (push action (stream-actions stream)))

(defmethod add-action-to-stream ((action <synchronise-action>) stream)
   (synchronise stream (stream-remote stream)))

(defmethod synchronise (stream (remote <remote-stream>))
   ;; as figure 1 ...
   ...)

(defmethod propogate-action-to-stream (action (stream
<remote-stream>))
   ;; as figure 1...
   ....)
```

Figure 2: Check-in/check-out strategy.

Example: Source Code Control

The second example is a traditional source code control system in a collaborative programming environment., using a check-in/check-out model for software components or modules, and a dependency mechanism which records relationships between them.

After the first example, most of the structure for this is already provided. We already have a means to accumulate and distribute sets of changes which arise in

[3] I use CLOS terminology here for object-oriented concepts. In Smalltalk, the closest relative of a "generic function" is a "message"; in C++, a "virtual function".

one place or another, which can be reused here. The most important change, as illustrated in figure 2, concerns user-initiated synchronisation. This code uses a new action class, `<synchronise-action>`, for operations which explicitly force synchronisation. In normal editing, the system accumulates the action records, as before; but for synchronisation actions, the synchronisation function is invoked.

Example: Multi-synchronous Editing

As a final example, let's consider the implications of multi-synchronous working.

```
(demethod synchronise (stream (remote <remote-stream>))
   (dolist (action (reverse (stream-actions stream))
      (integrate (propagate-action-to-stream action remote)))
   (stream-reset stream))

(defmethod propagate-action-to-stream (action (stream
<remote-stream>))
   (remote-call (stream-host stream) incorporate-action action))

(defmethod incorporate-action (action <edit-action>)
   (if (compatible-p action) (locally-perform action)
      (aggregate action)))
```

Figure 3: Supporting multi-synchronous activity.

With the exception of the possible use of consistency guarantees, omitted here due to space considerations, multi-synchronous activity is no different at the point of divergence Once again, we can accumulate actions until some synchronisation action occurs, either automatically or by user request. This, however, is the point at which a more complex strategy is required. In the first example, we could simply ignore data consistency problems, and in the second, asynchronous access ensured that such problems didn't arise. In this example, we have to be aware of the possibility of mutually inconsistent changes and act accordingly. So the focus of attention in this case is on the synchronisation procedures.

The code in figure 3 illustrates two points. The first is that synchronisation is now requires processing (i.e. it's not simply the transmission of information); and the second is that its now the mutual achievement of both parties (i.e. its no longer sufficient for the originating side to send the information and move on).

The approach is very simple. For the first time, the synchronisation procedure pays attention to the return value of `propagate-action-to-stream`, which can return information from the remote side. Here, we work to the model that integration work will be done by the remote stream, which may pass back modified data to reflect the resolution of conflicts; and so it must be reintegrated into the local stream's view. We also see the way in which `incorporate-action` is processes records of activities originating in some other stream. In this case, we use the simplest strategy; if the remote action is an edit action, and if it is compatible with local changes, then it is applied, and if not, then syntactic consistency is achieved through aggregation. Since the open strategy used in Prospero allows specialised definition of functions such as `compatible-p` and `locally-perform`, then we can be quite loose in what is accepted, and work to achieve semantic consistency when possible.

Specialisation in Prospero

These examples show the pattern of Prospero use. First, it provides default behaviours which embody mechanisms for collaborative data management. This is what toolkits do, and so in this respect, Prospero is not particularly different from other toolkits (although the detail of Prospero's management strategies differs from those of other toolkits) Second, and critically, Prospero structures these mechanisms in an object-oriented framework and reveals elements of this framework to applications as a means to introspection and intercession. Prospero, then, provides two, orthogonal interfaces the functionality of its collaboration support mechanisms. The first, *base-level* interface provides facilities which clients *use* to create collaborative applications. The second, *meta-level* interface allows internal functionality to be specialised to the needs of particular applications. Design decisions are not hidden behind traditional abstraction barriers but are open to manipulation, so the toolkit can support a wider range of application requirements than would otherwise be possible (Dourish, 1995a).

Summary

Managing the consistency of distributed data is a critical issue for many collaborative systems. However, the interactive nature of CSCW systems means that many techniques which might be adopted from other areas of distributed systems engineering are not appropriate. Even when they can be used, their implications often limit them to a restricted set of applications; and hence they are not suitable for a toolkit to support a wide range of applications.

I have outlined an alternative approach. Rather than creating the illusion of a single stream of activity, it is based on divergence and synchronisation between multiple, parallel streams. This approach is particularly suited to CSCW applications, and, as a *specialisable* model, it can be used as flexible basis for development. Along with the consistency guarantee mechanism, divergence forms the basis of the distributed data management in Prospero, a reflective toolkit for the design of collaborative applications. Prospero is a vehicle for the exploration of issues of flexibility and openness in the design and use of collaborative applications; and the use of divergence is a critical component of its open approach to CSCW design.

Acknowledgements

Alan Dix and John Lamping provided inspiration, while Dik Bentley, Jon Crowcroft and the conference reviewers improved the quality of exposition.

References

Ahuja, S., Ensor, J. and Lucco, S. (1990): "A Comparison of Application Sharing Mechanisms in Real-time Desktop Conferencing", in *Proc. ACM Conf. Office Information Systems COIS'90*, Boston, 1990.

Beaudouin-Lafon, M. and Karsenty, A. (1992): "Transparency and Awareness in Real-Time Groupware Systems", in *Proc. ACM Conf. User Interface Software and Technology UIST'92*, Monterey, Ca., November 1992.

Beck, E. and Bellotti, V. (1993): "Informed Opportunism as Strategy", in *Proc. Third Eruopean Conference on Computer-Supported Cooperative Work ECSCW'93*, Milano, Italy, 1993.

Dix, A. (1992): "Pace and Interaction", in *People and Computers VII: Proc. of HCI'92*, York, UK, 1992.

Dourish, P. and Bellotti, V. (1992): "Awareness and Coordination in Shared Workspaces", in *Proc. ACM Confe. Computer-Supported Cooperative Work CSCW'92*, Toronto, Canada, 1992.

Dourish, P. (1995a): "Developing a Reflective Model of Collaborative Systems," *ACM Transactions on Computer-Human Interaction*, 1995 (in press).

Dourish, P. (1995b): *"Consistency Guarantees: Exploiting Operation Semantics for Consistency Management in Collaborative Systems"*, EuroPARC Technical Report, Cambridge, UK, 1995.

Ellis, C. and Gibbs, S. (1989): "Concurrency Control in a Groupware System", in *Proc. ACM Conf.Manamagement of Data SIGMOD'89*, Seattle, Washington, 1989.

Greenberg, S., Roseman, R., Webster, D. and Bohnet, R. (1992): "Human and Technical Factors in Distributed Group Drawing Tools", *Interacting with Computers*, 4(3), pp. 364-392, 1992.

Greenberg, S. and Marwood, D. (1994): "Real-time Grouopware as a Distributed System: Concurrency Control and its Effect on the Interface", in *Proc. ACM Conf Computer Supported Coooperative Work CSCW'94*, Chapel Hill, North Carolina, 1994.

Haake, A. and Haake, J. (1993): "Take CoVer: Exploiting Version Management in Collaborative Systems", in *Proc. InterCHI'93*, Amsterdam, Netherlands, 1993.

Kiczales, G. (1992): "Towards a New Model of Abstraction in the Engineering of Software", in *Proc. Workshop on Reflection and Meta-level Architectures IMSA'92*, Tokyo, Japan, 1992.

Lauwers, C., Joseph, T., Lantz, K. and Romanow, A. (1990): "Replicated Architectures for Shared Window Systems: A Critique", in *Proc. ACM Conf. Office Information Systems COIS'90*, Boston, Massachussetts, 1990.

Munson, J. and Dewan, P. (1994): "A Flexible Object Merging Framework", in *Proc. ACM Conf. Computer-Supported Cooperative Work CSCW'94*, Chapel Hill, North Carolina, 1994.

Smith, B. (1984): "Reflection and Semantics in LISP", in *Proc. ACM Symposium on Principles of Programming Languages POPL*, Salt Lake City, Utah, 1984.

Suchman, L. (1987): *"Plans and Situated Actions"*, Cambridge University Press, Cambridge, UK, 1987.

Proceedings of the Fourth European Conference on Computer-Supported Cooperative Work,
September 10–14, Stockholm, Sweden
H. Marmolin, Y. Sundblad, and K. Schmidt (Editors)

A General Multi-User Undo/Redo Model

Rajiv Choudhary
Intel Corporation (rajiv_choudhary@ccm.jf.intel.com)

Prasun Dewan
University of North Carolina (dewan@cs.unc.edu)

A general multi-user undo/redo model must satisfy several requirements. It must be compatible with an existing single-user undo/redo model, give individual users autonomy in executing undo/redo commands, support undo/redo of remote commands and the remote effects of local commands, be independent of the coupling, multicast, and concurrency control model, and allow undo/redo of arbitrary commands. We have developed a multi-user undo/redo model for meeting these requirements. The model constructs the command history of a particular user by including all local commands and those remote commands whose results were made visible to that user. It allows a user to undo/redo corresponding commands in the command histories of all users of a program. Moreover, it allows a user to undo/redo both symmetric user-interface commands and asymmetric collaboration commands. We have implemented the model in a collaboration system called Suite. In this paper, we motivate, describe, and illustrate these requirements and our model.

Introduction

Undo/redo is an important interactive feature whose absence seriously degrades the usability of an interactive program. It provides automatic support for recovery from user errors and misunderstandings as well as a mechanism for exploring alternatives [11]. It is offered in some form or another by most popular single-user programs [2, 12, 13, 14]. But few of the multi-user programs known to us offer this feature although it is crucial in a group setting for several reasons. First, features available to users in the single-user case must also be available in the multi-user case. Otherwise users hesitate to use and adopt new environments. Moreover, in the multi-user case, the potential cost of an individual user's mistake is multiplied many times because it can adversely affect the work of a large number of collaborative users. Furthermore, in a collaborative setting, the number of alternatives to be explored increases due to the presence of many users. Thus undo/redo is even more useful in a multi-user application.

One reason for the absence of undo/redo from most multi-user applications is the lack of general requirements and models for multi-user undo/redo. We have identified an initial set of these requirements and designed an undo/redo model that satisfies them. The model determines how command histories of the users of a multi-user program are constructed, which commands are undone/redone by an undo/redo request from a particular user, and which users can undo/redo a command. It is an extension of the linear single-user undo/redo model [2, 14]. It constructs the command history of a particular user by including all local commands and the remote commands whose results were made visible to that user. It allows a user to undo/redo corresponding commands in the command histories of all users of a program. Moreover, it allows a user to undo/redo both symmetric user-interface commands and asymmetric collaboration commands.

This model is applicable to multi-user programs offering a variety of functionality, coupling, concurrency control, and multicast schemes. In particular, it is applicable to multi-user text/graphics editors, spreadsheets, mail programs, and code inspectors; coupling schemes offering WYSIWIS (What You See Is What I See) and WYSINWIS (What You See Is Not What I See) interaction; concurrency control schemes offering floor control and concurrent interaction; and multicast schemes supporting both atomic and non-atomic multicast.

We have implemented this model as part of a system called Suite [5]. In this paper, we motivate, describe, and illustrate our undo/redo model using the concrete example of Suite. The remainder of the paper is organized as follows. Section 2 outlines the set of multi-user undo/redo requirements we have identified. Section 3 explains the single-user undo/redo model used as the basis of our work. Section 4 motivates, describes, and illustrates how we have extended this model to meet the requirements. Finally, Section 5 presents conclusions and directions for future work.

Undo/Redo Model Requirements

We have identified a number of requirements that a multi-user undo/redo model should satisfy:

Compatibility Multi-user undo/redo should behave like single-user undo/redo when only one user is interacting with the system, thereby reducing the overhead of learning a new undo/redo model, which in turn hinders usability. This is especially true for a feature such as undo/redo that is expected to be used when the user makes errors and is thus not in a relaxed frame of mind to try new things. Compatibility allows the user to incrementally learn the new features of a multi-user undo/redo model.

Independence Multi-user undo/redo model should not require attention or intervention of all users in a collaborative session. This allows a number of users to participate in a collaborative interaction without being overloaded with the requirement of synchronizing with other users their use of recovery commands. It also allows each user to concentrate on the work he is performing.

Semantic Consistency When multiple users interact with an application simultaneously, a user's actions can affect other users. The undo/redo model must ensure that the effect of undoing a command is equivalent to the state the system would be in if the undone command had never been executed, thus guaranteeing that the degree of consistency ensured by the concurrency control policy adopted by an application is not compromised by the use of undo/redo.

Collaboration The model must allow users to undo/redo commands issued by other users, thereby allowing the users to collaborate on their undo/redo. This is a direct analogy of the ability of users to collaborate by executing 'do' commands on behalf of other users. The model must also allow users to undo the remote effects of command they issued, thereby allowing them to recover from mistakes made in their collaboration. This follows from the general semantic consistency requirement given above.

Genericity The model should be generic enough to allow its use in a number of applications with a variety of coupling, concurrency control, and broadcast schemes, thereby promoting uniformity and automation.

Undo of Arbitrary Commands The model must not be restricted to commands that manipulate the user-interface state. It must also support undoing of collaboration commands.

We describe below the model we have designed to meet these requirements.

Single-User Interactive Undo/Redo

Our multi-user undo/redo model is based on a minor variation of the linear single-user undo/redo model [13], which is provided in some popular tools such as the InterViews `idraw` editor. The model maintains a history list of executed commands and provides undo/redo/skip commands. These commands are metacommands, that is, they are themselves not added to the list. Each command in the command list has a status associated with it, which can be *executed*, *undone* or *skipped*. In addition, the model defines a *current command pointer* to point to a command in the list. When a new command is executed, it is inserted in the history list after the current command pointer and the pointer is then set to the new command. The undo metacommand undoes the command pointed to by the current pointer(if it has been executed) and moves the current command pointer to the previous command. The redo metacommand executes the command after the current command pointer(if such a command exists) and sets the pointer to the command just redone. The skip command marks the command after the current command pointer as skipped if it is currently undone and moves the pointer to the skipped command. In addition, each metacommand also sets the status of the command on which it operates.

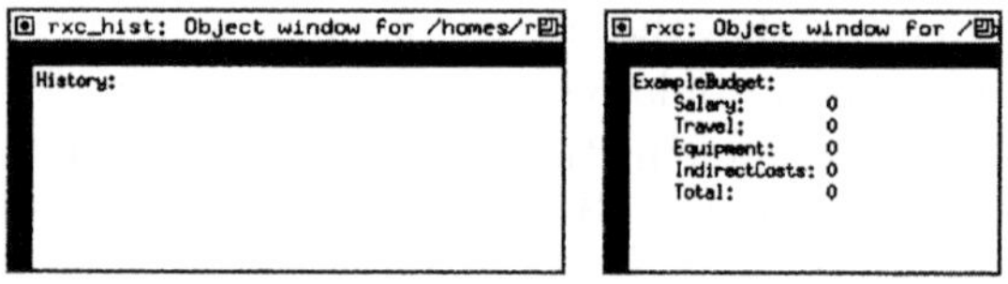

Figure 1: Initial display with the history list empty

To illustrate this model, consider a single-user interactive session with Suite that edits a simple budget. Figure 1 shows the initial display, which consists of an edit window (right window) showing the budget, and a history window (left window) displaying the history of commands executed in the edit window. The history list is initially empty and the fields of the budget are initialized to 0. [1] Figure 2 shows the contents of the two windows after the user edits the `Salary` and `Equipment` fields by moving the cursor to each field and inserting text. [2] [3] As each command is executed, it is appended to the history list. In the history list display, the last command is displayed in detail while all other commands are elided. The detailed display of a command shows a unique label for the command (motivated in Section 4.2 and 4.3), which user executed the command (a user, such as `rxc`, is indicated by the name of the Suite object, such as `/homes/rxc/objects/rxc`, that issued commands on his behalf), the

[1]In Suite, users do not edit simple lines of text. Instead, the display consists of a number of labeled fields and the user edits the text of these fields.

[2]It is not conventional to treat MoveCursor as an undoable history command in traditional editors. However in Suite, a number of other actions such as broadcast of a change can be tied to the moving of the cursor. Thus, as discussed later, Suite must treat MoveCursor as a history command.

[3]Successive `InsertChar` commands are combined together in to a single `InsertChar` command.

status of the command (Executed, Undone, Skipped), the name of the command (e.g. MoveCursor and InsertChar), and arguments of the command (e.g. field in which a character string was inserted, the insertion position, and the inserted string). [4] [5]

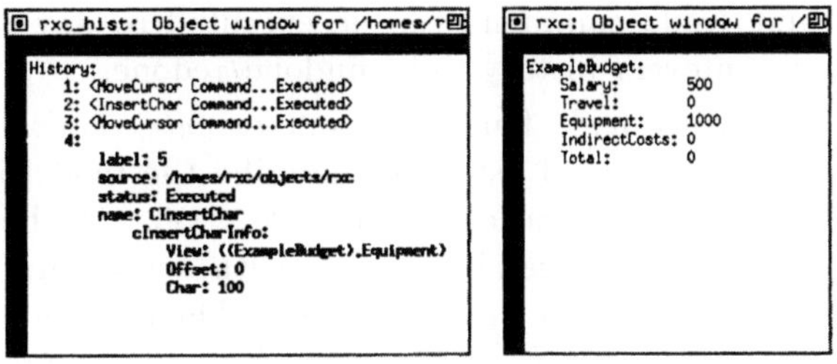

Figure 2: User edits Salary and Equipment fields

Figure 3 shows the editing window and history list after the user undoes the last two commands. As each undo is executed, the last executed command in the history list is marked undone and the effects of the command execution are removed from the display. Executing two more undo commands would return the edit window to the state represented by Figure 1 with all four commands undone, while issuing two redo commands would return the window to the state depicted in Figure 2.

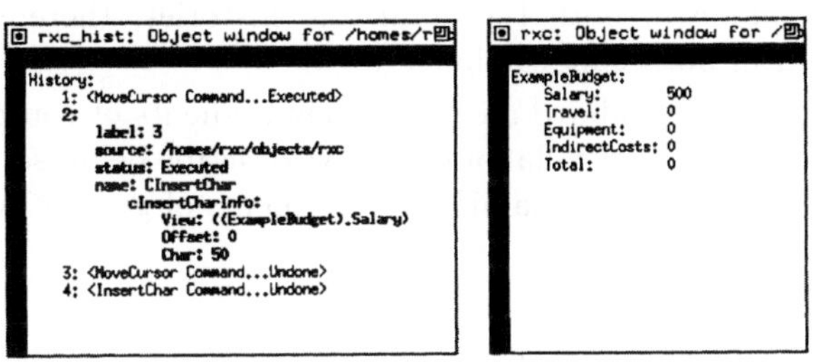

Figure 3: After two undos the Equipment field is reset

Designing Multi-User Undo/Redo

In this section, we incremently motivate, describe and illustrate the major components of our model.

[4] We expect most users would not be interested in these details. They have been expanded here to give the reader an idea of how the system works.

[5] We use a Suite dialogue manager to display the history list. The Suite dialogue manager provides facilities for eliding, and displaying different portions of the display in different fonts.

Basic Multi-User Undo/Redo

Here is a definition of a basic multi-user undo/redo model, which is a simple extension of the single-user undo/redo model above. All commands are shared by every user and commands appear in the same sequence in all command histories. An undo/redo command can be executed by any user and causes the last command in every history to be undone/redone.

More formally, we provide four operators *execute, undo, redo,* and *skip* which operate upon command lists. We describe the model in terms of the effect of these functions on the command lists. Let CL_i be the command list associated with the ith user interacting with a program. Let CL be a command list such that $CL = c_1, \ldots, c_{n-1}, c_n$. Then $execute(CL, c_{new})$ sets $CL = c_1, \ldots, c_{n-1}, c_n, c_{new}$, $CL_i = CL$ and $CurrentCommand_i = c_{new}$ for each user i. $undo_i$ executed by the ith user uses the same rule as the single user model for determining the target command. Thus $undo_i(CL = c_1, \ldots, c_{n-1}, c_n)$ results in setting $CurrentCommand_i = c_{n-1}$ and $c_n.status = Undone$ for each user i. We have ignored above undone and skipped commands. The redo and skip commands can be similarly defined by considering these commands.

We illustrate the model by using the example of a multi-user editing session in Suite. Figure 4 shows command lists and edit windows of two collaborating users, users `rxc` (top two windows) and `pd` (bottom two windows), after user `rxc` has edited the `Salary` and `Equipment` fields. When user `pd` autonomously issues an undo, the resulting state is shown in Figure 5. Note that the last command is undone in both the command histories, thereby resetting the `Equipment` field in both edit windows.

The model described above meets the requirements of compatibility, independence, consistency, and collaboration. We describe below several extensions to this design to meet the remaining requirements of genericity and arbitrary commands.

Corresponding Commands

The model above assumes that all command histories have commands in the same order. This requires the availability of an atomic broadcast facility or assumes the floor control model of interaction. Certain systems do not have(or use) an atomic broadcast facility. Some of these systems also allow simultaneous execution of commands by multiple users. In such systems, when two commands are executed by different users, the system can not guarantee that they are received in the same order by all users. Thus execution of commands c_p and c_q by other users may be received by users i and j in different order resulting in $CL_i \neq CL_j$. If we still assume that an undo/redo always operates on the last command in each command history, then an undo/redo invocation may operate on different commands in different command lists, since the last command in different lists is not guaranteed to be the same.

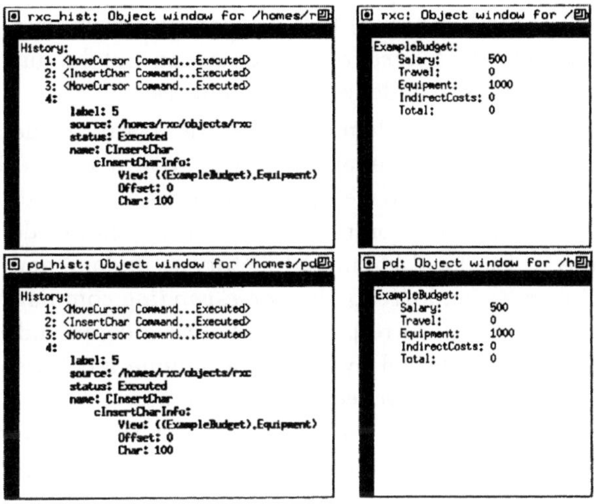

Figure 4: Local commands appear in remote histories

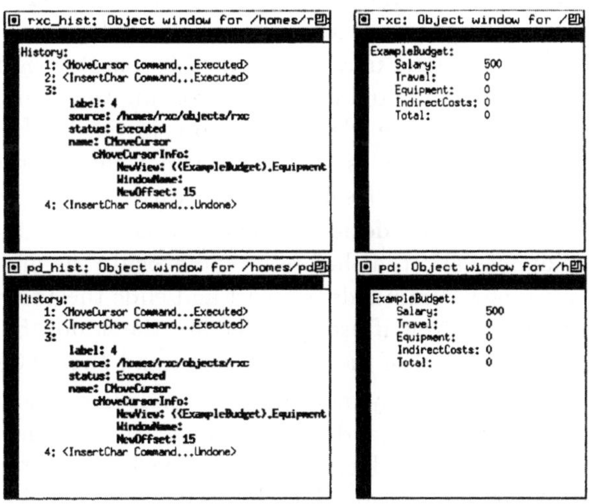

Figure 5: An undo undoes local and remote effects

More precisely, when the *ith* user issues an undo/redo command, it will result in the $CurrentCommand_j$ to be undone for each user j. But note that $CurrentCommand_i \equiv CurrentCommand_j$ can not be guaranteed and thus different commands gets undone for different users.

Our solution to this problem is to provide a way to identify all copies of a command in different command histories with a unique labels. Then semantics of undo/redo no longer need to depend upon all command histories having the same last command. When an undo/redo is executed, the last command in the local command history is undone and a request is sent to all other users to undo/redo the *corresponding* command in all the other command histories. The correspondence between commands in different command histories is established by using the unique label associated with each command. Thus $undo_i$ invoked by the ith user undoes the current command in the local command list CL_i. However the target command for the jth user is determined by $TargetCommand_j$ = Search c_k in CL_j such that $c_k.id = CurrentCommand_i.id$. We discuss and illustrate below the semantics of undoing a non-last (that is, non-current) command in a command history.

Undo by Reference

Now consider a system that also allows execution of undo/redo commands concurrently with other command execution. In such a system, when a user issues an undo to request the undoing of the last command in his command history, between the time the decision to invoke undo is reached and the undo is invoked, a new command may be executed by another user and become the last command in the command history. According to our model so far, this is the command that is undone when the undo is invoked. Thus the approach of always undoing/redoing the last command is not entirely satisfactory in such a system. For illustration, consider the multi-user editing session depicted in Figure 6. Suppose user `pd` decides to undo an accidental modification of the `Total` field. Suppose also that before he can execute the undo command, user `rxc` executes two new commands to select and elide the `IndirectCosts` fields, as shown in Figure 7. Now if user `pd` executes the undo, the `Elide` command would get undone instead of the desired command `InsertChar`.

We rectify this problem by modifying our undo/redo model to allow a user to explicitly mark the command to be undone. At most one command can be marked by a user, though different users can mark different commands. When an undo/redo command is invoked, it checks if a command in the command list has been marked. If a command is marked, that command is undone/redone. Otherwise, as before, the last command is undone/redone. Thus even if the referenced command is not the last command, this is the command that is undone/redone. To maintain the correctness of the interface state with respect to its command history, when a non-last undo/redo is requested, first all intervening commands in the command list are undone, then the referenced

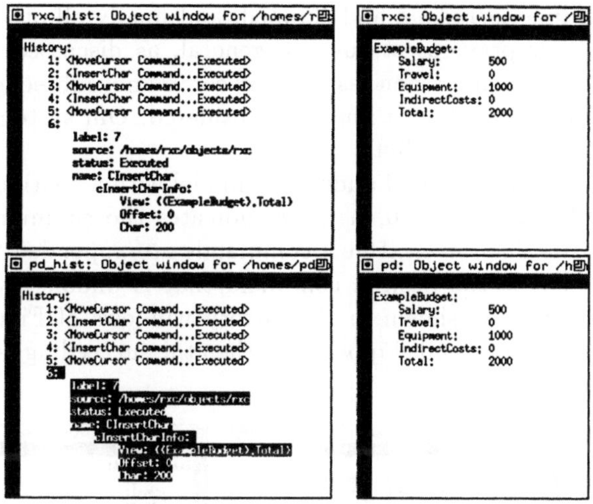

Figure 6: User pd decides to undo change to Total

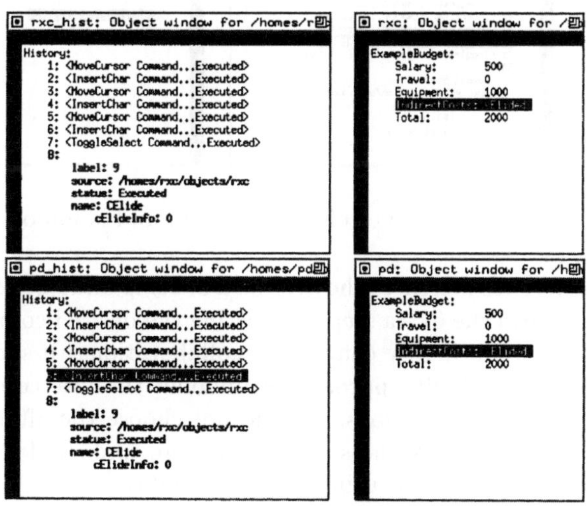

Figure 7: User rxc selects and elides IndirectCosts

command is undone/redone and skipped, and finally all other commands are restored to their previous status. In general, as discussed in detail in [10], before undoing/redoing a non-last history command, subsequent commands in the history that depend on it must be considered. Our system, currently, does not attempt to detect conflicts.

We illustrate our modified undo/redo model with a continuation of the previous example. In Figure 6, user pd indicates the command to be undone by selecting it. Then even if new commands are appended to the command list(Figure 7), it is the desired command that is undone by the undo command (Figure 8). As shown in the history windows of Figure 8, the target `InsertChar` is undone and skipped, and then the succeeding `Select` and `Elide` commands are redone.

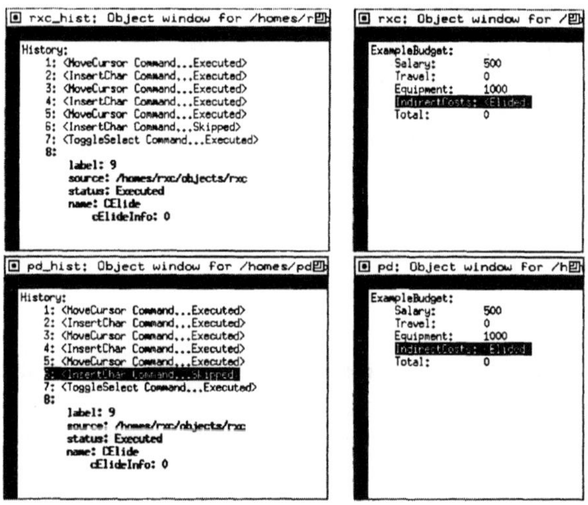

Figure 8: The referenced command is undone

Undo by reference increases the overhead of using undo/redo since it requires the user to perform the extra step of selecting the desired command. However, it is necessary only in highly concurrent collaborations. If such collaborations are rare, then the default approach of undoing the last command would be sufficient in most collaborations. We did not choose the alternative approach of requiring a user to lock the system before an undo/redo since that would increase the overhead of executing all undos/redos.

Selective Command Sharing

Now consider a system that provides non-WYSIWIS coupling [5, 9], that is, does not require the results of all commands to be shared immediately with all users. In these systems, our current approach of inserting all commands in every history is not applicable, since users expect that if their command histories are identical then so should be the state of their user interfaces. Therefore, we change our model to one that inserts into users' command histories only those commands that are shared with the users. More precisely, we introduce the concept of a *sharing* function. Given two users i and j and a command c_n executed by user i, the sharing function determines if the command will be (immediately) executed by the user-interface of user j. Different sharing functions can represent different collaboration schemes. When user i executes the command c_n, we insert c_n in CL_j for each user j if and only if $shared(i, j, c_n)$ returns *true*.

To illustrate undo/redo in non-WYSIWIS systems, consider the interaction shown in Figure 9. In this figure, user `pd` has executed a command to change the `Equipment` field. The results of this command are not currently shared with user `rxc`. (As we shall see in the next section, they will be shared later when an asymmetric collaboration command is executed). Therefore, according to our new command sharing policy, the `InsertChar` command does not appear in the command list of user `rxc`. Our undo/redo policy must now define the semantics of undo/redo when command sharing results in different histories. Consider what should happen when user `rxc` executes an undo. The last

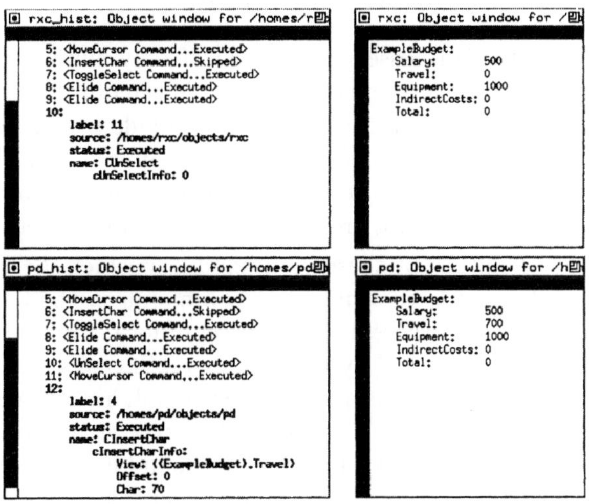

Figure 9: Only shared commands appear in a remote history

command in his history is an `UnSelect` command, which should be undone. But the `UnSelect` command is not the last command in the command list of user `pd`. Fortunately, using the unique labels assigned to commands, our existing undo/redo model can easily determine corresponding commands in command histories of all users and undo all of them. This is illustrated in Figure 10. An undo by user `rxc` undoes the last command in his interface and the corresponding (non-last) command in the interface of user `pd`.

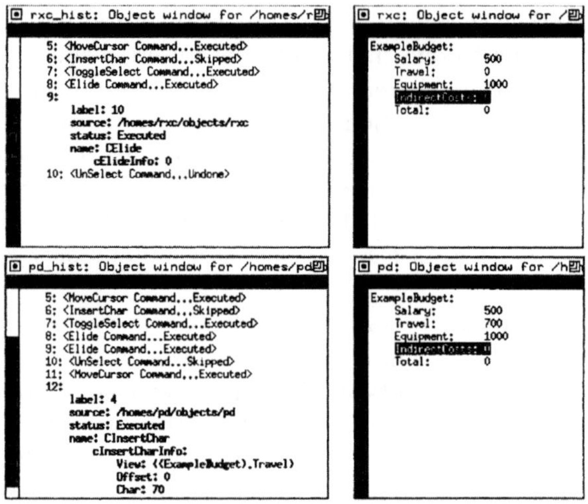

Figure 10: Undo with selective command sharing

Undo/Redo of Asymmetric Commands

So far, our model has addressed undo/redo of only symmetric commands - commands that have the same effect on local and remote user interfaces. Some non-WYSIWIS systems such as Suite [5], also provide asymmetric commands, commands that trigger the execution of previous commands in the local history in the user-interfaces of other users. These commands are asymmetric since the previous commands are not (re)executed in the local user interface.

To illustrate the nature of these commands, consider the Suite `Transmit` command, which transmits to other users commands in the local history that have not been shared with these users. The set of local commands transmitted to a remote user is determined by the Suite coupling scheme [5]. Continuing with the example, if user pd executes this command, his change to the `Travel` field, which has not been shared so far with user `rxc` (Figures 9 and 10), is now transmitted to `rxc` (Figure 11). This command is is an asymmetric command because its effects on local and remote user interfaces are different. In particular, a remote execution of it would yield results that have no correlation with the results of a local execution, since the remote execution would transmit pending changes of the remote user which have no correlation with the pending changes of the local user. Our model must now define the command sharing and undo/redo semantics of asymmetric commands.

According to our current command sharing scheme, an asymmetric command would not be inserted into remote command histories since it is not a (strictly) shared command. But that would not allow remote users to return changes they have received from other users. Therefore, we can modify our model to allow a user's history list to contain all commands, both local and remote, that modify that user's interaction state. But that would not allow a command such as `Transmit` to be inserted into the local command history (since it does not change the local interaction state), thereby not allowing users to withdraw changes they have sent to others. Therefore, we change our command sharing scheme to one that adds a command to the local command history and the histories of all users whose interaction states were modified by the command.

More precisely, we replace the sharing function described earlier with a more general *coupling* function. Given two users i and j and a command c_n executed by user i, the coupling function, determines the set of previous commands to be shared by user j. When user i executes the command c_n, we insert c_n in CL_j if and only if i is equal to j or $coupled(i, j, c_n)$ returns a non empty set.

The commands whose results are transmitted to remote users by a collaboration command are not added by our model into the histories of these users. Figure 11 illustrates our command sharing model. As shown in the figure, the `Transmit` command is added to both histories, but the `InsertChar` command that changed the `Travel` field is not added to the remote history. The remote user must undo the `Transmit` command to undo the effects transmitted by it.

Figure 12 demonstrates the effects of undoing the `Transmit` command in Suite. Recall that the effect of the `Transmit` was to transmit the result of the previous `InsertChar` command to a collaborating user (Figure 11). Thus, undoing of the `Transmit` command removes the effect of sharing the command. As before, either of the two users could have undone the command. Note that upon undoing, although the effects of the collaboration command are undone, the command sharing effects(namely the presense of the command in the remote command list) is not undone. This is the desired result since in single-user undo mode, the undo of the command removes the effects of the command, but does not remove the command from the command list. The presence of the command allows either user to redo the command. The `Transmit` command is an extreme form of an asymmetric command in that it has no effect on the local user-interface state. In general, an asymmetric command may change both local and remote states. For instance, the Suite `MoveCursor` command moves the cursor in the local user-interface and, depending on the coupling, may also transmit previous commands to other users. Our command sharing scheme described above accommodates such commands by including them in the histories of users who see their effects. It is for this reason that the `MoveCursor` command was included in the history windows of our example. Single-user applications do not usually put this command in the history, considering it a relatively insignificant command that users would seldom want to undo. In the multiuser case, several 'insignificant' single-user commands increase their significance since they can transmit significant changes to other users, and thus must be put in undo histories.

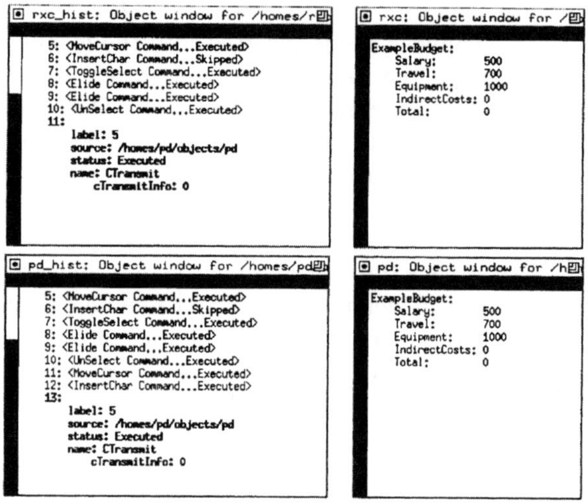

Figure 11: Transmit sends change to Travel

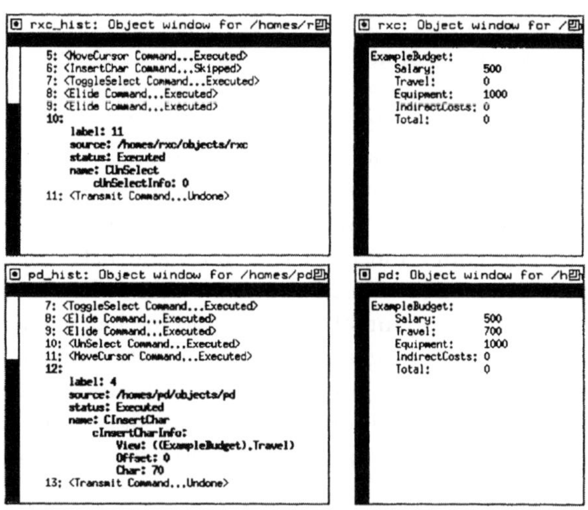

Figure 12: The transmission is undone

Conclusion

The contributions of this paper are a set of undo/redo requirements, a design that meets these requirements, and several detailed examples to motivate and illustrate the requirements and the design.

Multiuser undo/redo has also been addressed by other works [10, 3, 1]. These works and our model, which were developed independently and simultaneously, address mostly different issues arising in the design of multiuser undo/redo. In particular, none of these works addresses the undo issues that arise in a collaborative system allowing the histories of different users to diverge. The bulk of this paper presents these issues and an approach to resolve them. On the other hand, our model does not address some difficult issues raised by other works. In particular, it does not attempt to find conflicts that arise in the undo of a non-last command between the command be undone and subsequent commands in the history that are not be undone [6, 10].

The design described in this paper is only a first step towards a general multi-user undo/redo model and we propose to address the conflict issue in our future work. In particular, we propose to address the consequence of undoing a command that conflicts with only a subset of the histories that share the command. Moreover, we plan to consider extensions to single-user undo models other than the one assumed here. We plan to also explore how availability of a multi-user undo/redo facility may affect design of the access control and concurrency control facilities of collaborative systems. In particular, a multi-user undo/redo model must specify how a user's right to execute undo/redo is derived from his access rights to the data operated upon by these commands. Finally, due to lack of space, we have not discussed here undo of computation commands: commands that commands that request carrying out of computation. For instance, we have not discussed what happens if a user asks the application to compute the indirect costs of the budget and then wants to undo this computations. We address this issue in [4].

Acknowledgments

We would like to thank the reviewers for their detailed comments, which helped us improve the presentation of the paper. We would also like to thank the reviewer who pointed out the problem of a command conflicting with only a subset of the histories that share it. This research was supported, in part, by a grant from the Software Engineering Research Center at Purdue University, a National Science Foundation Industry/University Cooperative Research Center (NSF Grant ECD-8913133), and by National Science Foundation Grants IRI-9208319, IRI-9496184, and IRI-9408708.

References

[1] G. D. Abowd and A. J. Dix. Giving Undo Attention *Interacting Comput.*, 4(3):317–342.

[2] James E. Archer, Jr., Richard Conway, and Fred B. Schneider. User recovery and reversal in interactive systems. *ACM Transactions on Programming Languages and Systems*, 6(1):1–19, January 1984.

[3] Thomas Berlage A selective undo mechanism for graphical user interfaces. *ACM Transactions on Computer-Human Interaction*, 1(3):269–294.

[4] Rajiv Choudhary and Prasun Dewan. Multi-user undo/redo. Technical Report SERC-TR-125-P, Purdue University, 1992.

[5] Prasun Dewan and Rajiv Choudhary. Flexible user interface coupling in collaborative systems. In *Proceedings of the ACM CHI'91 Conference*, pages 41–49. ACM, New York, 1991.

[6] W. D. Elliot, W. A. Potas, and A. van Dam. Computer assisted tracing of text evolution. In *Proceedings of the AFIPS Fall Joint Computer Conference*, pages 533–540, 1971.

[7] R. F. Gordon, G. B. Leeman, and C. H. Lewis. Concepts and implications of undo for interactive recovery. In *Proceedings of the 1985 ACM Annual Conference*, pages 150–157. ACM New York, 1985.

[8] George B. Leeman, Jr. A formal approach to undo operations in programming languages. *ACM Transactions on Programming Languages and Systems*, 8(1):50–87, January 1986.

[9] C.M. Neuwirth, D.S. Kaufer, R. Chandhok, and J. H. Morris. Computer support for distributed collaborative writing: defining parameters of interaction. In *Proceedings of CSCW'94*, pages 145–152, October 1994.

[10] Atul Prakash and Michael J. Knister. A framework for undoing actions in collaborative systems. *ACM Transactions on Computer-Human Interaction*, 1(4):295–330, December 1994.

[11] Herold Thimbleby. *User Interface Design.* ACM, 1990.

[12] Jeffery Scott Vitter. US&R: A new framework for Redoing. *IEEE Software*, 1(4):39–52, Oct. 1984.

[13] Haiying Wang and Mark Green. An event-object recovery model for object-oriented user interfaces. In *Proceedings of the ACM Symposium on User Interface Software and Technology*, pages 107–115, Nov. 1991.

[14] Xerox PARC, Palo Alto, CA. *INTERLISP Reference Manual*, December 1975.

Proceedings of the Fourth European Conference on Computer-Supported Cooperative Work,
September 10–14, Stockholm, Sweden
H. Marmolin, Y. Sundblad, and K. Schmidt (Editors)

Supporting Cooperative Awareness with Local Event Mechanisms : The GroupDesk System

Ludwin Fuchs* , Uta Pankoke-Babatz, Wolfgang Prinz*
GMD – German National Research Center for Information Technology
Institute for Applied Information Technology
Schloß Birlinghoven
D-53731 Sankt Augustin , Germany
e-mail: ludwin.fuchs@gmd.de, uta.pankoke@gmd.de, wolfgang.prinz@gmd.de

Abstract

An event distribution model for a computer based cooperative working environment is presented. The proposed model aims to provide information about the ongoing and past activities of collaborating users, based on the semantics and contextual relationships of the shared artifacts and contributes to increase the awareness of the ongoing state of affairs without overloading the user with additional information.

GroupDesk, a prototype implementation of this model is introduced. The system provides a simple environment for the coordination of cooperative document production. Support for shared awareness is achieved by visualizing the event information using the desktop metaphor.

* This work has been supported by the European ESPRIT Basic Reasearch project COMIC (ESPRIT BR 6225)

1. Introduction

In the CSCW community the problem of supporting shared awareness among the users of systems for the support of cooperative work has gained much attention amongst researchers and is discussed quite controversially (Dourish and Bellotti 1992; Fuchs, Pankoke-Babatz et al. 1994; Pankoke-Babatz 1994; Sohlenkamp and Chwelos 1994). The discussion is motivated by two issues: on the one hand the problem of making the currently ongoing activities of interest visible to the users of the system and on the other hand to provide an overview about changes in the past concerning the objects of work.

Approaches to solve these problems differ very much in their respective orientation. They range from systems settled in traditional database technology, such as version and configuration management systems (Dittrich 1986; Belkathir and Estublier 1987; Kaiser and Perry 1987) to multimedia based information systems (Streitz 1992) or three dimensional virtual worlds (Benford and Fahlén 1993). All these systems have in common, that they focus on just one of the sub problems mentioned above. As an example, the spatial metaphor of Benford and Fahlén (Benford and Fahlén 1993) has proven to be especially suited to provide an awareness in synchronous cooperation and to support guidance of synchronous communication in potentially dense populated spaces, whereas the visibility of asynchronous changes seems to be more problematic to achieve. Conversely the traditional work on configuration management aims at object consistency in asynchronous work situations.

In this paper we present some ideas to enable an integrated description of the state of cooperation. Instead of conceptually separating the actors from the objects of work the model integrates the users, work artifacts, tools and resources, into a common organizational context and allows the provision of information concerning synchronous as well as asynchronous situations. The model is based on the representation of the working context as a semantic net. The nodes of the net represent the work artifacts, the actors (users), and organizational entities, such as departments, roles and procedures. The edges of the net are formed by different typed relations. Such a relation may describe similarities of artifacts in terms of content, or they can describe currently ongoing activities in the environment. They are also used to embed objects into the organizational context. The net is formed and continuously modified by the normal interaction of the users with the system.

A flexible event distribution strategy is applied, which distributes the events based on the user's interest in work situations. Users may get informed dynamically about events, that happen currently or that have happened in the past in the surroundings of their actual position in the work environment. This strategy has the advantage, that the visibility of events is bound to the user's current work occupation. Hence, the model provides a conceptual approach to prevent information overload. It allows the support for orientation in a very general sense: information about events is not only present at the directly involved objects, but also at objects that are related to them in some specific way. For modifications this behavior plays an important role, since the state of artifacts often cannot be determined clearly in isolation from related objects.

In the first part of the paper, we outline, which kinds of awareness the event model is capable to support. This is followed by a description of the representation of the work setting. We present the core event propagation mechanism and show how it uses this representation. and how it provides the necessary information, to support the respective modes of awareness in these situations.

In the second part of the paper, we introduce the GroupDesk system, a first prototype implementation of the event model, and show how the event related facilities of the system make use of these concepts and enable an implicit awareness of the users about the overall dynamics and state of work.

2. Modes of Awareness

Orientation in cooperative processes is based on events in these processes. In the following we use a notion of events, that allows a description of the state of cooperative situations and is suited to provide information to support each of the different modes of awareness, presented in Figure 1:

Synchronous awareness is concerned with events, that are currently happening, whereas asynchronous awareness considers events, that have occurred at some time in the past. Support for the latter mode needs to be derived by a summarizing interpretation of a whole sequence of events, that have happened in the meantime. Synchronous awareness should be supported by an immediate reflection of the ongoing affairs at the graphical user interface of the system.

	synchronous	**asynchronous**
coupled	what is currently happening in the actual scope of work ?	what has changed in the actual scope of work since last access?
uncoupled	What happens currently anywhere else of importance ?	Anything of interest happened recently somewhere else ?

Figure 1: Modes of awareness

Orthogonal to this classification we distinguish according to the current interest of the user between coupled and uncoupled awareness. Coupled awareness denotes the kind of overview, that is closely related to the current occupation of the user. An example for this kind of orientation is the knowledge of a user, who wants to edit a certain document, that this document is currently read by someone else. With asynchronous coupled awareness we mean situations, when a user is working on a certain object and gets informed about changes, that happened to this object in the past during a period of absence.

Uncoupled awareness applies in situations where information about events needs to be provided independent of the user's current focus of work. As an example for uncoupled asynchronous awareness consider a situation where a work flow system sends an object, such as a spreadsheet or a folder of documents to be worked over, to somebody who s currently on holidays. If there is a deadline attached to it, then it may be very important to notify the initiator of the work flow about this – even if he is at the moment concerned with something else.

3. The GroupDesk Model of a Working Environment

3.1. Objects

The basic units of information in the system are objects. Work artifacts in the environment, such as documents, tools or working resources of any kind, are modeled as respective objects. The same holds for more abstract entities, that compose the organizational context of work: groups, departments, organizational roles and rules are all simply objects in the system. Furthermore, we integrate objects that represent the users of the system. In terms of the model, they are basically treated in the same way as any other entity the system manages. In the following, we will however refer to objects representing users by the term actor, to distinguish them from the other objects in the system.

3.2. Relations

Relations are used to place the actors and artifact-objects into a collaborative context. Relations are typed and may be grouped into three basic categories: *structural* , *operational*, and *semantic relations*.

Structural relations are used to describe any kind of relationship between objects and an associated organizational context. Examples are all kinds of membership of entities and actors in specific contexts, such as projects and departments. Operational relations are always relations between an actor and an object. The general semantics of these relations is the fact, that the corresponding actor is currently involved in some kind of activity concerning the destination object. In an environment for document production, we would e.g. express the fact, that a user is editing a document by a corresponding operational relation. Semantic relations are used to express any semantic similarity between two entities in the system. They are highly dependent on the concrete nature of work to be performed.

The general form of the overall representation spans a semantic network. The actual maintenance and evolution of the network is triggered by the interaction of the users with the system: users may create objects and move them around as they like. The system performs the insertion and removal of the required relations. Also, the establishment of operational relations is derived automatically by the system, according to the actions, the users are performing. The system reflects the dynamics of the actions because the relations are only valid during the time the activity is happening. In many cases it is also possible to derive semantic relations by the system, e.g. a versioning system could introduce specific similarity relations between different versions of design objects.

3.3. Events

We distinguish two basic types of events: modifications and activities. Modification events are generated by the system, each time the state of an object changes due to some action of a user. Activities describe synchronous events, related to the users in the system. Their creation marks the starting point and their deletion the end point of the corresponding action. Here we may imagine events such as usage of tools, presence of a user in a certain working context or synchronous communication. Of course, this list is not complete. We can basically imagine any kind of event, that has a certain relevance when it comes to coordinating the work in a given setting.

Similar to the object class hierarchy there exists a class hierarchy for the events as well as for the relations. Furthermore there is a mapping between classes in the object class tree and classes in the event and relation hierarchy, in the sense that a particular class of objects may raise a particular set of events and can establish a well defined set of relations to other objects. This mapping is "inherited" to subclasses, but may be more specific as is illustrated in Figure 2. The vertical lines indicate the baseclass - subclass relationship.

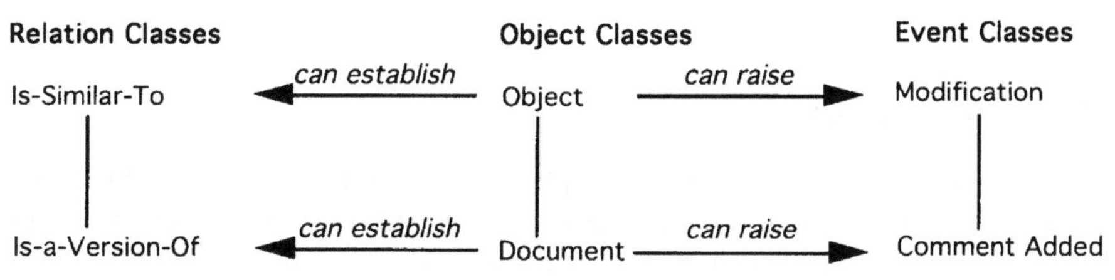

Figure 2: Relationship between Objects, Events and Relations

4. Awareness in Work Situations

4.1. Work Situations

A central requirement for the provision of awareness is to allow users to determine what they are interested in and what they are not. Thus notification of awareness information should not be prescribed by formal work representation. On the contrary the user should not be forced, to continuously register his interest for each and every object. So the system needs to offer a notion of work situation as a means to specify interest, such that each time the user is involved in one of these situations, he receives the awareness information, he is interested in.

Following the design rationale presented in the preceding chapters, we may consider a work situation for a given user a set of objects, interrelated in some specific way. An actor is involved in this situation, if one of the objects is interrelated to the actor by at least one relation. A simple example is the situation "working in a shared workspace" as illustrated in Figure 3: the situation consists of all objects that make up the workspace and the actor is involved in the situation until there is no longer some relationship between the actor an any of these objects.

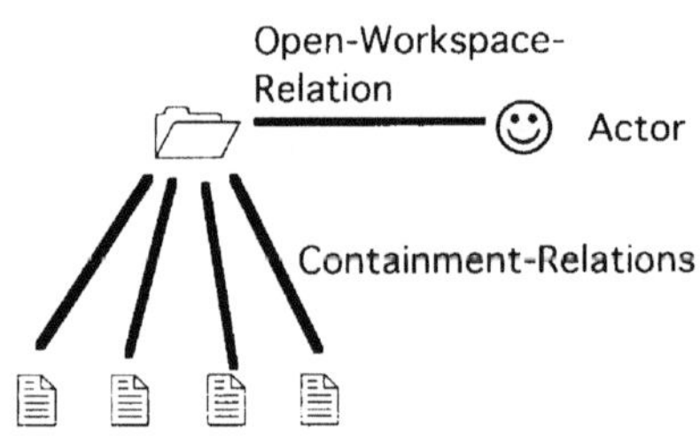

Figure 3: A work situation

4.2. Interest Contexts

Work situations form a suitable metaphor for the user to specify his interest in events. Interest in events for such situations is defined by interest contexts, which consist of a set of relation types, a set of event types and a list of interested users who have subscribed to the context. For any given object class in the system the user may define and/or subscribe to an interest context. The semantics of an interest context is, that the system maintains events of the indicated type raised by an object of this class in the surroundings of the object. The surroundings define a working situation and consist of all objects, that are linked to the original object by relations of the types listed in the context description. An example of an interest context for the class document involving the event "document modified", is shown in Figure 4.

This interest context is defined for situations where the subscribing user is the owner of the document. in which case he gets a synchronous awareness about all changes of documents he owns.

The concept of interest contexts can be fully integrated into the object oriented modeling paradigm. Each class in the system inherits the interest contexts of it's parent class. Furthermore users can override their subscription to interest contexts, i.e. they may subscribe to interest contexts of a base class, but not necessarily to the corresponding inherited contexts of the subclasses. Finally we can implement abstract interest contexts. An abstract context is a context which is defined for an abstract class. Also the specification of the relations or the events may be abstract as well.

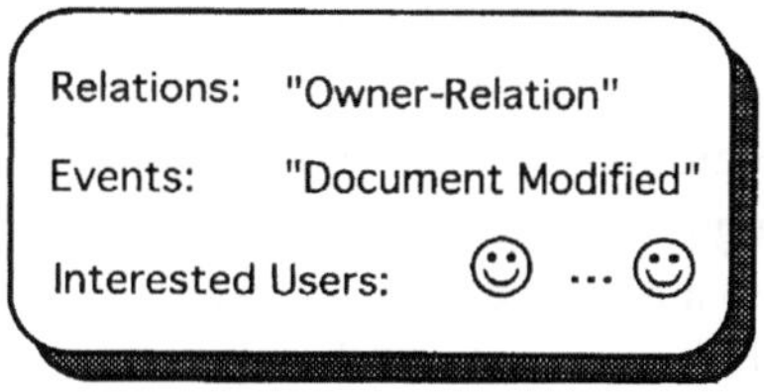

Figure 4: An interest context

4.3. Event Distribution

What happens, if an event gets raised by an object? First, the system checks, if there are matching interest contexts defined for the corresponding object class, i.e. that have the newly created event type listed in their event description. For all these contexts the system extracts the relation types and forwards the new event to all objects in the original object's surroundings, which are interconnected by one of the relations in this list.

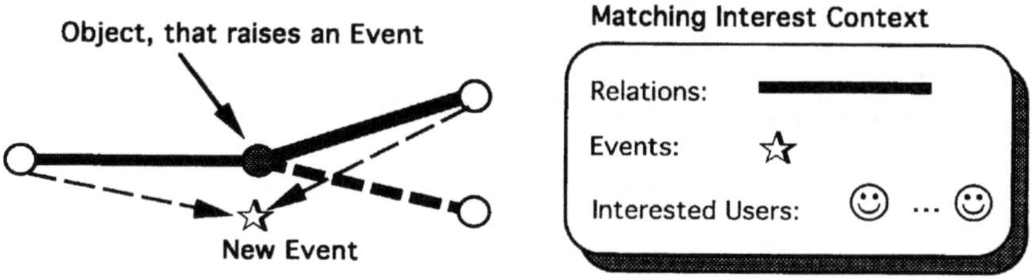

Figure 6: Event distribution

Distribution of events always means an accompanying passing of a reference to the interest context, that led to the event distribution along this specific relation.

This is necessary, in order to determine later on, which user wants to be informed about the event, if he is accessing this object. Furthermore the event object keeps a list of interested users as well. This list is formed by the union of all users that have subscribed to one of the interest contexts involved in the event distribution.

4.4. Event Notification

The distribution of the event according to the interest contexts leads to the presence of this event in a whole space of objects. Furthermore, there are different users that have expressed their interest in the event, and this space of objects is structured according to overlapping subspaces, for each of these users. If a user enters such a situation, i.e. if he is accessing one of the objects that take part in such a situation, the system performs a notification about all events that have occurred, since last access* .

The notification can be done in different ways and is independent of the core event model. We propose to have different urgency levels for subscription of interest contexts, which determine the form of presentation of event information at the user interface. A high urgency would typically lead to a disruptive notification, such as popping up a message window, whereas a low urgency could reflect the information by a change of color of the object's icon and leave the details of information to explicit user request. After the notification has been performed, the user is canceled from the list of interested users and will not be notified about the event again.

4.5. An Example

Consider the class "circulation folder" which is derived from class "folder". A circulation folder defines a list of recipients which sequentially receive the folder in their private workspace. The class defines the following relations that can be established to the actors in the list of recipients as shown in Figure 5:

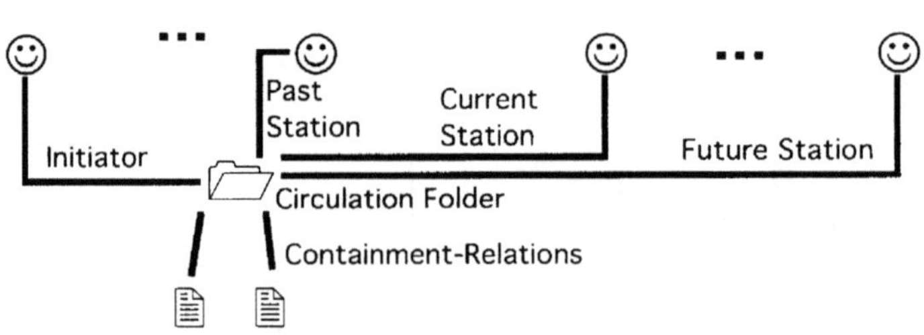

Figure 5: A circulation folder

* This can be determined by an inspection of the corresponing interest contexts for each event, i.e by checking, if this actor has subscribed to one of the contexts and by checking, if the user hasn't been informed before (via access of some other object).

- "Initiator" is a relation, which connects the originator of the work flow.
- "Past Station" connects all recipients, that have already finished their task.
- "Current Station" defines the actor, which is currently working on the circulation folder.
- The "FutureStation"-Relation identifies all the users, that will eventually receive the circulation folder.

Additionally a circulation folder inherits the Containment-Relation from it's parent class. Each time the folder travels from one station to the next, it raises a "Change Station"-event and the "Current Station"-relation of the former current recipient is exchanged by a "Past Station"-relation. The "Future Station"-relation of the successor station is exchanged by a new "Current Station"-relation.

The class "circulation folder" might define the following interest contexts:

- A "Progress"-context, which uses the "Initiator-relation to describe the situation. If this context is subscribed, users get an awareness about the state of any circulation folder, they have sent away. The class of events could e.g. be the "Change Station" events, such that they are informed, every time the folder changes from one station to the next.
- As a circulation folder inherits all interest contexts from his parent class, the user of the current station can make use of all awareness facilities he has subscribed for the class folder, e.g. he could subscribe to interest contexts that provide an awareness about the work, that has been performed by his predecessors, or he could be informed about things that happen synchronously, if he has opened the folder.
- We can additionally achieve awareness about work to be expected in the near future, with the following "Future Work"-context: the relations of this context are the "Future Station"-relations and as the interesting events we can simply define the "Creation"-event. A user subscribing to this context gets informed about the creation of each circulation folder, where he is contained in the list of recipients.

Interest contexts have to be defined for an object class only once and can be subscribed by any user in the system, who wants to share the corresponding awareness facilities.

5. GroupDesk

In the remainder of this paper we describe the GroupDesk system, a prototype CSCW application, that was specifically developed to demonstrate the event model, presented so far. The design of the system has dropped any features, that would have complicated the investigation of the event related concepts. As a result, GroupDesk has developed as a small platform, supporting distributed work in a simple environment for document production. The second design rationale behind the system has been the evaluation of novel object oriented development paradigms. For the implementation, a distributed development platform, compliant to OMG's CORBA standard, has been chosen (Object Management Group 1991; Object Management Group 1992).

5.1. GroupDesk Functionality

The system implements an environment for collaborative development and sharing of documents. The basic metaphor for coordinating and structuring cooperative work, used in the system, is the shared workspace. A workspace may be assigned the work artifacts and a set of members, which forms the group of users that have access to these objects and may freely modify them. Workspaces may be thought of as rooms in which the objects are visible and accessible and where the group members see each other and meet in order to perform shared tasks. In addition to the group workspaces, the system establishes a private workspace for each user that is registered in the system. Private workspaces may only be accessed by their respective owners.

Workspaces in GroupDesk allow members non sequential, unrestricted access of the objects they contain, thus supporting the accomplishment of tasks, that require continuous access of documents by the group members. The actual physical location of the artifacts in the distributed environment remains hidden from the users. In order to keep the design of the system as easy as possible, GroupDesk imposes no restriction or semantic prescription on the action of users. There are no conflict avoidance mechanisms implemented, e.g. to prevent two users from simultaneously modifying objects. The system addresses these problems by providing an implicit overview about all activities that are currently going on in the environment and thus enables an awareness of the users to prevent these situations.

The interface of the system presents workspaces as windows. The objects in the workspaces are shown as icons. The members of the workspace are also shown as labeled icons, showing the picture of the corresponding users. Interaction with the system is implemented by the usual drag and drop mechanism: objects may be moved freely around in the workspace and may be arranged as the users prefer.

Interaction with the system may be performed by double clicking on the respective object icon. If the object is a document, the system will launch the corresponding editing tool. Double clicking on folders and workspace icons opens a window, showing the contents of these objects. The system additionally supports synchronous and asynchronous communication facilities, which are attached to the actor icons. Double clicking on these symbols launches a video conference to the corresponding user. Artifacts may be moved into another location, i.e. workspace or folder, by simply dragging the object onto the destination's icon or window and dropping it. Each icon has additionally an associated menu attached, which gives users the possibility to delete, copy or rename the object.

5.2. Architecture

GroupDesk is designed as a distributed CSCW application, consisting of an object server and an arbitrary number of client applications, that may request services. The server manages a repository of objects and is responsible for administration and admission of the users, entering the system. The functionality of the system and the distribution of events and object changes is completely controlled by the server. Furthermore, the server is an instance that keeps the object repository consistent and enables a common view on the overall state of work.

The implementation is based on a CORBA compliant distribution platform which hides the aspects of localizing objects in the domain and granting access to remote objects from the clients. Clients may request services from any object in the system directly and don't have to be concerned with the interaction with the server. Interoperability between different domains is possible, although not yet based on the interaction of different domain servers. Currently users may start a client locally and access a server over the Internet. No matter where the server is running, communication with the server is completely hidden from the user.

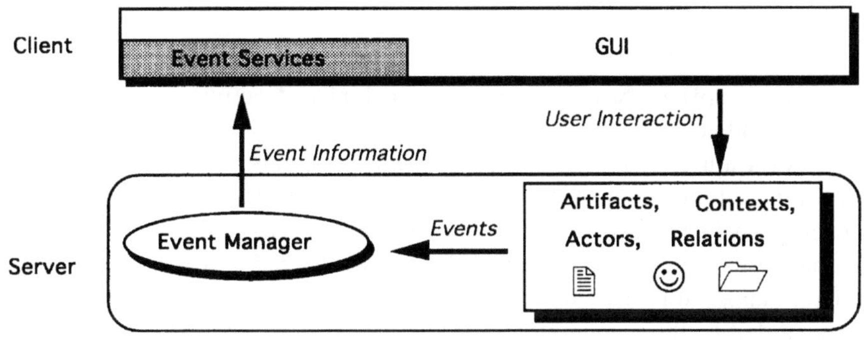

Figure 7: GroupDesk architecture

The system is structured according to Figure 7. On the client side, GroupDesk offers the services, that enables users to interact with the system. This basically consists of the graphical user interface, which is responsible for offering the functionality to access and manipulate objects. Additionally, the user interface displays the changes in the state of objects as well as the dynamics in the work setting, whenever the server notifies it about new events. The client side also provides the management facilities, that allow the user to explicitly request event related information via a history service.

On the server side, GroupDesk implements the common facilities to serve client requests for accessing objects, such as opening documents, deleting objects, or moving entities to another location in the repository. The object repository maintains the representation of the organizational context, i.e. the structuring of artifacts by different typed relations, to form a semantic network. At the current stage, the system supports structural and operational relation types. The server also implements an event manager, which handles the generation of events each time a user performs some action that results in a change of the object repository and subsequently performs the propagation of the events. The event manager further is responsible for storing events in object related event lists and notifies all interested clients about the changes, that took place. Additionally, it may receive event retrieval requests from clients and access and return event information.

5.3. Awareness Facilities in GroupDesk

The emphasis in developing the GroupDesk system has been the support of user awareness, by applying the strategy of local event distribution, that has been described previously. The event related services present the users the dynamics in the work process. Events caused by other actors and external influences are displayed by the system in an unobtrusive manner and include active notifications of changes in the work setting, as well as inactive presentation of event information on user request.

5.3.1. Events in GroupDesk

Currently GroupDesk has implemented two kinds of activities: presence in a workspace and generic working activities.

Whenever a user enters a workspace, the system adds an operational relation between the actor object and the workspace object. Furthermore an activity event is generated, which describes this action. The event contains a time stamp and a reference to the actor, who has entered the workspace. Subsequently all events, that have happened in the workspace since this user has accessed it the last time, are forwarded to the actor object and the user can immediately see what has changed. The system forwards modification events, that have happened in the past and the currently ongoing activities of other users in the workspace to the new user. Users may also request information about activities that are already finished. This helps to keep the amount of event information small and concentrate on the current state of work.

The generic work activities include any type of action the user performs on an artifact other than workspaces. Currently this involves editing a document or opening a folder. In both cases the system establishes an according relation between the actor and the corresponding object and presents event information related to the object. Among the types of modifications, GroupDesk has implemented object updates, which are generated whenever the content of a document, folder or workspace changes, creation, deletion and movement of objects. For each modification, the system generates a new event object and stores it in an object specific event list.

5.3.2. Event Propagation

Event distribution is currently statically defined: users cannot specify individual interest contexts. This is due to the fact, that the system is currently in an experimental stage and yet lacks many of the concepts that have been presented before. Similarly, the types of relations currently supported have to be complemented. They consist of structural and operational relations. The structural relations support the basic types of relations to structure the work artifacts in workspaces.

A typical GroupDesk scenario is shown in Figure 8. In this example, two workspaces are modeled. Structural relations place objects into the respective workspace context and are also used, to describe the contents of folders. Operational relations consist of two types, that describe presence of actors in a workspace and activities concerning artifacts, e.g. editing a document. Artifacts may be shared among workspaces. In the example, a document object is contained in two workspaces simultaneously.

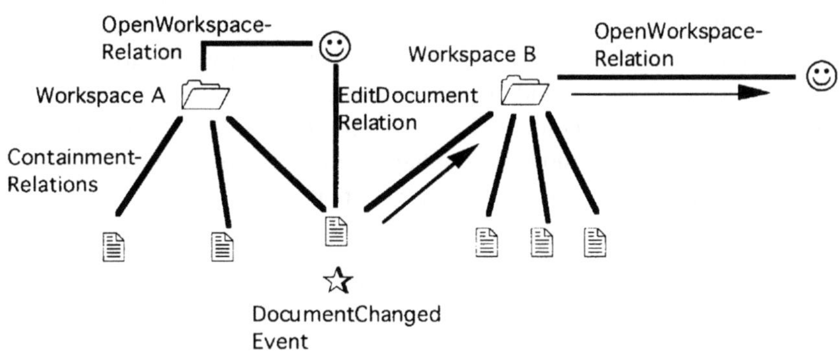

Figure 8: A GroupDesk scenario

In the example the user in workspace A edits a document, which in turn raises a "Document Changed"-event. This event is forwarded along the Containment-relations to all surrounding workspaces, such that the user in workspace B gets a peripheral awareness about the change.

To demonstrate the event model GroupDesk defines a global strategy for event distribution, which cannot be tailored by subscription of individual interest contexts. The distribution of events is defined as follows:

- Structural relations always forward events from the inferior object to the superior object, but not vice versa.
- Operational relations always distribute events to the involved actor.

5.3.3. Event Visualization

The display of event information is integrated in the standard user interface. Modifications on artifacts are indicated by changing the color of the object's icon.

Different colors are provided for the different types of modifications. The system however presents only the most recent modification on an object. It has turned out, that this is usually sufficient to give an overview at a glance about the state of affairs in the workspace. If more detailed information is needed, the user may request the complete summary of changes and activities concerning an object via the history service.

Synchronous events, i.e. currently ongoing activities of other users in the same workspace are shown on the graphical user interface by colored connection lines linking the icon of the actor, who is currently performing the activity, with the icon of the object, that is involved in the activity. The icons of workspace members are always shown in the workspace window, even if they are not currently active. If a member enters a workspace, this activity is shown by changing the member's icon from gray scale to colored. Non-members entering the workspace, are indicated by adding their actor icon in the workspace windows of all other users that have opened this workspace.

In general, the visibility of events is restricted to the visibility of objects in the user's view. This means that events are usually shown at the topmost object in the structural hierarchy, which is visible to the user. If the user wishes to see more details, he can open this object and inspect it's contents. As an example consider the modification of an object contained in a folder. If the folder is closed, the user may only notice that some modification happened to the folder. If he wants to see more details, he may open it and inspect it's contents.

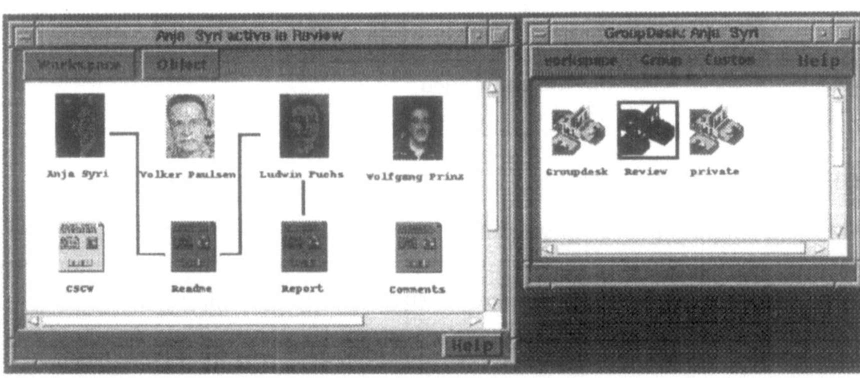

Figure 9: The GroupDesk Interface

A history service allows users to get a detailed description of the events that happened during an object's lifetime. The service is available for any type of object except actors. In the current version the description is text based, but it is planned, to implement graphical display of event information (e.g. charts, showing the appearance of events over time) as well as event filtering and interpretation. It has turned out however, that the current implementation is already quite useful when it comes to exactly determining what has happened in the past with an object.

Figure 9 shows a GroupDesk Interface. The right window displays a list of workspaces. Workspaces with ongoing activities or changes are displayed in another color. The left window shows an open workspace, with two active users and synchronous editing activities indicated by the connection lines. The modifications on the document are also indicated by different colors of the icons.

6. Future Work

The implementation of the GroupDesk prototype is currently only realizing a minimal environment for experimenting with the concepts of event propagation and support for shared awareness, presented in this paper. In order to capture the whole facilities of the model, many things remain to be done. Most notably, the representational issues need to be extended, i.e. the types of relations need to be extended by semantic relations. Additionally, the existing relation types have to be further diversified. To capture the dynamics, it is necessary to implement the concept of interest contexts for individual tailoring of event propagation.

Conversely the system needs to be enriched with more sophisticated event services on the client side. It is planned to extend the history service with facilities for graphical display of history information. To achieve support for uncoupled awareness, an event notification service has to be integrated. Last but not least, it would be necessary to provide full object persistency in order to make the prototype really usable for practical work. This is currently not realized to a full extent.

It has turned out however, that the approach of presenting the default event information graphically at the user interface results in an implicit overview for the participants in the work process about the state of affairs, without overloading them with too many details.

The concepts presented in this paper will be implemented in the German research project POLITeam (Hoschka, Kreifelts et al. 1994) on the basis of the CSCW platform LinkWorks.

7. Conclusion

In this paper we have presented an event mechanism which is capable of providing information to describe the dynamics and state of work in CSCW applications and thus may be applied to support shared awareness in systems for the coordination of cooperative work. The model proposes the representation of the environment as a semantic network. Awareness about changes and synchronous activities in the system is supported by the generation and distribution of events in the semantic network. The propagation mechanism provides the flexibility, to distribute the information, such that it may be accessed in places, where it is relevant, and on the other hand prevents overloading the user with unnecessary details.

GroupDesk, a prototype implementation of this model has been presented. The system is implemented on the basis of a distributed object service platform. The system implements a simple environment for coordination of distributed work and enables the support of shared awareness for the users by applying the event model and visualizing the event information using the desktop metaphor.

8. References

Belkathir, N. and J. Estublier (1987). *Software Management Constraints and Action Triggering in the ADELE Program Database*. First European Conference on Software Engineering, Strasbourg, France.

Benford, S. and L. E. Fahlén (1993). *A Spatial Model of Interaction in Large Virtual Environments*. Third European Conference on Computer Supported Cooperative Work, Milan, Italy.

Dittrich, K. W., et al. (1986). *DAMOKLES - A Database System for Software Engineering Environments*. International Workshop on Advanced Programming Environments, Trondheim, Norway.

Dourish, P. and V. Bellotti (1992). *Awareness and Coordination in Shared Workspaces*. CSCW '92 - Sharing Perspectives, Toronto, Canada, ACM Press.

Fuchs, L., U. Pankoke-Babatz, et al. (1994). *Ereignismechanismen zur Unterstützung der Orientierung in Kooperationsprozessen*. German Conference on Computer Supported Cooperative Work, Marburg, Unknown Publishers.

Hoschka, P., T. Kreifelts, et al. (1994). *Gruppenkoordination und Vorgangssteuerung*. Dritter GI Workshop des GI-AK 5.5.1 Betrieblicher Einsatz von CSCW Systemen, Sankt Augustin: GMD, GMD Studien.

Kaiser, G. E. and D. E. Perry (1987). *Workspaces and Experimental Databases: Automated Support for Software Maintenance and Evolution*. Conference on Software Maintenance.

Object Managemennt Group (1991). The Common Object Request Broker: Architecture and Specification. OMG.

Object Management Group (1992). Object Management Architecture Guide. OMG Tech. Document.

Pankoke-Babatz, U. (1994). *Reflections on Concepts of Space and Time in CSCW*. ECCE 7: Seventh European Conference on Cognitive Ergonomics. Human Computer Interactions: From Individuals to Groups, Sankt Augustin, Germany, GMD Studien.

Prinz, W. (1993). *TOSCA: Providing Organisational Information to CSCW Applications*. Third European Conterence on Computer Supportes Cooperative Work - ECSCW'93, Milan, Italy, Kluwer.

Sohlenkamp, M. and G. Chwelos (1994). *Integrating Communication, Cooperation and Awareness: The DIVA Virtual Office Environment*. Proc. Conference on Computer Supported Cooperative Work - CSCW 94, Chapel Hill, NC.

Streitz, N., et al. (1992). *SEPIA: a cooperative Hypermedia Authoring Environment*. ACM Conference on Hypertext, Milan, Italy

Proceedings of the Fourth European Conference on Computer-Supported Cooperative Work,
September 10–14, Stockholm, Sweden
H. Marmolin, Y. Sundblad, and K. Schmidt (Editors)

Why Groupware Succeeds: Discretion or Mandate?

Jonathan Grudin and Leysia Palen
University of California, Irvine, USA

Abstract: Single-user applications are designed with a 'discretionary use' model. In contrast, for large systems, upper management support is considered crucial to adoption. Which applies to groupware? The relatively low cost of groupware reduces high-level visibility, but some argue that social dynamics will force mandated use—the large system approach. Interview studies of recently adopted on-line meeting schedulers in two large organizations found successful, near-universal use achieved without managerial mandate. Versatile functionality and ease of use associated with discretionary products appeared to be factors leading to adoption. Other factors included organization-wide infrastructure and substantial peer pressure that developed over time.

Introduction

Many groupware developers hope to emulate the success of individual productivity software products such as word processors and spreadsheets. The use of single-user applications is often discretionary, and they are designed to appeal to discretionary users. Even corporate purchasers who do not themselves use such a product may consult users. Discretionary use and competition have led to emphasis on ease of use and more functionality. In contrast, a large system built or tailored for a specific setting has fewer resources for minor features and interface tuning, and requires users to adjust more. A large system has a range of users, not all of whom may benefit from or like it. Studies of the introduction of large systems invariably report that strong backing by upper management is critical to success.

Groupware lies between the two. Similarities to large systems include the need to tailor to individual settings and the likelihood of mixed reactions by group members. It has been argued that groupware success will require mandated use. On the other hand, the low (and downward-spiraling) cost of groupware gives it less visibility in a large organization; it is unlikely that upper management will become involved in promoting every groupware application or feature.

For example, Markus and Connolly (1990) examined social factors in the adoption of groupware tools and concluded that mandated use or other top-down measures appeared necessary for the use of these tools to reach 'critical mass.' In a widely-cited case of groupware adoption (Orlikowski, 1992), a high-level mandate to use LOTUS NOTES received a mixed response, but use continued at Alpha Corp.

However, conflicting signs are present. An interesting aspect of Orlikowski's study is that the technical support staff, under no mandate to use NOTES, adopted it successfully. Markus (1995) studied mandated use of electronic mail in one organization and found that *how* email was used was highly discretionary and varied. And of course the use of email often spreads without a high-level mandate, although email is a risky application from which to generalize about groupware.

By examining factors that underlie cases of successful groupware adoption, our study addresses the tension between the recognized importance of high-level support for large system adoption and the lower visibility groupware can expect.

We examined collaborative meeting schedulers, applications with recent successes that stand in contrast to early, documented failures. About 15 years ago, commercial office systems began to provide meeting scheduling features with electronic calendar applications. Computer-assisted meeting scheduling represented an appealing technical solution to a clearly identified problem: People spend a lot of time arranging and rearranging meetings. Nevertheless, it was difficult to find successful use of the software, even in the development organizations and research laboratories that produced the software and provided widespread access to it. In fact, Grudin (1988) used meeting scheduling to illustrate several factors that contribute to the lack of widespread adoption of some groupware applications.

Today, successful use is more widespread. Electronic meeting scheduling occurs in environments very similar to those where it was not found a decade ago. In this paper we review the findings of the mid-1980s, then describe two detailed interview studies conducted in environments similar in many respects to those examined a decade earlier, but where on-line meeting scheduling is now routine.

The settings we studied are not typical, and we do not claim that the software will soon be universally adopted. Quite the contrary, the settings are special: they are software development organizations. However, meeting scheduling was not adopted in comparable settings a decade earlier. What has changed in the software or in these environments that contributes to current use? What is the adoption process? The actual or potential presence in other settings of such factors, once identified, might signal the usefulness of this or other groupware and suggest adoption processes to expect or encourage.

Meeting scheduling in 1985

By the early 1980s, many organizations had installed office systems that provided word processing, spreadsheets, email, and on-line calendars. In settings in which on-line calendars are widely available, the concept of computer-assisted meeting scheduling is simple: A person scheduling a meeting identifies the participants and the application checks each person's calendar, finds a time when everyone is free, and schedules a meeting or issues invitations. The potential utility was clear: The time spent scheduling and rescheduling meetings is substantial. Opportunities lost through inefficiency in meeting scheduling had been identified (Ehrlich, 1987a).

However, a study conducted in a large organization that developed and marketed an early electronic calendar identified factors that contributed to a lack of use of the meeting scheduling feature (Ehrlich, 1987a; 1987b; Grudin, 1988). Electronic calendars were used as communication devices by executives, managers, and their secretaries, but only by about one in four individual contributors. The latter, if they kept any calendar at all, found portable paper calendars more congenial—available in meetings, for example. To maintain an on-line calendar would require more work of individual contributors, but the direct beneficiaries would be the managers and secretaries who called most meetings. In addition, although most employees had computer access, not everyone in the organization was networked tightly enough for the software to reach them. As a result, meetings were scheduled by traditional methods, despite the presence of the software on everyone's desks.

Research papers at early CSCW conferences described new approaches to meeting scheduling that did not fare much better. Woitass (1990) designed a system to address the access problem. Based on a distributed agent architecture, it consulted the electronic calendars of those maintaining them and engaged other users directly. Although a technical success, Woitass reported that the system was not used for much the same reason: It required work from those who did not see the benefit of using it. Beard et al. (1990) developed a priority-based visual calendaring system that performed well in controlled experiments, but in field tests encountered a range of problems, most notably a lack of integration with users' desktop applications. In their presentation, they suggested that these applications would become fully useful when portable computers eliminate some advantages of paper calendars. Finally, a 1991 survey of groupware use was directed at Internet distribution lists of "empirical researchers, system developers, and end-users of CSCW products and systems" (Butterfield, Rathnam, and Whinston, 1993). Respondents indicated that group calendaring systems were the most widely available of 10 groupware technologies by a substantial margin, but were judged to be the least likely to have a significant impact.

Collaborative meeting schedulers are not unique in requiring additional work (in this case calendar maintenance) from people who do not see a benefit in their use. Most large systems and major applications face this challenge when introduced.

But an important difference is that groupware is often not a large, expensive system: It can be a small application or even a feature. The collective benefit of using a feature or small application is not as evident, it does not have the visibility in the organization that an expensive system does, so it is unlikely to get the same degree of management support. To promote a large system, management may hire support staff such as system administrators and data entry personnel, change staff job descriptions, and encourage or even mandate use. In contrast, managers in the environments examined in the 1980s did not mandate that individual contributors maintain on-line calendars solely to facilitate meeting scheduling, nor were secretaries asked to maintain the on-line calendars of individual contributors.

Upper management advocacy is a key element in large system adoption. In contrast, the use of individual productivity tools or single-user applications has more often been discretionary; an application must offer each user a tangible reward. Groupware is caught in the middle: It often must appeal to all group members, yet can expect little in the way of top-down advocacy.

But the situation was never deemed hopeless: "The conclusion is not entirely negative. Automatic meeting scheduling could be targeted to environments or groups making the most uniform use of electronic calendars. Their value can be enhanced by adding conference room and equipment scheduling..." (Grudin, 1988). "Focus on improving the interface for those who receive less direct benefit... this may seem obvious but is very difficult" (Grudin and Poltrock, 1990).

It is difficult to focus interface design on "incidental" users because an application *must* appeal to its principal beneficiaries. A meeting scheduler that does not appeal to the manager or secretary who calls meetings has no chance. Interface development is usually directed toward those who will benefit most from using an application, not those who benefit least (Grudin, 1994).

Ehrlich's (1987a) data suggested one way to target existing calendar users. She reported a higher incidence of secretary-supported calendar use among managers and executives in the development organization she studied. Electronic support for scheduling meetings of managers was therefore feasible, and is often reported.

> "PROFS (Office Vision) is the single most used office system in the company. Most people with PROFS accounts do not use its calendar. Almost all managers/supervisors use the calendar, and secretaries maintain the calendar for 2nd level managers and higher... They collected data in (a group of primarily managers and secretaries) and found very large time savings and cost savings due to the online calendar." (Steven Poltrock, personal communication, 10/3/94.)

Obstacles hinder the wider use of this particular system:

> "In my [group] most people use an online calendar, but our calendars are not shared—we are not using PROFS." (Ibid.)

Our study involves engineering environments in which scheduling is not restricted to managers, engineering environments similar to those in which meeting scheduled failed in 1985. The prescription to improve interfaces for individual contributors is part of what we found has changed over the years, although it is not the full story.

Meeting scheduling in 1995

Although meeting scheduling is far from universal or even widespread—it not used in the authors' workplace, for example—reports of its use in engineering environments are encountered with growing frequency, even in the absence of portable computing. Questions prompted by these reports include:

- How widespread is calendaring and meeting scheduling at these sites?
- Who uses them?
- Are new application functionality and/or interfaces factors?
- Has the collective benefit of use been made more salient?
- Is adoption the result of top-down encouragement or mandate?
- How does adoption proceed over time?

Site Descriptions

Microsoft Corporation

Most of Microsoft's 15,000 employees are located in the Seattle area, where the interviews were conducted. The average employee age is 34, low for a large software company. For many of them, Microsoft is their sole or principal source of work experience. Most employees in the development divisions have their own office or share with one other person, and every employee has ready access to a common platform computer that is linked to the company-wide network.

Sun Microsystems

About half of Sun Microsystems' 13,000 employees work in the (San Francisco) Bay Area, with about 3,000 in the engineering departments where our interviews took place. The average age of Sun employees is 38. Each has an office or shares with one person, except for admins who are typically in cubicles in central locations. Employees have workstations connected to the company-wide network. ("Admins," short for "administrators" or "administrative assistants," are responsible for secretarial and other coordination functions.)

Method

The second author spent three months as a participant observer in a Microsoft development division, at which time she conducted five interviews on the topic of meeting scheduling. Based on experiential data and the Microsoft interviews, we developed a set of 40 questions that she used in twelve interviews conducted over a 3-day period at Sun. We had learned of widespread use of scheduling at these sites and sought active users. Our interest was in identifying possible success factors; the specific adoption contrast that frames this paper emerged during the analysis.

Participants

Microsoft. The five interviews were of people with different job titles across the development divisions. Each participant was in a different workgroup. All had been employed at Microsoft before the electronic calendar application was introduced, with an average of about 5 years' service. Listed in increasing order of time spent in meetings, the subjects were a developer, visual designer, program manager (project leader), development instructor and first level manager.

Sun. Eleven people from ten different workgroups in engineering organizations and one person in corporate marketing were interviewed. They had been at Sun over five years on average. Two arrived after the electronic calendar was introduced. Eleven now use the electronic calendar; the twelfth once used it but no longer does. Three participants were or had been on the CALENDAR MANAGER product team and provided technical implementation information, an historical account of the product's introduction, and data about their personal use. Listed in roughly increasing order of time spent in meetings: two administrative personnel, two technical writers, three developers, two human interface designers, one product marketer, one manager, and one corporate marketer.

Interview questions

We queried subjects about their use of paper and electronic calendars. Questions covered procedures and protocols for arranging or responding to meeting invitations, privacy, granting viewing access, peer pressure, managing one's calendar when away from the computer, using calendars for structuring work, and using calendars for handling resources such as conference rooms and equipment.

Description of the Electronic Calendar Applications

We next describe features of the two electronic calendars. These applications are maturing into versatile, flexible systems with a wide range of capabilities and multiple paths for achieving many goals. Readers familiar with them may prefer to skip to the discussion.

Microsoft's *SCHEDULE+*™

SCHEDULE+ runs on PCs under WINDOWS. Individual calendars are kept on the owners' machines with frequent updates to a central server. Users view a calendar by specifying its owner's email alias or name, the latter a recent enhancement.

Viewing the Calendar. SCHEDULE+ supports two on-screen calendar views. The day view provides complete textual information about each appointment and symbols that indicate if the appointment is a recurring meeting, a "locked" meeting not viewable by others, a tentative meeting, or a tentative meeting contingent on others agreeing. The planner view provides a quick check for availability over 17 days, with booked times blocked out graphically and no appointment content detail.

For printing, SCHEDULE+ supports day, week, and month views as well as a textual list of appointments. Printed views are designed to be put in appointment books and thus differ in appearance from on-screen views.

Navigation. Drop down menus allow users to jump to a specific day or week. Clicking on a specific day in a small monthly calendar graphic in a corner of the day view jumps directly to that day. Arrows enable one to advance by month or year.

Privacy Settings. Users can allow their calendars to be viewed by anyone in the company, by certain people, or by no one. Additionally, users can determine what level of access another person has: *restricted viewing* reveals when time is booked or free, but not the content of appointments; *complete viewing*; and *"assistant" privilege*, which allows another person to accept and send meeting requests on behalf of the calendar owner. Calendar owners can "lock" a meeting, making it completely private.

Booking Appointments. One way to book appointments is to select the time and duration in the day view, then type the description of the event directly into the view. Another way is to bring up the "Edit Appointment" dialogue box (either by clicking on a time or using menus), which provides input fields for appointment information, including whether a meeting is to recur every day, every work day, once a week, once a month, or in one of several other patterns. The dialogue window also allows one to set the lead time on alerts: a pop-up window and/or an audible reminder of an imminent appointment.

Group appointments are booked in one of two ways. 1) The meeting arranger enters the appointment details in the Edit Appointment dialogue box, then invites other people by specifying either their email aliases or full names. (An on-line rolodex tool can help locate names and aliases.) This spawns another window with a mini-planner view where the invitees' calendars are overlaid to reveal available times. Clicking on a booked slot causes a symbol to appear next to the email aliases of those who are booked at that time. 2) These steps can be reversed: The meeting arranger first specifies the people to attend, determines an available time from the overlaid calendars, and then enters the appointment details. This flexibility in sequencing allows meeting scheduling to proceed naturally in circumstances that vary regarding the availability of attendees, the importance of a meeting, and whether key people must be present.

Both scheduling procedures typically end with the meeting arranger initiating email from within SCHEDULE+. All attendees' email addresses appear in the *To* field, the meeting topic in the *Subject* field, and the meeting time in a special *When* field. The meeting arranger can also check a *Send Response* box, which generates response mail based on attendees' decisions to accept or decline the meeting. The meeting arranger can then track the status of the responses within another SCHEDULE+ dialogue window.

Receiving SCHEDULE+ Mail. An email message generated within SCHEDULE+ arrives with regular email. The message header includes *Accept*, *Decline*, *Tentative*, and *View Schedule* buttons. Selecting *View Schedule* launches

SCHEDULE+ (if it is not already open) to enable the recipient to review his or her schedule to confirm availability. If the recipient selects *Accept*, the meeting is automatically entered into his or her calendar and a mail window is generated to reply to the sender with "Yes, I will attend" as part of the header. If *Decline* is selected, a mail window is opened with "No, I will not attend" in the message header. *Tentative* produces the message "I might attend." With any of these, a responder can include additional information in the message body.

Sun's *CALENDAR MANAGER*™

CALENDAR MANAGER runs under OPENWINDOWS and CDE on SPARCSTATIONS. When open but inactive, it appears as an icon showing the current date. Calendars are maintained on their owner's host machines. Browsing other calendars requires specifying the host on which each calendar resides. Host names are listed in an on-line corporate rolodex of employee information.

Viewing the Calendar. CALENDAR MANAGER supports identical on-line and printed day, week, month, and year views, the latter including no appointment information. The day view presents meeting information in hour slots and provides small depictions of the current and next two months for navigation and context. In the week view, the view preferred by most employees interviewed, a full week is displayed two ways. Each day appears as a pane containing a simple text list of the day's appointments, including start times, end times and appointment details. In addition, the week is displayed with booked and free times shown graphically for an at-a-glance assessment. Appointments are shaded; overlapping appointments appear as progressively darker shading. The month view displays a given month with reduced appointment information.

Navigation. In the day view, advance and reverse buttons shift one day at a time. Clicking in one of the small month depictions jumps ahead. Similar buttons in the week and month views advance or go back a week or month. Users can thus jump to a week in a distant month by switching from week to month views, clicking to reach the desired month, and then returning to the week view.

Privacy Settings. As with SCHEDULE+, multiple levels of view access can be set for different appointments at the calendar owner's discretion. CALENDAR MANAGER specifies the same three levels of viewing access: *Show Time and Text*, *Show Time Only*, and *Show Nothing*. A global default is set and then overwritten as desired for specific appointments.

Privileges can also be assigned to specific people. *Browse* allows an assigned person to view one's calendar, with the viewable content level dependent on the access level assigned to each appointment. *Insert* allows a person to insert meetings into the owner's calendar and delete the same meetings later if necessary. *Delete* privilege allows a person to delete any meetings in the owner's calendar.

Booking Appointments. Appointments are booked by initiating the Appointment Editor dialogue box, either with a pull-down menu, by clicking on the desired meeting time in the day view, or by selecting the desired day in the week, month, or year views. The Appointment Editor has fields for the date, start and end times and a general content field for the subject and location. Privacy default settings can be modified and auto-reminders can be set in this dialogue box. Auto-reminder options are a pop-up window, beeping, screen flash, and sending email (typically to oneself, although any email alias can be specified for reminding). Any combination of auto-reminders with independently set warning intervals can be used, although a global default eliminates the need to set options for each appointment. Finally, appointments can be set to recur at a variety of time intervals.

Checking for Availability. There are several ways to arrange meetings, combining automated features and social protocols. The Multibrowser can be invoked to determine the availability of attendees. It overlays calendars that are specified by email alias and host machine name. Again, shaded time indicates unavailability; the darker the shading, the more people are unavailable. Once the Multibrowser is invoked, there are several ways to proceed. The meeting arranger can select an available time, enter the meeting details and then send email from within CALENDAR MANAGER by selecting the Mail button on the Multibrowser. This generates a Mail Tool window with invitees in the *To* field and an appointment icon in the attachments section of the mail message. Recipients can drag this icon to their calendars to automatically insert meeting and content information.

Another way to proceed is to use the Multibrowser to find two or three possible times and use the Mail Tool (outside CALENDAR MANAGER) to initiate normal email, asking invitees to choose among the possibilities. The arranger then chooses a time based on the responses and sends an official announcement, either as regular email, or from within the calendar to automatically include an appointment icon. Other ways to send the final notification through regular email are to drag appointment information from the Appointment editor and drop it into the email message or copy a template into the regular email and manually type in the fields.

Receiving Mail with CALENDAR MANAGER Information. Meeting invitees who receive email enclosing an appointment icon attachment or a template can drag it to their calendars for automatic entry. These attachments or templates are used for notification of large meetings ("all hands"), by administrators to distribute company holiday lists, and by meeting arrangers who confirm a meeting time by negotiating the time first and then sending automated information as a convenience to the invitees and to ensure that everyone has the same information.

Overview of Use

We had sought informants who used on-line meeting scheduling, so it was not surprising that high usage was reported in 16 of the 17 interviews (i.e., 15 of the 16 groups). The exception was the Sun corporate marketing representative, a former user, who frequently met with external contacts, people not accessible through the system.

At Microsoft, the most commonly used privacy setting was the application default, restricted viewing. This allows others to see booked and free time but not the details of scheduled appointments. People typically schedule a meeting by checking the availability of others and sending SCHEDULE+ mail with a proposed time, allowing the recipients to accept or decline with a keystroke. This approach, with no informal prior negotiation of time, can strike outsiders as very blunt when it involves, for example, initiating a one-on-one meeting with someone one does not know and who is not expecting the meeting request.

Only one Microsoft informant reported making hardcopies of her calendar and bringing them to a meeting. When people are away from their desks (e.g., in a meeting) and need to schedule something, common phrases are "Sched plus me" or "Plus me." Someone later finds an available time and sends out SCHEDULE+ mail.

A conference room has a calendar that is viewed and scheduled like any other. The conference room appears in the *To* field of the meeting invitation message. If meeting location information is omitted from the *Subject* line (which is read by SCHEDULE+ when the request is loaded into a person's calendar), a recipient can examine the *To* field to see which conference room has been "invited to" or booked for the meeting.

At Sun, the most commonly used privacy setting is also the application default, but in this case the default, *world browse,* allows others to see the descriptions of appointments as well as their times. Descriptions of private appointments, such as interviews and medical appointments, must therefore be "blacked out" individually. Employees use CALENDAR MANAGER to check weekly calendars to determine availability for formal meetings and for informal drop-ins. Seeing the content of a meeting can be useful: It can indicate whether a person is in their office or where they are and when they might be back, how interruptable they might be, how "reschedulable" a meeting might be in case of a conflict, and so forth. Browsing has other uses: Managers report locating subordinates and vice versa. "Browsing VP (Vice President)'s calendars is a lot more interesting," said one first-level manager, although perhaps not all VPs set their calendars to *world browse*.

To initiate a group meeting, Sun interviewees generally send regular email listing a possible time. Many are either unaware of the various ways a meeting template or drag and drop icon can be generated, or they find them inconvenient. But some of them take the trouble to type information in meeting template format so recipients can drop it into their calendars for automatic loading. People are more likely at Sun than at Microsoft to bypass the system to set up a one-on-one meeting, although they generally enter such appointments in their calendars after scheduling them.

Our Sun informants rarely print out calendars either (although we have evidence that managers and executives are more likely to do so). If a need to arrange a meeting arises, someone typically takes responsibility for setting it up, often in response to a request to "Browse my calendar" or "Browse me." Most groups use a separate application to schedule conference rooms, but special equipment in high demand is given a calendar for people to "browse" to find available time.

Factors Contributing to Successful Adoption

Many factors can contribute to a pattern of application use in a particular setting, not all of which may be clear to participants and thus not recovered from interviews. However, our interviews addressing calendar use in 15 groups in two organizations yielded evidence of conditions and patterns different from those prevailing ten years ago in similar environments. These differences, which plausibly contribute to the improved reception that meeting scheduling now enjoys, include:

- the infrastructure, including network, software, support, and behavior
- expanded application functionality
- the versatility and ease of access provided by graphical interfaces

The adoption of communication technologies occurs over time. Often a critical mass of use must be reached before a technology provides a net benefit (Markus, 1987). Virtually all group members must adopt some technologies before they are useful. Group calendaring has been described as one such application by researchers (Ehrlich, 1987b) and by some of our informants. How does one obtain universal compliance? The claim that management must mandate use has been made for groupware, but as noted in the introduction, groupware such as meeting scheduling may not be considered important enough for management to pressure people to do the substantial work of keeping their calendars on-line. Another approach found in the literature of success cases is that of the fervent product evangelist who persuades all group members to try the software, thus obtaining the critical mass that brings real benefits to the group.

Did we find management mandates or evangelist networks in our 16 groups? We found a few cases in which group leaders strongly encouraged group use, and we interviewed one self-described evangelist. But these did not explain the widespread use of meeting scheduling. Instead, we found widespread reports of peer pressure. Two notable aspects of this pressure were:

- aspects of the product interfaces that facilitate the delivery of peer pressure
- adoption was described several times as following a bottom-up pattern from developers to managers and administrative assistants ("admins"). Pressure on recalcitrant users could eventually come from every direction—managers, admins and peers—and adoption became nearly universal.

We now consider in turn each of the five bulleted items above.

Infrastructure

Both sites have organization-wide platforms supporting the calendar and scheduler. All employees with PCs (Microsoft) or workstations (Sun) were networked.

Ten years earlier, this was not true in large high-tech companies. Part of a company might rely on a mainframe, elsewhere minicomputers—the platform for groupware of that period—were in use, and PCs made inroads but were difficult to network. Email could not span these environments, much less meeting scheduling software. Members of a team might share a platform, but many meetings (other than regularly scheduled group meetings) included people from other groups; therefore scheduling software could not routinely replace traditional scheduling methods. Our informant who did not use the calendar was outside development, in corporate marketing; many of her meetings involved people external to the company whom the software could not reach. Ten years earlier, most developers were in comparable positions with respect to other groups *within* the company.

Both sites also provide strong technical support in installing and maintaining the software. This arose in several interviews. Group calendaring over a large client-server network is technically challenging. The failure of two releases of CALENDAR MANAGER was attributed by one informant to reliability problems, and occasional losses persist:

> About 2 years ago <sigh/laugh>, I lost all my data. And they had no idea what happened, it just was gone. So I mean all my personal data was gone too...I felt so stupid that I had to go back and call all these people. I lost all my birthday data, ... my work data ... I was lost, because I rely on my calendar to tell me where I am supposed to be and what I am supposed to be doing. I really was relying on it. When I lost the data, I had to go around and try to find it, or I'd get calls "where are you?" "well I am right here, where am I supposed to be?" So, you know it was an embarrassing time.

Clearly not much of this will be tolerated in a product.

Finally, although difficult to measure, behavior has changed. People are much more comfortable with technology and are heavier users of it now than was true ten years ago, even in engineering environments. Almost everyone in these settings can be counted on to read email regularly, one element of what Markus (1987) calls "message discipline," an important factor in promoting use. The casual use of phrases such as "Sched plus me" and "Browse me" is further evidence of structuration or an evolution of the culture around the technology. A "behavioral infrastructure" was also in place.

Functionality

Another change in ten years is product maturation. SCHEDULE+ requires about 2M RAM on each client and 5M disk space between client and server; CALENDAR MANAGER requires about 2-4M RAM and 1M or more disk space. Unlike earlier products and research systems, these applications were strongly integrated with desktop environments, email and corporate on-line rolodexes. The tight coupling with email was singled out as a factor in early adoption.

Conference room availability was sometimes described as the most critical aspect of scheduling a meeting, so the ability to schedule rooms or equipment through the system is another example of a feature that promotes use.

Both systems provide a broad range of privacy options. Informant attitudes toward privacy differed, so this flexibility could be important.

Seemingly minor features were often praised: the diverse mechanisms for reminding oneself of an upcoming event or a new release that increased the ways to define recurring meetings, such as 'Mondays, Wednesdays and Fridays at 9.' ('Feature creep' may afflict calendars but does not yet seem a problem.)

One admin had used CALENDAR MANAGER for six years to keep calendars for managers, but only started keeping her own three years earlier:

> [I started using it for myself] when I realized all the things it could do ... I don't remember it being that sophisticated before ... I mean it is an incredible thing. I mean now you can show multiple calendars on top of each other. So it's really just gotten so good, it's become a valuable scheduling tool ... I would say that with all of the increased capabilities of CALENDAR MANAGER that a lot more people have started to use it and realized that it's a very helpful thing.

Versatility and Ease of Access

In discretionary use situations, ease and enjoyment are powerful motivators. (If the MACINTOSH did not prove this, the success of interfaces such as EUDORA and MOSAIC have.) With the applications studied, many calendar and scheduling features are easily accessed and many tasks can be carried out multiple ways, with one or another way more natural depending on the context. With the earlier generation of schedulers, obtaining information was too time-consuming to promote some of the casual uses of calendar information that we observed. Even when unrelated to meeting scheduling, these promote the prerequisite on-line calendar use; they contribute to "calendar discipline," the behavioral infrastructure.

We found evidence that for applications that are only indirectly tied to people's principal work missions, interface transparency and efficiency are particularly important. Where a feature is even slightly obstructed, it can go unused. For example, CALENDAR MANAGER users greatly appreciate receiving invitations in the form of a "meeting template" which can be dropped into their calendar. Yet many message senders do not use either of the ways to drop a meeting template into their invitation, each of which involves an extra step or two: Instead they take more time to type an invitation character by character to conform to the message template.

One developer pithily summarized his attitude: "walk arounds are work arounds." If he felt blocked by the application, rather than looking for a way to work around the problem, he would arrange meetings "off-line," on foot.

An interface change that was widely praised at Microsoft was allowing users to enter employee's actual names, in contrast to their email aliases. At Sun, employees' calendars had to be identified by name and host machine. The integrated on-line rolodex renders this only a minor inconvenience; nevertheless, this was a common source of complaints, suggesting that small interface details are salient to users who may not be strongly committed to an application.

Universal Adoption and Peer Pressure

"The only way that makes it useful is that everyone is using it."

—Product marketing representative

Use was almost universal in the groups sampled, with some people unaware of anyone who did not use it. A Sun developer remarked "More people are running this stuff now, absolutely. It's probably almost 100% at this point." An admin estimated "Ninety-eight percent. I think that it probably went from like 50% when I [first] really started using it." Another developer said:

> The numbers have gone up dramatically. I think now ... everybody uses it, anybody who has a workstation uses it. It's hard to find someone who doesn't use it ... It'd probably be the janitor or someone like that because they just don't have access to the equipment. Everybody ... even non-technical people use it.

How did use become so widespread? When asked directly, some reported peer pressure to keep calendars on-line, some admitted exerting such pressure, others said they did not notice pressure, but might contradict themselves in subtle or not so subtle ways. "One person in this group refuses to use it and it drives people nuts," said a Microsoft designer. A Microsoft middle manager described a higher-level manager: "She doesn't use SCHEDULE+. That's a source of frustration." An admin at Sun reported telling the only non-user he knows: "Everyone on the team is available at this date and time, except I don't know whether you are even in your office." A Sun human factors engineer who said "I don't think that there's any pressure to use it" also said:

> Where I find that things become annoying is that a lot of people will call for meetings without using the calendar appointment embedded in their message ... then I've got to go into the CALENDAR MANAGER and schedule an appointment and it seems like a waste of time. And that happens all the time.

(He noticed and pointed out the contradiction himself.) A manager echoed this:

> I find it a real pain in the neck [when someone doesn't include the appointment icon]. It amazes me ... that people send out appointment notices that don't include them—irritating. They're lazy. I know they use CALENDAR MANAGER so I mean ... they haven't figured out how to do it, or it's just not important to them to think of that.

In environments where "sched plus me" or "browse me" are common phrases and future meeting dates are not set on the spot, non-users will quickly feel left out. In fact, they miss out. "Individuals were embarrassed about not having shown up to meetings. There was peer pressure to start." (Microsoft.) "Once people start sending you appointments then that behooves you to look at your calendar some and also suggests, 'well gee I've got appointments that other people are giving me, so maybe I should do the same.'" (Sun.)

Other forms of inducement include sending out lists of holidays or birthdays formatted to be dropped into calendars (which is a recent practice at Sun).

The application design can itself contribute to social pressure. Recognizable message templates remind non-users of a benefit they may be missing. Integration with email enables the technology to deliver peer pressure. A project manager at Microsoft reported "Some people don't look at my SCHEDULE+ [calendar] to see if I'm available. I will press decline, and say please see my SCHEDULE+." The recipient is left with little option other than to use the software.

The Adoption Trajectory

No single adoption pattern fit every group. A few reported pressure from managers, and at Microsoft group by group adoption occurred. Several developers and managers reported that developers—individual contributors—were the first adopters, exerting pressure on peers and then on managers and admins, with pressure continuing up the managerial ladder. Once admins adopt meeting scheduling they can exert pressure in all directions. (It may be a significant factor that admins appear to wield more influence than secretaries did ten years ago.)

People expressed a variety perceptions about adoption. A Microsoft program manager said: "I resisted for six months. When I had people under me, I needed it. Now I can't live without it." A Sun corporate marketing representative, who initially used CALENDAR MANAGER but has since stopped, reported:

> [In] Sun culture, engineers [say] 'You are not on CALENDAR MANAGER?' They're just shocked that you don't use your own technology ... I don't think marketing management uses [CALENDAR MANAGER].

A Microsoft trainer reported that "the first groups to get up to speed were the admins." Similarly, a Sun product marketing representative said:

> I think that most people keep a CALENDAR MANAGER because of the browsing capabilities.... When we are trying to set up appointments, admins ... rely on being able to look at other peoples' calendars to see when they are available.

A Sun developer described a bottom-up adoption pattern:

> Over time, they (managers) started to use it, they started seeing the benefit of using it ... but initially I can't say there were a lot of people using it. Initially ... it was mostly developers, then you start getting a scattering of managers, I bet you now we could go and browse Scott McNeely's (Sun CEO) calendar if we wanted to, so now all the way to the top ... now everybody.

However, a Sun technical writer reported a different experience: "pressure was from management, not coworkers. The attitude is 'Get into the 90s.'"

Conclusion

In these large organizations, groupware can succeed without mandated use, helped by the congenial functionality and interface features associated with discretionary use individual productivity tools. The features, some of which provide individual benefits (e.g., meeting reminders), may attract a critical mass of users, after which technology-abetted social pressure by peers and others extends use.

We do not say groupware use always follows this pattern; we found examples of mandated use, albeit from low management levels. Mandated use can clearly lead to or facilitate adoption. In addition, in contrast to these large established organizations, we have seen some new, small enterprises that organize themselves around groupware technologies, a de facto mandate. More study of the successful adoption of a variety of applications in diverse settings is needed to assess the significance and representativeness of these and other factors.

Acknowledgments

We are grateful to interview participants at both sites; to Ellen Isaacs for her enthusiasm and intellectual and operational support for the project; to Rick Levenson, Mark Simpson, Susan Denning, and the Microsoft Usability Group for their support; and to Susan Ehrlich Rudman, Steven E. Poltrock, and Lynne Markus for comments and help in identifying details of calendar use in different places and times. This material is based in part upon work supported under a National Science Foundation Graduate Research Fellowship awarded to the second author.

References

Beard, D., Palaniappan, M., Humm, A., Banks, D. and Nair, A. (1990): "A visual calendar for scheduling group meetings." *Proc. CSCW'90*, 279-290. New York: ACM.

Butterfield, J., Rathnam, S. and Whinston, A. B. (1993): "Groupware perceptions and reality: An e-mail survey." *Proc. 26th Annual HICSS*, 208-217.

Ehrlich, S. E. (1987a): "Social and psychological factors influencing the design of office communication systems." *Proc. CHI+GI '87*, 323-329. New York: ACM.

Ehrlich, S. E. (1987b). "Strategies for encouraging successful adoption of office communication systems." *ACM Transactions on Office Information Systems, 5*, 340-357.

Grudin, J. (1988): "Why CSCW applications fail: Problems in the design and evaluation of organizational interfaces." *Proc. CSCW'88*, 85-93. New York: ACM. Extended version in *Office: Technology and People, 4*, 3, 245-264.

Grudin, J. (1994): "Groupware and social dynamics: Eight challenges for developers." *Communications of the ACM, 37*, 1, 92-105.

Grudin, J. and Poltrock, S. E. (1990): "Computer Supported Cooperative Work and Groupware." *CHI'90 Tutorial Notes.* NY: ACM.

Markus, M. L. (1987): "Toward a 'Critical Mass' Theory of Interactive Media." *Communication Research, 14*,5, 491-511.

Markus, M. L. (1995). "Disimpacting use: How use of information technology creates and sustains organizational transformation." Working paper, February 1995.

Markus, M. L. and Connolly, T. (1990): "Why CSCW applications fail: Problems in the adoption of interdependent work tools." *Proc. CSCW'90*, 371-380. New York: ACM.

Orlikowski, W. (1992): "Learning from Notes: Organizational issues in groupware implementation. *Proc. CSCW'92*, 362-369. NY: ACM.

Woitass, M. (1990): "Coordination of intelligent office agents - applied to meeting scheduling." In S. Gibbs and A. A. Verrijn-Stuart (eds.), *Multi-User Interfaces and Applications*, pp. 371-387. Amsterdam: North Holland.

Proceedings of the Fourth European Conference on Computer-Supported Cooperative Work,
September 10–14, Stockholm, Sweden
H. Marmolin, Y. Sundblad, and K. Schmidt (Editors)

MAJIC Videoconferencing System: Experiments, Evaluation and Improvement

Yusuke Ichikawa, Ken-ichi Okada, Giseok Jeong, Shunsuke Tanaka and Yutaka Matsushita
Department of Instrumentation Engineering, Keio University
3-14-1 Hiyoshi, Kouhoku-ku, Yokohama, 223 Japan
Tel: +81-45-563-1141, Fax: +81-45-562-7625
E-mail: ichikawa@myo.inst.keio.ac.jp

We need to know the real intentions of participants that are not expressed by verbal languages. This means that not only verbal information but also non-verbal information (i.e., gestures, facial expression, eyes of participant, etc.) is a very important factor. We proposed and implemented MAJIC, a multi-party videoconferencing system that enables eye contact among people in remote places, with life-sized images of participants.

In order to evaluate users' perceptions of MAJIC, we have experimented with the size, background and boundary of the video images. These experiments verify the sense of presence in MAJIC environments where life-size video images without boundaries are supported. We developed a new MAJIC prototype based on these experiments.

Introduction

Face-to-face meetings are the best way to make decisions, but it is sometimes difficult to assemble participants at the same time and same place. There have been many studies on tele-communication support systems using video images [6, 7, 8], and we think video-conferencing systems could be developed in two categories. One attaches importance to portability, in order to be able to communicate with anyone, anytime and anyplace. An example of this is desktop conferencing systems [9, 10, 11]. We will be able to have meetings using multi-media notebook computers equipped with radio network facilities in the near future.

The other category attaches importance to reality, and, as a result, usually requires a large space. Some topics or keywords in studies of these systems are

(1) informal communication support [12, 13, 14],

(2) simulation of a multi-person round-table meeting [4, 15],

(3) eye contact support [3, 16],

(4) integration of communication space and work space [3, 17] and

(5) virtual reality [18].

In order to communicate with each other by videoconferencing with a sense of presence, one of the most important problems is how to support eye contact among participants and provide life-size portraits of them. Many systems use a half transparent mirror to support eye contact, while other systems use a large screen to provide life-size portraits, but it is difficult to provide both. Moreover, in the case of multi-party videoconferencing, multiple eye contact should be supported, and to support a sense of presence or feeling of togetherness, there should be no boundaries between the pictures.

In face-to-face meetings, we need to know the real intention of participants that are not expressed by verbal languages. This means that not only verbal information but also non-verbal information (i.e., gestures, facial expression, gaze of participant, etc.) is very important factor.

As the proverb says, "The eyes are more eloquent than the tongue." In many cases, we perceive one's true intention from his/her facial expressions and gestures. Moreover, the gaze serves to regulate the flow of conversation. Therefore, it is important for telecommunication systems to establish a method to enable non-verbal communication, such as communication made by facial expressions and gestures, as well as verbal communication. However, since cameras are mounted above display devices in conventional videophones or teleconferencing systems, natural communication with eye contact could not be achieved. We have developed a multi-party videoconferencing system, MAJIC, which supports teleconferencing with a sense of presence [1, 2].

The design of MAJIC

The MAJIC system has three concepts. The design concepts are:

Life-size portrait and background without boundaries

There are two important factors in achieving a sense of presence during videoconferencing. One is the size of participants' images on the screen. For example, we may feel participants are far away if their portraits are smaller than life-size. Moreover, it would be difficult to read facial expressions or gestures if participants are shown on a small display or displays. Another factor is the background behind the portraits. Although there are some systems that use multiple displays to provide for multi-party conferencing, to achieve a feeling of togetherness, there should be no boundaries between the portraits. If users are surrounded by other participants with a seamless background, they can feel as though they are together.

Multiple eye contact and gaze awareness

Multiple eye contact among participants should be supported to make multiparty conferencing effective since without eye contact or calling out the person's name it is difficult to speak to a specific participant in a multi-party environment. We usually become aware of one participant gazing toward another through eye movements and head turns in face-to-face meetings. With the Hydra system, it has been reported that movements in the periphery on the screen do not attract recipients' attention because of the problem of small screens [4]. Life-size portraits arranged around a table produce a situation in which the eye movements and head turns of the users attract the attention of the recipients.

Shared and personal workspace between participants

In face-to-face meetings, participants usually sit around a table on which material is piled up in front of them; some material is for individual participants and other material is shared. Of course eye contact is very important in communicating with one another, as mentioned above, but especially in Japan it is impolite to look into someone's eyes for a long time. What should we look at? Sometimes we look at other participants one after another, or we look at the material on the table. A space in front of participants provides each person with a personal workspace and a shared workspace on which to place material; at the same time, it gives participants a reason for averting their eyes.

Implementation of prototype MAJIC

The key feature of the MAJIC system is a screen composed of printed dots on a transparent sheet. The screen looks like a white screen from one side, but a transparent film from the other side. Therefore by setting the camera on the transparent side of the screen (i.e. behind the projected images), it is possible to achieve natural eye contact (Figure 1).

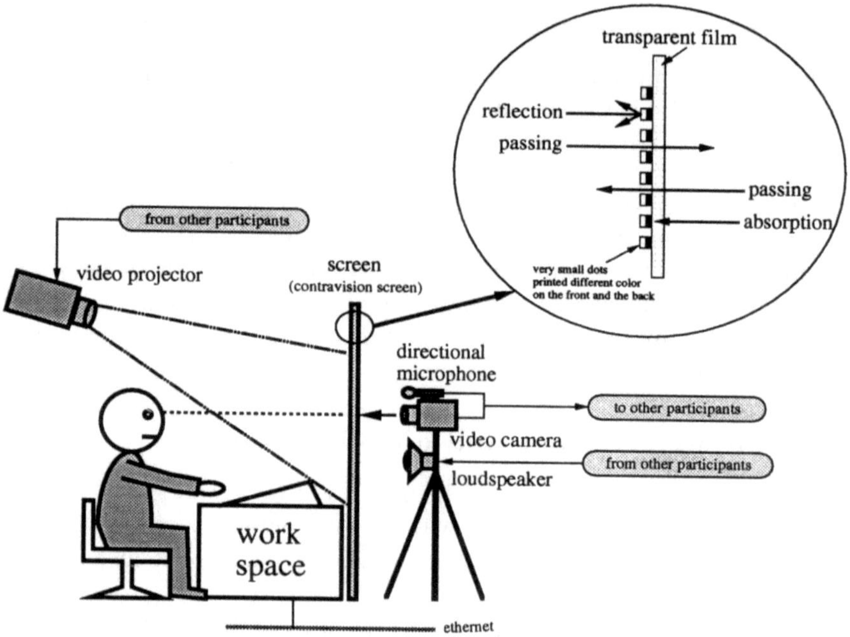

Figure 1. How to support eye contact

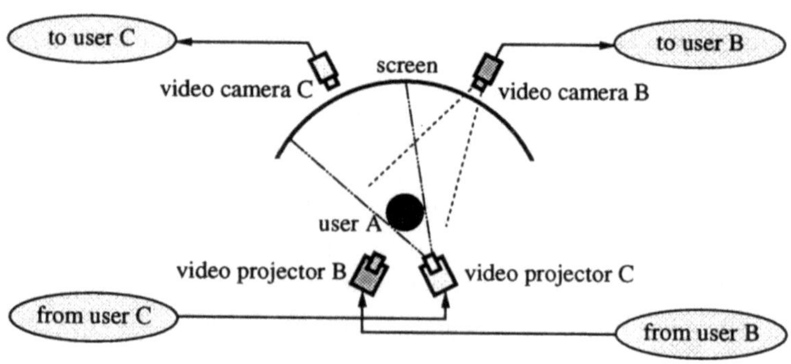

Figure 2. System constituents of MAJIC

Figure 2 illustrates three-way videoconferencing using MAJIC. When user A turns his head to the right to look straight at user B, user B sees user A full-face and user C sees the left profile of user A. In other words, user C becomes aware of user A gazing toward user B, and user B becomes aware of the head-turning of user A toward him/her and can make eye contact with user A if he/she likes. Thus the MAJIC system supports multiple eye contact and gaze awareness.

When user A sits at the center of the arc, the distance between user A and users B and C is around 4 feet. Distances between people vary according to their relationships and are classified as follows [5]:

(1) Intimate distance: 0 – 45 cm

(2) Personal distance: 45 – 120 cm

(3) Social distance: 120 – 360 cm

(4) Public distance: more than 360 cm

We have concluded that around 120 cm may be the best distance for face-to-face meetings with 3 or 4 colleagues, since the distance from people who work together tends to be shorter at a social distance, or it is sometimes than a personal distance.

Figure 3 shows multi-party videoconferencing using MAJIC.

Experiment using MAJIC

We have conducted experiments to explore the effects on to participants of various factors of the projected image (i.e., the size of participants' images, background and seams between images) using the MAJIC prototype. The data of this experiment were analyzed by factor analysis, and we improved MAJIC based on the results.

Method

Subjects

40 students in engineering participated: 10 women and 30 men.

Experimental Conditions and Apparatus

Subjects saw participants in experimental video conferencing in six conditions as follows. Condition 1 is basic MAJIC environment; that is, life size participants' images, with the same background behind other participants and seamless between images. In condition 2, the backgrounds of the participants were different; other factors were the same as in condition 1. There is a seam between images in condition 3. Large participants' images (twice as large as

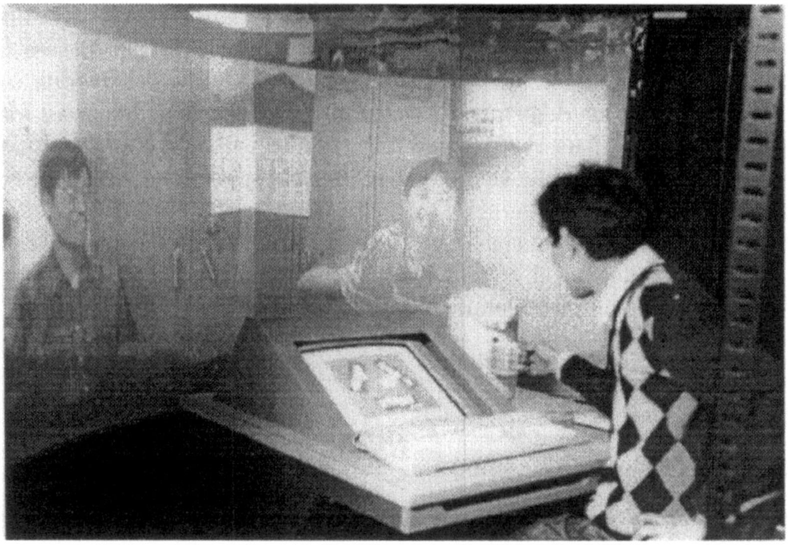

Figure 3. MAJIC in use

condition 1) were projected in condition 4; small images (.75 times) were projected in condition 5. Two small displays were used in condition 6. Hence, there were very small participants' images and a seam between them in condition 6.

	size of images	background	seams between images	apparatus
1	life size	same	seamless	MAJIC screen
2	life size	different	seamless	MAJIC screen
3	life size	same	10cm	MAJIC screen
4	large (×2)	same	seamless	MAJIC screen
5	small (×.75)	same	seamless	MAJIC screen
6	very small (×.3)	same	100cm	Using 14 inch display

Table I. Experimental conditions and apparatus

Procedure

Each subject watched a video conferencing movie filmed beforehand in each condition. The movie shows typical usual informal conversation (the participants in the movie sometimes speak to the subject). One minute later, subjects were asked to respond to 16 questions about the condition which they had just

Condition 1

Condition 2

Condition 3

Condition 4

Condition 5

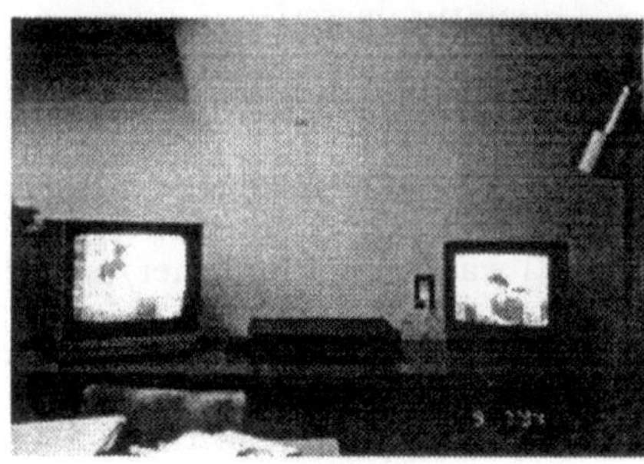

Condition 6

Figure 4. Experimental conditions

experienced. The questions concern sense of reality, virtual distance, gaze awareness and atmosphere. A score of 7 represents "Strongly Agree", while a score of 1 represents "Strongly Disagree". A score of 4 represents "Equal" for questions concerning distance; that is, Q2, Q7 and Q11. The questions are as follows.

Q1. I was able to understand what other participants did.

Q2. I felt other participants were larger than life size.

Q3. It's not unnatural when other participants "shook hands" or "linked arms."

Q4. I felt as though they were together.

Q5. The conversation was natural.

Q6. When I looked at other participants at the same time, I had a sense of congruity.

Q7. I felt participants were far/near.

Q8. When I moved my gaze from one image to the other image, I didn't feel unnaturalness.

Q9. It seemed other participants were able to communicate naturally.

Q10. I was able to recognize other participants' gaze.

Q11. I wanted to be farther/nearer to the images.

Q12. I could converse naturally, if there were pictures with a seam.

Q13. I was able to read the facial expressions of the participants.

Q14. The other participants seemed to be in the same room.

Q15. The conversation seemed highly interactive.

Q16. The atmosphere was impressive.

Factor analyses

The mean scores from the questionnaires averaged across 40 subjects are shown in Table II. But three questions concerning virtual distance were excepted, because these questions use different criterion. We discuss virtual distance later.

The data are analyzed by a principal components transformation method

	Condition1	Condition2	Condition3	Condition4	Condition5	Condition6
Q.1	6.45000	6.22500	6.00000	4.30000	6.35000	5.50000
Q.2	4.77500	4.90000	4.37500	6.92500	3.22500	1.87500
Q.3	5.25000	3.70000	4.37500	3.20000	5.60000	2.30000
Q.4	4.97500	3.27500	4.20000	3.47500	4.67500	2.65000
Q.5	5.72500	5.62500	5.17500	4.12500	5.92500	4.05000
Q.6	5.87500	4.10000	4.52500	3.72500	6.15000	2.50000
Q.7	3.97500	4.27500	3.92500	5.87500	3.05000	1.92500
Q.8	5.60000	4.37500	4.55000	4.65000	6.05000	2.50000
Q.9	6.15000	5.65000	5.65000	5.12500	6.27500	4.85000
Q.10	6.00000	5.37500	5.75000	4.95000	6.00000	4.45000
Q.11	3.85000	3.87500	3.77500	1.80000	4.65000	3.92500
Q.12	3.97500	3.97500	4.10000	4.15000	4.45000	2.75000
Q.13	6.22500	5.77500	5.90000	6.40000	5.95000	5.35000
Q.14	6.15000	2.87500	4.57500	4.27500	6.05000	3.62500
Q.15	5.87500	5.30000	5.65000	4.72500	6.00000	4.37500
Q.16	4.97500	4.90000	5.02500	5.30000	5.25000	3.62500

Table II. The mean scores from the questionnaire averaged across 40 subjects

using correlation coefficients which were calculated from Table II. As a results, two factors could explain 88.9% of all distributions. After Varimax rotation to these two factors is done [19], the model obtained is as follows:

$$\begin{aligned}
\textbf{Condition1} : \mathbf{X}_1 &= 0.298\mathbf{F}_1 + 0.934\mathbf{F}_2 \\
\textbf{Condition2} : \mathbf{X}_2 &= 0.845\mathbf{F}_1 + 0.318\mathbf{F}_2 \\
\textbf{Condition3} : \mathbf{X}_3 &= 0.834\mathbf{F}_1 + 0.516\mathbf{F}_2 \\
\textbf{Condition4} : \mathbf{X}_4 &= 0.864\mathbf{F}_1 + 0.042\mathbf{F}_2 \\
\textbf{Condition5} : \mathbf{X}_5 &= 0.210\mathbf{F}_1 + 0.951\mathbf{F}_2 \\
\textbf{Condition6} : \mathbf{X}_6 &= 0.852\mathbf{F}_1 + 0.415\mathbf{F}_2
\end{aligned}$$

Discussion

The first factor, F1, has high values when there are different backgrounds, a seam between images, or very large or small images. F1 has been named the "Sense of Incongruity" factor.

The second factor, F2, has high scores in condition 1 and condition 5. With a seamless display between participants, the same background, and a life sized image or a small image, the value F2 is. F2 has been named the "Sense of Presence" factor.

In summary:

- F1: The factor of the Sense of Incongruity.

- F2: The factor of the Sense of Presence.

These factors resulted in two clusters on the plot (Figure 5).

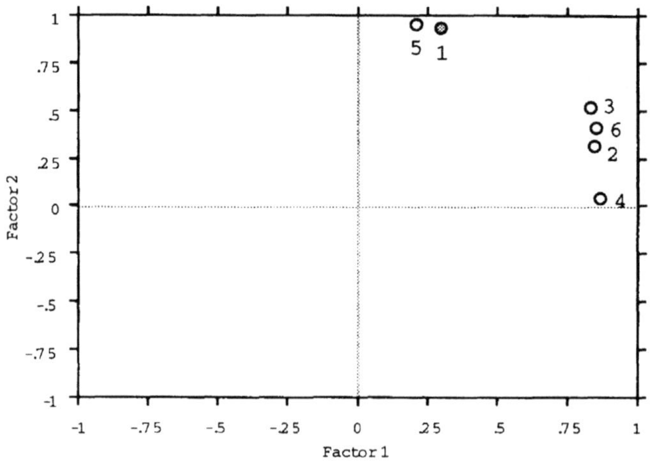

Figure 5. Factor Plot. (Condition 1 is the basic MAJIC environment.)

We diagrammatically depict the results from the questionnaire about the sense of virtual distance in Figure 6. Many participants felt that images are larger than their real size even though life sized images are projected. Therefore,we may say that it is effective to project the perceived image rather than a life sized image.

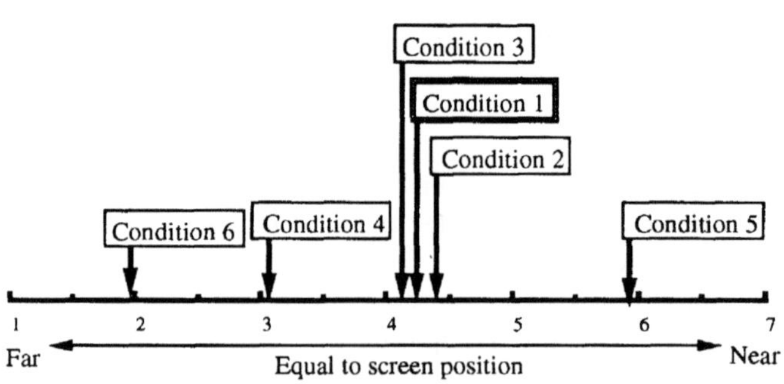

Figure 6. virtual distance

The improvement of MAJIC

The prototype of MAJIC has the following shortcomings:

(1) Only one user at each site can make eye contact with participants.

(2) Users cannot move around.

(3) The number of sites is limited, four-way video conferencing being the maximum possible with the prototype.

(4) The quality of images is not very good.

(5) The size of the prototype is very large.

(6) There is no seam between pictures, but there is a seam between backgrounds.

To overcome some of the problems of the MAJIC, we have improved the MAJIC system based on the conclusions of the experiments.

Miniaturization

The size of the prototype is very large. But from the experimant, it can be said that the sensed distance between a user and other participants is effectal by the projected image size. Therefore, it the user sits closer to the screen on which a small size video image is projected, the size of MAJIC can be miniaturized (Figure 7).

Seamless backgrounds by chromakey

The background influences the sense of presence. The improved MAJIC supports seamless backgrounds by chromakey. Figure 8 shows an example of seamless backgrounds. It will be interesting to observe virtual meetings in various backgrounds. For example, what is the effect of the background, or what kind of background relaxes users or inspires them?

Conclusion

We have explored the effects of the size of participants' images, the backgrounds of portraits and the seams between images on the sense of presence. We found that the sense of incongruity is increased by seams between images, differences in background, and unnatural size of participants' images. On the other hand, life size and slightly smaller images produce a sense of reality. From the results, we improved MAJIC by miniaturizing and providing the same background by chromakey.

We are designing "MAJIC-2" to offer several new functions:

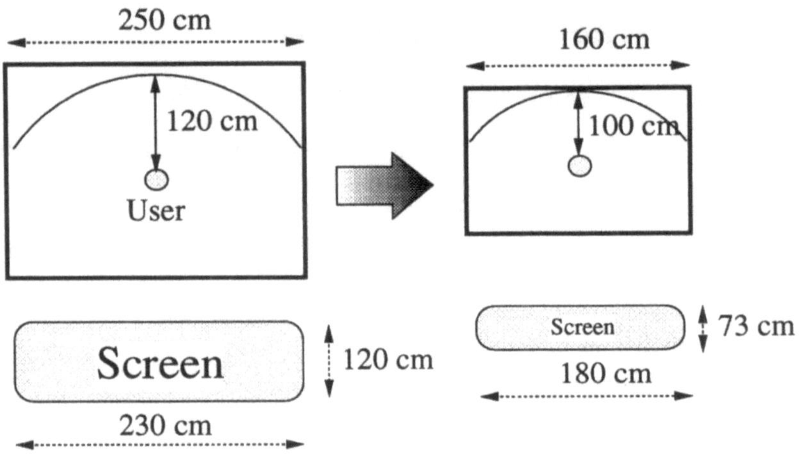

Figure 7. Miniaturization

Figure 8. Seamless background

(1) Support whispering. In a meeting we often speak to only one person. Hence, we design a tool by which participants can whisper. In order to provide this function some switches are attached to the inside of the chair, and switch whispering mode with the motion of a user. This chair is called "Whisper Chair".

(2) A video camera that pursues a person. MAJIC users cannot move around. This limitation is caused by the video cameras set behind the screen. They are mounted on a tripod and fixed on their target; that is, a user sitting at the center of the arc of the screen. In order to overcome this limitations, we introduce a video camera that pursues a person.

We currently have such a system in place and are running a second study to test these functions. We expect our approach will provide the next generation of teleconferencing system.

Acknowledgments

We thank Toppan Printing Co., Ltd. and NTT software laboratories for their support.

References

[1] Okada, K., Maeda, F., Ichikawa, Y. and Matsushita, Y. (1994): "Multiparty Videoconferencing at Virtual Social Distance: MAJIC Design", In *Proceedings of ACM CSCW'94*, Oct. 1994, pp. 385–393.

[2] Okada, K., Ichikawa, Y., Jeong, G., Tanaka, S. and Matsushita, Y. (1995): "Design and Evaluation of Majic Videoconferencing System", In *Proceedings of INTERACT'95*, June 1995.

[3] Ishii, H., Kobayashi, M. and Grudin, J., (1993): "Integration of Interpersonal Space and Shared Workspace: ClearBoard Design and Experiments", *ACM Transactions on Information Systems*, Vol. 11, No. 4, Oct. 1993, pp. 349–375.

[4] Sellen, A. J. (1992): "Speech Patterns in Video-Mediated Conversations", In *Proceedings ACM CHI'92*, May 1992, pp. 49–59.

[5] Hall, E. T. (1966): *The Hidden Dimension*, Doubleday & Company Inc., N.Y., 1966.

[6] Brittan, D. (1992): "Being There: The promise of multimedia communication", *Technology Revew*, May/June 1992, pp. 42–50.

[7] Buxton, W. (1992): "Telepresence: Integrating shared task and person spaces", In *Proceedings of Graphic Interface'92*, Morgan Kaufuman Publishing, Los Altos, 1992, pp. 123–129.

[8] Hollan, J. and Stornetta, S. (1992): "Beyond being there", In *Proceedings of CHI'92*, ACM, N.Y., 1992, pp. 119–125.

[9] Ahuja, S. R. (1988): "The Rapport multimedia conferencing system", In *Proceedings of Conference on Office Information Systems*, ACM, N.Y., 1988, pp. 1–8.

[10] Nishimura, T., Arikawa, T., Masaki, S. and Yamaguchi, H. (1992): "Communication environment over conference using a personal multimedia-multipoint teleconference system and its human machine interface", *IPSJ SIG Notes*, 92-GW-1, Tokyo, 1992, pp. 75–82.

[11] Watabe, K., Sakata, S., Maeno, K., Fukuoka H. and Ohmori, T. (1990): "Distributed multiparty desktop conferencing system: MERMAID", In *Proceedings of CSCW'90*, ACM, NewYork, 1990, pp. 27–38.

[12] Bly, S. A., Harrison, S. R. and Irwin, S. (1993): "MediaSpace: Bringing people together in a video, audio, and computing environment", In *Comunications of the ACM*, 36, 1, Jan. 1993, pp. 29–47.

[13] Fish R. S., Kraut, R. E. and Chalfonte B. L. (1990): "The VideoWindow system in informal communications", In *Proceedings of CSCW'90*, ACM, N.Y., 1990, pp. 1-11.

[14] Matsuura, N., Fujino, G., Okada, K. and Matsushita Y. (1993): "An approach to encounters and interaction in a virtual environment", In *Proceedings of ACM Computer Science Conference*, ACM, N.Y., 1993, pp. 298–303.

[15] Wellner, P. (1993): "Interacting with Paper on the DigitalDesk", *Communications of the ACM*, Vol. 36, No. 7, July 1993, pp. 86–97.

[16] Nakazawa, K. (1993): "Proposal of a new eye contact method for teleconferences", *IEICE Transaction on Comunication*, J76, 1, Jan. 1993, pp. 618–625.

[17] Tang, J. C. and Minneman, S. L. (1991): "Video Whiteboard: Video shadows to support remote collaboration", In *Proceedings of CHI'91*, ACM, N.Y., 1991, pp. 315–322.

[18] Takemura, H. and Kishino, F. (1992): "Cooperative work environment using virtual workspace", In *Proceedings of CSCW'92*, ACM, N.Y., 1992, pp. 226–232.

[19] Masuyama Eitarou, Shigeo Kobayasi (1989): *Sensory Evaluation*, Kakiuchi Publishing, Tokyo, 1989.

Proceedings of the Fourth European Conference on Computer-Supported Cooperative Work,
September 10–14, Stockholm, Sweden
H. Marmolin, Y. Sundblad, and K. Schmidt (Editors)

Multimedia Support of Collaboration in a Teleservice Team

Steinar Kristoffersen and Tom Rodden
Computing Department, Lancaster University, U.K.

Abstract: The purpose of this paper is to outline an architectural model for how multimedia can establish and support cooperative work. The proposed architecture emerged from empirical work in a large UK bank. Previous efforts have, as we see them, been largely experimental, and have focused on supporting informal work. Few examples concern the support of actual work tasks in companies outside a research context. The outlined model offers a conception of work as distributed across time, space, tasks, people, and artefacts. It aims to integrate informal and formal aspects of work by supporting the initiation and management of interaction as well as the cooperative work process itself.

Introduction

Multimedia communication has been a central part of CSCW systems development and research for a number of years. Considerable effort has been needed to establish the technical feasibility of multimedia. The development of conceptual demonstrators that highlight the possibilities offered by this form of technology, has as a result been limited to experimental use within laboratory settings. Limited possibility has existed for considering the use of cooperative multimedia in natural work environments. The development of commercial products based on ISDN technology means that it is now possible to examine the use of video systems in actual work settings and to consider the relationship between the work taking place and the technology supporting it .

This paper reflects on the use of the current generation of video systems and the implications for future cooperative systems that make extensive use of video. The paper is based on an empirical study of video communication in a large UK bank. The Bank is structured such that central units provide branches with the additional infrastructure and personnel needed to handle specialised products. The role of the Teleservice team, which is one of the service providers within the bank's national insurance centre, is to give customers advise about home insurance and related issues. They deal with existing customers, as well as those responding to advertisement campaigns. A video link has been introduced to support the communication with the customers and hosts in selected branches. The empirical study focuses on how the work is being performed today, as well as to what extent a multimedia conference system can establish and support cooperative sessions in the Teleservice team.

The empirical study reported in this paper is the result of observations and unstructured interviews in mundane working situations. The study was undertaken in conjunction with a wider ethnographic study of the bank. Focus was on the situated, everyday performance of work. The study included the manager of the Teleservice team, the project leader for video conference development and one of the branches connected to the Teleservice centre.

Unlike models that represent the details of the media (for example, QuickTime™ or MPEG) we wish to focus on the construction of an architectural model that more closely links multimedia communication and cooperative applications, based on the experiences of our empirical study. Several ways of structuring multimedia applications have been proposed. For example, HyTime is a hypermedia document structuring language that can represent relationships between datatypes with temporal character, like video, audio and animation (Newcomb et al. 1991). However, existing models for structuring media focus on multimedia documents rather than the interactive applications that are our principle concern.

The translation from detailed ethnographic descriptions into high-level, abstract, and general concepts is not trivial (Shapiro 1994; Hughes et al. 1994). In this effort, the system designer is also responsible for the ethnographic fieldwork, only guided by a sociologist with extended practical and theoretical experience from ethnographic work. This approach obviously hides the problem of translating between phenomena and concepts, and the need for debriefing meetings is reduced (Bentley et al. 1992). The problem of making this translation explicit for others to assess persists. In this paper we have attempted to document the appropriateness of the model by example scenarios showing how it could be implemented in a given situation. Sufficient as it might be as evidence within the scope of this paper, we appreciate that further research is called for in the CSCW field at large to solve the problems related to the use of ethnographic descriptions in system design.

The video based communication architecture developed here addresses the current detachment between video communication and the nature of the work taking place. The focus on informal cooperation prevalent in multimedia does not sit well with the very legal and procedural view of work evident in the Bank. Limited facilities exist to express the distribution of work and the relation between the video communication and the procedural representation of the work taking place. To address these issues the developed model aims to handle the control and workflow aspects of work together with open, more expressive channels like video. The model also allows integrated support of informal and formal work to be documented for future use. This paper presents in outline the study motivating our work and the resulting architectural model that has been informed from the empirical study.

Existing Limitations of Video

This paper is concerned with systems that combine audio, video, computing and networking technologies to provide an environment for cooperative work. To distinguish this class of technology from Videophones and systems based on analogue video-switches we focus on Multimedia systems as the flexible combination of communication and computing media with software applications. When examined in the context of real world settings, existing approaches to design of these systems present a number of shortcomings. This section focuses on these existing limitations and their implications for the work reported in this paper.

Unspecified support

The integration of video communication and computer systems is a relative recent technological development. As a result, many systems have the character of technical experiments rather than tools designed to support a dedicated task. The focus of research has been on demonstrating the technical feasibility of the emerging designs. For example, Watabe et al. (1990) focus on general meeting support in a research context to demonstrate the applicability of the MERMAID architecture. Bly et al. (1993) describe an experiment that aimed to study interpersonal computing in the context of systems design. A predominant focus of the work on media spaces is how awareness can be used to promote informal communication and cooperation independently on the work taking place. Gaver et al. (1992) report on how they implemented and used the Ravenscroft Audio Video Environment (RAVE) to allow physically separated colleagues to communicate. A software layer called Godard is implemented on top of the basic multimedia facility in RAVE to offer control over the video connections (Dourish 1993). The Porthole system intends to support social awareness as well as explicitly looking for colleagues by providing a database with images from video cameras in geographically separated public areas and offices (Dourish and Bly 1992).

Mantei et al. (1991) describe a media space called CAVECAT. Its purpose is to enable a small number of individuals or groups to participate in cooperative work without leaving their offices. The experiences of media spaces in use within research labs highlight the need for new interaction metaphors (these include Portholes (Dourish and Bly 1992) and office based metaphors (Mantei et al. 1991; Gaver 1992; Fish 1988)). The developed metaphors have considered the setting of the work taking place and the properties afforded by the technology rather than the relationship between the particular work undertaken by users, the properties of the communication media, and the nature of the support provided.

Formal and informal work

A prevalent advantage of video has been that it can support the informal aspects of work through spontaneous interaction, thus focusing on the use of video as a way to augment and coordinate work activities leaving more procedural aspects to be supported by structured applications. This is perhaps best characterised in the development of Cruiser (Root 1988); a tool specifically designed to promote social interaction rather than dedicated tasks. Cruiser aims to support the office as a social institution by facilitating communication, negotiation, spontaneous interpersonal communication. Based on the assumption that brief, unplanned encounters appear as a result of physical proximity, Root (1988) introduces the term "social browsing" to describe the dynamic process of person-to-person, mobility-based, social interaction. Experiments indicated that Cruiser is convenient, but not sufficiently expressive. Users found the use of the system to be more privacy invading than expected. It is described as marginally adequate to support spontaneous conversations, but did not did not manage to simulate face-to-face conversations (Fish et al. 1993).

The detachment between formal and informal work has continued as a dominant theme in video communications research. Users are expected to exploit their "natural" social skills to control and mediate the cooperation. One further illustration of this approach is the VideoWindow project (Fish et al. 1990) which aimed to extend a shared space over considerable distance without impairing the quality of the interaction. The core design intent was to provide "low cost" interaction, and the focus was on spontaneous, informal and socially situated communication afforded by a concentration of suitable partners, simulated co-presence, mechanisms to initiate the session, and a visual channel to facilitate coordination. Of the possible encounters however, very few resulted in prolonged conversation between people who were interested in each other's work. The degree of informality was also less than expected, a result attributed to the lack of reciprocity.

Moving into the real world

A significant limitation facing the development of video systems has been the need to construct these systems in experimental laboratory settings. Albeit the researchers have to some extent used the prototypes in their own work, the experimental nature of the technology involved has meant that most video systems have been developed and used within research labs (Ishii 1990), and use has often been limited because of the "prototypical" nature of the technology (Ishii et al. 1993). Whilst answering significant questions concerning video, a lab based approach has shortcomings for the designers of new technologies and techniques (Tang & Isaacs 1993). As Tang and Isaacs (1993) state in their consideration of video and desktop conferencing

".. we should strive to understand how new forms of interaction can be integrated with existing ones in people's day-today work. By understanding how these new technologies augment, complement and interact with people's existing work practice, we can design new technology that can be smoothly and naturally adopted " (Tang & Isaacs 1993, page 194).

Pagani and Mackay (1993) report from a study of video supported cooperative work in a real-world, albeit limited setting. In a similar move toward more realistic settings, Tang and Isaacs describe three studies of synchronous, distributed cooperation in small groups (Tang and Isaacs 1993). One of the central findings from this study was that as many as 57% calls did not lead to a conference session. These results motivated research on how to support the coordination activities that take place before the call, to facilitate cooperation. The early experiments with the Montage prototype, described by Tang and Rua (1994), did not, however, clearly demonstrate that the system was used as intended.

Systems like Montage and TeamWorkStation have given considerable insight into the possibilities offered by multimedia systems. We wish to complement this work with a study of the use of video within an actual work setting and the consequences for design. In particular we wish to consider:

- The role of video in supporting directed work in real world organisations.
- The integrated support of work that has a more formal and procedural nature.
- Mechanisms that embed video in the software support for a variety of work.

The motivation for our work is principally driven from the current isolated nature of video in cooperative applications. Video is seldom integrated or related to existing cooperative software and its use is characterised as an additional and independent communication channel. We seek to understand the use of video in commercial, non-research organisations and to develop techniques that allow video to be used in the support of planned and structured tasks as well as social and informal activities.

The Teleservice Team

The Teleservice Team is one of the bank's service centre teams, and receives approximately 1500 calls each day. Some of the calls are from the branches, others are from customers calling through on the freephone numbers associated with different campaigns. Each specialist enjoys on average 50 seconds of "idle" time before the telephone system distributes the next call to him. This time is used to keep the paperwork associated with calls up to date.

The Teleservice Team is situated in a dedicated room. The specialists sit side-by-side and face-to-face. A low wall on each side and a bookshelf in front define their private workspace. The manual documents created throughout the day are handled and archived by two clerks working in a back room, in which the Video Link is also installed. One person is handling the Urgents; files on existing business that needs to be amended immediately. The archives themselves are easily accessible at the side wall of the room.

The physical lay-out of the room is important considering the open availability of work, through which co-workers at a glance can get a picture of what is going on (Heath et al. 1993). The files in the archive are common artefacts. It is easy to see when people access them, and notes can be made on the covers as well as the individual document. In essence, files are instruments with functionality derived from the nature of work (Hughes et al. 1993).

Rather than present the work of The Teleservice Team in detail in this section we wish to focus on the relation between "formal" and "informal" work and the means by which interaction is managed. This focus allows us to consider the assumptions and shortcomings evident in existing video systems as video moves into the workplace and the lessons for developing support.

Formal and informal work

Work within The Teleservice Team is highly contingent and seldom follows a prescribed course of action. The specialists use glance and gesture continuously; they shout to each other across the desks that separate them and often call upon others to help meet the demands of the work. The specialists wear headsets all the time. As a result it is not possible to implicitly detect who is available. One has to ask "Are you on the phone?" or "Can I talk to you, please?". To leave their workstations they have to disconnect physically, by removing the plug from their headsets. Members of team demonstrate considerable skill in managing the communication technology in the room as part of their work. For example:

> Alice turned to ask Peter for some rates that she was not familiar with. She disconnected, and Peter handed her a binder that he kept in his drawer. It seems that they found the right rates in there, after thumbing through some of the pages. A few moments later, Alice did the same thing again, but this time without asking Peter. She disconnected and walked over to his desk to get the binder, but this time she didn't locate the right answers and turned around instead to ask Lou.
>
> Suddenly she shook her head and indicated with the finger to her head that she was unhappy with something the customer said. These gestures were intended for Lou as well as Peter. She disconnected and walked over to one of the supervisors and returned to her desk only to fetch the binder. The customer didn't want to pay the extra rate for a removable car stereo, and suggested that he would just not tell them that it was removable, rather than paying the extra rate. The reason Alice went to ask Jackie about it was that Peter had an old manual, and it wasn't clear on this point. The supervisor told her that a claim could be declined if the customer didn't give the right information about the type of stereo in the car, and Alice told him about that.

This type of contact is not purely social or informal and is often a means to support the formal aspects of the work. For example, specialists often receive calls regarding customers someone else has responsibility for, or need to find specialised expertise to support an enquiry. It might not be obvious who treated a particular case last time. During the highly social interactions that occur between calls specialists exchange important information and coordinate formal work. The following illustrates this fairly routine situation within the work:

> Jackie answered the phone, it was a customer that knew he talked to Anne earlier.

"Anne, there's someone who wants you for a couple of minutes", Jackie got up, and turned around to get eye-contact with Anne before addressing her. Because the two specialists were located closely together, Jackie did not have to leave her desk to talk to Anne. She asked for her extension number, sat down, keyed the number in and talked to Anne. She gave her the name and policy number before transferring the call. The critical moment here is between Anne acknowledging that she can take the call, and the call being transferred. If Anne does not log out, she will be given a call very soon by the telephone system before Jackie gets through to her. She would then have to get back to the customer and say, "Sorry, she's on the phone", maybe even after telling the customer that "Yes, she's here, hold on a minute and I'll get her for you,..."

Managing the interaction

It is not uncommon for a specialist to be working on several cases in parallel. When a call comes in, the current task is temporarily suspended. Often they have two instances of the same application up and running at the same time to handle these situations. The reason is that the system will not save a record unless it is complete and consistent. Since the work is extremely event driven, the specialist has little control over this condition when jobs are processed in parallel.

Specialists are very adept at managing the interaction with customers and software. When engaged in a lengthy discussion with a customer, specialists often manipulate the workflow aspects of the program by running two instances simultaneously, but they articulate their work in different ways; using pen and paper is as common as running one or several instances of the computer based systems for direct registration. Similarly, the specialists disconnect from their workstations to leave their physical workspace, or discuss with colleagues to meet the demands of interaction with customers and staff external to the service centre.

Video access to expertise

Selected members of The Teleservice Team have being using a video link for an 8 month trial period. So far, 1000 customers have used the video system, and given their response immediately by questionnaire. Given that the team currently manages perfectly well using only the telephone it is worth considering why the video link was suggested by the bank. The use of video was not a case of discarding the telephone as an insufficient medium of communication with customers. Rather, like many organisations the Bank has a complex development trajectory, implementing and evaluating new technologies whilst responding to a changing market, as well as managerial and organisational pressures. Like many financial institutions the Bank is looking for cost reduction through the centralisation of machine room processing. This requires technology research efforts whilst at the same time attempting to defend market shares and changing from an organisation that traditionally focus on administration to one that focus much more on selling. To put it simply, the Bank is looking for experiences with a set of technologies they feel make it easier to market and sell their products even when the people with product competencies are withdrawn from branches.

A goal of the video link is to make remote expertise instantaneously accessible to the branches and use this expertise to sell home insurance cover to the person in the branch. This is a highly competitive commercial situation, where the number of sales is paramount. Higher sales can be achieved either by dealing with more customers each day, or through a higher conversion rate between possible and actual sold policies. The duration of an average call using the video link is twenty minutes. The normal telephone call in the Teleservice Team lasts six minutes. The conversion rate in the team is 1 from 4. For the bank to conduct this type of business over the video link, a conversion rate of 3 from 4 or 5 calls an hour would be a minimum performance requirement. In the bank they hope that access to expertise in combination with a more personal touch will increase the conversion rate compared to use of the telephone.

The interview is designed as a procedure to be followed by the specialist. During this process, the customer and host in the branch are relatively passive, only responding to the questions asked by the specialist. With few exceptions, the possibilities for the specialist to manage the interview is removed. Because the customer can see her all the time, it is not a feasible alternative to "disconnect" and leave the workstation in order to discuss the case with others. This means that situations that integrate formal and informal aspects in The Teleservice Team, i.e. when the manager has to acknowledge an exception from the rule, cannot easily be supported. The system separates the articulation of the task from its formal structure, its legal aspects and business goals, and it is, among other thing, this separation that the model described below seeks to address.

To initiate a video session the specialist assigns a local host and the customer to a video link terminal. The local host then calls from their own workstation in the branch. Although one specialist told us that using the video link was "second nature to us now, eight months down the line,..." developing instantaneous access to expertise and a personal touch is problematic. The following example highlights some of the problems that can occur when the specialist finds herself dealing with an "awkward customer":

> The customer was hostile from the start, and did not respond to any of the small talk. Only reluctantly did he give out personal information. Suddenly he started to challenge the specialist's expertise, and asked about a life rather than home insurance. Because the video link is set up in a dedicated booth at both ends of the connection, the specialist only answered, although she could have disconnected and placed a call to the Life Department:
>
> -"We're not actually connected to the Life Department"

In the telephone supported Teleservice room, she could have asked nearby specialists, or suspended the call as she talked the matter through with someone from a different department. The lack of immediate access to expertise served to heighten an already tense situation.

> In addition this particular customer focused on the host in the branch, not the screen, so the experts "personal touch" could not help alleviate the situation. She moved on to tell the customer about restrictions he would have to comply with to receive a discount for having smoke detectors. The

customer then asked about another property that he owned, at the time rented to a professional couple.

-"I will just have to go back and amend this information to the system, it's going to take me a couple of minutes to do that."

The customer lost patience and told the expert to forget it, and the interview ended.

In this situation, the system's lack of flexibility and the shared application screen prevented the expert from using a second instance of the home insurance software to answer questions immediately. Her image as an expert was reduced requiring her to engage in an improvised effort to restore her position as a response to his antagonistic attitude. The system architecture restricted her responses to the situation, as the more formal aspect of the work is embodied in the workflow software and separated from the "informal" video support, reducing her ability to manage these in tandem.

Outlining a supporting model

The work of The Teleservice Team illustrates that the relationship between formal and informal working is highly flexible and that members of the team have considerable skills in managing the relationship. This coupling of the formal and informal does not sit well with the facilities maintained in existing approaches to video. To explore the implications of these initial studies of video in The Teleservice Team, this section seeks to formulate a general design framework that can embed temporal datatypes, like video, audio and animation as part of CSCW applications. It describes a basic data structure and some of the operations to manipulate it. It is also a perspective through which users can understand the organisation.

Requirements of the model

The work the Teleservice Team performs using the telephone introduces several challenges to multimedia systems. Work is subject to relaying, parallel processing and queuing, and any model reflect this flexibility. The model should treat formal and informal aspects of work in an integrated manner, to yield a uniform access to task-support as well as situated action. The model must offer a framework to describe distribution across people, time, space, tasks and resources in a meaningful and consistent way.

The following example of work as it was performed over the telephone, taken from the fieldnotes, will be used as an example situation that our multimedia communication support systems would have to support:

Karen was talking to an angry customer, and he introduced himself by asking "where is my money?" Karen was ready to help, but couldn't find him in the policy register, and the customer didn't have a reference number, so it wasn't obvious where to look. The customer admitted that he had not paid his premium yet, "how could I do that when you won't give me my money? I'm working myself into a right state here, I am."

His claim was from Feb. 8 and it wasn't clear from the database whether they had put the customer on cover at that time. Karen had to tell him that, "Mr. W.! If you are going to keep on swearing at me, I won't continue this conversation!"

While Karen is struggling with this customer, George (sitting diagonally to Karen's left) caught his name, "Mr. W? Karen, who is it?" The customer complained about how he can't tell Karen what the problem is because the loss adjuster wouldn't tell him what was wrong, "he just tells me that he can't tell me, and that there is something about my policy that he doesn't like, he found several thing that was unclear, he said, but he couldn't disclose what they were".

George had by now got the customer's name, and realised that he was the specialist who put him on cover originally. It gradually became clear that what the loss adjuster, among other things didn't like, was the fact that in the policy he couldn't find anything about the place being burgled twice before. In itself this is probably enough to decline liability, we were told, although the workflow system does not prompt this question at all, it only asks for previous claims. The customer claims that he told George about his and that he will sue him if he isn't given his money. George just shook his head and laughed.

"I've got naught in my house, someone threatened to burglar my place, that's why I got the insurance in the first place, isn't it, because I knew this was going to happen."

Suddenly Lisa interferes, because George went over to see her as soon as he found out that his old customer was on the phone. Lisa is currently dealing with this case, liaisoning with the Claims department.

On a logical level this situation is distributed across people, (George, Lisa and Karen in The Teleservice Team, Paul in the Claims department and an independent loss adjuster). Geographically, it is locally distributed between the desks, as well as globally (between the Teleservice room and the Claims department). The case in question has taken place over a period including three distinct steps, (the customer asking to be put on cover, the customer claiming, and the Claims department declining liabilities). It is also distributed across artefacts (the policy record, the police report and the written assessment from the loss adjuster), and it is treated using different media (like the telephone, letters, database records and face-to-face meetings). At the same time all of the above are used to articulate the process in an integrated fashion.

Cooperative work involves tasks that aim to manage the relationship between individuals in the organisation (Bannon and Schmidt 1991). Our model makes this relationship central, thus affording the articulation and coordination of work. Previous work on video indicates that simulation of physical co-location (Fish et al. 1990), explicit naming of the recipient (Tang et al. 1994), or spatial metaphors (Fish et al. 1993) do not appear to work as well as hoped. By focusing on the co-operative relation, easy access to the shared artefact (Sørgaard 1988) is also supported. The suggested model offers a lightweight implementation and makes no assumptions about the behaviour of the participants. This way the model encourages system implementations that support the unconstrained negotiation and articulation of task between the users.

Components of the model

The proposed model uses the data structure needed to support cooperative video as its point of departure. The elements in the structure are read out of the fieldwork. This allows the model to serve as an architectural framework on which tools and task oriented applications can be built, whilst still being founded in the social arrangements and processes in the workplace:

The ConnectionObject: The model populates a distributed object store with persistent objects that represent a potential cooperative session. The ConnectionObject enacts the cooperative sessions independently of their physical link, so that they can exist as entities before, during and after connection. The ConnectionObject may represent multiparty links. The relationship between Karen and George, or Karen and the customer, or Lisa and the loss adjuster are examples of binary relationship, but adding Lisa to the discussion between the customer, Karen and George shows how it can be extended.

The ParticipantObject: The ConnectionObject contains a list of participants. Examples of participants include Karen, George, the angry customer, and Lisa. The number of participants is unlimited, and so is the number of connections that a participant can be part of. These objects are simply representations of the potential collaborators.

The ServiceObject: The list of ServiceObjects specifies which tools the connection provides for its participants. In the case of a video channel, it describes its physical properties, the translation tables between participant identifier and addresses, and a Quality of Service specification. In the observed situation, the telephone, the workflow system, the manual documents from the loss adjuster, and the policy database are all examples of services.

The ReferenceObject: The ConnectionObject manages a list of ReferenceObjects that relate to the services the ConnectionObject offers. For example, the page in the customer script in which previous claims are registered, or the record in the policy database showing that Mr. A. Customer never paid the first installment, will both be paramount in the case described. The list of ReferenceObjects is a sequence of states that describe properties of a service at a given point in time. This list allows a connection to playback a set of services in concert.

Dynamic properties of the model

The components outlined above can in a static manner describe how people in the organisation relate to each other. Moreover, it can describe distribution along several dimensions in a way that supports localisation of participants and establishment of sessions according to a range of criteria. Dynamically, the model can be used to support and manage activities within the organisation. These aspects of the model will be supported through a range of device independent media managers that manipulate the model components. Access to the potential collaborators through explicit identification is supported by an ConnectionObject's ParticipantList containing the relevant actors in the organisation. Based on the excerpt of the fieldnotes describing the angry customer, the following example (figure 1) instantiates and illustrates the model:

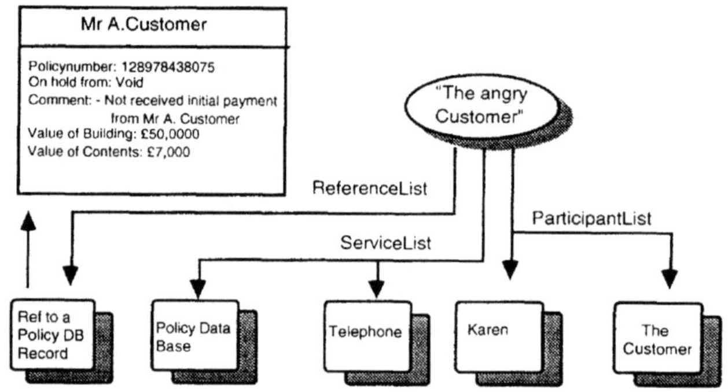

Figure 1. Instance of the model

Often a common task or shared material is the only link between parties. The ConnectionObject from which participants access the structure defines a perspective on the organisation. Many parallel structures are possible as an unlimited number of ConnectionObjects can point to each ParticipantObject. The implication is that the collaborators can create and maintain a set of perspectives on the organisation of work, that optimise specific tasks or situations. A group can dynamically redefine its structure and the model does not limit the users to describe formal organisation structures. In this situation George would have a ConnectionObject with this particular customer as one of the participants in his space of potential cooperative sessions, and we could imagine a mechanism alerting George about this customer being active again. If he responded to this call, the active instance of this part of the model would look like this (figure 2):

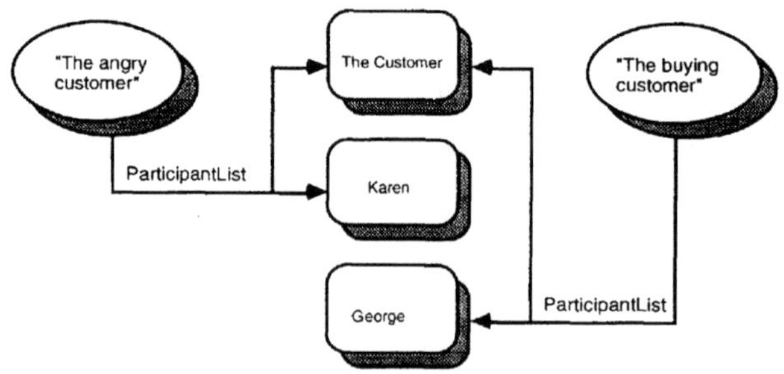

Figure 2. Instance of the model

George could in this situation generate a new ConnectionObject to make Karen available for conferencing without interfering with the established ensemble of herself and the customer, thus elaborating the network of connections. The model can be queried about the objects of work that can be reached from a ConnectionObject. Thus, a list can be compiled of shared artefacts, electronic records, or pointers to manual documents through which potential collaborators can be found and new cooperative sessions established, thus yielding a description of the actual communication patterns in the organisation.

The description is instrumental in the sense that mechanisms to localise potential collaborators and maintain the cooperative configuration can be build on it. In the above example George can chose between inviting Lisa to join the conference, i.e. attaching her own ParticipantObject to the "Who is this Mr. W?" ConnectionObject to engage in a synchronous discussion of the case, or he can suspend it and leave it for her to invoke later, asynchronously passing the conference, with context in the form of database records, workflow script pages and media connection to her for her to look at later (figure 3):

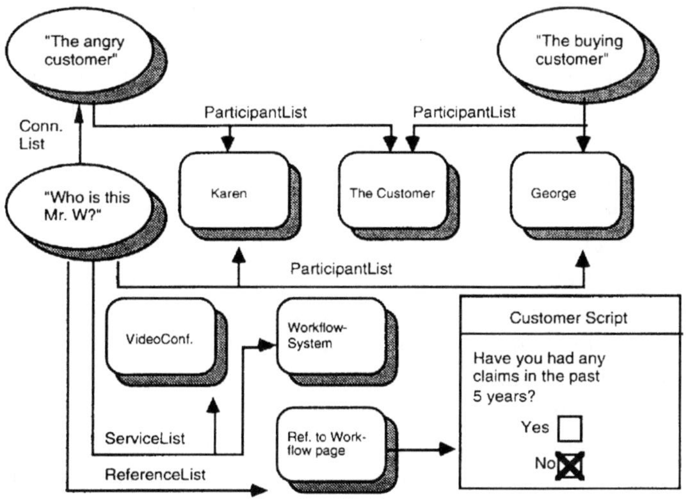

Figure 3. Instance of the model

It is possible to use the model to create a picture of how different activities create dependencies between ConnectionObjects. Each ReferenceObject can be viewed as a milestone along a path. Where two ConnectionObjects have a ReferenceObject in common, their paths have crossed, and the users can pursue this as a potential for further collaboration.

Because the ConnectionObject also contains pointers to the physical arrangement of the services, the model can describe distribution across geographical space. The ServiceObject also provides a related dimension of distribution, that of service types. From a ConnectionObject it is possible to issue queries for a given set of service specifications among those registered. The participants can use this information to coordinate the utilisation of resources.

Perhaps the most important issue that the model can address is that of synchronous versus asynchronous communication. Because the ConnectionObject is loosely coupled with the physical links, its state might change from active to passive and back again. This change of state is in reality a crossing of the borderline between synchronous and asynchronous communication.

Discussion

The most significant difference between the framework offered in this paper and previous work, is that it recognises the need for an architectural model in video based communication systems. The proposed model can through the view of organisations as relations between potential collaborators describe distribution across a wide range of dimensions, thus yielding a variety of addressing schemes. This is in contrast to earlier systems where participants can only explicitly identify each other by their name or picture (Mantei et al. 1991; Gaver 1992; Dourish 1993; Tang et al. 1994). Others rely on the physical location of people in offices or common areas to establish collaborative sessions (Fish et al. 1990; Bly et al. 1993). However, the model allows these metaphors to be implemented on top of such an architecture, like the media "space" (Bly et al 1993) or virtual "hallway" (Root 1988).

The Rendezvous Architecture represents a similar approach to the model described although it does not address multimedia issues (Patterson et al. 1990). Contrary to our approach however, support for users who need to join an advanced session is not addressed by Rendezvous, neither does it attempt to bridge the gap between synchronous and asynchronous communication.

Many modelling efforts have been criticised because they assume determinism in the performance of work and ignore the interpretation and improvisation that people depend on to articulate their work (Robinson and Bannon 1991). Our proposal is not prescriptive about the work it is intended to support and makes no assumptions about the behaviour of the collaborators. It is in this sense more similar to that of Reeves and Shipman (1992) when they aim to gradually populate an information space.

It might be of interest to compare the properties of the suggested model to the design principles for future workflow management systems set forward by Abbott and Sarin (1994). As an alternative to the vision of workflow as "simply another invisible capability that permeates all applications", we have outlined an architectural model that offers integrated multimedia support for the apparently social activities in the workplace as well as the tasks that are the purpose of the organisation. A strong point to make here is that the model reflects the organisational setting, rather than the current technological possibilities. The model offers a number of advantages:

- It associates the communication supported by video with the formal, directed work of the organisation.
- It provides a means of maintaining history and supporting a context for the work taking place.
- It provides an integration framework for video communication and existing CSCW applications.

- It offers a flexible basis to bring together and address a collection of resources in a particular set of activities.

The model represents our initial response to the fieldwork of multimedia communication within the Bank. Work will continue to implement tools and applications based on the proposed architecture and assess its properties in line with the demands of the Bank.

Acknowledgements

Support for this work was provided by the UK's Engineering and Physical Sciences Research Council under grant GR/ J 53409, the Research Council of Norway as part of project 100268/410 and Norsk Regnesentral for providing leave for the principle author. Thanks are due to the team itself and their manager for patiently and openly allowing us to learn about their work, as well as the Video Link project leader and our contacts in the Bank's research department. We are in debt to the anonymous reviewers whose constructive critique helped us improve the paper. We would also like to acknowledge our colleagues at Lancaster. Particular thanks are due to Mark Rouncefield for his continued support during fieldwork.

References

Abbott, K. R. & Sarin, K. S. (1994). Experiences with Workflow Management: Issues for the Next Generation. In *Proceedings of the ACM CSCW'94 Conference on Computer-Supported Cooperative Work*, (pp. 113-120).

Bannon, L. J., & Schmidt, K. (1991). CSCW: four characters in search of a context. In J. Bowers & S. Benford (Eds.), *Computer Supported Cooperative Work: Theory, Practice and Design* Amsterdam: North Holland.

Bentley, R., Hughes, J. A., Randall, D., Rodden, T., Sawyer P., Shapiro, D., & Sommerville, I. (1992). in *Proceedings of the ACM CSCW'92 Conference on Computer-Supported Cooperative Work*, (pp. 123-37).

Bly, S. A., Harrison, S. R. & Irwin, S. (1993). Media Spaces: Bringing People Together in a Video, Audio, and Computing Environment. In *Communications of the ACM*, January 1993, Vol. 36, No. 1, (pp. 28-47).

Dourish, P. (1992) and Bly, S. (1992). Portholes: Supporting Awareness in a Distributed Work Group. In *Proceedings of ACM CHI'92 Conference on Human Factors in Computing Systems* (pp. 541-547).

Dourish, P. (1993). Culture and Control in a Media Space. In *Proceedings of the Third European Conference on Computer-Supported Cooperative Work*, (pp. 125-137).

Fish, R. S., Kraut, R. E., & Chalfonte, B. L. (1990). The VideoWindow System in Informal Communications. In *Proceedings of ACM CSCW'90 Conference on Computer-Supported Cooperative Work*, (pp. 1-11).

Fish, R. S., Kraut, R. E., Root, R. W. & Rice, R. E. Video as a Technology for Informal Communication. In *Communications of the ACM*, January 1993, Vol. 36, No. 1, (pp. 48-61)

Gaver, W., Moran, T., MacLean, A., Lovstrand, L., Dourish, P., Carter, K., & Buxton, W. (1992). Realizing a Video Environment: EuroPARC's RAVE System. In *Proceedings of ACM CHI'92 Conference on Human Factors in Computing Systems,* (pp. 27-35).

Heath, C., Jirotka, M., Luff, P., & Hindmarch, J. (1993). Unpacking collaboration: the interactional organisation of trading in a city dealing room. In *Proceedings of the Third European Conference on Computer-Supported Cooperative Work*, (pp. 155-70).

Hughes, J. A, King, V., Rodden, T., & Anderson, H. (1994) Moving Out from the Control Room: Ethnography in System Design. In *Proceedings of the ACM CSCW'94 Conference on Computer-Supported Cooperative Work*, (pp. 417-28).

Hughes, J. A., Randall, D., & Shapiro, D. (1993). From ethnographic record to system design: some experiences from the field. In *Computer Supported Cooperative Work,* 1(3), 123-141.

Ishii, H. (1990). TeamWorkStation: Towards a Seamless Shared Workspace. In *Proceedings of ACM CSCW'90 Conference on Computer-Supported Cooperative Work*, (pp. 13-26).

Ishii, H., Artita, K., & Yagi, T. (1993). Beyond Videophones: TeamWorkStation-2 for Narrowband ISDN. In *Proceedings of the Third European Conference on Computer-Supported Cooperative Work*, (pp. 325-340).

Mantei, M. M., Baecker, R. M., Sellen, A. J., Buxton, W. A. S., Milligan, T., & Wellman, B. (1991). Experiences in the Use of a Media Space. In *Proceedings of ACM CHI'91 Conference on Human Factors in Computing Systems*, (pp. 203-208).

Newcomb, S. R., Kipp, N. A. and Newcomb, V. T. (1991) The "HyTime" Hypermedia/Time-based Document Structuring Language. In *Communications of the ACM*, November 1991, Volume 34, Number 11, (pp. 67-83)

Pagani, D. S. & Mackay, W. Bringing Media Spaces into the Real World. (1993). In *Proceedings of the Third European Conference on Computer-Supported Cooperative Work*, (pp. 341-356).

Patterson, J. F., Hill, R. D., Rohall, S. L., & Meeks, W. S. (1990). Rendezvous: An architecture for synchronous multi-user applications. In *Proceedings of the Conference on Computer Supported Cooperative Work (CSCW '90),* . Los Angeles, California: ACM Press.

Reeves, B. and Shipman, F. (1992). Supporting Communication between Designers with Artifact-Centered Evolving Information Spaces, In *Proceedings of the ACM CSCW'92 Conference on Computer-Supported Cooperative Work*, (pp. 394-401).

Root, R. W. (1988). Design of a Multi-Media Vehicle for Social Browsing. In *Proceedings of the ACM CSCW'88 Conference on Computer-Supported Cooperative Work*, (pp. 25-38)

Shapiro, D. (1994) The Limits of Ethnography: Combining Social Sciences for CSCW. In *Proceedings of the ACM CSCW'94 Conference on Computer-Supported Cooperative Work,* (pp. 417-28).

Sørgaard, P. (1988). A framework for computer supported cooperative work. In J. Kaasbøll (Ed.), *Report of the 11th IRIS, 10-12 August,* (pp. 620-639).

Tang, J. C. & Isaacs, E. (1993). Why Do Users Like Video? Studies of Multimedia-supported Collaboration. In *Computer Supported Cooperative Work (CSCW)*, 1(3), (pp. 163-196).

Tang, J. C. & Rua, M. (1994). Montage: Providing Teleproximity for Distributed Groups. In *Proceedings of the ACM CHI' 94 Conference*, (pp. 37-43).

Tang, J. C., Isaacs, E. & Rua, M. (1994). Supporting Distributed Groups with a Montage of Lightweight Interactions. In *Proceedings of the ACM CSCW'94 Conference on Computer-Supported Cooperative Work*, (pp. 23-34).

Watabe, K., Sakata, S., Maeno, K., Fukuoka, H., & Ohmori, T. (1990). Distributed Multiparty Desktop Conferencing System: MERMAID. In *Proceedings of ACM CSCW'90 Conference on Computer-Supported Cooperative Work,* (pp. 27-38).

Proceedings of the Fourth European Conference on Computer-Supported Cooperative Work,
September 10–14, Stockholm, Sweden
H. Marmolin, Y. Sundblad, and K. Schmidt (Editors)

What Are Workplace Studies For?

Lydia Plowman
University of Sussex, UK

Yvonne Rogers
University of Sussex, UK

Magnus Ramage
Lancaster University, UK

We have considered the role of workplace studies from the CSCW literature which are intended to inform system design and implementation. We present a critique of these studies, categorised according to which phase of the design process they most inform, and discuss the tensions between providing explanatory accounts and usable design recommendations, the pressures on fieldworkers to provide both, the purposes different approaches serve, and the transition from fieldwork to system design.

Introduction

Workplace studies intended to inform system design have become increasingly prominent in computer supported cooperative work (CSCW). Their primary role is to convey the importance of the sociality of work by shedding light on the complex actions and interactions that occur. Every workplace setting is unique and this is reflected in the interpretations of formal and informal work practices in various studies. But how effective is the field study approach for informing design? Is it desirable, practical, useful and economical for a workplace study to be carried out *ab initio* every time a CSCW system is to be developed or introduced into an organisation? Or is it now possible for the findings and insights gained from these disparate studies to be consolidated and generalised for application to other work settings and system designs? Our intention here is to begin to take stock by providing a critique of the various workplace studies and outcomes, elucidating themes and emerging areas of interest, and speculating about future directions.

We consider whether there are any commonalities in accounts of perceived problems, proposed solutions and actual input into system design, and assess workplace studies in relation to their applied and theoretical contributions to the field. Workplace studies are often claimed to be concerned with defining problems rather than providing solutions, but if studies are set up specifically with the purpose of informing system design then this is evasive. Clients or project partners are not impressed with pleas of intractable methodological or theoretical problems, and hybrid forms of workplace studies may be needed as a response. The contributions of other studies, not intended to feed directly into system design, may be more diverse and difficult to pin down. We discuss the tensions between providing explanatory accounts and usable design recommendations, the pressures on fieldworkers to provide both, and the purposes different approaches serve.

Selection of papers

As a focus for the selection of relevant papers we considered for inclusion all papers published in Proceedings of CSCW and ECSCW conferences and in the Journal of Computer Supported Cooperative Work since the first issue in 1992. Inevitably this determines the types of papers represented, as any editorial board biases will be perpetuated here, but they were also supplemented by papers from other sources. Our starting point for selection was 'accounts of workplace studies which have been undertaken with the intention of informing and evaluating system design'. For the purpose of this analysis we have interpreted 'workplace studies' more broadly than strictly ethnographically oriented studies and have considered quasi-real-world studies where the workplace is a research laboratory or academic department. We have also considered papers where ethnographic methods have been supplemented by a semi-experimental approach.

We each read through all the papers in the Proceedings of CSCW '92 and '94 to ascertain the extent of agreement on which papers should be included, based on our loosely defined criteria. There was a very high degree of agreement in our selections, and on the basis of this, we individually selected papers from other volumes. We initially selected 75 papers in total for consideration in this critique; not all these papers have been cited here but they have all informed the analysis we present. There is a risk of simplification and distortion as we have focussed on the main findings, perhaps at the expense of more subtle points, but we hope that having three authors' views means that no major injustices have been perpetrated.

After further analysis, papers were categorised into reports of i) studies resulting in detailed guidelines to inform the design of a specific CSCW system; ii) studies used to make more general design recommendations, either for a class of CSCW systems or a specific system; iii) studies carried out as basic research; and iv) implementation and evaluation of CSCW systems in the workplace. These categories provide the structure for this paper but this division is by no means absolute and there is inevitably some overlap between sections.

Questions of research methodology

The dominant research methodology used to study workplaces within CSCW to date has been ethnography, an interpretive method. It can broadly be characterised as research which aims to study work as it occurs, without imposition of specific research questions on the participants, as distinct from the experimental methods which are designed to investigate particular hypotheses.

There have been very few purely experimental studies in the CSCW literature. One such is that by Toth (1994), who presents a study of small-group computer-mediated communication using a laboratory setting, a set of clearly defined hypotheses, and various quantitative measures. In contrast, there have been far more ethnographic studies, such as Hughes *et al.*'s (1992) study of air traffic control. The method here is much less directive in its research questions, choosing instead to study the work performed on its own terms and to draw conclusions for system design from that. However, as Hughes *et al.* (1994) argue, it is often necessary to compromise the purity of the ethnographic method to make the results useful for system design. For example, the 'quick and dirty' study, which is much shorter (a few days) than the traditional study (several months or years) and uses predetermined research questions, is better accommodated within the timescales of a system design cycle.

Other studies use a variety of methods, including both quantitative and qualitative techniques (Okamura *et al.*, 1994; Ross *et al.*, 1995). For instance, methods in Ackerman's study (1994) of the use of an organisational memory system by a group of software engineers included an initial questionnaire, usage data at the 'mouse-stroke' level, critical incident interviews, final questionnaires, and field observations and interviews. There is a constant interweaving of quantitative measures and qualitative data in the presentation and the analysis of results.

Some studies are completely qualitative in their methods, but are quasi-real-world. Suchman (1987), for example, uses ethnomethodology and extensive analysis of conversation and interaction in a research laboratory setting. Other studies by researchers at Xerox PARC and EuroPARC (Harper, 1992; Goodman and Abel, 1986; Bellotti & Sellen, 1993) have this same characteristic of naturalistic methods used within quasi-real-world environments. This is not to downplay the importance of such studies or to suggest that they are as unsituated as a laboratory study: real work is still under study, but it is the real work of researchers rather than of more typical users.

There are two, more or less orthogonal, axes which characterise the methodologies used in CSCW workplace studies. Firstly, there is the qualitative-quantitative axis concerning the kinds of data under consideration; secondly, the extent of situatedness to be found in the study. These axes are of course continua rather than dichotomies: there are both 'semi-experimental' studies in real work settings using a hybrid of qualitative and quantitative methods and there are studies using qualitative methods in semi-situated environments.

Work studies and specific design guidelines

One of the precepts of ethnographically oriented workplace studies, and part of the rationale for favouring such approaches over more experimental methods, is that every work environment is unique, work practices are highly situated, and specific design solutions are needed for specific situations. Papers describing design guidelines for *specific* systems (as opposed to general design recommendations) may therefore be expected to constitute the largest of our categories.

However, such detailed design guidelines are typically absent from the standard format of CSCW conference or journal papers, which tend to offer a description of a case study, followed by an ‘implications for system design’ section at the end of the paper in which a number of highly generalisable or semi-intuitive recommendations are made. It is not our aim to devalue these findings - what may appear to be commonsensical requires the validation of studies undertaken in the context of use, and inevitably not all partners in a design team will share an understanding of how 'commonsense' relates to CSCW. The question is why so few ethnographic studies result in specific design guidelines.

The growth in the number of projects involving liaison between academic researchers and industrial partners may suggest some reasons. Although researchers conducting field studies for an industrial partner often produce design guidelines for an intended specific system, they may meet a number of obstacles in delivering their findings to a wider audience, thus accounting for the apparent dearth of such studies. Recent funding initiatives in the UK often require the main consortium partners to be from industry, and one of the main purposes of research is now considered to be generation of revenue. This militates against basic research which has no obvious application, but also makes dissemination of findings from industry/academia partnerships more difficult as commercial sensitivity of information is paramount for projects aiming to find a competitive advantage in the marketplace. Publication of accounts of workplace studies may therefore be inhibited by the industrial vetting process. Specific design guidelines are more likely to be restricted to confidential internal reports with only high level findings being published in the CSCW literature. By the time that specific design guidelines can be made public, generally when the system is in use or commercially available, findings may be of less interest. Researchers may also meet resistance from other parts of the team, such as sales, finance or marketing departments, who feel that various design inputs are inappropriate or too expensive to implement. Once design guidelines are offered there is a focus for disagreements, factions may surface within the team, and major recommendations can be overturned, ignored or diluted.

Within the CSCW literature selected for this paper, studies which resulted in the most specific system requirements describe workplace studies supplemented by other methods (Streitz *et al.*, 1994; Tang & Isaacs, 1993) and as the main objective of these two projects was to develop a prototype, it is not surprising that their emphasis is on specific design. Examples of specific design guidelines may be found in other sources, where the emphasis is more on technical issues than their genesis. For instance, Ian Rogers (1995) describes a 'to do' list on a tool to support the process of complex electronic systems design by a salesperson. The 'to do' list guides the user to a correctly constructed design artefact by allowing any sequence of changes rather than imposing a pre-ordained sequence. If the changes introduce errors or mean that certain requirements have not been met a short description appears as an aide-mémoire. This is a specific design feature, implemented in a prototype, which is an outcome of findings from workplace studies which showed that the sales team simultaneously capture requirements and design the equipment in the customer's presence and they do not want to be hindered by a system which constrains their existing methods of working. However, the fact that this design feature was implemented as a result of the designer's creative response to the workplace study is not mentioned in the paper. It is difficult to ascertain how many other similar examples exist, in which the relationship between specific design features and the workplace study is invisible to those outside the project. But this example is also a demonstration of how a designer interprets the general findings of a workplace study through reading internal reports and discussions with the researcher rather than being presented with a specific design guideline which they then implement.

The paucity of papers detailing specific design guidelines can therefore be attributed to the lack of reported research which has developed to the stage of a system prototype (see figure 1) and to the constraints within which researchers working with industrial partners operate. It does not constitute enough evidence for the assertion that workplace studies do not produce specific design guidelines; it is more likely that our selection of CSCW literature has failed to capture papers which fall into this category, either because they are published elsewhere or because they do not make clear the provenance of described design features.

Work studies and general design recommendations

One of the strengths of an ethnographic approach is that detailed analyses of work can provide rich material on which to ground *general* design recommendations which are publishable and therefore more potentially influential than specific design guidelines. This category of papers has the highest output and the presentation of recommendations ranges from sets of bullet points to hypothetical scenarios, and from the tokenistic to the highly influential.

It is as iniquitous to expect researchers to produce highly specified design guidelines for systems designers as it is to expect systems designers to 'assume responsibility for the redesign of work' (Shapiro, 1994) but these expectations still appear to be widespread. They are perpetuated in promises of such outcomes in proposals for funding and exacerbated to some extent by researchers' self-imposed demands to produce something obviously useful. This can result in zealous but inadequate attempts to meet these expectations, and perhaps accounts for the claims for contributions to design being very modest.

Studies are generally described as *informing* system design in the sense of 'imparting knowledge to', rather than 'giving form to'. Typical of this reticence are claims to offer only 'insights' (Heath & Luff, 1992), 'directions' (Filippi & Thereau, 1993), 'input' (Grønback *et al.*, 1992), 'suggestions' (Luff *et al.*, 1992), 'implications' (Beck & Bellotti, 1993), and 'options' (Egger & Wagner, 1993) for design. There is a strong impetus to provide recommendations, even when couched in these terms. Authors of studies which make a valuable theoretical contribution to CSCW feel obliged to force design guidelines from their data, resulting in the classic 'implications for design' section at the end of a paper. Even those bold enough to state that it is 'no part of our remit to produce actual design solutions' (Rouncefield *et al.*, 1994) seem driven to provide such a section.

How to present design recommendations in a way that is practically useful is a central concern. Hughes *et al.* (1992) comment that findings from workplace studies may appear troublesome or strange from a software engineering or HCI perspective because there is no formal modelling, data flow analysis or separation between function, implementation and interface. As a way of tackling the problem of translating from ethnographic analysis to design recommendations they opt for the unusual approach of positing different examples of electronic alternatives to the flight strip used during air traffic control. Although the various strips appear to fulfil requirements, they use the ethnographic analysis to demonstrate how some design options would offer impoverished support within the specific work context (Hughes *et al.*, 1993).

Alternative methods of structuring design recommendations are also found in Heath *et al.*'s (1993) analysis of share trading in a securities house in the City of London. They discuss different types of technological innovation, such as voice recognition, as an example of misinformed design and instead recommend adoption of a pen-based, handwriting recognition system. Beck and Bellotti (1993) take the approach of demonstrating the disparity between flexible low tech solutions and constraints imposed by new technologies by explicitly referring to design features of available systems for collaborative writing. This approach is also taken by Plowman (forthcoming) in her discussion of the interfunctionality of talking and writing. She speculates about ways in which these processes could be replaced or augmented technologically and discusses the limitations of systems which rely on text to support collaborative writing. In their presentation of design guidelines, Katzenberg and McDermott (1994, p.204) use three imaginary scenarios 'as a basis for exploring solutions for support'.

Many studies aim to contribute both to broadening our understanding of work and to informing system design within the confines of one paper. Grønbaek *et al.* (1992), for example, state their aim to provide feedback for specific product development and for a long term vision of CSCW. Anderson and Sharrock (1993) claim that their paper is mainly an investigation of the sociology of cognition, but also provides a level of detail sufficient for 'design decisions to be framed and options to be ranked'. As this is an ambitious undertaking, it is not surprising that many offer little more than semi-platitudinous 'implications for design'. This entanglement is noted by Heath and Luff (1992), who criticise a number of studies which offer contributions to our understanding of collaborative work but have implications for the design and development of technology which 'appear to be difficult to draw'. Undeterred, they claim both to bridge the gap between naturalistic analyses of collaborative work and the design of technology, and to discuss implications for the development of systems in the Line Control Room of the London Underground, perhaps demonstrating the difficulty of escaping these pressures. Nevertheless, concepts such as surreptitious monitoring and the ways in which activities are rendered visible have permeated the field of CSCW so that designers now consider whether the location of screen information impedes or enhances this necessary, and often invisible, means of communication. Findings have therefore been of value beyond the particular system initially under consideration, but it would be difficult to make an assessment of this value. Whether we should be trying to measure outcomes as a way of validating workplace studies or whether we should avoid succumbing to these pressures is an unresolved issue.

Work studies as basic research

Several studies of the use of various technologies for work are primarily concerned with revealing interesting social phenomena and/or conceptual and theoretical concerns (Anderson *et al.*, 1993; Goodwin & Goodwin, 1995; Harper & Carter, 1994; Hutchins, 1995; Linde, 1988; Murray, 1993; Nardi & Miller, 1990; Suchman, 1987). Although they are sometimes dismissed with 'so what?' by designers, who may not use their findings explicitly, such studies can play an important role in shaping the concerns, issues and central questions of CSCW; as theoretical and conceptual contributions they are not susceptible to a checklist approach, but suffuse thinking about these issues. For example, Suchman's (1987) classic study is considered essential reading for sociologists, system designers and students of CSCW alike and has been much cited.

The influence of these field studies on system design is significant, albeit diffuse and difficult to quantify, and their findings have become distilled over a period of time to become almost part of the early folklore of CSCW. Some authors attempt to demonstrate their relevance to design by resorting to somewhat cursory generalising of their findings, as either a few bullet points or as a brief 'implications for design' section. If employers, funding bodies and others in the CSCW community were willing to value such research in its own right, these gestures at design 'relevance' would be unnecessary.

Some studies persuade researchers and designers to rethink some of the mainstays of CSCW. Although their study is brazenly non-applied, claiming that 'technological matters are eschewed', Harper and Carter (1994) provide a riposte to the commonplace that CSCW is concerned with bringing people together in demonstrating that keeping people apart may in some circumstances be more productive. Murray (1993) suggests that 'the group which most obviously appears to work together in teams may not be the most suitable one to consider when introducing new technology'.

The large research laboratories associated with companies such as Sun, Bell, Hewlett Packard and Xerox are responsible for a significant proportion of the output in publications considered here. Although they belong to multinational corporations in which one might expect many of the constraints of working with an industrial partner to operate, they may paradoxically offer more freedom to engage in 'blue sky' research. Opportunities for system designers and ethnographers to work in close proximity, and the saturation of research environments with communications technologies or radical innovations can be informative and result in valuable cross-fertilisation of ideas. For instance, research output from Xerox PARC and EuroPARC has provided a framework for thinking about privacy, control and feedback issues (Bellotti & Sellen, 1993) and interface design for media space technologies (Dourish & Bly, 1992).

Studies of the implementation and evaluation of CSCW systems in the workplace

There have been far fewer studies of the procurement, implementation and use of CSCW systems in places of actual work than studies intended to inform either CSCW in general or the design of specific systems. One reason for this imbalance is that groupware and multi-user systems for office support have only recently become widely commercially available. Another reason is that the focus of research has primarily been understanding the nature and requirements of existing cooperative work and communication practices for the purpose of informing the design of future systems. The need to inform the design and redesign of systems through evaluating the implementation of CSCW systems in actual work settings has only recently been acknowledged (Bowers, 1994; Rogers, 1994; Sanderson, 1992).

The discrepancy problem and ways of managing it

Despite persistent appeals to engineer the 'the social' in with the technical, many CSCW systems have been developed and introduced into organisations without heed to such advice. Not surprisingly, field studies which have analysed the implementation of CSCW systems in work settings note how they have fallen short of expectations, being used sub-optimally, not at all, or in different ways than intended. It appears that there is a mismatch between the promises of software companies promoting their groupware products, management's expectations of how these can be realised in their particular organisations, and the changes in work practices that have to be adopted by employees to enable the groupware to work in the ways intended and projected. Accordingly, researchers have concerned themselves with describing the different ways in which this 'discrepancy problem' has manifested itself in organisations together with proposals for how collaborative work could be supported and facilitated more effectively.

The now 'classic' groupware failure, described by Grudin (1988), is the lack of uptake of electronic calendars which have automatic meeting scheduling facilities. The disruptive effects of implementing CSCW systems in work settings which benefit one group of users (usually management), but in doing so constrain those of another group using the same system, is explored further by Rogers (1994). Her field study of a new system in a travel centre analyses how it was designed to allow management and the accountancy department to carry out their work in a flexible and unconstrained manner. But the consequences are propagated to the sales consultants using the system further downstream, requiring them to carry out their tasks in a highly inflexible way and often resulting in extra work.

The different expectations of CSCW system developers and of users are another instance of the discrepancy problem. Star and Ruhleder (1994) point out how, in order to use a piece of customised communication software run over the Internet, the users (who are biology researchers) have to learn a vast array of skills and tap knowledge which is taken for granted by the developers.

Several studies make the general point that teething problems are inevitable when implementing CSCW systems into organisations. To manage 'the work to make a CSCW network work' (Bowers, 1994) requires supporting the process with various methods, conceptual tools and mechanisms. These need to co-evolve, so the CSCW system fits in with the current organisational structure whilst work practices are concurrently adapted to enable the system to support collaboration. One mechanism is the intervention of local technically skilled mediators, 'gardeners' or 'tailors', who take on board the responsibility of customising and shaping other users' adoption and understanding of the new system together with deciding on which work procedures to standardise (Gantt & Nardi, 1992; Okamura *et al.*, 1994; Trigg & Bødker, 1994). Here, the emphasis is on empowering and formally acknowledging key individuals within an organisation to facilitate the transition to collaborative working.

Resistance to collaboration

The need for co-adaption of CSCW tools and organisational practices so that they will be perceived to be of benefit by the employees is illustrated in two further field studies. Both used extensive in-depth interviewing and observational studies of work practices to analyse the implementation of Lotus Notes (Orlikowski, 1992) and networking software tools (Bowers, 1994) in established organisations. A general observation was employees' considerable resistance to working more collaboratively so that they could benefit from the functionality afforded by the new groupware tools. The reasons why they should share information and collaborate with others were not obvious to them given the individualised and competitive nature of the organisations.

The extent to which employees are willing to accept a new CSCW system also depends on how much it invades their privacy. In a study of active badges used to generate information about location of personnel, Harper (1992) found that there were significant differences in their use according to work roles: those whose job it was to keep tabs on people (especially receptionists) found them very helpful, while researchers perceived them to be an intrusion into their working patterns. This kind of observer-observee dichotomy was also found by Ramage (1994) in a study of the use of a workflow system within a financial services company. Workers felt that the system, while useful for scheduling work and providing summary information, had a 'big brother' nature in as much as managers could observe how much work they had done in some detail, but the manager found this useful as a way of ensuring her team was meeting its targets.

A further problem with implementing supplementary groupware support (tools which are not essential to the existing way of working but which are considered potentially useful for improving collaboration) is how it might aggravate or interfere with existing 'work arounds' that employees have developed informally. The clash between employees' self-constructed coping strategies and externally imposed groupware solutions is well illustrated in a field study by Harper and Carter (1994), who observed the outcome of installing a video link which was intended to facilitate collaboration between two groups working in the same architectural company. The anticipated benefits did not materialise as the two groups quickly realised that the video link was not helpful to them in their work. The study was also able to expose the nature of the actual problems that the two groups were experiencing, allowing the researchers to suggest quite different requirements for technological support.

Discussion

We have constructed a diagrammatic overview to show the various ways in which work studies have been used to inform system design and facilitate the implementation of CSCW in organisations. The figure is divided into three merging phases, each showing the kinds of research activities that take place at that stage in the design cycle and their potential outcomes. These are i) initial research and its implications, ii) the design and change phase, and iii) the evaluation and development phase. Invariably, workplace studies take place in phase (i) although others may follow the design and change phase.

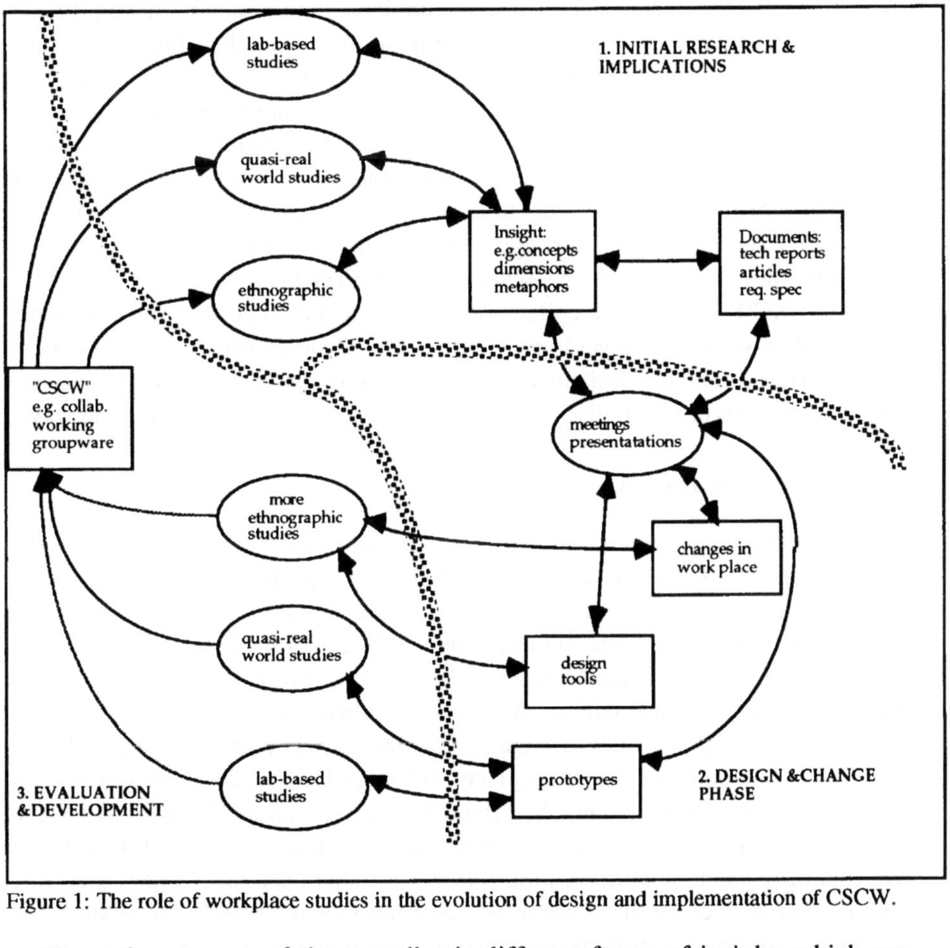

Figure 1: The role of workplace studies in the evolution of design and implementation of CSCW.

The main outcome of these studies is different forms of insight, which are usually reconceptualised at a more abstract level. Depending whether the study is government funded, self-funded or industrially-based, the abstractions are elaborated and documented in academic articles, technical reports or requirements specifications. Because only the first two have tended to be available or cited in the CSCW community it is difficult to assess the extent of more formal documenting.

The findings are also disseminated and discussed at meetings with other interested parties (industrial sponsors, company managers, users, designers, other academics) and verbally presented at conferences. Many of the papers described in the section on studies leading to general design recommendations fit into this category. By and large, it is at this point that the research stops - at any rate, few further publications reporting further developments are to be found. Notable exceptions include researchers who have built software prototypes and design tools based on their initial workplace studies (e.g. the Lancaster CSCW research group), whilst one or two others, described in the implementation section, have proposed and instigated change in work practices during or following their fieldwork. These follow-ons are indicated by the arrows in phase (ii) of the diagram.

Further meetings and presentations may follow and other workplace studies may ensue, although not necessarily as a continuation of the original fieldwork. This is currently the most advanced stage of the evolution of CSCW design reached by any workplace project. At the same time, others who entered at phase (ii) have progressed to phase (iii), through commencing quasi-real-world studies of prototypes developed in the lab (Ackerman, 1994; Tang *et al.*, 1994). The ultimate goals of CSCW - to improve collaborative working and to design useful and used groupware systems - have yet to evolve convincingly and explicitly from the fruits of the earlier research-based activities. The question remains as to when and how this final phase will materialise. There are, however, several obstacles in the way.

The translation process

Many of the approaches advocated by social scientists for informing CSCW design are similar to those that have been applied by the cognitive sciences to interface design for single-user systems in HCI, such as design recommendations and building software prototypes and evaluation tools. So far there have been very few attempts to translate findings from workplace studies beyond the provision of a few general design recommendations. Moreover, fieldworkers are only too aware that their practical offerings are meagre and commonsensical compared with their rich and poetic accounts of the workplace. Whereas HCI researchers have found numerous ways of transforming their findings into practical implications and formal prescriptions that, arguably, have proved useful for designers, CSCW researchers are finding it much more difficult to follow suit. There is a real danger, therefore, that the 'nuggets of useful information' (Sommerville et al, 1993) generated from workplace studies may become marginalised before they have had the opportunity to show their value (Blomberg *et al.*, in press).

There are several issues at stake here. Firstly, workplace studies carried out primarily to understand a particular working practice are making a valuable contribution to the body of CSCW knowledge in their own right. As pointed out in the section on basic research such studies can *inform* CSCW design through raising awareness of important conceptual issues and questioning taken-for-granted assumptions about work activities and how they should be supported. In essence, 'the main virtue of ethnography is its ability to make visible the 'real world' sociality of a setting' (Hughes *et al.*, 1994).

Secondly, is it unfair to expect any more from social scientists? As argued by Button (1993) and Shapiro (1994) the descriptive language and sociologically-generated analytical categories constructed in ethnographic studies are likely to be of little relevance to the practical problem of designing computer systems. Those who attempt to show explicitly the relevance of their research, may find that in the process of translating their detailed accounts into more formal requirements, the richness and significance of their work gets lost, distorted or misconstrued. But if researchers find it problematic reconceptualising their findings, what is it like for designers and consultants (whose job it is to implement new technology and redesign work) to translate descriptions of 'the sociality of work' into the language of design and workflow procedures?

Although some designers have been able to consider researchers' findings and implement them in their design of CSCW systems, we suspect that they are atypical. The majority of designers do not have the time, inclination or expertise to do so. Given the multiple constraints and deadlines that many have to work to, most designers are likely to prefer the translation work to be done for them, by using easily available 'cookbooks' containing step-by-step recipes for incorporating social aspects. But unlike other aspects of design, where it has been possible to provide such guidelines (e.g. ergonomically-based standards for screen and keyboard design) the sociality of work cannot be reduced to metrics.

What this reveals is a big discrepancy between accounts of sociality generated by field studies and the way information can be of practical use to system developers. This observation could lead us into thinking that bridging the gap between the social sciences and system design has proved to be too problematic and should perhaps be abandoned. Certainly, there is evidence of this kind of impatience influencing research funding bodies and commercial R&D departments. We believe that this market-led view of the value of work studies is short-sighted and needs to be reconsidered.

Given all the difficulties, what contribution can workplace studies make? It is clear that their contribution can be significant, if difficult to chart, whether they are intended to inform the design of specific systems, to produce more amorphous insights, or to increase our understanding of implementation processes. Following the aforementioned tradition, we propose:

- researchers who are directly involved in projects where system design guidelines are a required outcome may need to consider developing hybrid and tailored forms of ethnography which can play different practical roles in the various phases of design and implementation;

- researchers should not feel obliged to force design implications from their material;
- researchers and designers should engage more in a continuous dialogue to help bridge the gap and misunderstandings between 'techno-talk' and 'ethno-talk';
- workplace studies for 'their own sake' have played an important role in shaping CSCW and should continue to be supported unfettered to provide further insight into the social, the cognitive and the technical aspects of work.

Acknowledgements

Lydia Plowman is funded by EPSRC and DTI grant GR/J/53454. Magnus Ramage is funded by the EPSRC and the Digital Equipment Corporation. We thank John Hughes, Jonathan Grudin and the anonymous reviewers for their valuable comments.

References

Citations have been abbreviated as follows:

CSCW'86	*Proceedings of the Conference on Computer Supported Cooperative Work* (Austin, Texas, Dec. 3-5, 1986). ACM Press, NY.
CSCW'88	*Proceedings of the Conference on Computer Supported Cooperative Work* (Portland, Oregon, Sept. 26-28, 1988). ACM Press, NY.
ECSCW'89	J.M. Bowers & S.D. Benford (eds.) *Studies in Computer Supported Cooperative Work. Theory, Practice and Design.* (Proceedings of the First European Conference on Computer Supported Cooperative Work, 1989). North Holland, Amsterdam.
CSCW'90	*Proceedings of the Conference on Computer Supported Cooperative Work* (Los Angeles, CA., Oct. 7-10, 1990). ACM Press, NY.
ECSCW'91	L. Bannon, M. Robinson & K. Schmidt (eds.) *Proceedings of the Second European Conference on Computer Supported Cooperative Work.* (Amsterdam, 24-27 Sept., 1991). Kluwer, Dordrecht.
CSCW'92	J. Turner & R. Kraut (eds.) *Proceedings of the Conference on Computer Supported Cooperative Work* (Toronto, Canada, Oct.31-Nov.4, 1992). ACM Press, NY.
ECSCW'93	G. de Michelis, C. Simone, & K. Schmidt (eds.), *Proceedings of the Third European Conference on Computer Supported Cooperative Work.* (Milan, Italy). Kluwer, Dordrecht.
CSCW'94	R. Furuta & C. Neuwirth, (eds.) *Proceedings of the Conference on Computer-Supported Cooperative Work* , (Chapel Hill, North Carolina, Oct. 22-26, 1994). ACM Press, NY.

Ackerman, M. (1994). 'Augmenting the organizational memory: a field study of Answer Garden', in *Proceedings of CSCW'94*, pp.243-252.

Anderson, R., G. Button & W. Sharrock (1993). 'Supporting the design process within an organisational context', in *Proceedings of ECSCW'93*, pp. 47-60.

Anderson, R. & W. Sharrock (1993). 'Can organisations afford knowledge?' *Journal of Computer Supported Cooperative Work* 1 (3) 1993 pp. 143-161.

Beck, E.E. & V. Bellotti (1993). 'Informed opportunism as strategy: supporting coordination in distributed collaborative writing', in *Proceedings of ECSCW'93*, pp. 233-248.

Bellotti, V. & A. Sellen (1993). 'Design for privacy in ubiquitous computing environments', in *Proceedings of ECSCW'93*, pp. 77-92.

Blomberg, J., L. Suchman & R. Trigg (forthcoming). 'Notes on the Work-Oriented Design Project in Three Voices'. To appear in G. Bowker, L. Star, & B. Turner (eds.) *Bridging the Great Divide: Social Science, Technical Systems and Cooperative Work.* MIT Press, Cambridge, Mass. (in press).

Bowers, J. (1994). 'The work to make a network work: studying CSCW in action', in *Proceedings of CSCW'94*, pp. 287-298.

Button, G. (ed.) (1993). *Technology in Working Order.* Routledge, London.

Dourish, P. & S. Bly (1992). 'Portholes; supporting awareness in a distributed work group', in *Proceedings of CHI'92*, (May 3rd-7th, Monterey, CA.), pp. 541-547. ACM, N.Y.

Egger, E. & I. Wagner (1993). 'Negotiating temporal orders - the case of collaborative time management in a surgery clinic.' *Journal of CSCW* 1 (4) 1993, pp. 255-275.

Filippi, G. & J. Thereau (1993). 'Analysing cooperative work in an urban traffic control room for the design of a coordination support system', in *Proceedings of ECSCW'93*, pp. 171-186.

Gantt, M. & B.A. Nardi (1992). 'Gardeners and gurus: patterns of cooperation among CAD users', in *Proceedings of CHI'92, Human Factors in Computing Systems* (May 3rd-7th, Monterey, CA.), pp. 107-118. ACM, N.Y.

Goodman, G. & M. Abel (1986). 'Collaboration research in SCL', in *Proceedings of CSCW'86*, pp. 246-251.

Goodwin, C. & M.J. Goodwin (in press). 'Formulating planes: seeing as a situated activity', in *Communication and Cognition at Work*, eds. D. Middleton & Y. Engeström. CUP, Cambridge.

Grønbaek, K., M. Kyng & P. Mogensen (1992). 'CSCW challenges in large-scale technical projects - a case study', in *Proceedings of CSCW'92*, pp. 338-345.

Grudin, J. (1988). 'Why CSCW applications fail: problems in the design and evaluation of organisational interfaces', in *Proceedings of CSCW'88*, pp. 85-93.

Harper, R. & K. Carter (1994). 'Keeping People Apart.' *Journal of CSCW* 2 (3) pp.199-207.

Harper, R. (1992). 'Looking at ourselves: an examination of the social organisation of two research laboratories', in *Proceedings of CSCW'92*, pp. 330-337.

Heath, C., M. Jirotka, P. Luff & J. Hindmarsh (1993). 'Unpacking collaboration: the interactional organisation of trading in a city dealing room', in *Proceedings of ECSCW'93*, pp. 155-170.

Heath, C. & P. Luff (1992). 'Collaboration and control: crisis management and multimedia technology in London underground control rooms.' *Journal of CSCW* 1 (1/2) pp. 69-94.

Hughes, J., V. King, T. Rodden & H. Andersen (1994). 'Moving out from the control room: ethnography in system design', in *Proceedings of CSCW'94*, pp. 429-439.

Hughes, J., D. Randall & D. Shapiro (1993). 'From ethnographic record to system design. Some experiences from the field.' *Journal of CSCW*1 (3) pp. 123-141.

Hughes, J., D. Randall & D. Shapiro (1992). 'Faltering from ethnography to design', in *Proceedings of CSCW'92*, pp. 115-122.

Hutchins, E. (1995). *Cognition in the Wild.* MIT Press, Cambridge, MA.

Katzenberg B. & J. McDermott (1994). 'Meaning-making in the creation of useful summary reports', in *Proceedings of CSCW'94* , pp. 199-206.

Linde, C. (1988). 'Who's in charge here? Cooperative work and authority negotiation in police helicopter missions', in *Proceedings of CSCW'88*, pp. 52-63.

Luff, P., C. Heath & D. Greatbatch (1992). 'Tasks-in-interaction: paper and screen based documentation in collaborative activity,' in *Proceedings of CSCW'92*, pp.163-170.

Murray, D. (1993). 'An ethnographic study of graphic designers', in *Proceedings of ECSCW'93*, pp. 295-309.

Nardi, B. & J.R. Miller (1990). 'An ethnographic study of distributed problem solving in spreadsheet development', in *Proceedings of CSCW'90*, pp. 197-208.

Okamura, K., M. Fujimoto, W. Orlikowski & J. Yates (1994). 'Helping CSCW succeed: the role of mediators in the context of use', in *Proceedings of CSCW'94*, pp. 55-66.

Orlikowski, W.J. (1992). 'Learning from Notes: organisational issues in groupware implementation,' in *Proceedings of CSCW'92*, pp. 197-370.

Plowman, L. (forthcoming). 'The interfunctionality of talk and text', to appear in *Journal of CSCW*.

Ramage, M. (1994). *Engineering a smooth flow? A study of workflow software and its connections with business process reengineering.* Unpublished MSc dissertation, University of Sussex, UK. Available from author.

Rogers, I. (1995). 'The use of an automatic 'to do' list to guide structured interaction', in *Proceedings of CHI'95*, (May 7-11, Denver, Colorado). ACM Press, N.Y.

Rogers, Y. (1994). 'Integrating CSCW in evolving organisations,' in *Proceedings of CSCW'94*, pp. 67-78.

Ross, S., M. Ramage & Y. Rogers (1995). '*PETRA: Participatory Evaluation Through Redesign and Analysis*', CSRP no. 375, School of Cognitive and Computing Sciences, University of Sussex.

Rouncefield, M., J. Hughes, T. Rodden & S. Viller (1994). 'Working with 'constant interruption': CSCW and the small office', in *Proceedings of CSCW'94*, pp. 275-286.

Sanderson, D. (1992). 'The CSCW implementation process: an interpretative model and case study of the implementation of a videoconference system', in *Proceedings of CSCW'92*, pp. 370-377.

Shapiro, D. (1994). 'The limits of ethnography: combining social sciences for CSCW', in *Proceedings of CSCW'94*, pp. 417-428.

Sommerville, I., T. Rodden, P. Sawyer, R. Bentley & M. Twidale (1993). 'Integrating ethnography into the requirements engineering process', in *Proceedings of the IEEE Requirements Engineering Conference*, San Diego.

Star, S.L. & K. Ruhleder (1994). 'Steps towards an ecology of infrastructure: complex problems in design and access for large-scale collaborative systems', in *Proceedings of CSCW'94*, pp. 253-264.

Streitz, N., J. Geissler, J. Haake & J. Hol (1994). 'DOLPHIN: Integrated meeting support across local and remote desktop environments and liveboards', in *Proceedings of CSCW'94*, pp. 345-358.

Suchman, L. (1987). *Plans and Situated Actions: The Problem of Human-Machine Communication*. Cambridge University Press, Cambridge.

Tang, J., E.A. Issacs, & M. Rua (1994). 'Supporting distributed groups with a Montage of lightweight interactions', in *Proceedings of CSCW'94*, pp. 23-34.

Tang, J. & E. Isaacs (1993). 'Why do users like video? Studies of multimedia-supported collaboration.' *Journal of CSCW*1 (3) 1993, pp. 163-196.

Toth, J. (1994). 'The effects of interactive graphics and text on social influence in computer-mediated small groups', in *Proceedings of CSCW'94*, pp. 299-310.

Trigg, R. & S. Bødker (1994). 'From implementation to design: tailoring and the emergence of systematization in CSCW', in *Proceedings of CSCW'94*, pp. 45-54.

Proceedings of the Fourth European Conference on Computer-Supported Cooperative Work,
September 10–14, Stockholm, Sweden
H. Marmolin, Y. Sundblad, and K. Schmidt (Editors)

Chalk and Cheese: BPR and ethnomethodologically informed ethnography in CSCW

Dave Randall
Manchester Metropolitan University, UK

Mark Rouncefield, John A. Hughes
Lancaster University, UK

Recently a number of methodological approaches have been presented as proffering radical solutions to organisational change. This paper discusses one such approach, Business Process Re-engineering (BPR) and contrasts it with Ethnography, a method that has gained some prominence in CSCW. The paper suggests, using a number of empirical examples, that despite some superficial similarities, the two approaches differ markedly in their analytical purchase. In particular, ethnography's emphasis on understanding 'systems' within the situated context of the work setting rather than as an abstract model of process, has consequences for the successful identification and implementation of system re-design.

Introduction

> "Do you know what you are asking? You are asking, 'Could you tell me, without knowing what kind of world we are in, what a theory would look like?' ...."
>
> Harvey Sacks

Sack's reply to a fellow sociologist's request concerning method was designed, as Lynch points out (1991), to question the widely held presumption that, regardless of subject matter, there can be a unitary method for scientific enquiry.We also wish to suggest that Sack's insight has as much relevance for recently developed policies for organisational intervention as much as it has for developing theories of human conduct.

Our particular concern in this paper is to contrast one such programme of organisational intervention, Business Process Re-engeering (BPR), with ethnography, a sociological approach to work study prominent in CSCW. Both approaches challenge orthodox structured methods for system design and stress the vital importance of investigating organisations as a preliminary for proposing changes. However, beyond this there are some crucially significant differences between the two approaches which have a bearing on CSCW. We focus here on Business Process Re-engineering (BPR), not because it is the 'best' or even the 'trendiest' of the available programmes, but because it is self-confessedly the most 'radical', systematic, and far-reaching of the change management techniques now available.[1] We feel that an examination of its promise and some of its limitations is overdue not least because it poses a challenge to sociologists working in CSCW.

There is by now a substantial literature on BPR (see for example Hammer and Champy, 1993; Harrington, 1991; Davenport; 1993; Jacobson et al, 1995), and we do not propose to re-invent the wheel by elaborating its practices unnecessarily. Instead, we are concerned with the degree to which, if at all, BPR's systematic approach to work, organizations, and IT systems is likely to supercede the 'ethnographic'[2] practices of sociologists within CSCW. In examining the methodological presuppositions of BPR, therefore, we are not seeking to make a moral point, nor attempting to assess whether BPR can and does live up to its radical promise. Our interest lies precisely in the fact that a challenge to CSCW generally and to the sociological practice of ethnography is, implicitly or explicitly, being made.

The commitments of BPR

We suggest that, despite its varied guises, BPR can be distilled into a few essential methodological commitments.

Although BPR can be variously characterised as a recipe for fundamental change[3] or as a more modest and progressive refinement of business objectives in terms of core processes (Harrington, 1991), the role of IT is almost universally seen as critical. In particular, IT is significant because it is capable of magnifying the accuracy and the scope of measurement. Thus, "Measurements are key. If you cannot measure it, you cannot control it. If you cannot control it you cannot manage it. If you cannot manage it you cannot improve it." (Harrington, 1991). Nevertheless, despite placing IT at the centre of the change management process, BPR is predicated on the recognition that traditional design has, in many instances, failed to produce the productivity gains anticipated for business, especially in its 'white collar' sectors. That is, whilst being fundamentally a method for changing the organization, implicitly at least, it problematises and challenges both orthodox structured approaches to systems design and also some characteristic stances in CSCW. In the first instance, BPR proponents

---

1 Proponents of BPR can make some startling claims. Jacobson et al for instance point out, "There are estimates that 50 to 70% of companies that try it fail. I think the risk of failure is even higher." (1995, preface). They are, of course, implying very high risk but even higher reward. In other words, the word radical here has a surgical sense.

2 We are extremely conscious of the extent to which this is a gloss on many and varied practices.

3 For instance by Hammer (1993) in his famous injunction to stop 'paving over the cowpath'.

create a distance from the modelling activities associated with traditional design by arguing that,

> "all these techniques come from the computer world. It is as though we learned to think in a way that works for computer systems, and we realized we could apply the same way of thinking to describe an organization ... we find this unacceptable .... we shall introduce .... the basis for a modelling technique for people, not machines." (Jacobson et al, 1995: 36)

In this respect, it appears that BPR proponents are establishing analytic procedures which go to the very heart of CSCW concerns. It is certainly hard to read the claim that the design and implementation of IT systems must orient to business goals as anything but a demand for new approaches to 'requirements'.

The distinction between BPR and traditional approaches to design is further established by an argument which respecifies the relationship between 'what happens now' and procedures for respecifying activity. Whereas structured design has to a greater or lesser extent reduced the importance of the physical model of the current system (see Yourdon and Constantine, 1979; Benyon, 1992a; Benyon, 1992b), BPR seems to re-establish the problematic relationship between the two, something that ethnographers have also tried to do (Randall et al 1992). That is, it seems, as with ethnography, to be interested in the gap between actual practice and idealised conceptions of practice. Thus, Davenport argues that BPR "implies a strong emphasis on *how* work is done within an organization, in contrast to a product focus's emphasis on *what.*" (Davenport, 1993) For those who see ethnography merely as a matter of data collection in naturalistic environments, BPR advocates seem to be suggesting something which is both consistent with 'ethnographic' enquiry whilst providing an answer to some critics of ethnography by providing strategies for 'envisioning' alternatives which meet at least one criticism levelled against ethnography, namely, that it is inherently conservative.[4] Harrington (1991) provides a more complete description of the appropriate methods, for instance, by emphasising the 'process walkthrough' as a principal method for understanding how work is done. Hence one finds:

> "One of the key activities in the BPI [Business Process Improvement] walk-through process is to observe the activity being performed. Immediately after the interview, the interviewer and the interviewee should go to the work area to observe the activity discussed in the interview. Observing the individual tasks being performed will stimulate additional questions. As Dr. H. James Harrington puts it, "You never really understand the activity until you do it yourself. If that isn't possible, the next best alternative is to observe the activity while it is being performed, and ask a lot of questions." (Stowell, 1991)

Such insights would, at least as far as CSCW is concerned, be both modest and somewhat unoriginal were it not for the extra dimension which BPR seems to provide, that of socio-technical systematicity. The typical 'problem specifications' and comparisons one finds in BPR, for instance between the formal process and actual practice, the differences in the way employees perform tasks, the relevance of training requirements, the existence of process problems and 'roadblocks', and so on, constitute foci which all overlap to some degree with those of typical ethnographic studies.

Moreover, analysts such as Harrington recognise, as do ethnographers, that not only are process specification and the activity in question not the same thing, but that deviation from the specification is explicable by a whole range of factors, including the

---

4 We do not, of course, accept that ethnography is a 'conservative' enterprise and have argued elsewhere that orienting to design is the fundamental problem (see Hughes et al , 1992).

possibility that there may be potentially positive reasons such as finding a better way to do things, or at least compensating for problems. In particular, BPR stresses the role of 'chronic' problems in working life, because, it is argued, chronic problems are often difficult to see. This in turn is because methods for completing processes often adapt to chronic problems. That is, people often find ways round persistent obstructions and the fact that work can be done effectively is sometimes despite problems of this sort. This is both an argument that ethnographers have advanced, and one which has a considerable, but sometimes unrealised, importance in the evaluation of technologies.[5]

To return to the main point, however, and in a nutshell, the systematicity that BPR offers may appear attractive because it addresses both the weaknesses of traditional IT design and the glosses on organizational context which CSCW has tended to provide by, on the face of it, providing both a concern for current context and practice and a systematic technique for producing alternatives. By way of example, an adequate picture of what is going on in the organization and how to transform it requires, for Davenport, a holistic approach which encompasses not only every dimension of an organization's activities, but also a method for designing the future. Thus, "The term process innovation encompasses the envisioning of new work strategies, the actual process design activity, and the implementation of the change *in all its complex technological, human, and organizational dimensions.*" (Davenport, 1993)

That is, BPR promises a complete and systematic understanding of how the organization currently functions and what has to be done in both work and technological terms to provide radical success in redesign. Nevertheless, asserting that one has provided an 'all singing, all dancing' solution to the problems raised within CSCW and elsewhere is a long way from demonstrating that the assertion is valid. Merely because a system is offered which *claims* to deal with problems of appropriate technology as well as appropriate organizational structure does not make it so. We reiterate that we are not trying to provide either an ethical critique of BPR nor trying to argue that it is unlikely to achieve the goals it sets. We do want, however, to raise issues that spring from the apparent similarity of some of its procedures to ethnography and, quite distinctly, from the apparent systematicity it offers.

BPR's commitment, and distinctively from ethnography, is conceptualizing what goes on in organizations as a matter of *understanding and defining 'processes'*. Moreover, these processes are unequivocally defined according to their measurable relationship to the customer. Thus, Harrington[6] describes a process as:

> "any activity or group of activities that takes an input, adds value to it, and provides an output to an internal or external customer. Processes use an organization's resources to provide *definitive* results."

A Business Process in turn is defined as,

---

[5] One caveat here is that occasional problems may be equally significant, but in different ways. For instance, in Safety Critical environments occasional problems are potentially disastrous precisely because operators may be unfamiliar with them. One argument for ethnography is that prolonged exposure to the domain usually prompts recognition of occasional but nonetheless important 'problems'.

[6] We cite Harrington more than other proponents of BPR not out of any conviction that his work is the 'best' or even the most 'typical' of the field, but because he, in our view spells out the method in rather more detail than most.

"All service processes and processes that support production processes. A business process consists of any *logically related* tasks that use the resources of the organization to provide defined results in support of the *organization's objectives*." (our italics).

In other words, BPR makes use of an orthodox rationalistic perspective on organizational goals, but orients it to a set of explicit change management objectives, such as improving effectiveness, efficiency, and adaptability or implementing control systems. The analytic work involves identifying a set of defined tasks which are to do with meeting organizational objectives, and which are construed in terms such as determining where the process boundaries will be, and what the inputs and outputs to the process are. Key aspects of this work might, for instance, include identifying suppliers to, and customers of, the process identified, along with "who is performing the key operations.". Thus, and for instance, determining process boundaries has to do with "identifying the ownership of the process and where it begins and ends." (Harrington, 1991), with a view to assessing the strategic relevance of each process.[7]

As one might expect from a largely top-down methodology, the point of investigating how operations are performed is to establish the 'health' or otherwise of the processes in terms of the business objectives of the organization. A sample method advocated by Harrington for doing precisely that is to identify 'multiple buffers', which produces the 'queuing up' of stages. Indeed, a recurring theme in all BPR versions is the distinction between the logical connection between activity, which tends to be horizontal, and the vertical connections of the organization. It is this distinction, perhaps more than any other which has informed the developing interest in Workflow. Workflow is defined in BPR as the method for transforming input into output, and is one of the primary characteristics of a process, and in many respects is the key to understanding what is distinctive about BPR.

That is, and to summarise, the analytic force of BPR, its interest in the observation of current practice is solely to identify, from the top down, what is wrong in terms of the specified business goals and the means for pursuing them. Further, what is wrong is to be defined in terms of measurable obstructions to efficiency with a view to producing alternative structures in which those obstructions have been eradicated. These obstructions may, of course, be of more than one kind and may include, for example, the generation of error, the existence of 'poor quality' costs (waste), and 'multiple buffers'. In any event, the presupposition is that analysing current work can unproblematically lead us to conclusions concerning what it is that causes 'problems' to arise. The presumption is that measurable benefits will be obtained precisely from the identification, measurement, and respecification of process. These benefits, and we highlight them only to provide a flavour of the direction in which this kind of analysis takes us, conventionally include the elimination of duplication, error proofing, automation, and standardization. It is the latter that will primarily concern us below.

7 It would, therefore, be a mistake to view BPR as a *naive* reformulation of Taylorist principles for the white collar world. Although aspects of BPR are unmistakeable Taylorist in their force, the method recognises that 'informal' aspects of organization may impinge on the success or failure of objectives. Thus and for instance, Harrington refers to the problem of qualifying the 'culture and politics' surrounding the process.

The view from ethnography

It will come as no surprise that we do not, in fact, accept that the practices of the process walkthrough and related techniques are similar to the conduct of ethnography in any but the most superficial ways. Although on the surface, at least, much of what is being advocated here is similar to what has been claimed for ethnography, to restate a point we and others have made elsewhere (see Hughes et al, 1994; Button and King, 1992; Anderson, 1994; Pycock et al, 1994), ethnography is not in any sense a unitary method, if indeed the word method is applicable at all to its varied practices, but is a gloss on various and different *analytic* frameworks. Nevertheless, an ethnographic stance arguably entails a minimum orientation, which has to do with seeing the social world from the point of view of participants. One 'take' on this, and one which has strongly influenced our own work, is the ethnomethodological one, in which member's methods for accomplishing situations in and through the use of local rationalities becomes the topic of enquiry. The relevance of such a perspective to systems design issues lies in the fact that this respecification of sociology draws attention to the way in which orderliness can be viewed, *inter alia*, as a feature of the sense making procedures participants use *in the course of their work*.. The explication of sense making machinery has often invoked work activity as a manifest 'working division of labour' (See Anderson, et al, 1989, Hughes et al, 1994). In other words, and to put it simply, although individual workers have individual tasks to perform, they are also and necessarily individuals-as-part-of-a-collectivity, and much of their work consists in the ability to organise the distribution of individual tasks into an ongoing assemblage of activities *within* a 'working division of labour'. Individuals, that is, orient to their work according to 'egological' principles and their own 'horizons of relevance' but have to be attentive to the work of others in order to organise the flow of work in a coherent way. This focus has arguably provided an important analytic tool for the examination of work as lived experience, providing important clues as to both how work was accomplished and perhaps, from a systems analytic perspective, why work was done the way it was.

Our point is that, despite the apparent similarities, the *analytic* interest of BPR investigation is irrevocably different from that of ethnography as outlined above. This is not to claim that BPR is somehow mistaken or misguided, but that methods must be judged on the problems they are designed to deal with. BPR's strategy is decompositional. It derives from its clearly stated objectives, which include providing a measurement system for organizations and a means to standardize processes. 'Problem' and 'solution', that is, exist in a hermetic relationship in which each can only be understood as aspects of 'healthy' and 'unhealthy' processes. Observation of the current state of play is conceived in terms of the analysis of task performance, the obstructions which may be associated with it, and evaluation and comparison of different task performances. In other words, and put simply, when a BPR analyst is observing work, s/he is either looking for what is wrong with it, and defining it as process failure, or at examples of 'good' strategies which can be codified into the new processes. At root, although sources of discretion and variation may be of some interest, the task of BPR is either to eliminate them or provide methods for their universal application. The solution to organisational 'problems' lies in understanding how, for instance, 'culture and politics', methods of 'task performance', or what have you can be conceived as variations which can be removed, wherever possible.

Now there may be many good reasons from a business point of view, for undertaking such analyses, and discovering sources of error, redundancy, or obstruction is likely as not going to prove valuable to the organization. The key question, however, is whether understanding these issues as *process failures* is either necessary or adequate. After all, practitioners of differing styles of observation, whether it be ethnography, task analysis, BPR process walkthroughs, or participative design techniques, will all recognise occasions when they have construed situations as 'obstructions', 'duplications', or 'problems'. In BPR, however, they are problems of process because the analyst has defined them that way according to the hierarchy of measurable goals and means which constitute the organization's objectives. That is, any possibility that such problems can be understood in several ways, including the perspective of the participant to the work, *and that participants' perspectives may have consequences for organizational objectives*, is excluded.

Specifying a 'problem' in other words is not, as it would be for the ethnomethodologically informed ethnographer, a matter of understanding local rationales for 'doing work'. The point is that the strategies for 'doing work' uncovered by the latter analytic are likely to be explications of *reasons for doing it this way* as well as some problems encountered.

The particular claim of ethnography, at least as we understand and practise it, lies less in its ability to identify 'why a current system is not working', which is the force of BPR analysis but, at least in a sense, 'how it *is* working'. That is, the ability of the BPR analyst to identify processes as meeting, or not as the case may be, the organisation's objectives, depends critically on the system-oriented approach. In contrast, the value of ethnography for systems design cannot be separated from its focus on the accomplishment of work from the point of view of parties to the work. Ethnographic methods seek to uncover features of the sociality of work and its organisation; how the work 'gets done'; the conversations, gossip and asides; the interruptions and mistakes; the details of the how the paperwork and computer work are practically accomplished as part of routine, ordinary, taken-for-granted, 'real world' work activities. A related focus is *making visible the judgement and discretion* that workers need to use in response to the various contingencies that arise in even apparently routine activities. Making visible because the range of tacit skills and local knowledge can be elusive, 'taken for granted' and so on such that they may otherwise, perhaps, become visible only when routines or organisations break down.

This approach to work as socially organised is designed to illuminate the rationale brought by people at work to the various tasks, their 'problems', and the 'things to do' that they are confronted with in the course of their daily working lives. In a nutshell, the ethnomethodological interest in how work is done highlights the fact that human activity in work may be deeply relevant to the working of the organization in ways that are not apparent when one only looks for what is wrong. The consequences of such a choice, we would argue, are substantially different from those that result from BPR analysis. That is, the point of ethnography is not to highlight various obstructions and 'blockages' that exist in the system, for this is something that may be more or less adequately done by various kinds of analysis, including those done by members themselves, of which BPR is only one.

We should perhaps stress that our task is not to deny the possible benefits of process redesign exercises to particular organisational interests, for it would be quite plausible to claim that such benefits do indeed, at least sometimes, accrue. Rather, we are attempting to problematise BPR as a *systematic* solution to business problems by proffering ethnographic analysis as a complementary mode. In what follows we use vignettes drawn from organisations in the retail financial sector where both ethnographic studies and process re-design activities of some kind have been undertaken. What we are aiming to show is how some typical categories that might be deployed in ethnographic analysis are radically different in consequence to those typical of BPR, such as 'duplication elimination', 'error proofing', 'standardization' and so on. Here, and they are merely exemplars, we utilise categories such as skill and local knowledge, although we might equally well have dealt with issues of time, unpredictability and interruption, and hope to do so elsewhere.

Ethnographic approaches seem especially valuable and insightful in discovering and 'unpacking' the often highly situated and tacit notions of skill that promote the practical accomplishment of work as a 'routine, everyday' activity; subtle notions that may well prove essential if 'skills' are to be understood as relevant to system design. The sense of 'skill' that we are interested here is that of 'knowing how', or competency. In this respect the competencies involve making sense of, and thereby being able to make available to others, what is 'going on'. These could be described as competencies required for 'mutual intelligibility' on the part of the members of a work team - in producing what might be accepted as visibly 'rational' decisions or actions - 'rational' that is, in the context in which the decision is made. Space precludes detailed analyses of the various 'skills' we might find deployed in different contexts within the sector, and we focus here on one specific example - the skills of lending- specifically because it resonates with the use of decision support technology which was implemented precisely with standardization and error proofing in mind.

Skill

In this financial organization, the production of 'rational' lending decisions are seen as important in both the 'mass market ' and the 'small business' sector. In both instances, software exists to support lending decisions, and in the mass market the 'risk grades' produced by the software, as one Assistant Manager said, are;

> "... a lot more process driven ..the machine will give you a recommendation ...if the machine says 'no' and that decision is overridden, its 90% likely to 'go down the pan'... loans "down the pan" have reduced considerably since the introduction of machines.."

In this way, we can see that the standardization of decision-making here was introduced by the codification of 'expert' rules into software, along with a number of structural changes which need not concern us here. The Lending Process was respecified in order to address the unacceptably high number of 'bad' decisions. This does not, however, mean that the process is no longer accompanied by skilful work, and in higher value lending this became particularly clear, especially in terms of the work of accounting for, or justifying, decisions. A number of features of 'business' lending appeared to involve the utilisation of a range of 'skills'; an appreciation of 'paperwork' and the affordances of paper; the use of computers to support relationship building, local knowledge and decision making; the deployment of local knowledge and local 'logics' in guiding and supporting notions of 'rationality' and rational decision-making - notably in the lending acronym 'campari and ice' (character-ability-means-purpose-amount-repayment-insurance-interest-commission-extras) which relates to lending proposals.

It is a mechanism for assessing risk and reward which is enshrined in the Bank's manual, but is more 'honoured in the breach' than in practise in one important respect. Attention to all its details, as opposed to its general spirit, appeared relatively rare. It is in the appreciation of this balance, between application and non-application of 'the rule' that at least part of the 'skill' of lending resides. The other part of the 'skill' is in the construction of a rationale to justify any decision. In the following extracts a Business Manager is making lending judgements supported by a range of local and informed knowledge of the customer accumulated from the skilful use and linkage of information from paperwork, computerwork and personal interview. He, along with an assistant, is considering a request for a £100K loan to a college for more building work;

1. Looking at draft accounts - some problem over ownership of land.

2. Developing some questions for answers from college - agreement in principle to loan with some conditions - fixed price contract; staged payments; site visits.

3. Discussion of criteria for borrowing

4. Assistant- GAPPing accounts[8]

5. Interruption - instructions for GAPPing - talk about problems.

6 Phoning college - arranging papers - Principal not available

- another problem over the constitution of the College - whether they are legally allowed to borrow money etc. - lending - problem of powers of college to borrow money. 3 main worries - land; powers; ability to repay - re: £40K deficit.

7. Calculating depreciation.

8. Using computer - BAF - to work out possible repayments - problems with password.

9. Inquiries menu - repayment info menu - various options = O/D; loan - fixed term; loan - fixed repayment; actuarial structured loan (BDL) - types in figures - £23K per annum.

Business Manager's Assistant - GAPPing

Next.

1. Balance sheet carding - taking college accounts and putting onto balance sheet card - 'Balance Sheet Carding for individuals and Firms' - when finished will put on screen and then GAPP them

2. Problem with GAPPing - advice from Region applies to Polys and Unis not Colleges

3. Still working on Balance sheet

4. Using screen - 'update financial accounts' - enters figures from balance sheet onto screen

5. Looking at guidelines from UKBB on Colleges

6. Interr - C...- has found diff set of accounts - show a surplus - management figures - "Which shall I enter?" "I don't know"

7. Back looking at instructions/guidelines

8. GAPPed - Risk Grade 6 - "I just followed the instructions - I'll send it to Region now and they can play around with it"

---

[8] Grading and Pricing Policy- the decision support software.

Next.

1. Still working on college report/interview preparation.

2. Discusses with C....- rates for loan; had phone conversation with principal re: land; talk about alternative uses etc. (alternative uses of buildings and land etc. - effects valuation for security) (tape)

3. Filling out 2 loan forms - 50K OD; 150K 10 yr. BDL.

4. Calculating rates for loans

5. C...dictating letter to college - Assistant still filling out forms.

6. Asks C...to sign and then she'll key it in. Gives him to sign - looking at form "its a matter of interpretation isn't it?" - filling in managerial details.

This extract shows the ways in which computer support for decision-making is enmeshed within a working division of labour, and its usage as part of the process of rational decision-making. The various programs were intended both to support decision making and to improve the speed of processing thereby giving staff more time to be 'pro-active'. The GAPP was used to calculate Risk Grade of Businesses (1-9; 1 = "substantially risk free"; 9 = "loss likely"); and the pricing policy that should be adopted. The program gave a margin within which pricing could be negotiated.

It is important to recognise and emphasise that GAPP was an addition to the existing risk assessment and pricing 'devices' - in some senses simply automating what had previously been done (and continued to be done) manually. The fact that GAPPing, although incorporated into the lending process appeared as a mere additional check in that process rather than integral to it, meant that GAPPing seemed less important as a decision-making device than as a 'security blanket' for decisions already made; and the starting point for negotiation (particularly over pricing) with the business concerned. As an Assistant Manager said;

> "you cannot say straightaway...just because the computer program says 1% higher...you cant just impose a 1% rise...you've got to use it as a tool..."you've got to sum up how much the overdraft is and whatever.."

Using the software to confirm rather than determine decisions - may have arisen as a consequence of the inclusion in the program of 'non-financial' information which could significantly influence the risk grade obtained and which was dependent on the Manager's store of local and anecdotal knowledge; e.g. "are there any signs of creative accountancy?"; "are there any anecdotal signs of problems?". Such 'anecdotal' evidence should not, however, be sneered at since in at least one instance - a double glazing firm - no indication of trouble was revealed by any of the computer packages or printouts and only became evident when the firm appeared on the 'receivership and liquidation' perusal form.

Local Knowledge - "he's a God to this Branch."

It is a commonplace observation (e.g., Suchman, 1987) that work 'routines' are not slavishly adhered to but, typically, involve the considerable exercise of judgement and the deployment of a variety of 'skills'. Such discretion 'typically' concerns the circumstances under which a routine is to be strictly followed and the circumstances under which modifications or 'short-cuts' may be employed through, for example, the utilisation of informal teamwork or 'local knowledge' and is a matter for 'occasioned determination' in the course of the work. The significance of such an observation can be assessed by the fact that problems arose, for example, when staff absence, or a need to clear a back-log of work, required the employment of part-timers unfamiliar with the particular office or the redeployment of staff unfamiliar with the particular processes. This was noted in the fieldwork observations with reference to attempts to clear a backlog of Standing Orders following a Bank Holiday;

"for these staff, the first day or two in a branch are largely unproductive. A considerable amount of time is spent in orienting to local practice ... staff were not always familiar with the available technology...and frequently had to ask others what the appropriate codes for various screens were..".

A number of other comments and typical exchanges from the fieldnotes support this view;

"Ask X, she might know"

"To be honest with you, I don't know how it works...I've only done this job for a week...what's your phone number? I'll find out and ring you back."

On the phone.."Your charging structure...we used to charge them...how does it work now?"

"The girl there thinks its...but she's not that sure"

This seems to problematise the relationship between standardised processes and 'local' knowledge. That is, the above examples demonstrate that in important senses standardised operations articulate with local knowledge to produce practise. It may, of course, do so in ways that are inconsistent with the bank's purposes. In one instance complaints arose from the fact that customers were charged as a result of the delayed processing of standing orders which, at the time of the observations, had a five day backlog of work. The failure to cancel standing orders in time occasionally meant that the account became overdrawn and incurred charges. Bank charges were automatically triggered on the computer when the agreed limit for the account was exceeded. When the initial mistake was rectified - typically after a customer complaint - and the money paid back into the account, the charges levied were often overlooked, so initiating a further complaint from the customer. As a Manager commented: "people aren't instructed to think through the effect of that change - they're only interested in putting it right". This example serves to make the point that it is in the articulation of standardised procedures- rules- and local knowledge and practise that work gets done. When assessed according to some hierarchy of goals or means it may or may not be done well, but in either event it makes no sense to emphasise the procedure alone, as though the procedure guarantees meeting objectives.

Fieldwork observations in the Bank have consistently identified the extent to which the accomplishment of work tasks was frequently associated with informal teamwork, 'constellations of assistance' and the use of 'local knowledge'. Such 'local knowledge' consisted of knowledge of individual customers or particular processes and routines and was used mainly to avoid lengthy perusal of 'action sheets' or the 'PIF' manual of job processes. 'Local knowledge' incorporates ideas about methods for short-cutting or facilitating tiresome and time-consuming routines comprising what Bittner (1965) calls 'gambits of compliance'; that is, techniques that enable workers to 'get the work done' whilst giving the appearance of complying with the formal rules. An example from the fieldwork notes on the cashiers illustrates this point;

"Customer who wants to cash a cheque from another branch...handed over to section head to ring for authorisation...rang several times, branch continually engaged....phone still engaged, trying to contact bank via switch message...after 35 minutes no reply to switch and phone still engaged...customer asked if he wanted to reduce the amount to £300...his cheque was then cashed"

The existence and utilisation of informal teamwork and 'local knowledge' is hardly a novel discovery but a persistent finding of most empirical CSCW research. Nevertheless their importance needs to be recognised, particularly with regard to attempts to redesign the work process. In the bank study, for example, while occasionally semi-formal teams were created to deal with a particular 'problem' or task, usually a backlog of work, these often appeared to be inefficient, primarily because they often failed to incorporate the personnel possessing the kinds of local knowledge that would facilitate task completion.

One of the intentions behind the re-design of Bank operations, through the creation of specialised processing units, was to increase standardisation of operations and thereby remove any dependence on 'local knowledge'. However, and perhaps surprisingly, the use of local knowledge remained a regularly observed feature of the work in the specialised units. In the Foreign section, for example, workers were familiar with the specific requirements of particular (usually 'awkward') customers but there were also other instances when local knowledge was used to speed up the work process;

5. Phoning - re: urgent fax - transfer of funds. Unable to identify the customer on the phone and therefore there is a problem over the release of funds.

6. Goes to see Supervisor.

7. Back on phone - decides to phone customer and tell them to go to Branch and ask for original with signatures - or if manager is prepared to sign fax (some faxes they will accept - they have a list - but this is not one)

8. Phoning customer - wants identification.

9. Decides to send money - explains to Supervisor that customer was always getting trouble with X Branch; that he knew people in Commercial & Foreign; that he sounded genuine(?).

10. Gets details of Bank for correspondence book.

11. Keying details into screen.....

Although this might be viewed as merely a reconfiguration of local knowledge, the important point to make is that it remains local and derived directly from the experience and knowledge of the work itself and provides a resource by which the procedures are made to work more smoothly than they might otherwise in avoiding problems that might arise through a strict use of procedure. Such an advantage is most clearly seen when processes, automated into some form of 'expert system' suddenly become redundant or inapplicable as a consequence of change. One example of this in the bank was the 'TS' software package, used for the taking, maintaining and releasing of securities guaranteeing loans. This system was heavily rule driven with each set of 'formalities' having to be completed before continuing to the next stage. Consequently, when action had to be taken quickly and securities released before the paperwork became available workers were forced to the expedient of 'telling lies' to the machine in order to expedite the process.

Conclusion

A key insight of BPR is that technology is but one feature of a wider 'system' and that its design must orient to the system in the large. Insights obtained from ethnography's focus on social organisation is that 'functionality' cannot be considered to be a systematic property at all, but rather a relation between system and the use to which that system is put, understood in and through the mutually accomplished purposes of participants. Ethnographic approaches view computers, procedures and rules as enmeshed in a system of *working* - incorporated into the flow of work in highly particular ways, including being misused, modified, circumvented and ignored. One of the virtues of ethnography lies in revealing these myriad usages in the context of 'real world' work settings; highlighting those 'human factors' which most closely pertain to system design, whether 'system' in this context is restricted to technology, or is expanded to include organizational processes. Ethnographic methods thus seek to understand 'systems' within the situated context of the work setting and not an abstract model of process, thereby identifying the subtle and often unremarked cooperative aspects of work, the small scale constellations of assistance and deployment of local knowledge that enable the work to be accomplished. Ethnography involves, therefore, far more than 'mere' detailed description but bring a particular focus to the analysis of systems in use and thereby outline the 'play of possibilities' for systems design;

> "to enable designers to question the taken-for-granted assumptions embedded in the conventional problem-solution design framework" (Anderson 1994:170)

Or, as it has been put elsewhere, ethnography affords the prospect of 'respecifying the problem' (COMIC Deliverable 2.1). Once this is recognised, the apparent similarity between ethnography and some of methods employed by BPR practitioners dissolves. Thus, conceptualising 'doing work' as egologically organised, through 'bridesmaid' concepts like skilfulness and local knowledge, enables us to demonstrate not only that it can be counterposed to notions of standard process, but that it examines aspects of organizational life which are entirely, and necessarily, left out of BPR analysis. Where BPR should be assessed in terms of standardisation and suchlike, ethnography must in contrast be assessed by what it says about aspects of working which are complementary to process.

Standardized procedures in principle confer a number of advantages, notably that they should be easy to understand, the training overhead is reduced, staff should become to a degree interchangeable and ambiguity is removed. However, our argument has been that, even when standard procedures are implemented, local knowledge and skills are both persistent and indeed necessary to the very flow of work that is presumed to result from process design. Further, and given BPR's emphasis on new technologies as a vehicle for providing organisational gains, it is as well to remember that the fieldwork observations further suggest that in a number of instances the deployment of local knowledge and instigation of informal teamworking, such as asking for codes to enter screens, how to complete routines; etc., was effectively constituted as 'ways to cope' with the inadequacies of the computer systems; that is, and to adapt a phrase of Garfinkel's (1967), there are 'bad organisational reasons for good organisational practices". What local knowledge and skill is, and how it is deployed is hardly likely to be incidental to the concerns of process redesign. After all, even if one accepts that it is a sensible task to reduce discretion down to a lowest common denominator, it is likely to prove useful to know how it is constituted and how it relates to existing processes, technologies, and what have you. The importance of, for instance, the computer interface in making the machinery 'useable' is by now well-attested. However, here and elsewhere, we have tried to emphasise how 'useability' itself can be a function of the mutually elaborated character of work activities, whether it is accomplished by operatives, or as we have observed elsewhere (Randall and Hughes, 1994; King and Randall, 1994) by operatives and customers working together. In the later case, our interest lay in the work of the clerk or cashier processing transactions, generated either by interactions with customers or by organisational requirements. Our interest in 'what needs to be done' led in turn to an understanding of the role of the customer in initiating, structuring or enabling the work of the cashier. The inherent unpredictability of customer demands, we argued, had considerable significance for the design of the interface. Customers in a very real sense are participants to the ordering of the flow of work and the use of systems, especially the direct interaction of officers with the database, can usefully be comprehended as customer driven. It was one of our purposes, in short, to demonstrate how it is that in and through the demands, enquiries, requests, and so on that customers bring to encounters that the ordering of the process, the structure of database interrogation, work priority, and the spatial organisation of work in hand is determined. As we have seen, BPR has the customer as the primary focus of the process chain, but nowhere is it recognised that what customers *do* might be just as important as their statements of need, and the fact that customers can be construed as 'doing work' just as operatives can is very relevant to the technologies that are intended to support the business process.

Our brief examination of some features of 'working' in the financial services sector raises a number of questions which we can only attend to in outline. They are nevertheless important questions for BPR if we are to accept it at face value as a systematic strategy for addressing the problem of technologies in organisational contexts.

Firstly, the question of the allocation of function is pertinent. As we have seen in our discussion of lending, the use of instinct, 'gut feeling' or intuition is hardly eradicated when a standardising system is brought in, and this seems to suggest that it is not adequate to effective performance.

Secondly, the question of what kind of knowledge base is relevant, and how should it be distributed is raised. Workflow, however it is conceived, is unlikely in our estimation to provide methods for recognising or supporting those aspects of the 'process' in which tacit, invisible, taken for granted local knowledges are responsible for the quick and straightforward accomplishment of the task.

Thirdly, and related to the above points, there is in our view a question concerning what standardisation actually is. What is construed as standardisation is, we believe, in reality nothing quite so simple. In particular, we have serious doubts about the universal appropriateness of measurement as the basis of standards, because on this assumption processes are only externally identical to the observer. This kind of measurement gives us no purchase on the significance of activities to the participant. This may have some fairly obvious consequences. In the first instance, it means we may have no means to distinguish between on the one hand wasteful duplication of effort and on the other checking work which is designed precisely to avoid wasteful mistakes. Similarly, because to a very large degree measurement processes are averaging processes, and our observation suggests this is a particular problem of workflow measures, no means is available for understanding the significance of rare events. In contrast, we would argue, these are analytic issues which ethnography specifically does provide for.

The sociological attentiveness to the routine and ordinary way in which work is mutually accomplished as meaningful activity specifically complements the focus on data and process associated with most models, including that of the business process model. None of this would matter a great deal outside of our own sociological 'church' were it not for the claim that the analytical attentiveness brought by the kind of enquiry we advocate does have consequences for effective design decisions, even when these design decisions orient to the business process rather than 'mere' technical functionality. We remain convinced that it does. Our purposes are not 'conservative' in that we are not making an implicit defence of current practice, nor or they in any way a political critique of BPR. Rather, they are to understand how, while some aspects of work activity can be shown to be constraining in that they are time consuming, repetitive, or unnecessarily complex, they at the same time may afford certain possibilities that good design should not merely ignore. Of course design work must orient to problems of efficiency, effectiveness and adaptability, but these objectives may be a function of complex articulations of process, technology, and the skilful deployment of situated knowledge. The latter, one of the proper concerns of ethnographic enquiry, is precisely what the modelling activities of BPR wish to gloss as either 'healthy' or 'unhealthy'. Real organisational life will always be complex, and this is no argument against the design of procedures to ensure the success of working arrangements in principle. It is an argument about the likelihood of success in practice.

Bibliography

Abbott, Kenneth, and Sarin, Sunil, (1994) 'Experiences with Workflow Management: Issues for the Next generation, in *Proceedings of CSCW '94*, eds. R, Furuta and C. Neuwirth, ACM Press, New York

Anderson, R. J., (1994), 'Representations and Requirements: The Value of Ethnography in System Design.' *Human-Computer Interaction,* Vol. 9 pp. 151-182.

Anderson, R. J., Hughes, J.A., and Sharrock, W. W. (1989) *Working for profit; The Social Organisation of Calculation in an Entrepreneurial Firm.* Aldershot, Avebury.

Benyon, D. (1992) a) 'The role of task analysis and system design'. *Interacting with Computers,* Vol 4 No. 1 pp102-123.

Benyon, D. (1992) b) 'Task analysis and system design: the discipline of data', *Interacting with Computers.* Vol. 4 No. 2. pp246-259.

Bittner, E. (1965), 'The concept of organisation', *Social Research*, 23, pp. 239-255.

Button, G. and King, V., (1992) Hanging around is not the point: Ethnography in system design', Paper delivered at workshop, CSCW'92, Toronto.

COMIC Deliverable 2.1, *Informing CSCW System Requirements,* Computing Department, Lancaster University

Davenport, T. H., (1993), *Process Innovation,: Reengineering Work Through Information Technology*. Harvard Business School Press, Boston, Mass.

Garfinkel, Harold, (1967), *Studies in Ethnomethodology*, Polity Press, Cambridge

Hammer, M., and Champy, J. (1993) *Re-engineering the Corporation: A Manifesto for Business Revolution*. Nicholas Brealey Publishing.

Harrington, H.J., 1991, *Business Process Improvement: The breakthrough strategy for total quality, productivity and competitiveness*, McGraw-Hill, New York

Hughes, J. A., King, V., Rodden, T., and Andersen, H. (1994) 'Moving out from the control room: Ethnography in system design'. In *Proceedings of CSCW '94,* Chapel Hill, North Carolina.

Hughes. J.A., Randall, D. and Shapiro, D. (1992) 'Faltering from Ethnography to Design', *Proceedings of the ACM 1992 Conference on CSCW, 'Sharing Perspectives',* ACM Press, 1992, pp. 115-122.

Hughes, J.A., Rodden, T., Rouccfield, M., Viller, S. (1994), 'Working with Constant Interruption: CSCW and the Small Office', *Proceedings of CSCW94,* New York, ACM Press.

Jacobson, I., Ericcson, M., and Jacobson, A., (1995), *The Object Advantage: Business Process Re-engineering with object technology*, Addison- Wesley, Wokingham, England

King, Val, and Randall, Dave, (1994), 'Trying to keep the customer satisfied', *Proceedings of the 5th IFIP Conference on Women, Work, and Computerisation*, July 2-5th, Manchester, England.

Lynch, Michael, (1991) "Method: measurement- ordinary and scientific measurement as ethnomethodological phenomena", in G. Button (ed.), *Ethnomethodology and the Human Sciences*, 1991, Cambridge University Press, Cambridge, England.

Pycock, J., Calvey, D., Sharrock, W., King, V., and Hughes, J., 'Present in the plan: Process models and ethnography', Comic Document MAN-1-7

Randall, D. and Hughes, J. A. (1994) 'Sociology, CSCW and Working with Customers', in Thomas, P (ed) *Social and Interaction Dimensions of System Design*. Cambridge University Press Cambridge.

Randall, D., Hughes, J. A., and Shapiro, D. (1992) 'Using Ethnography to Inform Systems Design'. *Journal of Intelligent Systems*, Vol. 4, Nos 1-2.

Stowell, D. M., (1991) Appendix to H.J. Harrington *op cit*

Suchman, L., (1987) *Plans and Situated Action: The Problem of Human-Machine Communication*. Cambridge University Press. Cambridge.

Yourdon, E. and Constantine, L. C. (1979) *Structured Design: Fundamentals of a Discipline of Computer Program Nd System Design,* Prentice- Hall.

ECSCW '95 Directory: Authors and Committee Members

Liam J. Bannon
Department of computer Science & Information Systems
University of Limerick
Limerick
Ireland
phone: (+353) 61-202 632
fax: (+353) 61-202 572
email: bannonl@ul.ie

Steve Benford
Department of Computer Science
The University of Nottingham
Nottingham NG7 2RD
United Kingdom
phone: (+44) 115-951 4203
fax: (+44) 115-951 4254
email: sdb@cs.nott.ac.uk

Richard Bentley
GMD FIT CSCW
Schloß Birlinghoven
D-53754 Sankt Augustin
Germany
phone: (+49) 2241-142 699
fax: (+49) 2241-142 084
email: bentley@gmd.de

Jeanette Blomberg
Xerox Palo Alto Research Center
3333 Coyote Hill Road
Palo Alto, CA 94304
USA
phone: (+1) 415-812 4751
fax: (+1) 415-812 4380
email: Blomberg@PARC.Xerox.com

John Bowers
Department of Psychology
University of Manchester
Oxford Road
Manchester M13 9PL
United Kingdom
phone: (+44) 161-275 2599
fax: (+44) 161-275 2588
email: bowers@hera.psy.man.ac.uk

Tone Bratteteig
Department of Informatics
University of Oslo
P.O. Box 1080 Blindern
N-0316 Oslo
Norway
phone: (+47) 22-852 427
fax: (+47) 22-852 401
email: tone@ifi.uio.no

Graham Button
Rank Xerox Research Centre
Cambridge Laboratory (EuroPARC)
61 Regent Street
Cambridge, CB2 1AB
United Kingdom
phone: (+44) 223-341 500
fax: (+44) 223-341 510
email: button@europarc.xerox.com

Susanne Bødker
Department of Computer Science
Aarhus University
Ny Munkegade 116
DK-8000 Aarhus C
Denmark
phone: (+45) 89423 256
fax: (+45) 89423 255
email: bodker@daimi.aau.dk

Matthew Chalmers
Ubilab
Union Bank of Switzerland
Bahnhofstrasse 45
CH-8021 Zurich
Switzerland
phone: (+41) 1-236 7504
fax: (+41) 1-236 4671
email: chalmers@ubilab.ubs.ch

Rajiv Choudhary
Intel Corporation
Mail Stop JF2-52
2111 NE 25th Avenue
Hillsboro, Oregon 97124-6497
U.S.A
phone: (+1) 503-264-8480
fax: (+1) 503-264-6055
email: rajiv_choudhary@ccm.jf.intel.com

Claudio Ciborra
Theseus Institute
BP 169
Rue Albert Einstein
06903 Sophia Antipolis Cedex
France
phone: (+33) 92 945 100
fax: (+33) 92 653 837
email: ciborra@theseus.fr

Andrew Clement
Faculty of Information Studies
University of Toronto
140 St. George Street
Toronto, Ontario M5S 1A1
Canada
phone: (+1) 416-978 3111
fax: (+1) 416-971 1399
email: clement@flis.utoronto.ca

Prasun Dewan
Department of Computer Science
CB 3175, Sitterson Hall
University of North Carolina
Chapel Hill, NC 27599-3175
USA
phone: (+1) 919-962 1823
fax: (+1) 919-962 1799
email: dewan@cs.unc.edu

Paul Dourish
Department of Computer Science
University College, London
Gower Street
London WC1E 6BT
United Kingdom
and
Rank Xerox Research Centre
Cambridge Laboratory (EuroPARC)
61 Regent Street
Cambridge CB2 1AB
United Kingdom
phone: (+44) 1223-341512
fax: (+44) 1223-341510
email: dourish@europarc.xerox.com

Lennart Fahlén
SICS
Box 1264
S-164 28 Kista
Sweden
phone: (+46) 8-752 1539
fax: (+46) 8-751 7230
email: lef@sics.se

Geraldine Fitzpatrick
Department of Computer Science
The University of Queensland
Queensland 4072
Australia
phone: (+61) 7-365 2097
fax: (+61) 7-365 1999
email: g.fitzpatrick@cs.uq.oz.au

Ludwin Fuchs
Institute for Applied Information Technology
GMD - German National Research Center for Information Technology
Schloß Birlinghoven
D-53754 Sankt Augustin
Germany
phone: (+49) 2241-14 2721
fax: (+49) 2241-14 2084
email: ludwin.fuchs@gmd.de

Chris Greenhalgh
Department of Computer Science
The University of Nottingham
Nottingham NG7 2RD
United Kingdom
phone: (+44) 115-951 4225
fax: (+44) 115-951 4254
email: cmg@cs.nott.ac.uk

Jonathan Grudin
Information and Computer Science Department
University of California, Irvine
Irvine, California
USA
phone: (+1) 714-824 8674
fax: (+1) 714-824 4056
email: grudin@ics.uci.edu

Jörg M. Haake
IPSI - Integrated Publication and Information Systems Institute
GMD - German National Research Center for Information Technology
Dolivostr. 15
D-64293 Darmstadt
Germany
phone: (+49) 6151-869 918
fax: (+49) 6151-869 966
email: haake@darmstadt.gmd.de

Christian Heath
King's College
University of London
Campden Hill Road
London W8 7AH
United Kingdom
phone: (+44) 171-333 4097
fax: (+44) 171 333 4486
email: christian.heath@kcl.ac.uk

John A. Hughes
Department of Sociology
Lancaster University
Lancaster LA1 4YL
United Kingdom
phone: (+44) 1524 594174
fax: (+44) 1524 594256
email: J.Hughes@lancaster.ac.uk

Andrew Hutchison
Department of Computer Science
University of Zurich
Winterthurerstrasse 190
CH-8057 Zurich
Switzerland
phone: (+41) 1-257 4581
fax: (+41) 1-363 0035
email: hutch@ifi.unizh.ch

Yusuke Ichikawa
Department of Instrumentation Engineering
Keio University
3-14-1 Hiyoshi, Kouhoku-ku, Yokohama
223 Japan
phone: (+81) 45-563 1141
fax: (+81) 45-562 7625
email: ichikawa@myo.inst.keio.ac.jp

Hiroshi Ishii
NTT Human Interface Laboratories
1-2356 Take, Yokosuka-Shi
Kanagawa, 238-03
Japan
phone: (+81) 468-59 3522
fax: (+81) 468-59 2332
email: ishii.chi@xerox.com

Gen Ishimoda
Institute of Engineering Mechanics
University of Tsukuba
1-1-1, Tennoudai, Tsukuba, Ibaraki 305
Japan
phone: (+81) 298-53 6187
fax: (+81) 298-53 5207
email: ishimoda@kz.tsukuba.ac.jp

Giseok Jeong
Department of Instrumentation Engineering
Keio University
3-14-1 Hiyoshi, Kouhoku-ku
Yokohama 223
Japan
phone: (+81) 45-563 1141
fax: (+81) 45-562 7625

Simon M. Kaplan
Department of Computer Science
University of Illinois at Urbana-Champaign
1304 West Springfield Avenue
Urbana, Illinois 61801
USA
phone: (+1) 217-244 0392
fax: (+1) 217-333 3501
email: kaplan@cs.uiuc.edu

Viktor Kaptelinin
Department of Informatics
Umeå University
S-901 87 Umeå
Sweden
phone: (+46) 90-165 927
fax: (+46) 90-166 550
email: vklinin@informatik. umu.se

John King
ICS Department
University of California
Irvine, CA 92717
USA
phone: (+1) 714-824 6388
fax: (+1) 714-854 4994
email: king@ics.uci.edu

Andrew Kirby
Computing Department
Lancaster University
Lancaster LA1 4YR
United Kingdom
phone: (+44) 15-246 5201 x5835
fax: (+44) 15-245 93608
email: ak@comp.lancs.ac.uk

Konrad Klöckner
Institute for Applied Information Technology
GMD - German National Research Center for Information Technology
Schloß Birlinghoven
D-53754 Sankt Augustin
Germany
phone: (+49) 2241-14 2055
fax: (+49) 2241-14 2084
email: konrad.kloeckner@gmd.de

Sabine Kolvenbach
Institute for Applied Information Technology
GMD - German National Research Center for Information Technology
Schloß Birlinghoven
D-53754 Sankt Augustin
Germany
phone: (+49) 2241-14 2721
fax: (+49) 2241-14 2084
email: kovenbach@gmd.de

Kimio Kondo
Research and Development Division
National Institute of Multimedia Education
Ministry of Education
2-12, Wakaba, Mihama, Chiba-shi Chiba 261
Japan
phone: (+81) 43-276 1111
fax: (+81) 43-275 5117
email: KFH001464@niftyserve.or.jp

Laszlo Kovacs
Computer and Automation Institute of the Hungarian Academy of Sciences
MTA-SZTAKI, ASZI
H-111 Budapest XI
Lagymanyosi u. 11
Hungary
phone: (+36) 1-269 8286
fax: (+36) 1-269 8288
email: laszlo.kovacs@sztaki.hu

Steinar Kristoffersen

Computing Department
Lancaster University
Lancaster LA1 4YR
United Kingdom
phone: (+44) 15-246 5201, ext. 4537
fax: (+44) 15-245 936 08
email: steinar@comp.lancs.ac.uk

Hideaki Kuzuoka

Institute of Engineering Mechanics
University of Tsukuba
1-1-1, Tennoudai, Tsukuba, Ibaraki 305
Japan
phone: (+81) 298-53 5258
fax: (+81) 298-53 5207
email: kuzuoka@kz.tsukuba.ac.jp

Paul Luff

Department of Sociology
University of Surrey
Guilford GU2 5XH
United Kingdom
phone: (+44) 1483 300800
fax: (+44) 1483 306290
email: Paul.Luff@soc.surrey.ac.uk

Kalle Lyytinen

Department of Computer Science and Information Systems
University of Jyväskylä
P.O. Box 35
SF-40 351 Jyväskylä
Finland
phone: (+358) 41-603 025
fax: (+358) 41-603 011
email: kalle@jytko.jyu.fi

Peter Mambrey

Institute for Applied Information Technology
GMD - German National Research Center for Information Technology
Schloß Birlinghoven
D-53754 Sankt Augustin
Germany
phone: (+49) 2241-14 2710
fax: (+49) 2241-14 2084
email: mambrey@gmd.de

Nelson R. Manohar

Department of Electrical Engineering and Computer Science
University of Michigan
Ann Arbor
MI 48109-2122
USA
phone: (+1) 313-662 1191
fax: (+1) 313-763 1503
email: nelsonr@eecs.umich.edu

Marilyn Mantei

Department of Computer Science
University of Toronto
10 Kings College Road
Toronto, Ontario M5S 1A1
Canada
phone: (+1) 416-978 5512
fax: (+1) 416-978 4765
email: mantei@dgp.toronto.edu

Gloria Mark

IPSI - Integrated Publication and Information Systems Institute
GMD - German National Research Center for Information Technology
Dolivostr. 15
D-64293 Darmstadt
Germany
phone: (+49) 6151-869 917
fax: (+49) 6151-869 966
email: mark@darmstadt.gmd.de

Hans Marmolin

IPLab, NADA
KTH
100 44 Stockholm
Sweden
phone: (+46) 8-790 9106
fax: (+46) 8-790 0930
email: hanmarm@nada.kth.se

Yutaka Matsushita
Department of Instrumentation Engineering
Keio University
3-14-1 Hiyoshi, Kouhoku-ku
Yokohama 223
Japan
phone: (+81) 45-563 1141
fax: (+81) 45-562 7625

Giorgio De Michelis
Department of Computer Sciences
University of Milan
Via Comelico 39
201 35 Milan
Italy
phone: (+39) 2-55006 311
fax: (+39) 2-55006 276
email: gdemich@hermes.dsi.unimi.it

Othmar Morger
Department of Computer Science
University of Zurich
Winterthurerstrasse 190
CH-8057 Zurich
Switzerland
phone: (+41) 1-257 4581
fax: (+41) 1-363 0035
email: morger@ifi.unizh.ch

Thomas Mühlherr
Department of Computer Science
University of Zurich
Winterthurerstrasse 190
CH-8057 Zurich
Switzerland
phone: (+41) 1-257 4581
fax: (+41) 1-363 0035
email: muehlher@ifi.unizh.ch

Christine Neuwirth
Carnegie Mellon University
Pittsburgh, PA 15213
USA
phone: (+1) 412-268 8702
fax: (+1) 412-268 5288
email: cmn+@andrew.cmu.edu

Yushi Nishimura
Institute of Engineering Mechanics
University of Tsukuba
1-1-1, Tennoudai, Tsukuba, Ibaraki 305
Japan
phone: (+81) 298-53-6187
fax: (+81) 298-53-5207
email: ynishimur@kz.tsukuba.ac.jp

Ken-ichi Okada
Department of Instrumentation Engineering
Keio University
3-14-1 Hiyoshi, Kouhoku-ku
Yokohama 223
Japan
phone: (+81) 45-563 1141
fax: (+81) 45-562 7625

Agneta Olerup
Department of Informatics
Lund University
Ole Römers väg 6
S-223 63 Lund
Sweden
phone: (+46) 46-222 9764
fax: (+46) 46-222 4528
email: agneta.olerup@ics.lu.se

Leysia Palen
Information and Computer Science Department
University of California, Irvine
Irvine, California
USA
phone: (+1) 714-824 5086
fax: (+1) 714-824 4056
email: palen@ics.uci.edu

Uta Pankoke-Babatz
Institute for Applied Information Technology
GMD - German National Research Center for Information Technology
Schloß Birlinghoven
D-53754 Sankt Augustin
Germany
phone: (+49) 2241-14 2707
fax: (+49) 2241-14 2084
email: uta.pankoke@gmd.de

Encarna Pastor
Department of Telematics Systems Engineering
Technical University of Madrid
ETSI Telecommunicacion
Ciduad Universitaria
E-28040 Madrid
Spain
phone: (+31) 1-336 7328
fax: (+31) 1-543 2077
email: encarna@dit.upm.es

Lydia Plowman
School of Cognitive and Computing Sciences
University of Sussex
Falmer, Brighton
BN1 9QH
United Kingdom
phone: (+44) 1273-678 647
fax: (+44) 1273-671 320
email: lydiap@cogs.sussex.ac.uk

Atul Prakash
Department of EECS
University of Michigan
Ann Arbor, MI 48109-2122
USA
phone: (+1) 313-763 1585
fax: (+1) 313-763 1503
email: aprakash@eecs.umich.edu

Wolfgang Prinz
Institute for Applied Information Technology
GMD - German National Research Center for Information Technology
Schloß Birlinghoven
D-53754 Sankt Augustin
Germany
phone: (+49) 2241-14 2730
fax: (+49) 2241-14 2084
email: prinz@gmd.de

Magnus Ramage
Department of Computing
Lancaster University
Lancaster, LA1 4YR
United Kingdom
phone: (+44) 1524-65201 x4537
fax: (+44) 1524-593608
email: magnus@comp.lancs.ac.uk

Dave Randall
Department of Interdisciplinary Studies
Manchester Metropolitan University
Manchester, M15 6BG
United Kingdom
phone: (+44) 161 247 3037
fax: (+44) 161 247 6321
email: D.Randall@mmu.ac.uk

Mike Robinson
GMD FIT CSCW
Schloß Birlinghoven
D-53757 Sankt Augustin
Germany
and
SAGEFORCE LTD
61 Kings Road
Kingston-upon-Thames
Surrey KT2 5JA
United Kingdom
phone: (+44) 81-546 5099
fax: (+44) 81-255 1365
email: robinson@gmd.de

Tom Rodden
Computing Department
Lancaster University
Lancaster LA1 4YR
United Kingdom
phone: (+44) 15-2459 3823
fax: (+44) 15-2459 3608
email: tam@comp.lancs.ac.uk

Yvonne Rogers
School of Cognitive and Computing Sciences
University of Sussex
Falmer, Brighton
BN1 9QH
United Kingdom
phone: (+44) 1273-606755 x2414
fax: (+44) 1273-671320
email: yvonner@cogs.sussex.ac.uk

Mark Rouncefield
Department of Sociology
Lancaster University
Lancaster LA1 4YL
phone: (+44) 15-2459 4186
fax: (+44) 15-2459 4256
email: soa031@cent1.lancs.ac.uk

Christian Sauter
Department of Computer Science
University of Zurich
Winterthurerstrasse 190
CH-8057 Zurich
Switzerland
phone: (+41) 1-257 4581
fax: (+41) 1-363 0035
email: sauter@ifi.unizh.ch

Kjeld Schmidt
System Analysis Department
Risø National Laboratory
P.O. Box 49
DK-4000 Roskilde
Denmark
phone: (+45) 4237 1212
fax: (+45) 4675 5170
email: kschmidt@risoe.dk

Abigail Sellen
Rank Xerox Research Centre
Cambridge Laboratory (EuroPARC)
61 Regent St.
Cambridge, CB2 1AB
United Kingdom
phone: (+44) 12-2334 1513
fax: (+44) 12-2334 1525
email: sellen@europarc.xerox.com

Wes Sharrock
Department of Sociology
University of Manchester
Manchester, M13 9PL
United Kingdom
phone: (+44) 61-275 2510
fax: (+44) 61-275 2514
email: wes.sharrock@man.ac.uk

John Sherry
Department of Anthropology
Haury Building Room 219
University of Arizona
Tucson, AZ 85721
USA
phone: (+1) 520-621 2966
fax: (+1) 520-621 2088
email: jsherry@anthro.arizona.edu

Carla Simone
Department of Computer Sciences
University of Torino
Corso Svizzera 185
I-10148 Torino
Italy
phone: (+39) 11 7429 236
fax: (+39) 11 7712002
email: simone@di.unito.it

Markus Sohlenkamp
Institute for Applied Information Technology
GMD - German National Research Center for Information Technology
Schloß Birlinghoven
D-53754 Sankt Augustin
Germany
phone: (+49) 2241-14 2872
fax: (+49) 2241-14 2084
email: sohlenkamp@gmd.de

Norbert A. Streitz

IPSI - Integrated Publication and Information Systems Institute
GMD - German National Research Center for Information Technology
Dolivostr. 15
D-64293 Darmstadt
Germany
phone: (+49) 6151-869 919
fax: (+49) 6151-869 966
email: streitz@darmstadt.gmd.de

Lucy Suchman

Xerox Palo Alto Research Center
3333 Coyote Hill Road
Palo Alto, CA 94303
USA
phone: (+1) 415-812 4340
fax: (+1) 415-812 4380
email: suchman@parc.xerox.com

Yngve Sundblad

IPlab, NADA
KTH
S-100 44 Stockholm
Sweden
phone: (+46) 8-790 7147
fax: (+46) 8-790 0930
email: yngve@nada.kth.se

Ryutaro Suzuki

Research and Development Division
National Institute of Multimedia Education
Ministry of Education
2-12, Wakaba, Mihama, Chiba-shi Chiba 261
Japan
phone: (+81) 43-276 1111
fax: (+81) 43-275 5117
email: KFG00535@niftyserve.or.jp

Anja Syri

Institute for Applied Information Technology
GMD - German National Research Center for Information Technology
Schloß Birlinghoven
D-53754 Sankt Augustin
Germany
phone: (+49) 2241-14 2762
fax: (+49) 2241-14 2084
email: syri@gmd.de

Shunsuke Tanaka

Department of Instrumentation Engineering
Keio University
3-14-1 Hiyoshi, Kouhoku-ku
Yokohama 223
Japan
phone: (+81) 45-563 1141
fax: (+81) 45-562 7625

Stephanie Teufel

Department of Computer Science
University of Zurich
Winterthurerstrasse 190
CH-8057 Zurich
Switzerland
phone: (+41) 1-257 4335
fax: (+41) 1-363 0035
email: teufel@ifi.unizh.ch

William J. Tolone

Department of Computer Science
University of Illinois at Urbana-Champaign
1304 West Springfield Avenue
Urbana, Illinois 61801
USA
phone: (+1) 217-333 4201
fax: (+1) 217-333 3501
email: tolone@cs.uiuc.edu

Ina Wagner
Abteilung fuer CSCW
Institut für Gestaltungs- und
Wirkungsforschung
Vienna Technical University
Argentinierstrasse 8
A-1040 Vienna, Austria
phone: (+43) 1-588 01 4439
fax: (+43) 1-504 2478
email: iwagner@email.tuwien.ac.at

Yvonne Wærn
Department of Communication Studies
Linköping University
S-581 83 Linköping
Sweden
phone: (+46) 13-282 937
fax: (+46) 13-282 299
email: yvowa@tema.liu.se

Index of Authors

MIX
Papier aus verantwortungsvollen Quellen
Paper from responsible sources
FSC® C105338

If you have any concerns about our products,
you can contact us on
ProductSafety@springernature.com

In case Publisher is established outside the EU,
the EU authorized representative is:
Springer Nature Customer Service Center GmbH
Europaplatz 3, 69115 Heidelberg, Germany

Printed by Libri Plureos GmbH
in Hamburg, Germany